Wind Power in China

T0331379

Whilst China's growing economy is widely regarded as being responsible for severe environmental degradation and a high reliance on energy from fossil fuels, China is emerging as a potential leader in new green energy technologies. Outlining the extraordinary growth in China's wind power capacity since 2005, this book explores the deliberate creation of a whole industry and the strategy of transitioning the power sector to renewable energy by accelerated experimentation and through literally pushing the emerging wind power sector to its limits. Investigating how wind power may not always be considered as sustainable in a wider Chinese developmental context, the book traces the struggle China has had in getting this high technology sector to qualify as truly Chinese scientific development, whilst often being opaquely at the mercy of foreign expertise, technology, and certification. The book furthermore exposes the surprising nuances, dynamics, and potency of unexpected players in Chinese wind power marketisation. Complex interplays are revealed between wind turbine control systems, algorithms in critical software technology, relationships between suppliers, wind farm developers, financiers, the electrical grid itself, the coal lobby, the broader Chinese state, and much more. The book has important implications far beyond wind power and contemporary China studies, highlighting the much wider story of China's fragmented and experimental style of innovating, upgrading, and greening.

Julia Kirch Kirkegaard is a Postdoctoral Fellow at Stanford University, as well as at Copenhagen Business School and the Technical University of Denmark

Routledge Studies on the Chinese Economy
Series Editor:
Peter Nolan
Director, Centre of Development Studies

Chong Hua
Professor in Chinese Development; and Director of the Chinese Executive Leadership Programme (CELP), University of Cambridge

Founding Series Editors:
Peter Nolan
University of Cambridge

Dong Fureng
Beijing University

The aim of this series is to publish original, high-quality, research-level work by both new and established scholars in the West and the East, on all aspects of the Chinese economy, including studies of business and economic history.

Wind Power in China

Ambiguous Winds of Change in China's Energy Market

Julia Kirch Kirkegaard

Routledge
Taylor & Francis Group

LONDON AND NEW YORK

First published 2019
by Routledge
2 Park Square, Milton Park, Abingdon, Oxon OX14 4RN

and by Routledge
52 Vanderbilt Avenue, New York, NY 10017

First issued in paperback 2020

*Routledge is an imprint of the Taylor & Francis Group,
an informa business*

British Library Cataloguing in Publication Data
A catalogue record for this book is available from the British Library

Library of Congress Cataloging in Publication Data
A catalog record has been requested for this book

ISBN 13: 978-0-367-58315-6 (pbk)
ISBN 13: 978-0-415-78711-6 (hbk)

Typeset in Times NR MT Pro
by Cenveo® Publisher Services

To my father, Peter Kirkegaard,
in loving memory

Contents

Figures

Tables

Text boxes

Preface

This book has been a long journey, traversing both time and space, as well as languages, metaphors, scientific disciplines, fields of expertise, and relations.

First and foremost, *Ambiguous Winds of Change* is a result of several years of research, with shifting periods of intense work and intermittent breaks. It all started when I embarked on my PhD study of the Chinese wind turbine industry in 2011 and led to three years of intensive study. When I first arrived in China I expected a story of success and the formation of 'global innovation networks', but all I heard about was quality crisis and power struggles. Over time, as I investigated the weighty issues and socio-technical details of the multi-faceted rhizomatic account, the central actors in the account would turn out to be the least expected: software algorithms. It is not an easy task for a (not so technology-savvy) socio-technical cartographer to be faced with software algorithms, aeroelastic codes, control systems, simulation tools and many other more or less expected entities and actors.

During my extensive ethnographic fieldwork in China and elsewhere, the contours of a constructivist controversy study took shape, a shape that continued to take form in my follow-up research upon completion of my PhD. My analysis, founded in the Anthropology of Markets and Actor Network Theory within Science & Technology Studies (STS), has resulted in an account that does not resemble most ordinary accounts of Chinese catch-up, upgrading, innovation, or greening. Instead, it illustrates Chinese upgrading as an ambiguous and often contested pathway of disruptive catch-up and leapfrogging, as China increasingly enters the global scene as a potential 'green leader'. It emerges that China's strength has really come about by benefiting from its self-inflicted 'failures', because failures are treated as effective stepping stones for learning.

Throughout my work, a great many metaphors have arisen and have helped me on my journey before fading away again. Traversing this sea of metaphors, there eventually emerged one that was to stay with me to the end of the journey: a metaphor of electromagnetic waves. This has proved its worth not only because it fits to the physical properties of the object of inquiry, that is, the alternating current (AC) electricity generated from the wind, which is wave-like in nature: the electrical flow rises and falls, albeit very quickly, but still periodically and definitely very wave-like. More, it was used to guide my sensemaking of China's mode of industrial upgrading through oscillating wave-like movements towards the brink of tipping over into disruption and stalemate in Chinese wind power development. As a metaphor for a specific mode of Chinese industrial development, the wave metaphor is also coupled to China's governance mode of fragmented authoritarianism, namely the wave-like oscillations between centralised control and fragmented experimentation that the development of Chinese wind power displays.

As well as spanning time and metaphors, the book traverses three continents: Asia, Europe, and the USA. *Ambiguous Winds of Change* has been written in China,[1] Denmark,[2] Norway,[3] and finally Northern California's Silicon Valley in the United States of America.[4] Accordingly, it has involved the use of several languages – not only the language of metaphors, but also body language, from Danish to English and Chinese (Mandarin), as well as the diverse languages of social science and engineering due to the inter-disciplinary nature of my study.

Indeed, as the study developed over time and I delved into the socio-technical nitty-gritty details of software algorithms and other turbine components, lateral moves were necessary that at times tended to dissolve the boundary between me and my respondents as 'expert' versus 'practitioner': I endeavoured to learn the 'local' scientific and technical language of the field, so that I could speak with respondents in their own terms. I had to take their science and expertise seriously – and even try to grasp it to the best of my ability. Accordingly, I gradually built up an engineering vocabulary during my fieldwork and through my trips to the Technical University of Denmark where I interviewed researchers and scientists in wind energy, as well as during my later postdoctoral research at their Wind Energy Department. Further abiding by the principle of reduction-resistant research, I started to read engineering journals and asked my respondents about more and more technical details – often to their sheer surprise – and they patiently drew me pictures of wind turbines, control systems, and power grids. As I gradually delved deeper into the weighty details of wind turbine technology, I painstakingly built up a new working vocabulary (in English, Danish, and Chinese) about wind turbines, algorithms, control systems, simulation tools, aeroelastic codes and much more. In time, this made it possible for me to explore an increasing array of the technical aspects, which unexpectedly turned out to be critical to the story line. Over and over again, much of my understanding inevitably had to be demolished and modified during my PhD work, since my first, rather 'blackboxed', understanding of the different components proved unstable in many situations. However, I was later afforded the opportunity to collaborate with a wind power engineer 'in the field' during the critical final stages of summarising my findings into the present book volume. This turned out to be fundamental in order to unleash the full synergistic potential of what may be an interdisciplinary 'science-without-borders'.

What is more, often in my fieldwork it seemed as if I were being drawn into the field, as I was treated as a consultant or 'soul-searcher' to render advice and recommendations for Chinese and Western respondents alike. This emergent 'hybrid' role of mine – to some extent due to my acquaintance both with Chinese and Western cultures and languages – meant that my treatment of the sometimes highly 'sensitive' (and 'politicised') issues became quite a balancing act, requiring a great degree of reflexiveness on my part. It was a hybrid status that continued to be enhanced as I increasingly was becoming an 'expert' in unforeseen fields such as software algorithms and aeroelastic codes, which forced me to cross-disciplinary boundaries between social and engineering sciences, building new bridges between the sciences.

This long journey into the technical landscape of the wind turbine's machinery, components and algorithms did not come easily or automatically. It required me to literally climb – and some would say, to sometimes 'tilt at' – wind turbines, just like some other misfortunate Don Quixote. And so, just as China's wind turbine industry has experienced a bumpy path with oscillating stages of crisis, and tipping towards the brink of stalemate, I myself have felt the challenges of writing this book as a sometimes rocky route. It did not make it easier that things in China are often not what they seem to be, or that they may change overnight, leaving everything highly ambiguous. Indeed, the research has required experimental tactics and an ability to steer through troubled waters of messy ethnographic research – feeling, living and surviving the resulting productive 'creative chaos' of my own constitution, and of my mode of working and thinking (sometimes a blessing, at other times an excruciating curse) – which, now that I come to think of it, may be a 'birth gift' from my mother and father with their blend of a perfectionist sense for structured, analytic order, versus the fragility of artistic freedom-seeking creativity and improvisation, and an addition of stubbornness on my part. This research has been scattered with stages of doubt and concern, as I engaged in coupling and binding fields and sciences together in unique ways, building bridges and seeking new pathways for research, and seeking new modes of conversation between disciplines as well as cultures.

As a result, this adventurous research journey has been marked by curiosity and joy, together with iterative stages and various levels of confusion. Whilst an integral part of my anthropological method, the experimental mode of research was also felt in the very choice of what to 'follow' in the analysis. In the beginning, I adhered to the principle of no censorship in the hope that something new and unexpected could be discovered, and so the idea to follow software algorithms and other turbine components only gradually emerged through the fieldwork. However, it was only at a much later stage in my research that I realised the peculiar resemblances between my own experimental research journey and the fragmented and experimental mode of Chinese 'greening' detected in the book. In some ways, it thus seems in retrospect that my interest in China's experimental and somewhat messy mode of developing new industries through fragmented experimentation can be likened to my own personal journey of disruption, chaos, and crisis, followed by stages of clarity and disruptive breakthrough, sometimes feeling as if trapped in the creative chaos of my mind and in traversing the alternating constructive and destructive interferences of the wind turbine's electromagnetic waves.

After all is said and done, the analysis complete and conclusions drawn and redrawn – with a total reframing of my PhD thesis, not a single sentence in the present volume standing as before, after ongoing struggles to find my 'own (expert) voice' – I have one overriding humble hope for you, the reader. That hope is that, through reading this book, you will come to appreciate the fascinating way in which it is possible to explain so much about an unfathomable, complex assemblage such as China and the greening of China's electrical power sector, just by looking at seemingly innocuous small players such as software algorithms and individual wind turbine components. By conducting a journey through the wind turbine and some of its more critical core components, this book renders some of the micro-foundations and controversies of China's green transformation and industrial and economic development visible. To me, it continues to be an avenue for learning and surprise to study China, and to do it not only through the pioneering lens of the Anthropology of Markets within Science & Technology Studies, but also by employing a controversy mapping approach, which is new to China Studies, but extends a budding conversation between the two fields.

The open-mindedness that is characteristic of the ethnographic fieldwork and controversy mapping that Science & Technology Studies preaches is something that I hope the reader will appreciate and take away with them. Whatever your field is - China Studies, Science & Technology Studies, Industry or Market Studies, Economic Geography, Innovation Studies, International Business, New Economic Sociology or even engineering - or no matter whether you are an academic, industrial practitioner, or policy actor in China or abroad, then I hope that I can convince you how such an inquisitive approach can benefit the field of contemporary China area Studies and extend our understanding of China's greening. Alas, there is no doubt that the courage and rationality of the exploratory journey riding the electromagnetic waves of Chinese 'greening' in the electrical power sector can only be judged at its completion. This I leave up to you.

Acknowledgements

The book not only spans time, continents, languages, and culture, continents and disciplines. It also spans a broad network of people, from my highly valued interviewees who showed the confidence to speak with me, to those who assisted, encouraged, and helped me from diverse backgrounds and fields of expertise. It goes without saying that the book would not have been here without any of them. Whilst my respondents – Chinese and foreign wind turbine manufacturers, component suppliers, grid companies, research institutes and universities, certification bodies, design houses, 'agents', and more – have had to be treated anonymously, I want to thank them all. In the following, however, I want to personally thank some of the people on my journey by name.

After my PhD was completed and I had done my follow-up fieldwork, it was time to write up the present volume. This also required that my 'lay person' and social science-based understanding of wind turbines and software algorithms had to be double-checked with an engineer in the field. This entailed numerous iterative discussions with Senior Engineer Tom Cronin who,[5] amongst other things, has been essential because of his assistance with drawing and explaining me the inner workings of software algorithms and wind turbines, for helping me out when the electromagnetic waves seemed too abstract or the wind turbine components too technical, as well as for helping with his 'cooling' and sometimes 'blackboxing' engineering perspective as my mind and thoughts during the final phase of writing sometimes became 'too creative'. Indeed, this cooperation evolved at times into lateral work, with the social and engineering sciences almost intertwined. During my PhD, I have also enjoyed the benefits of discussing insights with economic sociologists such as Professor Peer Hull Kristensen[6] with whom I have always loved to discuss the patterns and broader perspectives that emerge out of the seemingly 'small' 'micro'-relations and processes. A deepfelt thanks I owe to Professor Susse Georg who has acted as academic and personal mentor over the last ten years or so,[7] providing insightful comments on the book (and sometimes harsh but fair and helpful critique (!)) from a Science & Technology Studies perspective and the Anthropology of Markets, along with mental support and understanding throughout.

Professor Kjeld Erik Brødsgaard[8] has commented in depth on the China-geeky issues and helped me through with numerous encouragements,[2] and Associate Professor Stine Haakonsson[9] has discussed issues related to economic geography, innovation, and upgrading with me as well as joined me in some of my initial 'GIN-hunting' (global innovation networks) fieldwork in China – great fun![2]

During my stay at Stanford University, I have also been honoured with inputs from my mentor, renowned organisational sociologist Professor Woody W. Powell, and I have been lucky to receive fruitful comments on drafts of the book from students in his Networks and Organisations Workshop held bi-weekly at the Scandinavian Consortium for Organizational Research (SCANCOR), Stanford University, where I am currently residing as a postdoctoral fellow.

Apart from this, I have engaged in discussion about my findings with renowned China-scholars at the Shorenstein APARC China Program at Stanford University, hereunder Professors Andrew Walder and Jean Oi, and with renowned Science & Technology Studies-scholars at the Department of Communication at Stanford University. Discussions at Georgetown University, at the Mortara Center for International Studies, Washington D.C. of my findings, and with the American expert on China and renewable energy and wind, Joanna Lewis, have informed my work. Professor Liu Xielin at the (University of) Chinese Academy of Sciences has provided vital comments and contacts at an early stage, as has Associate Professor Liu Zhigao at the Chinese Academy of Sciences, who was so kind to lend me a desk during my fieldwork and many hours to discuss pressing socio-political issues in China. I am also very grateful to my PhD panel opponents Associate Professor Koray Caliskan, Bogazici University, and Professor Gary Herrigel, University of Chicago: they have provided useful advice for later publication, teaching me how to strengthen my thinking, theorisation, and argumentation. Postdoctoral Fellow Marius Korsnes at NTNU, Norway, also helped with insightful comments at the early stage of book writing, sharing his expertise on both Science & Technology Studies and China, as well as offshore wind power, together with other scholars during my research stay in Norway. And last, but not least, I owe much to my long-term 'partner-in-crime', PhD Louise Lyngfeldt Gorm Hansen with whom I spent months in China, following and sharing our separate paths of exhaustive and exhausting fieldwork, laughing, yelling, discussing and crying our way through our journey. Simon Tornby, my brother-in-law, has assisted very much with his professional skills in drawing figures.

The book would not have been here today without their, or the others', help. I should also not forget to mention reviewers at Routledge, Peter Sowden and Peter Nolan, who supported through their productive comments in the finishing stage. I am thankful for the support and time in ushering this book through to publication. Further, and plainly, this book would not have been possible without the financial support and administrative assistance from multiple sources. Bo Bøgeskov at the (now previous) Department of Business and Politics (CBS) always offered me essential help through the regulations of the Sino-Danish Center for Education and Research, and Head of Department Peter Hauge Madsen at the Technical University of Denmark, Wind Energy, made it possible for me to go to the Norwegian University of Science & Technology, NTNU in Trondheim, Norway, for three months to get a good start in writing this book with funding from the European Union-funded IRPWind Mobility Programme and the European Energy Research Alliance (EERA) Joint Programme on Wind Energy (JP WIND) so that I did not any longer only have my weekends, evenings, and holidays to spend on it for a while. I am also grateful to Department Head, Professor Margrethe Aune at NTNU for lending me a desk and an environment where a Science & Technology Studies scholar can feel at home. In financial terms, the Otto Mønsted Foundation and the Head of Department Fund at Department of Business and Politics, Copenhagen Business School, have co-funded my fieldwork and book publication, whilst the Sino-Danish Center for Education and Research in Beijing made the whole adventure possible by funding my PhD that laid the foundation for this study in the first place.

Last but not least, it goes without saying, that this book couldn't have happened without support from friends and family and reviewers and commenters too numerous to mention. In particular, though, my husband, Christian Hollitsch'es, never-ending love, wit, intelligence, down-to-earth constitution, patience, and cooking skills – not to forget his willingness to move to California and start a family with me here for two years – and my family's support have been invaluable to arrive at the end. It seems just right that as I am writing the last sentence of this book, the process of giving birth to a book is now taken over by the growing life inside me, little Erik, that will manage to meet our world just shortly before this book comes out. Also, my friends Dorte Munch Nielsen has offered valuable proof-reading skills and mental support, while Vanessa Roin (McGrail) has given mental support and deep friendship throughout. This is something that I treasure highly. Thank you all.

And, finally, I want to thank my mother, Kirsten Kirch, and my father, Peter Kirkegaard, whom I think I owe to have been given the courage and skills to undertake such crazy journey in the first place. My mother, by chance, managed to help me out in one of my last writing sprints as the metaphor of electromagnetic waves was consolidated, by reminding me of links between Danish literature and 'the Danish Golden Age' ('Guldalderen', appr. 1800–1850) when great poets and scientists discussed freely across later divisions between the sciences. This helped with the building of the metaphor around electromagnetism through links to the famous Danish fairytale-writer Hans Christian Andersen and the Danish chemist and engineer - and poet artist (!) – Hans Christian Ørsted. The former was fascinated with the material world, including electromagnetism, and how it could unveil hidden fairytales, whilst the latter forever changed the way scientists think about electricity and magnetism, by discovering that electric currents create magnetic fields, at the same time as he sought for the holy spirit in nature. In a way, my father also participated in this inquiry of building bridges, as some of the missing pieces of the emerging metaphor she found in the basement, sorting out my father's old papers and notes. Combining these insights with engineering insights from Tom Cronin, and my own understanding of the Chinese wind power market from the fieldwork, has helped to construe an overall narrative that binds the empirical and theorised storylines together through the metaphorical 'thread of life', the electromagnetic waves. Indeed, in seeking the potential wonders of interdisciplinary research - following my fascination with building bridges and tunnels between natural and social sciences (not a construction engineer in real life (luckily, due to my left-handed (*fummelfingrede*) nature, just like my father gave up the engineering dream from his own father who built actual bridges), but building bridges nonetheless – I may claim myself a 'new Ki(e)rkegaard' arising, even though this evidently seems a bit of an over-statement taking the world-famous Danish philosopher Søren Kierkegaard's (1813–1855) fame into account: Nevertheless, let us say that whilst Kierkegaard did not feel enthusiasm for the nerd's fascination with the material physical world, but insisted on taking a leap of faith to engage with the metaphysics as a realm for higher insights, I, as a Ki(e)rkegaard 2.0. have endeavoured to take a new 'leap of faith': Engaging in interdisciplinary research and being deeply fascinated by how we can learn something larger about the world by tracing seemingly mundane or trivial physical entities. I have done this, in large part, through improvisation and chance, believing in how it would all come together in the end, much like China seems to have done in its experimental moves and waves of development. It is endeavouring to dare greatly.

This finally brings me to the person I dedicate this book to: my loved and loving father, Peter Kirkegaard. Almost up to his very last day, and as I finished my PhD, he provided insightful and meaningful comments and reflections, not least on connections to poetry, chance, improvisation in jazz and bebop that come together to create new beauty, detective stories and spy plots, but also on a great many other matters besides.

It is for him that I have written this book. Be Babalula[10].

Abbreviations

AC	Alternating Current
AMSC	American Superconductor
AoM	Anthropology of Markets
ANT	Actor–Network Theory
CCC	China Compulsory Certification
CCCPC	Central Committee of the Communist Party of China
CGC	China General Certification
CPC	Communist Party of China
CRESP	China Renewable Energy Scale-Up Program
CWEA	China Wind Energy Association
DC	Direct Current
DNV	Det Norske Veritas
DNV GL	Det Norske Veritas merged with Germanischer Lloyd (and Garrad Hassen, GH)
DSO	Distribution System Operator
FDI	Foreign Direct Investments
FIT	Feed-In Tariff
GATT	General Agreement on Tariffs and Trade
GDP	Gross Domestic Product
GIN	Global Innovation Network
GVC	Global Value Chain
GW	Gigawatt
GWh	Gigawatt hour
HAWC2	Horizontal Axis Wind turbine simulation Code 2nd generation
IEC	International Electrotechnical Commission
IP	Intellectual Property
IPR	Intellectual Property Rights
ISO	International Organization for Standardization
KIBS	Knowledge-Intensive Business Services
LAC	Loads, Aerodynamics, and Control
LCOE	Levelised Cost of Energy
LLL	Linkage, Leverage, and Learning
LVRT	Low-Voltage Ride-Through

M&A	Mergers and Acquisitions
MIIT	Ministry of Industry and Information Technology
MMS	Mandatory Market Shares
MNC	multinational corporation
MOST	Ministry of Science and Technology of the People's Republic of China
MW	Megawatt
NDA	Non-Disclosure Agreement
NDRC	National Development and Reform Commission
NEA	National Energy Administration
OECD	Organisation for Economic Co-operation and Development
OEM	Original Equipment Manufacturer
PLA	People's Liberation Army
PPA	Power Purchase Agreements
PRC	People's Republic of China
R&D	Research and Development
RPS	Renewable Portfolio Standard
S&T	Science & Technology
SASAC	State Asset Supervision and Administration Council
SDC	Sino-Danish Center for Education and Research
SOEs	State-Owned Enterprises
STA	Socio-Technical Assemblage (*agencement*)
STS	Science & Technology Studies
TBT	Technical Barriers to Trade agreement
TIS	Technological Innovation System
TRIPS	Agreement on Trade-Related Aspects of Intellectual Property Rights
TSO	Transmission System Operator
WFOE	wholly foreign owned enterprise
WIPO	World Intellectual Property Organisation
WT	Wind turbine
WTM	Wind turbine manufacturer
WTO	World Trade Organization

Notes

1. The Sino-Danish Centre for Research and Education (SDC), the Graduate University of Chinese Academy of Sciences, and the Chinese Academy of Sciences.
2. Copenhagen Business School (CBS), previously at Department of Business & Politics, now at Department of Organization, and the Technical University of Denmark, Department of Wind Energy.
3. NTNU, Norwegian University of Science and Technology, Department of Interdisciplinary Studies of Culture.
4. Stanford University, Graduate School of Business, Graduate School of Education, SCANCOR/Scandinavian Consortium for Organizational Research.
5. Department of Wind Energy, Technical University of Denmark.
6. Copenhagen Business School, CBS, Department of Organization (previously at Department of Business & Politics).
7. Aalborg University in Copenhagen, cDIST, Centre for Design, Innovation and Sustainable Transition.
8. Copenhagen Business School, CBS, Asia Research Center, Department of International Economics and Management.
9. Copenhagen Business School, CBS, Department of Organization (previously at Department of Business & Politics).
10. Title of song by the Danish music band, tv2, in the album 'Nutidens Unge' (1984) – with reference to bebop - which my father would often quote or sing.

Part I

Setting the context for the controversy study of Chinese 'greening' through accelerated wind power development

Prologue
The algorithmic universe of wind power – mapping controversies over China's 'wind power miracle'

'Give me one matter of concern and I will show you the whole earth and heavens that have to be gathered to hold it firmly in place'
(Bruno Latour (2004:246), 'Why Has Critique Run out of Steam? From Matters of Fact to Matters of Concern')

Stepping into the wind turbine, it dawns on me for the first time: what I thought to be a relatively simple machine is actually assembled from thousands of components, some visible and some hidden. I start to understand why there may be so many quality issues in China's booming wind turbine industry – if these assembly blocks are not fitted perfectly together or optimised, each and every one of them, I reckon there may be some quality implications. And I assume there may be some implications for China's long-held strategy of technology transfer in the wind turbine industry. What they are, though, I have not yet found out. I get a hint of this during my first field trip to China in 2011, where I, to my big surprise, am not told about the great successes of Chinese wind power deployment – China's heralded 'wind power miracle' – but instead more about the abundance of quality issues surfacing in the Chinese wind power sector. And so my project of tracing China's great ascendance on to the global scene through its integration into global innovation networks becomes more complicated.

Not an engineer by training, I have an idea that it is important to understand how collaborative relations are formed not just at an industrial level, but at a more fine-grained level: what I am curious about is the role of specific technologies, particularly the 'core technologies', and their role in ensuring the 'quality' of the wind turbine. Where things are considered 'core', 'key', 'strategic', and 'political', this is where they are likely to become messy and controversial, especially in a developmental context such as China's. This sets me on a detective story, gradually disassembling the wind turbine into its constituent components and inquiring into what the core of the wind turbine is, as I want to trace the formation and transformation of collaborative and competitive relations that are formed around it.

Little did I know that this would take me to the software algorithms of the wind turbine's supervisory main controller or the simulation tool used for certifying wind turbine designs. These algorithmic components are both invisible components to the outsider. Yet they are critical in ensuring the quality of the turbine, its reliability, and its performance. Functioning as the 'spine' of the wind turbine, the 'core algorithm' of the control system is key to the wind turbine's performance, one of my respondents, a foreign control system supplier, tells me in a dark corner of my favourite café in Beijing. The core algorithm is positioned at the centre of all the different source code scripts. As such, it binds together all information from the different components to regulate the wind turbine in the most efficient and safest way. Much later in my research, another respondent working in a foreign wind turbine design house informs me in his kitchen, while his Chinese wife makes us excellent pancakes for dinner, about the importance of the simulation tool for certification and standardisation of new and optimised wind turbine design. Here, aeroelastic codes in simulation tools form the 'stomach' of the entire turbine, helping to tame the potentially disruptive powers of the stochastically fluctuating wind. However, while being critical of the upgrading of Chinese wind power, which has stumbled upon a severe quality crisis in recent years, such proprietary software codes are being 'locked, sealed, and protected in every possible and impossible way'. And so, as it turns out, this is where power struggles unfold in the supply chain around software as Chinese actors strive to turn an unfolding quality crisis in Chinese wind power towards a turn to quality: around software algorithms so critical to China's 'scientific development' on its path towards a 'Harmonious Socialist Society'.

It is only later, as I unpack my luggage in Denmark after yet another trip to China, filled with new data and technical information that I, to my great frustration, do not fully comprehend, that I recall the voice of the female engineer who joined one of my first ethnographic field trips. At that point I did not understand why she kept asking various Chinese scientists, researchers, and wind turbine manufacturers about how they had got hold of their control system software and design tools. And so I write to her. She invites me to see a wind turbine at the national wind energy research centre in Roskilde, Denmark. Drawing the drive-train of the wind turbine for me on the whiteboard, she elaborates further on why some components are considered core components of the wind turbine. Though much of this is still a riddle to me, I nod. I have a feeling that I still need to build up the technical engineering language to understand what she and my respondents in China and at home are speaking about.

It is the beginning of a journey whose ending is unknown to me. It is a journey that I decide to embark on by myself, largely without guidance, and where I have to educate myself. The only advice I get is from my respondents during iterative fieldwork trips in China and Denmark; they help to guide my enquiries, even though they don't know what I am looking for. And so it becomes a journey where I feel like a detective, first without much of a lead, but as the plot grows thicker around core algorithms, it becomes a detective story with multiple leads. It takes me to a power struggle over access to critical software algorithms to tame the wind, but also to unexpected fields, entities, and actors: By travelling through the algorithmic universe of the wind turbine, a much broader story about the Chinese greening of its electrical power sector through renewable energy market development and expansion, enmeshed in China's fragmented authoritarianism, is provided. This story illustrates, amongst other things, the wind power sector's entanglement in a Chinese spider's web-like mesh of state-business relations, entangled in a 'system problem' of China's socialist market economy. And so the algorithmic story unveils a much broader story about the contested and negotiated nature of Chinese catch-up, greening, and industrial development, one that reveals underlying socio-material power struggles between fossil fuels and renewables, but also over the very mode of what I find to be a particular Chinese pragmatics of experimental market construction and its implications for constant trials of strength in transforming Sino-foreign supply chain relations that are based on software.

And so the algorithmic journey through the wind turbine begins…

Entering into the round tower of a wind turbine for the first time, putting on the elaborate safety gear, and climbing the long, sparsely lit and confined access ladder, one emerges into the turbine nacelle on top of the wind turbine. It is a vast place, far bigger than expected and packed with equipment. The nacelle is the machine room that houses many of the core components of a wind turbine, with the electrical generator at its heart. By this stage, it will have dawned on most people that a wind turbine is not the simple machine that it may appear to be from the outside. Indeed, even though most conventional three-bladed wind turbines may look the same to the layperson, they can be more or less advanced and be worlds apart in terms of performance.

As a complex energy conversion system, a wind turbine constitutes a complicated assemblage of thousands of components – blades, gearbox, generator, brakes, bearings, yaw drives, transformers, and power electronics – all on a scale that is likely to impress any spectator when they see them for the first time (refer to Figure 0.1 for visual representation of modern wind turbine and its main components). Indeed, signs of the turbine's primary function, to convert the kinetic energy of the wind into electrical power, are everywhere, as evidenced by all these engineering components (Manwell, McGowan & Rogers 2010). But the electrical energy itself is nowhere to be seen. The main shaft turns, the generator rotates, and the transformer hums. To appreciate the energy conversion and its flow, one has to 'see' into the components as an electrical engineer does.

As the precisely designed rotor of the generator is turned by the wind, its carefully controlled electromagnetic field meshes with that of the stator, sending pulsating waves of newly generated electricity through the cables and down the tower. Here, the low-tension energy is intensified by the electromagnetic fields of the transformer, and the energy is pushed on further as high-voltage electric waves carry the electricity into the lengthy overhead lines that transport

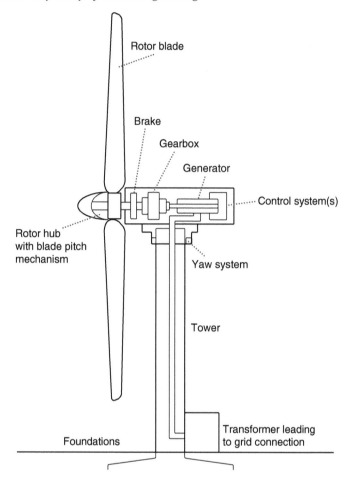

Figure 0.1 A modern wind turbine and its main components.

Source: Bieksha 2013.

the electrical energy into the powerful national grid. Only now can one sense the power of the energy flow that journeys through all these components, and which powers factories, houses, vehicles, and much more, all around the globe.

And yet much smaller and less obvious components have come to play an increasingly critical role in today's globally competitive wind turbine industry. As wind turbines over the last few decades have grown considerably in size, and as wind power provides ever larger shares of the electrical energy consumed in mature wind power nations (for instance 45 per cent in Denmark and 20 per cent in Germany), wind turbines have required increasingly more (algorithmic) 'intelligence' built into them. To ensure an optimised power output and the safe operation of massive rotating machinery, and to minimise the risk of disruption to the grid from the stochastically fluctuating forces of the wind, more and more computing power is employed to control turbines. This 'intelligence' is written into line after line of computer code, calculation algorithms, and data handling software. It is used not only in control systems that serve to control, manage, and monitor the turbine itself, and in the simulation tools employed to develop an optimised turbine design, but also in those programmes that are an integral part of certifying a modern wind turbine (see Box 0.1 for more details on algorithms). Strikingly, the impression of the turbine one gets from inside the nacelle machine room is a very different one from what is presented when one visits a wind turbine research establishment. Here the same wind turbine that was experienced as a mighty physical machine is represented in a virtual world by thousands of lines of computer code on a screen, where the calculations embedded in algorithms model the turbine's design and simulate its control.

Much of the competition in today's global wind turbine industry revolves around such continuous efforts to optimise the turbine's energy output using advanced algorithms – often protected from copying through intellectual property rights (IPRs) or encryption devices and technical locks – that are programmed into number-crunching software. But it is not only the

---

Box 0.1

Algorithms – what's all the fuzz about?

Algorithms as a concept have been around for centuries. The idea goes back to the era of the great Greek mathematicians. All algorithms display – in a series of logical steps – how an output is obtained based on a set of inputs and a particular inscribed behaviour that is desired. They are designed to solve a problem (or series of problems) and today often form the basis for transcription into software code for implementation by a computer.

They can be very straightforward or highly complex, but what they have in common is that they attempt to simplify (or model) a system such that there is a good chance of controlling it and providing predictability. The nightmare of the author of an algorithm is that the system encounters a situation in reality that he/she has not thought of. There are always 'corners' of uncertainty of the operational envelope that are not covered, but good algorithms have a flexibility and a robustness that tries to ensure the system does not get stuck in an endless loop or a situation it cannot recover from.

So, whilst the objective function of an algorithm may be obvious ('find the optimum pitch angle for maximum power output', for example), the most sought-after implementations will not only be able to do just that under every conceivable situation, but will also maintain safe operation when the turbine finds itself in a situation the algorithm author had not thought of. In short, algorithms are devices to regulate risk and uncertainty, taming and controlling the potentially disruptive forces of the wind, whilst trying to cope with the unforeseeable.

output of individual turbines that is regulated by software, but also that of whole wind farms and even the operation of the entire electricity system. Increasingly, simulation and prediction tools are being relied upon for the forecasting of power production and demand, and in some countries, such as Denmark, for the pricing of energy. It therefore follows that a wind turbine and its 'competitiveness' is not only a function of the effectiveness of its software algorithms and other turbine components, but that it is also dependent on cost and price calculations that are inscribed into system operators' databases. These price characteristics often filter through to the spreadsheets and asset portfolios displayed on computer screens of investment banks or in the turbine manufacturer's annual reports.

Continuing the journey around the less obvious and unseen wind turbine components, let us look at the specific example of the wind turbine's main supervisory controller. Its software algorithms regulate the turbine's operation, making sure it accurately adjusts the pitch angle of the blades in accordance with the changing speed of the wind (Bianchi, de Battista & Mantz 2007). Additionally, the controller signals motors to rotate (or 'yaw') the nacelle to align the rotor when the wind changes direction. Thus, the supervisory main controller functions as the turbine's 'brain' or 'central nervous system' (interviews), as it ensures the systemic interplay of the many sub-controllers that regulate the various individual components of the turbine. With such fundamental influence on the turbine's performance and energy output, the main supervisory controller, and in particular the algorithms and source code that it uses, constitutes one of the turbine's most vital components, or what can be called a 'core technology' (interviews). Without it, there is no control over the rotor's inertia, the generator's electromagnetic fields, the energy fed into the grid, nor the balance between energy production and operational safety. Less dramatically, the turbine would be significantly less efficient, unable to convert as much of the wind's kinetic energy as otherwise would be possible.

Another example of a core technology that is central to the development of a modern wind power sector is the simulation software used when certifying a new wind turbine design to an accredited standard. Being able to demonstrate compliance with, for instance, the widely recognised international standard for wind turbines, the International Electrotechnical Commission (IEC) 61400, is the goal for any manufacturer wishing to sell turbines internationally. Simulating the heart of the wind turbine, the aeroelastic code in the simulation tool is decisive in assessing whether the turbine is compliant or not, being fundamental in modelling the relationship between wind velocity (speed and direction), blade pitch, rotational rotor speed, and structural loads. The code is thus critical in assessing the safeguarding of the structure of the turbine, whilst the supervisory controller works to maximise the energy harvested from the kinetic energy of the wind.

Although invisible to an observer in the nacelle, these algorithmic source codes in the supervisory main control and simulation tool represent the turbine's 'algorithmic intelligence' and the basis for decisions in the certifi-cation process. At the same time, these algorithms play an important role in a broader sense: the transition from fossil fuels to renewable energy. This is because they are key constituents in the struggle to reduce the cost of wind energy: the more the turbine design is capable of harvesting energy out of the kinetic forces of the wind owing to optimised control and/or aerody-namic design, the lower the cost of energy that will be produced, and the better wind power can compete against fossil fuels in terms of cost.

This constant need to crunch and optimise numbers is linked to the socio-technical character of the wind: it is uncontrollable and stochastically volatile. When the wind blows, energy can be produced, but when it does not, no energy can be produced. What instead can be controlled is how well a turbine (and thus a wind farm) harvests and converts the wind into energy, and how it is distributed into the grid. In turn, once generated, electricity cannot be readily stored in bulk, but must be fed into the system as it is being produced, to be distributed and consumed.[1] Such an optimisation of use and output is of great importance for the cost effectiveness of wind power.

Today, a turbine's 'algorithmic intelligence' can be argued to have come to represent wind turbine 'quality', as it helps to control and tame the poten-tially disruptive impact of the stochastically fluctuating wind on the stability of the grid. That is, it contributes to making wind power more economically viable by helping to ensure more predictable and controllable wind power. In this way, algorithms contribute to delivering green (renewable) energy in a sustainable manner, and the heightened importance of these algorithms signifies a particular milestone in the development of wind power tech-nology. Wind turbines have, of course, been continually optimised, start-ing from the simple and relatively cumbersome, stiff, and rigid induction machine generators of the 1980s–1990s that employed a basic fixed-speed generator.[2] Over time, this led to the doubly fed generator, and eventually to today's sophisticated synchronous generators operating at variable speeds – little brothers of those used in coal-fired power stations – this advance in some instances having enabled manufacturers to get rid of the fault-prone gearbox in modern wind turbines. Now, with full-range power electronics and the ability to actively pitch the elastic blades, full variable speed can be achieved, requiring that the wind turbine controllers and their algo-rithms regulate the turbine so that it reacts nimbly to both the wind and the grid's conditions, signals, and needs – requirements that have become more demanding as more and more wind turbines and wind power operate in the national grids (Tande & Jenkins 2003). Thus, wind turbines have gradually developed from relatively crude machines, with upgrades in efficiency, size, and controllability. These improvements – afforded amongst other things by enhanced aeroelastic blade design, inertia control, power electronic con-verters, advanced forecasting tools, pitch control systems that can regulate the mechanical power in the rotor transferred to the gearbox by pitching the blades according to shifting wind speeds, generator control systems that can change the rotor's electromagnetic fields in a split second – have brought technological and scientific breakthroughs in the flexibility of operation, along with increased interdependencies between components and actors. Overall, the technological advancements and the present moment of 'algorithmic quality' reflect a much broader story of the transition of the power system to accommodate larger shares of fluctuating renewable energy. This is a story of making both the grid and the turbines more flexible, capable of balancing the needs of harvesting the variability of the wind, whilst not disturbing the stability of the electrical grid.

What follows is not, however, an engineering textbook for optimising software algorithms in wind turbines. Rather, this work undertakes a trip into the previously unseen socio-technical algorithmic and kaleidoscopic universe of wind power development in a country relatively new to wind power, one which has experienced unprecedented growth in installed capacity along with an ensuing quality crisis and a still imminent turn to quality, but which today represents the world's largest wind power market in terms of gigawatts (GW) of installed capacity. This country is China. The ethnographic inquiry into Chinese wind power development, though, is conducted in an unconventional manner, namely by following the power as we journey through different key components of the wind turbine, down the tower, through the transformer, and into the Chinese state-controlled grid system, where wind power constitutes an ever-increasingly important part of the country's transition to renewable energy, now around 4 per cent of the national electricity supply. What is revealed in travelling through the wind turbine are the often opaque and frequently hidden socio-material contestations playing out in China's drive to increase the proportion of renewable energy in the country's power system: contestations over the imminent greening of China's coal-based and state-controlled electrical power sector. This work further exposes critical aspects of the relationships, and their transformation and contestation, between Chinese manufacturers and foreign suppliers, state–industry relations, and between certification and standardisation bodies, research institutions and universities, consultancies, design houses, and laboratories, around software algorithms – as Chinese actors rapidly catch up.

Meanwhile, and as will be shown – maybe to some surprise – the algorithmic story reflects a much broader story about what is here hypothesised as what might be a particularly Chinese mode of experimental, pragmatic, and fragmented industry creation (or market construction) within renewable energy, and the contestations this produces. The story also uncovers aspects of the legitimacy struggle(s) in which the Chinese Party-State finds itself. These struggles relate to not only the balancing act of finding the right degree of opening up the Chinese economy to global competition and of protecting its strategic sectors and state-owned enterprises (SOEs), but also to finding the right balance between rapid scaling up and experimentalism, versus a more cautious growth path. Meanwhile the political monopoly of the Communist Party of China (CPC) needs to be preserved through maintenance of social stability and ensuring 'sustainable' development. Accordingly, by tracing algorithms, a story of power is provided, not only in physical terms of electrical power struggles, but also in terms of socio-political power. It is a story of the fight to gain 'algorithmic power' over the potentially disruptive powers of the wind in China's current coal-based power system; that is, by taming ambiguities, uncertainties, and risks of the wind through algorithms. But it is also a story of increasingly complex technological and socio-material interdependencies that render it impossible to entirely rule out such latent ambiguity and uncertainty. Indeed, as will be uncovered, while algorithms are deployed to reduce uncertainty, they often turn out to operate at a deeper level, producing even more uncertainty as they raise new concerns and controversy. Through understanding the controversies raised by the complex and intricate algorithms, it will also be discussed how the experimental mode of industry creation in wind power that has been detected may prove more risky, wasteful and costly in relatively high-tech sectors such as wind power, than in sectors that are technologically less advanced. Thus, the volume is concerned with the contested viability of Chinese 'experimentalism', and touches upon the importance of having a more fine-grained understanding of the applicability of such experimentalism in different sectors and at different levels of technological complexity.

In short, this book presents the previously untold story of the accelerated development of Chinese wind power, with its socio-material cycles of volatility and phases of (potential) self-disruption. It uncovers and articulates some of the complex and often hidden socio-material struggles that are taking place as China emerges as a potential green leader of the world – a role particularly strengthened as China's President Xi Jinping in 2017 reasserted China's commitments to the United Nations Paris Agreement on Climate signed in 2016 (whilst President Donald Trump has withdrawn the USA from it). To set the context for the ethnographic journey, this study first provides a brief overview of the development of China's wind power sector (Chapter One), which leads to a presentation of the unique analytical lens that this work brings to bear, namely the Anthropology of Markets within Science and Technology Studies (STS), and a controversy mapping method (Chapter Two). Next, a brief review of the existing China Studies literature sets the context for understanding Chinese particularities of wind power development. The brief review is concluded by a brief outline of a 'relational gap' in the literature, which this book argues can be filled in by the Anthropology of Markets and the relational 'pragmatist tunnel' and socio-technical lens that the book brings to bear (Chapter Three). Together, the Prologue and Chapters One to Three of Part I set the stage for Part II (Chapters Four to Eight), which conducts an algorithmic controversy study, diving into five different but enmeshed 'sites of controversy' (over 1) the ongoing quality (qualification) crisis (Chapter Four); 2) access to the electrical power grid (Chapter Five), 3) access to money (Chapter Six); 4) access to Intellectual Property Rights (IPRs) (Chapter Seven); and 5) access to standards and certificates (Chapter Eight)). In Part III (Chapters Nine and Ten), the volume concludes: In Chapter Nine the book reflects on contributions to China Studies as well as to the Anthropology of Markets within STS, while Chapter Ten reflects on the broader implications for related literatures such as Economic Geography (particularly notions of global innovation networks/GINs and value chain upgrading and governance) from the perspective of the Anthropology of Markets, concluding in a brief discussion of the need to cross-fertilise relational and structural perspectives in New Economic Sociology more broadly.

Overall, what you will find on this journey is:

- A mapping of controversies in Sino-foreign supply chain relations around software and in the overarching transition to renewable energy, whose *socio-material* constitution is often overlooked in the extant literature.
- A discussion of the development of Chinese wind power as an example of a potentially particular – and contested – fragmented, experimental pragmatics of green market construction.
- An account of how Chinese fragmented authoritarianism makes the seemingly paradoxical experimental mode of Chinese wind power development 'logical' in a Chinese developmental perspective, that is driven by a growth imperative of upscaling and upgrading. The account also reveals how this mode of development becomes contested as some of the hidden costs and risks of such development in a high-tech sector reveal themselves;
- An inquiry into the shifting configuration of Sino-foreign customer–supplier relations around core technologies, exploring implications for Chinese upgrading, learning, and catchup around software algorithms, set into the politicised context of Chinese ambitions for scientific development and the schism between accelerated industrial development through applied science versus gradual learning through basic research.
- An account of controversies over what 'sustainability', 'quality', 'science', and 'innovation' are and should be, and who and what should be allowed to define them.

Meanwhile, the multifaceted and algorithmic story that follows has only been made possible through the unique perspective from the Anthropology of Markets within STS, one which has not previously been introduced to China Studies (see, however, Kirkegaard 2015). This book therefore offers a unique and innovative contribution to the budding conversation between STS and China Studies, one which extends its implications not only into China Studies, but also into STS and market studies, and New Economic Sociology more broadly, such as Innovation Studies, International Business, Transition Studies, the literature on Institutional Fields, and more. Before going further, it is necessary to lay out some of the specific characteristics of Chinese wind power development, and its volatile waves of disruption. This empirical context is provided in Chapter One. It is time to turn on our torch, check our safety harness, ensure our hard hat is securely on, and move on to the next section of the wind turbine nacelle.

Notes

1. Electricity can be stored in hydro-dams and in batteries. However, this depends on the availability of hydropower and on huge investments into still inefficient batteries. Today, vast amounts of R&D investments are going into the development of cheaper and smaller batteries. Still, however, this is a technology that must be developed further before it can be part of the solution to the issue of fluctuating wind power and grid balancing. Apart from these developments, China boasts vast hydropower resources (Gorm Hansen 2017), which can act as a battery/storage for wind power.
2. Induction refers to electromagnetic induction: moving electromagnetic fields will induce a current in a stationary wire. This enables the transfer of mechanical power from the rotor to electrical power in the generator.

References

Bianchi, F.D., de Battista, H. & Mantz, R.J., 2007, *Wind Turbine Control Systems, Principles, Modelling and Gain Scheduling Design*, Springer, Berlin.

Bieksha, J., 2013, *Market Facts – Wind Energy*, 2 September 2013, http://www.connectorsupplier.com/021913-cs-ff-wind-energy/.

Gorm Hansen, L. L., 2017, *Triggering earthquakes in science, politics and Chinese hydropower. A controversy study*, PhD thesis, Dept. of International Economics and Management, Asia Studies Centre, Copenhagen Business School.

Kirkegaard, J. K., 2015, *Ambiguous Winds of Change – Or Fighting against Windmills in Chinese Wind Power: Mapping Controversies over a Potential Turn to Quality in Chinese Wind Power*, PhD thesis, Department of Business & Politics, Copenhagen Business School.

Manwell, J. F., McGowan, J. G. & Rogers, A. L., 2010, *Wind Energy Explained: Theory, Design and Application*, 2 edn., Wiley: Hoboken, NJ.

Tande, J. O. G., & Jenkins, N., 2003, 'Grid Integration of Wind Farms', *Wind Energy*, 6:281–295, DOI: 10.1002/we.91.

1 Upgrading in software algorithms at the core of Chinese wind power development

China entered the wind turbine industry relatively late. Nevertheless, within the last decade, Chinese wind turbine manufacturers have emerged as 'Dragon Multinationals' (Mathews 2016). These companies are increasingly able to manufacture competitive, state-of-the-art wind turbine systems, and are claimed to be integrating into global learning and innovation networks as they experiment with control system software, software applications, and indigenous (homegrown) design (interviews; Lewis 2013:166; Mathews 2016; Silva & Klagge 2013). Despite being the world's largest CO_2 emitter, China is now greening its electrical power sector at an unprecedented rate through world-record investments in renewable energy, and particularly in wind power. This is a process that coincides with the country's rise as the world's largest electricity consuming nation (from hydropower, coal power, wind power, nuclear, and natural gas), owing to the simultaneous rapid growth in its industrial sectors, and coinciding with the Chinese government's stimulus package designed to ensure the recovery from the global financial crisis that hit the world around 2007–2008.[1] As a recent sign of serious intention, China's proclaimed 'Energy Revolution' (*néngyuán géming*, 能源革命) strategy, promulgated through 'Document #9', lays out the clear ambition to strengthen grid capacity, expand distributed generation, and improve the integration of renewable energy into the electrical power system, and gradually introduce spot electricity markets[2] (Chung & Xu 2016; Communist Party of China Central Committee and the State Council 2015; Dupuy 2016; Göss 2017; Liu & Kong 2016; National Energy Administration (NEA) 2015).

In this way, the 'Coal Kingdom' of China, which has suffered (and still suffers) from a long-held reputation of politically contentious pollution problems and policy enforcement problems, particularly on environmental issues and the implementation of environmental laws (Economy 2004 and Stern 2013 in Gorm Hansen 2017:112), is greening its electrical power system. For some, this emerging 'Beijing model' of a sustainable transition to renewable energy, which has spurred Chinese industrial development and development in green technologies, is laid out as a potential route for other developing and emerging economies to follow (Mathews & Tan 2015). Boasting a total cumulative installed wind production capacity of 188 GW

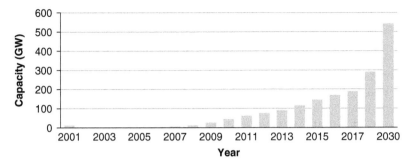

Figure 1.1 Cumulative installed wind power capacity in China.

Sources: GWEC 2016:21; 2018.

and an astounding 35 per cent of the world's cumulative total of 540 GW installed wind power by the end of 2017 (Global Wind Energy Council (GWEC) 2018), China is now poised to become the world's global 'green leader' (Mathews & Tan 2015; Mathews 2016). The virtual explosion in wind power since 2005 speaks for itself in Figure 1.1.

Growth rates in installed wind power capacity took off in China after 2005 following the introduction of the state-led auction-based concession programme (2003–2009) and, in particular, after the groundbreaking Renewable Energy Law was issued in 2005 (enacted 2006), more or less simultaneously with the revolutionary 11th Five-Year Plan (2006–2010) that provided a watershed in the focus on renewable energy (Fan 2006).

Paradoxically, the clear policy intent and regulatory framework that these policies and plans provided – particularly with ambitious installation targets and support mechanisms for investments into wind power development – did not only result in the rapid upscaling of China's wind power sector in terms of installed wind power capacity (measured in GW), but soon also brought with it unintended externalities in terms of a tsunami of quality issues. In 2010 there were already 'visible flaws in China's wind power industry' (Riley & Vance 2012). The reasons were manifold, one of which was the production quality of wind turbines:

> Since the government planners demanded [installed] quantity [GW], and not performance [measured in gigawatt hour, GWh, generated electricity], wind farm developers tended to cut corners. Thousands of China's turbines lack the more expensive technology that keeps them operating when there is a disturbance on the power grid. (Riley & Vance 2012)

More precisely, as there were no clear incentives for wind turbine performance – for the level of electricity generation – wind turbines were developed and wind farms were installed without regard to their ability to actually deliver power to the grid. This is what a "planned economy" can look like at times[3]. One of the main problems for wind turbines and wind farms was the lack of investment into research and development (R&D) (interviews), and the lack of adequately advanced control system software – with advanced and optimised algorithms – that was designed to fit Chinese conditions, as well as the lack of certification requirements according to any conventional international quality standards (interviews; Kirkegaard 2015). As a result, turbines and their control and design systems were plainly not of sufficient (algorithmic) quality. This, in turn, resulted in surging numbers of curtailed/downrated wind farms that were simply not allowed to connect to the grid even when the wind was blowing, as they could threaten grid stability. As a result, grid companies (transmission system operators/TSOs) and power-generating companies soon viewed wind power as a 'trouble-maker' that threatened to destabilise the grid and their balance sheets.

This emergent 'quality crisis' (interviews; Kirkegaard 2015; Li 2015) in Chinese wind power was, however, significantly troublesome, and prompted central government to nimbly intervene in an attempt to reinstall wind power as a reliable power source. This was done, for example, through the introduction of certification requirements and an emphasis on the need for developing domestic, or indigenous (i.e. homegrown), IPRs and standards. Most particularly, this was aimed at core technologies such as wind turbine software (both control systems and simulation tools) to reduce dependence on Western technology, as dictated in particular in the 12th Five-Year Plan on the Scientific and Technological Development of Wind Power (MOST 2012).

Turning the Chinese wind turbine industry from a sector experiencing a quality crisis into one that focuses on quality does not, however, happen overnight. Indeed, even though there are signs that a 'turn to quality' has been instigated (interviews; Kirkegaard 2015; Li 2015), the signs remain ambiguous. What is certain, though, is that amongst all the ambiguity, core technologies such as software tools have been constituted as critically important and strategic for the survival of the Chinese wind power sector. The critical nature of these technologies during this potential turn to quality means that Sino-foreign supply chain relationships around these very tools and technologies have become volatile because of their strategic, or political, nature. The relationships are now far more prone to power struggles. Chinese actors are increasingly struggling to design and develop their own software tools in order to become independent from foreign technology, at the same time as foreign actors (suppliers of simulation packages, for instance) strive to protect their own core competence through proprietary IPRs or by setting standards that are difficult to achieve and depend on advanced simulation tools, as well as long-term experience and basic research.

Sustainability contested in Chinese wind power

The quality crisis and the subsequent focusing on core technologies during the ongoing turn to quality have done more than just instigate power struggles in and around turbine technology. They reflect a broader underlying struggle to legitimise wind power as a sustainable renewable power source both in terms of provision of energy, but more importantly in terms of China's state focus on using wind power as a means of industrial policy to sustain China's growth model (Kroeber 2016; Lardy 2016; Naughton 2014): using the sector as a means for industrial upgrading and technological catch-up, by tapping into foreign resources and via sometimes radical government intervention (or, as will be illustrated, radical lack thereof).

The legitimisation of wind power as sustainable was, however, destabilised owing to the poorly operating and/or curtailed (downrated) wind farms that seemed a 'resource waste of unimaginable dimensions'. Industry reports during the growth spurt consistently reported that between one fourth and one third of installed wind power was being curtailed or disconnected from the electrical grid (interviews; Bloomberg 2012; Klagge, Liu & Silva 2012; Lewis 2013). As the wind was blowing but turbines were not allowed to connect to the grid, the result was 'a lot of coal-based power plants, which just stand there and burn off a lot of power, and they actually don't care. They are just producing like crazy. And that's not sustainable' (Interview with foreign control system supplier 2013). With turbines that did not function properly and a lack of experience in developing indigenous tools that could remedy the quality issues and/or boost China's green or techno-scientific reputation, China's comprehensive mode of understanding sustainable development as a matter of 'scientific development' was being seriously challenged: In China, 'sustainability' and 'sustainable development' are inextricably coupled to the ambitious, yet ambiguous, vision of a so-called Chinese 'Harmonious Socialist Society' (*Shèhuì zhǔyì héxié shèhuì*, 社会主义和谐社会) (Fan 2006), which was introduced in 2004 under former President Hu Jintao. In turn, whilst a harmonious society is the objective, 'scientific development is the method to reach it' (Naughton 2005 and The New 2005 in Fan 2006:709).

A comprehensive mode of understanding sustainable development through scientific development

The influential notion of the portmanteau term 'scientific developmentalism' (*kēxué fāzhǎn guān*, 科学发展) (Naughton 2011) was first introduced in 2003 by President Hu Jintao (Christensen 2013:85-86),[4] and later enshrined in CPC doctrines, which marked its legitimisation (Christensen 2013:86). To achieve scientific development, the development of indigenous innovation capabilities (*zìzhǔ chuàngxīn*, 自主创新) in science, research, and within core technologies, has been construed as indispensable (Andrews-Speed 2012; Christensen 2013; Fan 2006:709–717; Lewis 2013; Mathews & Tan 2015; Meidan, Andrews-Speed & Xin 2009; Serger & Breidne 2007). China's emphasis on core technologies and the pursuant '[i]ncreasing investments in research and development underscores this trend' and reveals an underlying emphasis on applied science (Gorm Hansen 2017:113). According to the Organisation for Economic Co-operation and Development (OECD),

China's spending on R&D, as a percentage of gross domestic product (GDP), has risen from 0.7 per cent in 1991 to 2 per cent in 2014, and is 'now higher than that of the 28 European Union countries' whose aggregate spending on research and development was at 1.9 per cent of GDP in 2014 (OECD 2016 in Gorm Hansen 2017:109). This emphasis on R&D and applied science suggests an exploitative and utilitarian view on science, namely as a matter of 'solving practical problems' and of producing new products or improving technical capabilities (Gorm Hansen 2017:113), rather than expanding the scientific status quo or reaching new (sometimes unexpected) radical insights, by undertaking more exploratory basic research (Cao 2004a, 2014). Overall, Hu Jintao's view of science 'as a tool to aid state development' largely continues to this day under President Xi Jinping (Gorm Hansen 2017:108), who several times has stressed the importance of scientific development for China's global competitiveness. For instance, Xi Jinping urged 'Greater Innovation' in 'Core Technologies' in an official speech on the issue of Science & Technology (S&T) in 2014, reiterating how China's 'past as a victim of invasion and subjugation' is 'a lesson in the price of scientific backwardness', whereby the country's future competitiveness is linked to its 'scientific and technological strength'. That is, scientific and technological strength 'determines changes in the world balance of political and economic power, and determines the fate of every nation' (Xi Jinping in Buckley 2014). Recently, though, the contentious notion of 'indigenous innovation' has been downplayed slightly for diplomatic reasons, as it created controversy amongst foreign governments over what was often construed as a matter of (c)overt protectionism (Breznitz & Murphree 2011; McGregor n.d.:33). Instead, the notion of open innovation has recently been promoted to overcome the contested 'translation issues' with respect to 'indigenous innovation' (interview 2016 with Chinese scientist and government advisor on S&T, who (co-)coined the original notion of 'indigenous innovation').

A genealogical timeline of the intricate web of key concepts around China's sustainable and scientific development is laid out in Figure 1.2, reflecting how research related to China often has to focus on slight changes in rhetoric and discourse to unravel the shifting priorities of the Chinese Party-State (Christensen 2013; Gorm Hansen 2017:113; Kirkegaard 2015).[5]

Overall, 'sustainable development' in China continues to be consistently and inherently coupled to developmental concerns about Chinese industrial upgrading, technological catch-up, and leapfrogging through indigenous innovation capabilities in core technologies and standard-setting (Christensen 2013:88; Ernst 2013). This coupling is seen, for instance, in the Chinese Ministry of Science & Technology's (MOST) influential 15-year National Plan for the Development of Science and Technology in the Medium and Long Term (2006–2020) (MOST 2006, State Council).

Encapsulating the vision of a Harmonious Socialist Society, the influential plan envisions Chinese upgrading and indigenous innovation in 'frontier technologies' and 'frontier scientific basic research issues', which will,

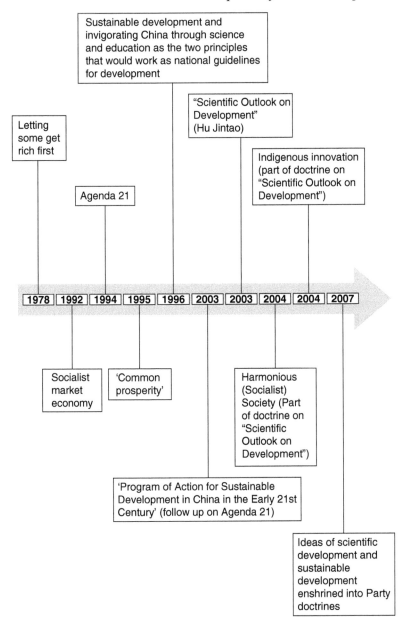

Figure 1.2 Timeline of concepts of sustainable and scientific development in China.

Source: Kirkegaard 2015; based on Christensen 2013; Fan 2006; Serger & Breidne 2007; Meidan et al. 2009.

in turn, create new market demands and new industries expected to lead the future economic growth and social development' (MOST 2006, preface, s. II(1)). Through such development, China should be able to leapfrog in priority fields, and to 'lead the future' in the realisation of the 'great renaissance of the Chinese nation' (MOST 2006, Preface, s. II(1)). The different frontier technologies and basic research areas include, amongst other things, software, IT, renewable energies, manufacturing, and core mathematics. Accordingly, the plan emphasises the need to raise the capability of equipment design, manufacturing, and integration, for example by promoting technological innovation, realising proprietary design, and manufacturing high-end programmed machine tools and key components, which highlights the need to transform and upgrade China's manufacturing industry using high technology and IT (MOST 2006, s. III; V2(6, 7, 8); VI3(6), 3(10)). Overall, by referring back to China's past and forward to China's renaissance, the plan construes a narrative around an imagined future for China, largely manifested through techno-scientific development, one which can also link up to the vision of a strong Chinese wind turbine sector.

And so, since 2004, the Chinese leadership has systematically promoted the paradigm of indigenous innovation 'as a way for China to climb up the global value chain' in different strategic sectors (Christensen 2013:88) and to become independent from foreign technology. Overall, '[t]here is no question that anything related to knowledge in China is also linked to politics' (Gorm Hansen 2017:113). Along the same lines, anything related to science, scientific disciplines, expertise, and even technology is 'political', as evidenced in the Chinese state's competitive race and struggle to win the Nobel Prize, to take out the most patents, and to publish the largest number of scientific papers (Cao 2004a, 2004b, 2014; Gorm Hansen 2017). This evident link between science and politics revealed its flipside during the Cultural Revolution of Mao Zedong and his attack on academics and scientists, but since then moved 'towards modern "Western" science under Mao, over Deng's turning Mao's ideas around to today where the push for innovation and upgrading relies heavily on applied science' (Gorm Hansen 2017:113). To this day, science and experts are used extensively, and increasingly, in Chinese policy-making, with scientifically educated personnel dominating the state bureaucratic apparatus and Party memberships (Gorm Hansen 2017:113).

Sustainable and scientific development as a matter of China's socialist modernisation

As such, sustainable development through scientific development has become a matter of ensuring China's comprehensive, balanced and sustainable development (Christensen 2013:85–86). The gradual development of a comprehensive discursive complex around sustainability, scientific development, and indigenous innovation reflects, in turn, a broader shift on China's path towards a socialist modernisation, namely towards a more 'social' vision of socio-economic development, which also entails a shift in the type of industrial production that is to be promoted (Christensen 2013:86–87). Thus, as China seeks to move from an economic model of extensive growth based on quantity – constituting China as a 'global factory' – towards an intensive economic growth model of quality and innovation (Christensen 2013:83; Ernst 2013), the CPC doctrine of sustainable development through a 'Scientific Outlook on Development' can 'be seen as the substantiation of the milestones of the second phase in the national tale' (Christensen 2013:86): While industrial growth was the overarching mantra of the first generations of China's communist political leadership, the gradual incorporation of more social concerns for sustainability reflects how the long-term official ideology of 'socialism with Chinese characteristics' associated with Deng Xiaoping's Open Door Policy (1978) and the construction of a 'socialist market economy' 'with Chinese characteristics' (1992) (Christensen 2013:84) has gradually changed its flavour,[6] in China's protracted transitioning process from a so-called planned to a (paradoxically) market-based yet social-ist planned economy (Meidan et al. 2009:593). Indeed, the 11th (2006–2010), 12th (2011–2015), and 13th (2016-2020) Five-Year Plans have sought to shift the economy away from the export-led model, 'which has benefited China for a generation but is no longer sustainable, towards a more consumption- and innovation-based economy' (Naughton 2015 in Mertha & Brødsgaard 2017:2) – a trend which has been enhanced during the recent 'new normal' of below-two-digit growth rates. Along with a more social vision of sustainable development, environmental concerns have increasingly come to the fore, as pollution issues have become politically more contentious. And so China's political leadership increasingly focuses on quality, innovation, high-tech production, and market-based sustainable growth in general, as also empha-sised in the recent 'Made in China 2025' strategy (State Council May 2015). So far, though, the transition of China's manufacturing industries from a scaling-up to an upgrading strategy still seems to have a fair way to go. These industries have generally benefited from second generation innovation and competition in terms of scale and pace that could lead to higher levels of innovation, rather than 'leading at the cusp of novel-product innovation' (Breznitz & Murphree 2011). However, enhanced global competition and strengthened ambitions for China's scientific development may produce ten-sions between the preference for industrial pace and scale through applied science and reverse engineering versus the ambition for indigenous innova-tion through more long-term frontier basic scientific research.

Linking renewable energy and wind power to sustainable development

Along with the gradual development of a comprehensive, developmental discourse around China's sustainable and scientific development, a host of plans, regulations, and policies for innovation and science and technology

(S&T) have been issued. A number are relevant to renewable energy and wind power in particular. Apart from the influential 15-year National Plan for the Development of Science and Technology in the Medium and Long Term 2006–2020 (MOST 2006), the doctrines of scientific development and sustainable development have also had an impact on China's Energy Policy (The Information Office of the State Council 2012), for instance:

> China will continue to take the Scientific Outlook on Development as its guiding principle, and work hard to transform its development pattern, giving prominence to building a resource-conserving and environment-friendly society. (The Information Office of the State Council 2012, Preface)

This implies, amongst other things, that China intends to 'further develop new and renewable energy resources'. In addition, the Energy Policy mentions the strategic role of core technologies (and the need to reduce dependency on their foreign importation), key equipment, and the need for further R&D, international cooperation, standardisation, and technological upgrading as well as a more environment-friendly energy mix (The Information Office of the State Council 2012). With specific regard to renewable energies, apart from being inscribed into the discourse of sustainable and scientific development (e.g. in the Renewable Energy Law) (Standing Committee of the National People's Congress 2005) and the Medium- to Long-Term Renewable Energy Plan (NDRC 2007), these have recently been promoted as constituting an increasingly important 'strategic sector' in China, playing a critical role in the sustainable development of China's economy and society (Lewis 2013). This is even though they still only account for a minor role in the overall energy mix. For instance, China's 12th Five-Year Plan (2011–2015) promotes renewable energy as 'new energy' under encouraged development (nuclear, solar, wind, and biomass). Renewable energy constitutes here one amongst several other 'strategic and emerging' industries,[7] replacing the often state-owned strategic pillar industries such as coal, oil, national defence, telecoms, electricity, airlines, and marine shipping (Lewis 2013:23; People's Daily Online, 11 May 2011).

Wind power, in turn, has recently been very firmly targeted. Five-Year Plans were previously issued referring to the development of wind power in general terms. It was only in 2012 that the scientific development of wind power was targeted specifically (signifying that the quality crisis had reached an unsustainable level), with the issuing of the Five-Year Plan for the Scientific and Technological Development of Wind Power (MOST 2012). Linking wind power development to the doctrine of sustainable and scientific development, the plan problematises the issue of China's technological and science-based backwardness, which means that 'there are still large gaps' when 'compared with the international advanced level'. To reinstate wind power in China as 'sustainable' and align it with the strategy of scientific development, these gaps have been targeted as ones to be filled, and the plan thus outlines a number of technological and scientific areas that need extra attention. In particular, the development of indigenous IPRs, software tools, and control system technologies are singled out, together with design and simulation tools, and technologies for certification and standardisation (MOST 2012), a theme that reiterates the mantra about the importance of indigenous (homebred) IPRs and standards in the 15-Year Plan for China's medium- to long-term scientific and technological development (2006–2020) (Ernst 2013; MOST 2006).

Wind power as a matter of (un)sustainability? China's 'turbine wave attack'

Meanwhile, the Chinese 'quality crisis' around wind power in about 2010–2011 soon started to raise questions about the sustainability of wind power, as explored in great detail in Chapter Four, as wind power could hardly be aligned with Chinese ambitions of scientific development.

What seems even more intriguing is how, somewhat paradoxically, it appears that the quality issues that had surfaced in China's wind turbine industry were pragmatically allowed by the state. This happened for instance through setting local forces loose, and through a radical lack of intervention until the very last minute. Indeed, it seems that China's wind power sector was deployed through a so-called 'human wave attack' (*rénhǎi zhànshù*, 人海战术) (interview with Chinese government advisor and wind turbine industry association 2013 in Kirkegaard 2015; also see Kirkegaard 2017). This draws a parallel with the old Chinese military offensive tactic, in which an attacker conducts an unprotected frontal assault with densely concentrated infantry formations against the enemy line, intending to over-run the defenders. China's wind turbine industry seemed to have conducted a similar frontal attack in its upscaling: In a veritable tsunami, a virtual 'turbine wave attack', the country had been flooded not with infantry but with (poor quality) wind turbines. This soon resulted in:

> massive quality problems. Massive grid break downs. Enormous problems. And you see that because you have been installing gigawatt by gigawatt of very poor quality. […] Without any of the key things you need to make a sustainable market… That's the direct consequence of that policy'. (Interview with foreign wind turbine manufacturer 2013)

In doing so, China had done it 'the Chinese way. You know, we call [it the] "Human Wave Attack"' (Interview with Chinese government advisor and wind turbine industry association 2013). There is an extra layer of meaning attached to the metaphor, as it also denotes a strategy of mobilising myriads of heterogeneous local actors, enrolling them in a strategy of distributed agency or Chinese 'crowdsourcing' – a particular mode of Chinese co-creation. In other words, local forces join together with only limited guidance from the state, and are able to act with great synergistic force to co-create a virtual 'marketquake' – one that could shake the tectonic plates of the sector as well as industry relations.

Learning from practice rather than imagination – on pragmatism as experimentalism

In turn, even though the Chinese state may not have intended to induce the number of quality issues that surfaced, it also did nothing to prevent them from happening. This strategy is linked to learning through 'failure' – rather than cracking down on failure at the outset:

> in China it's very strange, maybe different from Europe, but in China, we first do it then solve it! First do it then solve it! *(Xiān zuò, cái jiějué,* 先做, 才解决!) (Interview with Chinese government advisor and wind turbine industry association 2013)

As quality issues have emerged during this experimental strategy, central government has eventually intervened, such as through the Five-Year-Plan for the Scientific and Technological Development of Wind Power (MOST 2012) and the introduction of certification requirements. In this way, China has been able to manage the issues – but only when direly needed – flexibly and nimbly. This reveals a potentially unique Chinese experimental and pragmatic mode of green market creation. In other words, the accelerated upscaling of Chinese wind power capacity, which led to overcapacity and environmental issues - a general phenomenon in Chinese industrial policy (Rock & Toman 2015; Economy 2004) - curtailment, and quality issues, produced 'problems, which force people to solve them. [...] If the problem had not appeared, nobody would have considered that [a potential problem].' Thus, China pushed the problems to emerge faster and with greater intensity, in order to benefit from the forced accelerated learning (Interview with Chinese government advisor and wind turbine industry association 2013). Indeed, this may even be dubbed an extreme form of 'creative destruction 2.0', albeit pushing Schumpeter's notion of the gale and breeze of creative destruction and its implications for economic innovation to the limits of what is conventionally conceived as 'sustainable' (aka 'Schumpeter's gale', cf. Schumpeter 1934).

Pursuing such an apparently precarious trial-and-error approach, the development of China's wind power sector reflects how 'to learn from the practice is much better than learning from the theory or learning from imagination. It's the Chinese way' (Chinese wind expert and government advisor 2013). Curiously, in Chinese, even the very notion of pragmatism translates directly as experimentalism *(shíyàn zhǔyì,* 实验主义) (Heilmann 2008:18). Such an experimental approach has historical roots, and is variously discussed in the context of China's Special Economic Zones, which from the late 1970s were pragmatically allowed to engage in local experiments with market reforms, including free-trade areas and industry and innovation parks in designated areas, before they were cautiously scaled up to implementation at a larger (national) scale (WTO n.d.). And so Chinese leaders since Mao have picked up ideas from the philosophy of American pragmatism (in particular, of John Dewey 1927, cf. Wang 2007, though not his ideas of democracy), namely adopting ideas of experimentation as 'guided by intentional anticipation instead of being blind trial and error' and learning through direct practical experience rather than abstract theory (Heilmann 2008:18). As explained by a Chinese wind turbine manufacturer (2011), while 'in Europe, you have developed wind energy for many years, so you know how it works, they know how to walk. China is just a beginner and we are walking and running, and learning. Sometimes we fall. Maybe I should walk or run with slower speed.'

In short, rapid but uncoordinated actions of upscaling pushed development to the brink of potential disruption and stalemate, reflected in the quality crisis that threatened to delegitimate wind power's sustainability. As will be shown later, such stages have occurred repeatedly, namely in three different phases identified in Chinese wind power development (Chapter Four). These, in turn, have been followed by timely and agile government intervention, leading on to a new stage of rapid development. This seems to be what we may term a precarious strategy of balancing at the very pivot or on the edge of a tipping point, which is what makes the industry, and Sino-foreign supply chain relations, so volatile. From this it follows that allowing for problems and challenges to occur on a scale and at a pace that sometimes amounts to an imminent crisis can sometimes prove to be an effective solution, as long as it forces you to find new and innovative solutions faster than would have been the case if the problems had not surfaced. The problems were, therefore, if not intentional then at least to some extent expected, as they could help to spur disruptive and accelerated moves of learning, catch-up, upgrading, and leapfrogging (also refer to Kirkegaard 2017). Somewhat paradoxically, and as will be illustrated in the following chapters, China's 'policy flexibility and institutional adaptability' (Korsnes 2014:175) through 'directed improvisation' (Ang 2016:66) have created space for catch-up and leapfrogging. Indeed, and as is so often noted, the Chinese word for crisis contains both the character for 'threat' and 'opportunity' (*wēijī*, 危机).

Fragmentation in Chinese wind power development and balancing at the brink of the tipping point

The experimental characteristics of Chinese governance of the wind power sector and iterative stages that tip towards potential disruption and/or impasse also indirectly reveal an underlying oscillating movement between centralised, coordinated control by the state versus fragmented decentralised experimentation relating to planning and development at the local provincial level (Kirkegaard 2017; Korsnes 2015). This, in turn, exposes the inherently fragmented nature of the sector's development, and how it has been characterised by so-called fragmented authoritarianism (e.g. ed. Brødsgaard 2017; Lieberthal 2004; Lieberthal & Oksenberg 1988; Mertha & Brødsgaard 2017). This relates to the division of China into different 'crisscrossing jurisdictions at both the vertical and horizontal levels', which produces complex and entangled vested interests and negotiations across administrative silos (Lieberthal 2004:187). Meanwhile, even though Chinese fragmented authoritarianism may cause lax and protracted implementation of policies at a local level, fragmented authoritarianism has in contemporary China Area Studies (hereafter China Studies or the China literature) also been linked to a specific mode of experimentalism and creative tinkering: In essence, fragmentation can create space at the local level to pragmatically experiment with and learn from central policies, at the same time as local experiments as evidenced by the Special Economic Zones, for example, have served as a basis for cautious learning from local practice and experiments before reforms have been rolled out at a larger scale (Heilmann 2008, 2010; WTO n.d.). At the same time, the account of excessive volatility above may counter the commonly held layperson's view of China being caricatured by an image of a monolithic central state, with one-party control and an innately poor ability to innovate. This volume exposes the paradoxical coexistence of state control in China with extensive experimentation and 'local tinkering'. This, perhaps surprisingly, forms the basis for volatile upgrading and catch-up, and vastly accelerated innovation in terms of market creation.

Contesting China's fragmented pragmatism of green energy development in wind power

As a 'quality crisis' seems to have been pragmatically allowed in Chinese wind power development, characterised by pragmatism, fragmented planning and development, radical neglect, and government intervention at the very last minute, the sector has been problematised over time, as explored in the following chapters. Indeed, according to the same Chinese industry expert and government advisor who argues that experimentalism can serve as disruptive learning, catch-up, and upgrading, the Chinese mode of developing wind power without proper reference to quality – and largely allowing SOEs to continue to do so – constitutes 'a big trouble for the future. No good for the people, no good for the country' (Interview with Chinese government advisor and wind turbine association 2013). This issue, in turn, is being described as a pressing 'system problem' caused by China's lack of a 'pure market economy' (Chinese certification body 2013) and exacerbated by China's investment-driven growth model (Kroeber 2016; Lardy 2016; Naughton 2014), which means there is 'no driving force for manufacturers to improve their quality'. [...] 'I'm so worried about it' (Interview with

Chinese government advisor and wind turbine industry association 2013). This system problem indicates a potentially more severe crisis of legitimacy, which may even be directed against the CPC. That is, whilst the quality crisis means that 'the reputation of the whole industry suffers' (Interview with European research institute 2013), the political leadership and developmental and political sustainability behind the Chinese mode of fragmented market construction, which has allowed for the quality crisis, is also being questioned.

Indeed, wind power may be in danger of being dismissed not only as socially, environmentally, and economically' unsustainable, owing to the vast amounts of wasted resources, but also as technologically and scientifically unsustainable if the quality crisis is not solved. This, in turn, may allow wind power to be construed as developmentally and politically unsustainable, the latter denoting the delicate structural balancing act of the Chinese Party-State. Its fragmented and experimental governance of wind power development is entangled in a state-controlled power sector that faces conflicting pressures, being motivated either to open up the Chinese economy to global competition or to protect SOEs that continue to bear extended social responsibilities in the country's socialist market economy.[8] Indeed, by producing a quality crisis, China may be instigating a 'fight against (its own) wind turbines', in a paraphrasing of Cervantes' (2003) famous novel from 1605 about Don Quixote's vain 'fight against windmills'. Hereby, while acknowledging the potential to learn from "failure", the volume exposes the contested nature of the seemingly idiosyncratic Chinese 'green fragmented experimentalism'. In particular, it reveals today's underlying negotiation of how and whether China's 'authoritarian growth machine' (Naughton 2017:21) – accelerated by an underlying 'system of incentivized hierarchy' and the fiscal stimulus package (Naughton 2017:21) – is indeed sustainable in the long-run, or rather a matter of blunt 'policy failure', in particular as it plays out in a relatively high-tech sector such as wind power. Thus, the volume digs into the issue of 'contested (policy) failures'.

Fragmented experimentation spinning out of control – or catching up through and in spite of experimentalism?

This work is concerned with the risk of fragmented experimentation spinning out of control and with the contested sustainability of what Ang (2016) has recently dubbed a Chinese 'crisis-and-response' development model. That is, the book exposes how the extension of fragmented experimentalism to a national high-tech sector such as wind power may lead to wasting resources to such an extent that it risks undermining the very system that constructed the sector in the first place. This may indeed make the argument for how experimentalism may be more suitable for low-tech sectors, and at a smaller scale rather than nation-wide sector building. Meanwhile, this book argues, somewhat paradoxically, that China has so far been able to green its electrical power sector – through the integration of larger shares of wind power and other renewable energy sources, at the same time as it catches up – because and in spite of the particular Chinese mode of fragmented, experimental, and pragmatic development. That is, the (somewhat counter-intuitive) hypothesis here is that China may have been able to upgrade and upscale its wind power sector with unprecedented pace through and in spite of its fragmented, experimental, and pragmatic mode of greening that has allowed for repeated advances towards the brink of disruption and/or stalemate that the Chinese state has allowed to emerge, even though sometimes on the way it has threatened to produce socio-material lock-in into fossil fuels as unintended externalities have become too vast and detrimental.

The above further entails a productive dilemma and tension owing to the inherent risk of ultimate (self-inflicted) disruption. Through the development of indigenous innovation capabilities, China seeks to become independent from foreign technology assistance and technology transfer. This has destabilised Sino-foreign supply chain relations around core technologies such as software tools, as these have become constituted as politically 'critical' and 'strategic' in the ongoing potential 'turn to quality'. This produces a paradoxical dynamic of simultaneous collaboration and competition around strategic core technologies. The political nature of these core technologies, however, may risk destabilising some of the very relations on which China still depends, and could benefit from in terms of mutual learning in emerging globalising innovation networks. In this way, Chinese experimental governance can have both benefits and disadvantages, as it constitutes both China's greatest advantage for achieving disruptive catch-up and its emergence as a 'scale-up nation', but it can also become China's sorest and weakest Achilles' heel.

Opening up to different modes of doing science and innovation

The Chinese mode of fragmented experimentation basically raises questions over what sustainability, quality, innovation, and even science mean, and for whom, and on whose terms. In China, could it be that what is sustainable or innovative is something quite different from the conventional views held in 'developed countries' (or in Europe, or what is often described as 'the West')? And is it possible that 'failures' in China are not deemed uncommon or shameful (contrary to most conventional perceptions of innovation in Europe), and that they may instead constitute fruitful sources of innovation? Indeed, the argument here is that we should acknowledge how China does *not* necessarily hinder innovation, albeit it may look different from what we know of as 'proper' innovation in Europe.

What we may be witnessing could be a purposeful Chinese strategy of innovation and sustainability. Even at the level of innovation processes in companies and research institutes engaging in product development, we may be seeing how China establishes its own path, not following the traditional Western methods of controlled experimentation, verification, external validation, testing, theorisation, and certification. This Western analytical mode of doing things is characterised by a constant effort to reduce uncertainty and risk, taming the untameable wind through the constant optimisation of algorithms and documented, codified certification – representing a view on 'quality by algorithm' – all the while the physical scale of wind turbine technology is increasing. The "Western" model of designing, prototyping, testing, and improving, all at full physical scale, was commonplace 50–100 years ago, but - over time - computer design and test-through-simulation has become the only viable way to conduct product development experiments. This is not only due to the increased costs of experiments on ever–increasing large-scale prototypes but also because of the significantly increased pressure to speed up the innovation processes (interview with senior advisor in foreign research institute 2018). Meanwhile, this cautious 'Western' model of designing, prototyping, testing and improving could very well collide with a Chinese corporate innovation strategy that seems less risk-averse. Indeed, many Chinese companies involved in wind power seem to have pursued a model of 'launch, test, improve' (O'Connor 2006) and a paradigm of 'open innovation' (cf. ed. Chesbrough, Vanhaverbeke & West 2006; Hyland 2008), which has 'accelerated innovation' (Williamson & Yin 2014) though not enhanced radical innovation. This strategy stands in direct opposition to the 'improve, test, launch' model typical of most Western multinationals (O'Connor 2006), which have used slower, rigid, and more risk-averse innovation management tools to reduce the risk of wasted investment in failing products (Cooper 1990). China at times may be pursuing a risky strategy, through its open, fragmented, and experimental mode of innovation, in particular when a push for pace and applied science overrules the need for long-term basic research and radical innovation. However, some 'Western' wind turbine manufacturers have realised that the corollary of the risk-averse innovation process is that 'thinking outside the box' has become restricted, limiting the potential for radical and accelerated innovation (interview with senior advisor in foreign research institute 2018; interview with foreign wind turbine manufacturer 2015). As a response to this, some of them are considering a redefinition of their innovation model, for example by developing a discovery–incubation–acceleration model (O'Connor 2006). This is based on open and radical innovation, to accelerate their innovation process (interviews 2015, 2016; O'Connor 2006) and to overcome the innovation-stifling effect that too much testing, simulation, and certification may produce. As Western companies try to accelerate their innovation, China may on the other hand over time put more emphasis on basic research, as already indicated in China's Medium- to Long-Term Plan for S&T 2006–2020 (MOST 2006), the 12th Five-Year Plan for the Scientific and Technological Development of Wind Power (MOST 2012), and the 13th Five-Year Plan for China's Economic and Social Development. The latter for instance argues for greater autonomy for educational and research institutions with more medium- and long-term objectives being considered, and more importance being attached to 'the quality, originality, and contribution of research' (NDRC 2016, s. 1).

The aim of this book is to move beyond accounts that frame Chinese wind power development as either a 'success' or a 'failure'. Instead, it is open to the view that quality and innovation in a Chinese context might imply something quite different from what is conventional wisdom in the developed countries, but also that these notions are shifting and negotiated. In order to do this, we need to pry open the way in which the Chinese state instigates *market construction*: the manner in which it experimentally 'innovates' new industrial sectors. However, at the same time as it illustrates how such experimental pragmatics of market construction play out, we look at how it is also being co-constructed e.g. by algorithms, firms, universities, research institutes, and certification bodies engaging in experimental practices of *product development innovation*. In doing so, the book traces Sino-foreign supply chain relations around software algorithms, as the study enquires into the quality crisis in Chinese wind power, and the ongoing struggle to qualify/frame wind power as sustainable through a turn to quality. Indeed, this study can be said to trace how software algorithms have become critical as they ascribe associations of developmental worth to wind power, which has gained currency in the current 'qualification struggle' of Chinese wind power; that is, the struggle to qualify wind power as sustainable in accordance with the developmental ambitions of scientific development. Further, as algorithms have become powerful actors in today's wind power sector – driven by ever larger wind turbine structures that require increased use of simulation, testing, and certification – this volume digs into a *specific moment* and *site* of wind power market construction. Accordingly, the volume conducts a brief comparison in Chapter Ten of industry development across sectors, taking into account that the fragmented mode of experimental marketisation may be more applicable in certain (lower-tech) sectors and technologies such as solar power and different infrastructure-building manufacturing sectors, while also comparing the Chinese mode of wind power development with other wind power nations (Denmark and the US).

A story of power(s), contested 'qualities', and entangled transitions

Overall, and as will be shown, this volume exposes how algorithms – rather than constituting mundane, simple, and non-controversial artefacts – have become contested and controversial in Chinese wind power. This is even more the case when it turns out that they are locked (by encryption devices, IPRs, and standards) to outsiders, who have no access to the algorithmic content of the source code. And so we are back to a story of power: of attempts to control and tame wind power through algorithms, but also of socio-political power struggles between fossil fuels and renewables, as well as between Chinese and foreign actors engaged in simultaneous competition and collaboration as algorithms designed to tame uncertainty reveal themselves as ambiguous, contestable, negotiable, and controversial. Indeed, the very mode of measuring quality by algorithm in today's global wind turbine industry is not necessarily uncontested in China. Rather, it may well engender power struggles; for instance, over the very right to define what is quality, and to set standards accordingly, as well as over the proprietary access to the IPRs of software algorithms.

Rather than taking the stance that Chinese turbines are lagging behind or poor quality, this work is concerned with how China is being regarded (and regarding itself) as a laggard, and what the outcome is of this. It is also concerned with how wind turbine quality is being framed and measured, and in particular how it may be increasingly qualified by algorithm; that is, what may be termed 'quality through and by algorithm'. In conducting such an algorithmic account, this investigation is a multifaceted and much broader study of China's wind power development, showing it to involve entangled and contested transitions, as the country transforms itself from black to green, from coal to wind, from quantity, pace and growth to quality, from manufacturing to innovation, from follower to leader, and from plan to market. It does so by zooming in on algorithms, rendering China's alleged 'wind power miracle' as richer, more ambiguous and 'messy'. To best appreciate these insights and to climb through the wind turbine, as it were, we first need to be properly equipped with the tools of the Anthropology of Markets, which has made these findings possible in the first place.

Notes

1. While explosive growth rates in wind power installations had already started in 2005, this rapid growth can be argued to have been further supported around 2008 when the Chinese government responded promptly to the global financial crisis. China made the world's largest fiscal crisis response, the stimulus package, mobilising an investment effort equal to over 10 percent of GDP (Naughton 2014:11). As a result, vast sums of money were poured into Chinese infrastructure build-out (Kroeber 2016; Lardy 2016; Naughton 2014:14), including not only building of highways, buildings, and railways, but also the electrical power system and renewables such as wind farm projects, and much more. The stimulus was a great success in terms of steering China free of the repercussions of the global financial crisis and ensuring continued economic growth. This investment-driven growth model based on infrastructure build-out has however recently been claimed to have reached its limit, as explored later in the volume (Kroeber 2016; Lardy 2016; Naughton 2014:14).
2. This study focuses on the emergence and development of a wind power sector (a 'wind power development market'), which constitutes the infrastructural basis for a potential electricity market emerging later on. The introduction of competitive electricity trading markets has long been a contentious issue in China, but has so far not been realised due to protracted negotiations and the controversial nature of the issue, as discussed later in the study. Nonetheless, just as the Chinese government seeks to reform the power market even

further, accelerating its efforts to liberalise power prices it currently sets by the state, the National Energy Administration (NEA) declared in April 2018 its plans to introduce its first real-time electricity trading spot markets. This is to be done through the introduction of pilot spot markets in eight provinces and regions by 2019 (hereunder, Guangdong and Zhejiang are well into the detailed rulemaking), to help to provide a local price signal (Reuters 20 April 2018; Romig 22 August 2018). Among the main aims of these competitive markets are 1) to bring down industrial power prices, 2) to curb overcapacity through price signals (that is, 'new capacity should come online when needed, rather than based on capacity targets set by policymakers') (Romig 22 August 2018); and 3) to solve 'China's curtailment challenge by replacing the plan with markets' (Romig 22 August 2018). The spot markets form part of a major programme of structural and market reforms that was put in place with the Energy Revolution's blandly named 'Document #9' (2015), which, amongst other things, introduced competitive markets at wholesale and retail levels, with incentive-based transmission and distribution pricing rolled out across the country, at the same time as China seeks to introduce private capital into distribution networks (Romig 22 August 2018). With the introduction of spot markets, NEA has now issued guidelines to set up the 'real-time trading platforms that will set prices for the cash market as well as those for a day ahead, allowing power generators, industrial users and distributors to trade power in real time' (Romig 22 August 2018). As a consequence of these initiatives, '[t]housands of new power retail companies have been registered and are now experiencing first-hand the challenges familiar to European or American counterparts', e.g. the integration of multiple electricity markets through coupling across and between provinces (Romig 22 August 2018). While not the focus of this study, as it still only a plan, it is worthwhile to notice how these new plans mark a remarkable shift in China's power reforms. How China will deal with the challenges ahead in the construction of its emerging electricity market is an interesting area for future studies.

3. Bearing in mind, though, that, formally, China's planned command economy, 'with central plans that purported to steer the economy' was already abandoned by the late 1990s. However, long-range plans and industrial policies still play a strong role, and China is today operated by national plans and literally hundreds of local government plans (Naughton 2017:11). Five-year plans are at the centre of this, combining 1) a vision statement, 2) a handful of binding targets, and 3) a panoply of associated sectoral and local plans (Naughton 2017:12).

4. The idea that science, technology, and education are critical to sustainable development had already been expressed earlier, for example in 1996 when China adopted '"sustainable development" and "Invigorating China through science and education" as the two principles that would work as national guidelines for development' (Christensen 2013:84; Kirkegaard 2015).

5. The idea of sustainable development entered Chinese political discourse in 1994 when China formulated its own Agenda 21, two years after China's participation in the United Nations Conference on Environment and Development held in 1992 (Christensen 2013:69; Kirkegaard 2015).

6. Whereas the third generation of China's leadership (1992–2003/Jiang Zemin) was relatively liberal in economic terms (Meidan et al. 2009:593), promoting the notion of 'common prosperity' (Jiang Zemin 1995:12 in Christensen 2013:84), a more 'social' vision for China's economic and social development was developed during the subsequent fourth generation (Hu Jintao-Wen Jiabao 2003–2012). During the fourth generation, while holding back on giving freer rein to market mechanisms although continuing market reforms

(Meidan et al. 2009:592), more emphasis was put on social equity and a balanced growth pattern (Christensen 2013; Fan 2006; Meidan et al. 2009:593). This is reflected in slogans such as 'the Moderately Well-Off Society'/'a well-off society in an all-round way', which through people-centred growth and putting people first (*Yǐrén wéi běn*, 一人为本) should contribute to ensuring common prosperity (*Gòngtóng fùyù*, 共同富裕) (Christensen 2013:85–86; Fan 2006). Meanwhile, it was only with the fourth leadership generation that 'sustainability' as a matter of 'sustainable development' was taking centre stage in plans and policies, being linked to a web of other ideas (Fan 2006), which all form part of the overarching objective of establishing a so-called Harmonious Socialist Society (Fan 2006; Kirkegaard 2015; Meidan et al. 2009) with long-term, environmentally, and socially sustainable, economic development. This social vision for China's sustainable economic and social development, which denoted a remarkable shift away from the previous development philosophy of 'letting some get rich first' (Christensen 2013; Deng Xiaoping 1978 in Fan 2006), is being continued by China's current political leadership (Xi Jinping–Li Keqiang-administration, 2013–). This is reflected in the recent slogan of the 'China Dream' (*Zhōngguó mèng*, 中国梦) (PWC 2013), which reflects a goal of achieving a harmonious, stable, peaceful, equitable, and sustainable development. Meanwhile, even though the 'objective of China's state intervention has clearly shifted from growth at any price to a more complex set of goals that includes 'redistribution and social and economic security' (Naughton 2017), there is long-standing debate as to the 'socialist' features of China. Indeed, even though China seems to move 'towards a version of "socialism," (albeit a very particular flavour of socialism that is authoritarian and top-down, but with a market economy based primarily on private ownership'), a more sceptical view is that China's 'growth miracle' is now coming to an end. That is, with the "new normal" of below two-digit growth rates, China is still facing severe challenges in terms of ensuring universal social security, modest income redistribution, and amelioration of environmental problems (Naughton 2017:22).

7. While renewable energies have been included in earlier plans and policies (for instance, alternative energy was already included in China's fifth Five-Year-Plan, and the Electricity Law (1995) encouraged supply of power in rural areas through wind, solar energy, and biomass in 1995), it was particularly during the 'revolutionary' 11th Five-Year Plan (2006–2010) that emphasis on the renewable sector was linked to the emerging, comprehensive notion of sustainability (Fan 2006). This was further emphasised with the Renewable Energy Law in 2005.
8. These responsibilities have roots in the now formally dismantled Communist work unit system (*danwei*, 单位). Traditionally, under Communist party rule, Chinese SOEs played a critical role for social security in the old communist 'iron rice bowl'. This gave them extended social responsibilities as part of their role as a work unit, but also meant that they enjoyed relatively soft budget constraints as they were not driven exclusively by profits, but also by social concerns of providing jobs and social stability (Clark & Li 2010; Oi 2005:115; Wei 2003:101).

References

Andrews-Speed, P., 2012, *The Governance of Energy in China. Transition to a Low-Carbon Economy*, Palgrave Macmillan, Basingstoke.

Ang, Y. Y., 2016, *How China Escaped the Poverty Trap*, Cornell University Press, New York.

Bloomberg (New Energy Finance), 2012, Will China's New Renewable Portfolio Standard Boost Project Development? *Renewable energy: Research note*, 11 May.

Breznitz, D. & Murphree, M., 2011, *Run of the Red Queen: Government, Innovation, Globalization, and Economic Growth in China*, Yale University Press, New Haven, CT.

Brødsgaard, K. E. (ed.), 2017, *Chinese Politics as Fragmented Authoritarianism: Earthquakes, Energy and Environment*, Routledge, Abingdon.

Buckley, C., 2014, 'Xi Urges Greater Innovation in "Core Technologies"', Sinosphere, *New York Times*, 10 June 2014, viewed 14 August 2014, http://sinosphere.blogs. nytimes.com/2014/06/10/xi-urges-greater-innovation-in-core-technologies/ ?_php=true&_type=blogs&_r=0.

Cao, C., 2004a, 'Chinese Science and the "Nobel Prize Complex"', *Minerva* 42, 151–172.

Cao, C., 2004b, *China's Scientific Elite*, Routledge Curzon, London and New York.

Cao, C., 2014, 'The Universal Values of Science and China's Nobel Prize Pursuit', *Minerva* 52, 141–160.

Chesbrough, H., Vanhaverbeke, W. & West, J. (eds.), 2006, *Open Innovation. Researching a New Paradigm*, Oxford University Press, New York.

Christensen, N. H., 2013, 'Shaping Markets: A Neoinstitutional Analysis of the Emerging Organizational Field of Renewable Energy in China', PhD thesis, Dept. of Business & Politics, Copenhagen Business School.

Chung, S-w. W., & Xu, Q., 2016, *China's Energy Policy from National and International Perspectives – The Energy Revolution and One Belt One Road Initiative*, City University of Hong Kong Press, Hong Kong.

Clark, W. W. & Li, X., 2010, '"Social capitalism" in Renewable Energy Generation: China and California Comparisons', *Utilities Policy* 18(1), 53–61.

Communist Party of China Central Committee and the State Council, 2015, 关于进一步深化电力体制改革的若干意见,中发(2015)9号文'全文 ['Several Opinions of the CPC Central Committee and the State Council on Further Deepening the Reform of the Electric Power System', No. 9 Text Full Text], 'Energy Revolution' ('*Policy #9*'/'Document No. 9'), 15 March 2015, http://www.ne21.com/news/show-64828.html.

Cooper, R. G., 1990, 'Stage-Gate Systems: A New Tool for Managing New Products', *Business Horizons* 33(3), 44–54.

Dupuy, M., 2016, 'China Power Sector Reform: Key Issues for the World's Largest Power Sector', *The Regulatory Assistance Program (RAP)*, March 2016, viewed 8 December 2016, https://www.raponline.org/wp-content/uploads/2016/07/ rap-dupuy-key-issues-china-power-sector-2016-march.pdf.

Economy, E. C., 2004, *The River Runs Black: The Environmental Challenge to China's Future*, 2nd edn., Cornell University Press, Ithaca, NY.

Ernst, D., 2013, 'Standards, Innovation, and Latecomer Economic Development: A Conceptual Framework', *East–West Center Working Papers*, Economics Series 134.

Fan, C. C., 2006, 'China's Eleventh Five-Year Plan (2006–2010): From "Getting Rich First" to "Common Prosperity"', *Eurasian Geography and Economics* 47(6), 708–723.

Gorm Hansen, L. L., 2017, *Triggering Earthquakes in Science, Politics and Chinese Hydropower. A Controversy Study*, PhD thesis, Dept. of International Economics and Management, Asia Studies Centre, Copenhagen Business School.

Göss, S., 2017, 'China's Renewable Energy Revolution Continues on its Long March', *Energypost*, 13 February 2017, http://energypost.eu/chinas-renewable-energy-revolution-continues-long-march/.

Global Wind Energy Council (GWEC), 2016, Global Wind Energy Outlook 2016, Oct. 2016, http://files.gwec.net/files/GlobalWindEnergyOutlook2016. GWEC, 2018, *Global Wind Statistics 2017*, 14 February 2018.

Heilmann, S., 2008, 'From Local Experiments to National Policy: The Origins of China's Distinctive Policy Process', *The China Journal* 59, 1–30.

Heilmann, S., 2010, 'Economic Governance: Authoritarian Upgrading and Innovative Potential', in J. Fewsmith (ed.), *China Today, China Tomorrow. Domestic Politics, Economy, and Society*, pp. 109–128, Rowman & Littlefield Publishers, Plymouth.

Hyland, J., 2008, 'Innovation and Corporate Entrepreneurship – Success Comes from the Future … Not the Past', Powerpoint presentation at OECD Innovation Strategy Workshop, 29 May 2008, on file with author, Founding partner of Radical Innovation Group.

Kirkegaard, J. K., 2015, 'Ambiguous Winds of Change – Or Fighting against Windmills in Chinese Wind Power: Mapping Controversies over a Potential Turn to Quality in Chinese Wind Power', PhD thesis, Department of Business & Politics, Copenhagen Business School.

Kirkegaard, J. K., 2017, 'Tackling Chinese Upgrading through Experimentalism and Pragmatism: The Case of China's Wind Turbine Industry', *Journal of Current Chinese Affairs* 46(2), 7–39.

Klagge, B., Liu, Z. & Silva, P. C., 2012, 'Constructing China's Wind Energy Innovation System', *Energy Policy* 50, 370–382.

Kroeber, A. R., 2016, *China's Economy – What Everyone Needs to Know*, Oxford University Press, New York.

Korsnes, M., 2014, 'Fragmentation, Centralisation and Policy Learning: An Example from China's Wind Industry', *Journal of Current Chinese Affairs* 43(3), 175–205.

Korsnes, M., 2015, 'Chinese Renewable Struggles: Innovation, the Arts of the State and Offshore Wind Technology', PhD thesis, Department of Interdisciplinary Studies of Culture, Norwegian University of Science and Technology (NTNU).

Lardy, N. R., 2016, 'The Changing Role of the Private Sector in China', Conference Volume.

Lewis, J. I., 2013, *Green Innovation in China. China's Wind Power Industry and the Global Transition to a Low-Carbon Economy*, Columbia University Press, New York.

Li, X., 2015, *'Decarbonizing China's Power System with Wind Power: The Past and the Future'*, The Oxford Institute for Energy Studies (OIES), EL11, January 2015.

Lieberthal, K., 2004, 'The Organization of Political Power and its Consequences: The View from the Outside', in K. Lieberthal, *Governing China: From Revolution through Reform*, pp. 171–205, 2nd edn., W.W. Norton & Co, New York.

Lieberthal, K. & Oksenberg, M., 1988, *Policy-Making in China: Leaders, Structures and Processes*, Princeton University Press, Princeton, NJ.

Liu, X. & Kong, L., 2016, 'A New Chapter in China's Electricity Market Reform', *Energy Studies Institute*, Policy brief, March 21 2016, http://esi.nus.edu.sg/docs/default-source/esi-policy-briefs/a-new-chapter-in-china-s-electricity-market-reform.pdf.

McGregor, J., n.d., 'China's Drive for 'Indigenous Innovation'. A web of industrial policies,' *APCO Worldwide, US Chamber of Commerce, Global Intellectual Property Centre*, Global Regulatory Cooperation Project viewed 29 November 2014: https://www.uschamber.com/sites/default/files/documents/files/100728chinareport_0_0.pdf.

Mathews, J. A. & Tan, H., 2015, *China's Renewable Energy Revolution*, Palgrave Macmillan, New York.

Mathews, J. A., 2016, 'China's Continuing Renewable Energy Revolution – Latest Trends in Electric Power Generation', *The Asia-Pacific Journal, Japan Focus* 14(17), 6 September 2016.

Meidan, M., Andrews-Speed, P. & Xin, M., 2009, 'Shaping China's Energy Policy: Actors and Processes', *Journal of Contemporary China* 18(61), 591–616.

Mertha, A. & Brødsgaard, K. E., 2017, 'Revisiting Chinese Authoritarianism in China's Central Energy Administration', in K. E. Brødsgaard (ed.), *Chinese Politics as Fragmented Authoritarianism: Earthquakes, Energy and Environment*, pp. 1–14, Routledge, Abingdon.

MOST (Ministry of Science and Technology of the People's Republic of China, 2006, State Council, 国家中长期科学和技术发展规划纲要 (2006-2020)[National Outline for Medium and Long Term Science and Technology Development (2006–2020)], 9 February 2006, http://www.gov.cn/jrzg/2006-02/09/content_183787.htm.

MOST (Ministry of Science and Technology of the People's Republic of China), 2012, State Council, The Central People's Government of the People's Republic of China, 关于印发风力发电科技发展'十二五'专项规划的通知 ['The 12th Five-Year Plan for the Scientific and Technological Development of Wind Power], 国科发计, 197号, National Branch No. 197, 24 April 2012, http://www.most.gov.cn/fggw/zfwj/zfwj2012/201204/t20120424_93884.htm.

NDRC (National Development and Reform Commission), 2007, Medium and Long-Term Development Plan for Renewable Energy in China, September. http://www.chinaenvironmentallaw.com/wp-content/uploads/2008/04/medium-and-long-term-development-plan-for-renewable-energy.pdf.

NDRC (National Development and Reform Commission), 2016, The 13th Five-Year Plan for economic and social development of the People's Republic of China (2016–2020), transl. Central Committee of the Communist Party of China, Beijing, China, http://en.ndrc.gov.cn/newsrelease/201612/P020161207645765233498.pdf.

NEA (National Energy Administration) of the National Development and Reform Commission, 2015, 国家发展改革委 国家能源局关于改善电力运行调节促进清洁能源多发满发的指导意见 发改运行[2015]518号 [The NEA of the NDRC's Guiding Opinions on Improving Electric Power Operation Regulations and Promoting the Reform of Full Release of Clean Energy Development and Operation, No. 518], September 2015 http://www.nea.gov.cn/2015-04/09/c_134136821.htm.

Naughton, B., 2011, 'What Price Continuity?', *China Leadership Monitor* 34.

Naughton, B., 2014, 'China's Economy: Complacency, Crisis & the Challenge of Reform', *Dædalus, the Journal of the American Academy of Arts & Sciences* 143(2), 14–25.

Naughton, B., 2015, 'Reform Retreat and Renewal: How Economic Policy Fits into the Political System', *Issues & Studies* 51(1), 23–54.

Naughton, B., 2017, 'Is China Socialist?', *Journal of Economic Perspectives* 31(1), 3–24.

O'Connor, G. C., 2006, 'Open, Radical Innovation: Toward an Integrated Model in Large Established Firms', in H. Chesbrough, W. Vanhaverbeke & J. West (eds.), *Open Innovation. Researching a New Paradigm*, Oxford University Press, New York.

OECD (Organisation for Economic Co-operation and Development), 2016, 'Gross Domestic Spending on R&D', available at: http://www.oecd-ilibrary.org/content/indicator/d8b068b4-en.

Oi, J. C., 2005, 'Patterns of Corporate Restructuring in China: Political Constraints on Privatisation', *The China Journal* 53, 115–136.

People's Daily Online, 'China Fine-Tunes Wind Turbine Industry with New Guidelines', 11 May 2011, http://english.peopledaily.com.cn/90001/90778/90857/7376036.html.

PWC (Price Waterhouse Coopers), 2013, 'New Roadmap for Achieving the China Dream. Business and Economic Implications of the Third Plenary Session of the CPC's 18th Central Committee'. http://www.pwc.ch/user_content/editor/files/publ_tls/pwc_new_roadmap_achieving_china_dream_e.pdf.

Reuters, 2018, 'China plans first spot electricity trading as Beijing reforms power market', 20 April 2018, https://www.reuters.com/article/us-china-electricity/china-plans-first-spot-electricity-trading-as-beijing-reforms-power-market-idUSKBN1HR1LA.

Riley, M. & Vance, A., 2012, 'Inside the Chinese Boom in Corporate Espionage', *Bloomberg/Bizweek*, 15 March 2012, http://www.businessweek.com/articles/2012-03-14/inside-the-chinese-boom-in-corporate-espionage.

Rock, M. T. & Toman, M. A. 2015, *China's Technological Catch-up Strategy: Industrial Development, Energy Efficiency, and CO_2 Emissions*, Oxford University Press, New York.

Romig, C., 2018, 'Powering the Dragon: the rise of Chinese renewables', *Poyry/PEI (Power Engineering International)*, 22 August 2018, https://www.powerengineeringint.com/articles/2018/08/powering-the-dragon-the-rise-of-chinese-renewables.html.

Schumpeter, J. A., 1934, *The Theory of Economic Development*, Harvard University Press, Cambridge, MA.

Serger, S. S. & Breidne, M., 2007, 'China's Fifteen-Year Plan for Science and Technology: An Assessment', *Asia Policy* 4, 135–164.

Silva, P. C. & Klagge, B., 2013, 'The Evolution of the Wind Industry and the Rise of Chinese Firms: From Industrial Policies to Global Innovation Networks', *European Planning Studies* 21(9), 1341–1356.

Standing Committee of the National People's Congress, 2005, Renewable Energy Law, 28 February 2005, http://www.npc.gov.cn/englishnpc/Law/2007-12/13/content_1384096.htm.

State Council 2015, 国务院关于印发《中国制造2025》的通知国发〔2015〕28号 [Notice of the State Council on Printing and Distributing 'Made in China 2025'], 8 May 2015, http://www.gov.cn/zhengce/content/2015-05/19/content_9784.htm.

Stern, R. E., 2013, *Environmental Litigation in China: A Study in Political Ambivalence*, Cambridge University Press, Cambridge.

The Information Office of the State Council, Energy Policy 2012, First edition 2012. October 2012, http://www.gov.cn/english/official/2012-10/24/content_2250497.htm.

Wang, J. C.-Z., 2007, *John Dewey in China. To Teach and to Learn*, State University of New York Press, New York.

Wei, Y., 2003, *Comparative Corporate Governance – A Chinese Perspective*, Kluwer Law International, The Hague.

Williamson, P. J. & Yin, E., 2014, 'Accelerated Innovation: The New Challenge from China', *MIT Sloan Management Review*, Research Feature, 23 April.

WTO (World Trade Organization), n.d., 'China's Special Economic Zones, Experience Gained in the Development of China's Special Economic Zones', China Development Bank, http://www.worldbank.org/content/dam/Worldbank/Event/Africa/Investing%20in%20Africa%20Forum/2015/investing-in-africa-forum-chinas-special-economic-zone.pdf.

2 Introducing a unique analytical strategy – the Anthropology of Markets

The account of Chinese wind power development, which provides a broader story about Chinese fragmented experimentalism with greening, has only been made possible by viewing the industry through a unique analytical lens: the relational, lateral, socio-technical, and processual lens of the Anthropology of Markets (AoM) (Caliskan & Callon 2009, 2010a, 2010b) and a controversy mapping approach within STS (Blanchet & Depeyre 2016; Callon, Lascoumes & Barthe 2001; Latour 2005a; Sismondo 2010; Venturini 2010; Yaneva 2012), both with roots in American Pragmatism (see Chapter Three). The analytical strategy of this study will contribute to China Studies as well as to STS, going further than conventional and narrower accounts of STS. In doing so, this volume offers a unique and innovative approach to STS, conveying a much bolder and broader account of Chinese greening through an algorithmic study.

Moving from the science laboratory to the (Chinese) market laboratory

The Anthropology of Markets (Caliskan & Callon 2009, 2010a, 2010b) has its roots in STS in general and draws on Actor–Network Theory (ANT) (e.g. Callon 1986a, 1986b, 1991, 1998, 2007, 2009; Callon, Méadel & Rabeharisoa 2002; Callon et al. 2001; Latour 1982, 1983, 1987, 1992, 2004, 2005a, 2005b; Law 1994, 2003, 2009).[1] The predecessor to the Anthropology of Markets, ANT started out with studies that were literally conducted 'in the (scientific) laboratory' (e.g. Latour 1983, 1987) – illustrating how scientific facts, knowledge, expertise, and technology are assembled and produced (Muniesa 2015). Overall, ANT is not a theory, but more of an analytical strategy or prism which constitutes a fusion of sociological and technological theory, and which is characterised by a (somewhat paradoxically) materialist (socio-technical), radically constructivist, and yet realist approach to social theory and empirical research (Muniesa 2015). Over time these studies have moved out of the scientific laboratory and into studies of engineering and technological innovation (e.g. Callon 1986b), as well as into organisation studies, political science, anthropology, and economic sociology. ANT has been deployed to understand how the economy (looked upon as processes of economisation) is socio-materially constructed by economic theory and economic calculative devices (Callon 1998). More recently, an emerging strand of this line of thought has embedded itself directly into Market Studies within New Economic Sociology (e.g. Beckert & Zafirovski 2011; Dobbin (ed.) 2004; Granovetter 1985; Padgett & Powell (eds.) 2012; for a critical review of this literature, refer to Caliskan & Callon 2009, 2010a, 2010b), by taking the constructivist study of the economy into one specific site, namely markets (Caliskan & Callon 2009, 2010a, 2010b). This emerging 'performativity programme' of the (Sociology and) Anthropology of Markets is the foundation of this work, as it enquires into the arduous socio-material process of constructing a Chinese 'market' for wind power development, looking upon this as a process of marketisation. A market study is thus conducted of China's wind power sector, moving into the 'laboratory' of wind power deployment, so to speak. As expressed by a respondent regarding the development of Chinese wind power development, 'Chinese is like a humongous laboratory': In Europe,

> we don't really understand the scale in China [...] So we think that it's terrible that wind turbines are failing, while the Chinese just say, 'it's fun trying it off... There's a long way to 2020, so now we've got this, and then we'll figure out what to do next' [...] Maybe that's how they [the Chinese Government] have looked at it. 'Let's try to start up something. Let's see what happens!' [Then] they [the Chinese Government] make some policies, and then people follow those policies. And then they stop them. And then they look to see, 'what did we get out of that?' And then they make some new [policies]. (Interview with foreign control system supplier 2012)

And so this study is moving laboratory studies from the technology lab to the market site, proposing a 'laboratory study' in its own right.

Ten main reasons for adopting the lens of Anthropology of Markets

There are several reasons why an Anthropology of Markets lens (and its underlying ANT) can prove helpful in shedding light on previously often disregarded processes of Chinese greening and wind power development. Ten of these are listed below.

Processes of assembling market networks (assemblages)

First, a shared trait of studies of scientific laboratories, technological innovation, economy, and markets is the affinity to a so-called 'ecology of practice' (Stengers 2005) and network/assemblage perspectives. By this is meant a common interest in the *'hows'* (the practices) of assembling heterogeneous entities (humans, non-humans, and hybrids) into temporarily stabilised wholes (e.g. markets, economy, technologies, experts, scientific facts, sustainability, society, global value chains (GVCs), or GINs). This means that entities that are often assumed to 'just be there' and 'exist in the first place' cannot be taken for granted any longer. Instead, an ecology of practice means that we need to trace how the world as we know it has come to be configured in the way it has: this means the use of a profoundly relational and processual lens. Founded in an ecology of practice, the unit of analysis becomes the very practice (the action, or so-called performance/translation) of connecting and relating heterogeneous entities into temporarily stabilised networks/assemblages (such as markets), which is known to entail processes of problematisation, interessement, enrolment, and mobilisation (Callon 1986a). Translation is also known to contain so-called obligatory passage points (OPP) (Callon 1986b:26–27) through which entities must pass to be legitimised and associated as constituting parts of the network, and for the network to be assembled and stabilised. Looking upon the Chinese wind power sector as an emerging network that must be mobilised, the Anthropology of Markets is a useful tool for capturing issues of genesis and emergence, rather than looking at it 'after the fact'.

Reintroducing the missing masses of markets by slowing down enquiry into controversy

Second, an Anthropology of Markets lens can help to shed light on the potential role and effect of often overlooked material artefacts in the forging of network relations around technologies and products. Taking the role of these material artefacts seriously, the Anthropology of Markets lens provides a perspective of so-called radical symmetry. It treats all actors and entities – both human and non-human – in the same way, at least at the outset, in order not to ignore the (potential) role of technology and the scientific facts behind it from the beginning.

The inclusion of these often neglected material artefacts – such as software algorithms – in social analysis enables us to trace the socio-material/socio-technical constitution of things. This seems fitting in the case of Chinese wind power development, where wind turbines, the power grid, and the algorithms hidden in control systems and simulation tools have produced a severe 'quality crisis' that cannot be readily understood without understanding their hybrid social and material nature. This also means that, whilst constructivist in perspective, the Anthropology of Markets (and its underlying perspective of ANT) is anything but *social* constructivist. Instead, things (even 'the social') are always socio-*materially* constituted. And so this research can help to reintroduce 'the missing masses' of technical artefacts (Latour 1992, 2004) to market studies, reassembling 'the missing markets' by making visible their socio-material construction and maintenance.[2]

To take the heterogeneous nature of market construction seriously (involving both human and non-human actors and entities), the book traces and engages with many of the (often neglected) techno-scientific details of

Chinese wind power development. This entails an engagement with theoretical and methodological 'promiscuity' and the collection of rich ethnographic data from China, taking to heart the principle of engaging in the 'painstaking ethnography' of 'slowing down inquiry into controversy' (Yaneva 2012:3). The resulting inclusion of material actors in the account allows an understanding of the socio-material construction of the wind power sector, and the socio-material struggles that it entails.

Mapping controversies over markets – shedding light on genesis, dynamics, and agency

Third, the inherently relational and processual perspective of the world of the Anthropology of Markets implies that markets are conveyed through the adjectival form of 'market', namely as processes of marketisation (Caliskan & Callon 2009). This denotes how the marketisation of wind power development is seen as an emergent network effect: it forges and mobilises socio-technical relations around the wind, through the construction of (an) associated monetary and non-monetary value(s) of wind power. This builds on the basic presumption that no market actors would be gathered around developing components, wind turbines, wind farms, or even wind power in the first place, if no value were associated with it. This 'pragmatics of valuation' builds on the American pragmatist John Dewey's (1859–1952) 'Theory of Valuation' (1915, 1939): he argued that for things to be circulated and traded, associations of value must first be attributed to the thing. Thus, 'things circulate because they are valued and it is because they are valued that they become goods' (Caliskan & Callon 2009:389 paraphrasing Dewey 1915). Taking into account how valuation processes are part and parcel of market construction, an Anthropology of Markets does not look at 'The Market' as something that readily exists, but instead treats it as dynamic processes of marketisation. Over time, marketisation may mobilise a socio-technical 'arrangement or assemblage (and power field) of heterogeneous elements' that include, for instance, rules and conventions, plans and policies, certificates and standards, IPRs, technical devices, algorithms, control systems, infrastructures, discourses and narratives, technical and scientific knowledge, and competencies and skills embodied in living beings (Caliskan & Callon 2010a:23).

The concept of a (market) socio-technical assemblage denotes a high level of agency, as indicated through the French word *agencement*. Meanwhile, even though Caliskan & Callon (2010b) have argued that this Francophile notion better describes the entailed agency in marketisation,[3] and despite this study ascribing to the impetus of agency, we use here the notion of 'assemblage', as this is more readily understood in English. In doing so, this work looks at the arduous mobilisation and maintenance involved in enrolling and mobilising heterogeneous actors that are engaged in distributed agency (Akrich, Callon,& Latour 2002; Callon 2007; Doganova 2009) into an emerging socio-technical assemblage around wind power development,[4] as they display 'resourcefulness and improvisation on the part of involved actors' (Garud & Karnøe 2003:278). Indeed, the notion of distributed agency in marketisation can be related to China's strategy of a 'turbine wave attack' at both central and local levels, as actors seem to have engaged in 'Chinese crowdsourcing 2.0'.

And so, this volume traces how wind power has been de- and reassociated and qualified with monetary and non-monetary value for Chinese society before, during, and after the 'quality crisis', producing a still unfolding 'qualification struggle' that has de- and restabilised the emerging socio-technical assemblage. Drawing on the Anthropology of Markets and ANT to develop a methodological approach for studying (or 'mapping') controversies over and in markets (Blanchet & Depeyre 2016:41), marketisation becomes a site of controversy as heterogeneous market agents engage in politicised bargaining about the terms of exchange and the 'price, quantity, and quality of goods, but also quarrel over the very organization of markets' (Blanchet & Depeyre 2016:41). Meanwhile, through the lens of the Anthropology of Markets, controversy is not seen as inherently negative, but as a site of potential learning (Callon et al. 2001).

By tracing the socio-material valuation processes of wind power development, an inherently dynamic account emerges, one which is adept at accounting for market maintenance, instability, change, and transformation (dynamics). In sum, the Anthropology of Markets is a productive lens that is interested in exploring issues not only of emergence and genesis, but also of agency and dynamics. This seems timely, as an overarching 'qualification struggle' over wind power's sustainability is taking place in China, with resulting heterogeneous actors, such as software algorithms, coming to the fore.

Defining 'wind power development marketisation'

Fourth, and as a matter of definition, when talking about 'market', this book refers to the marketisation of wind power development and deployment in its entirety, indicating the processual lens of continuous market emergence: the arduous mobilisation of a socio-technical assemblage around monetary and non-monetary investments to create a wind power sector. Through this lens, 'wind power development marketisation' encompasses the trading of, and investment in, the equipment needed for wind power generation, such as wind turbines and wind farms, and the generation of electrical energy from the wind and its integration from wind farms into the electrical power grid, together with its transmission by the TSO/grid company and distribution to the electricity off-takers (in this case provincial governments). This can be seen as an investment market for wind power, including the installation of wind turbines and the infrastructure for wind power development, deployment, and distribution, as well as the establishment of an infrastructure for R&D, certification and standardisation. This also includes, for instance, the pricing and support mechanisms for wind turbines and electricity, and the IPRs and certificates, narratives and discourses that make the economisation and marketisation of the investment attractive to investors.[5] Thus, the overall object of exchange is the wind resource itself, its socio-material and algorithmic translation into generated power, through framing tools such as wind turbines, but also through control systems, simulation tools, IPRs, standards, algorithms, the power grid, price-setting mechanisms, and the epistemic work of discourses and narratives.

By focusing on wind power development, the book takes a different approach from most contemporary social studies of energy markets within the Anthropology of Markets; these have focused on wind power development marketisation as a matter of competitive electricity trading markets, such as those that have been developed in the Nordic electricity trading market Nordpool, are under negotiation in the European Union,[6] and are being introduced by the emerging Danish retail electricity demonstration market EcoGrid, or involve capacity markets connected to wholesale electricity markets in the United States (Breslau 2013; Jenle 2015; Jenle & Pallesen 2017; Karnøe 2013; Kurunmaki et al. 2016; Pallesen 2016; Silvast 2017; windeurope n.d.). However, these competitive electricity markets are not liberalised in the popular idea of being 'free' and regulated by the 'invisible hand of the market' (as imagined by Adam Smith 1776) rather than by government intervention. That is, like most other markets, these competitive markets are not adhering to the idealistic (and neo-liberal) imagination of supposedly naturally 'liberalised' markets of automatically intersecting supply and demand curves arriving at the perfect equilibrium. Rather, they are specifically socio-materially organised and regulated according to the balancing requirements of physics, with only TSO-qualified actors allowed to trade.

Meanwhile, such a market with competitive prices does not yet readily exist in China, primarily for two reasons. First, as wind power is still a new sector in the country and provides only a relatively small fraction of the energy in China's primarily thermal coal-based power system, electricity trading for grid balancing purposes is less crucial. This is because as long as wind turbines and wind farms are properly controlled and planned, wind power does not constitute a large threat to grid stability. (It did, though, during the 'turbine wave attack', with large and poorly coordinated and controlled wind farms being rapidly connected to the grid). Second, despite multiple attempts in China at liberalisation of state-controlled sectors (Central Committee of the CPC (CCCPC) 2013; Energy Policy 2012) the wind power sector in China is inherently entangled in China's state-controlled and state-owned electrical power sector, where the state continues to set prices and where cross-provincial grids and power trading are not easily set up for political, bureaucratic, and technical reasons. Meanwhile, there are indications of radical change as China has recently started experimenting with competitive markets at the wholesale and retail levels. While not the focus of this study, another recent signal of the emergence of an actual future electricity trading market is NEA's draft rules issued in April 2018, to launch real-time pilot spot electricity markets by 2019 in eight regions and to be established by 2020 (Romig 22 August 2018; Reuters 20 April 2018)).

Opening up a market perspective on Chinese wind power development allows us to study marketisation in a socialist context, which can teach us new things about China, wind power, and 'emergent markets'.

Processes of framing and overflowing and staying sober with power

Fifth, the book draws on the notions of 'framing' and 'overflowing' to account for the overarching qualification struggle in Chinese wind power development. To mobilise a socio-technical assemblage around wind power development, the association of value must be construed and (temporarily) stabilised. This entails framing wind power investments as valuable (e.g. sustainable), and the use of calculative framing devices to bracket some associations in or out.[7] These framing tools are constituted, for instance, by property rights, standards, or rules for market exchange,[8] which can help to construct a simplifying 'blackbox' around the object,[9] construing it as something that can be taken for granted as an objectified 'fact'. Meanwhile, framings are inherently fragile and bound to fall apart, or 'overflow' (Callon 1998). This fragility of framings is linked to how they de- and reconfigure relations of domination, since only

> [t]he most powerful agencies are able to impose their valuations on others and consequently to impact strongly on the distribution of value. (Caliskan & Callon 2010b:13)

Not only framing, but also framing devices can become contested, as proposing a frame is a matter of power exertion, with elements included or excluded (Callon 1998; Caliskan & Callon 2010b; Garud & Gehman 2012). When the framing falls apart, maybe just for a brief moment, it 'overflows', with unintended externalities. The overflowing nature of framings indicates a latent perspective of power, albeit the dictum in ANT is to always 'stay sober with power' (Latour 2005:260). That is, instead of assuming power structures to be there at the outset, the 'power struggles at the heart of any market' (Caliskan & Callon 2010b:12) must be traced in minute detail, following how agency and power is mounted, and following their socio-material construction and configuration. This implies a non-foundational, processual, and relational approach to power, inspired by American pragmatism, whereby 'power is not a hierarchical concept, but a figurational one based on associations' (Garud & Gehman 2012:990).

Overflowing as the norm – and Politics with a capital P in China

Sixth, frames that tend to overflow are 'the norm' when one observes through the lens of the Anthropology of Markets. That is, rather than assuming framing and stability to be the norm, the Anthropology of Markets assumes 'instability and trials of strength' (Callon 1998:33, 252–254). Such overflowing is particularly prone to happen in environments such as China where everything has the potential to become political, strategic, or sensitive. In such cases, markets may even produce 'hot situations' (Callon 1998:260). This happens particularly when there exists no stabilised consensus, certainty, or knowledge base, as this tends to engender feelings and entangled 'matters of concern' (Callon 2007, 2009; Latour 2004) that cannot be readily solved, mobilising a myriad of unforeseen heterogeneous actors into 'hybrid forums' (Callon 1998:260, 2007:158).

The propensity to overflow is inherently linked to how marketisation cannot be seen as separate from the economy or economics (processes of economisation), politics (processes of politicisation), or science (processes of scientification) (Callon 2007, 2009). These processes are different but insep-arable like the north and south poles of a magnet, like the attraction and repulsion of an electromagnetic field. This entanglement makes qualification and valuation processes in marketisation – as the framing processes they constitute – fragile, as complete framing/bracketing/blackboxing becomes impossible. Politicisation, especially, can be expected to play a large part in wind power development marketisation, for instance owing to contestations over subsidisation, China's ambition to create a Harmonious Socialist Society through scientific development, and over state ownership and state control. In a marketising Chinese socialist context, in particular, it can be argued that politicisation abounds, as the power sector is controlled and owned by the state, for example with electricity prices being set by the state, albeit this is being gradually liberalised. Whilst the Anthropology of Markets lens tends to observe the potentiality of politics and negotiations everywhere, this is often a 'politics' with a lower-case 'p'. In China, though, owing to the entangled nature of the Party-State, everything tends to become 'Political' with a capital 'P'.

Stretching marketisation studies by moving to a socialist context

Seventh, by moving marketisation studies from the conventional Western con-text into the context of China's socialist planned economy, we are reminded that markets are but one potential modality of economisation, and that mar-ketisation can take many different shapes. By taking marketisation studies to a context, which does not necessarily follow the prototypical 'Western', 'capitalist' model of markets, we are reminded of the multiple modes of marketisation and economisation, as well as of its 'political dimension'. This is particu-larly the case when studying the marketising of 'objects and behaviours that have previously defied marketization' (Caliskan & Callon 2010b:23). It may be argued that China's energy sector is stranded uncomfortably somewhere between the plan and the market (Andrews-Speed 2012:81). This illustrates that marketisation is not an irreversible effect of economisation (Caliskan & Callon 2010b:23). Whilst processes of economisation and marketisation in Chinese wind power development have taken place alongside each other, China has so far economised wind power without fully marketising it. This book therefore stretches marketisation studies by taking it to a context where wind power development and (the as yet non-existent) electricity markets are closely controlled, owned, and monitored by the Chinese socialist state in intricate ways. By acknowledging that 'the movement towards markets is by no means irreversible, other forms of economization can always be envisaged' (Caliskan & Callon 2010b:23). The present case of marketisation in Chinese wind power development offers a chance to open the blackbox of China's state-led energy sector, which is entangled in unfinished market reforms. Indeed, in a socialist context such as China's planned economy, it is necessary 'to be clear that one can economise a domain without marketising it (take the example of Soviet economic planning)' (Kurunmaki et al. 2016:396). Hereby, by taking the Anthropology of Markets to the 'socialist' market economy of China, we get the chance to explore how '[m]arkets have a history; they also have a future that cannot be reduced simply to an extrapolation of the past' (Caliskan & Callon 2010b:24).

Reflexivity and multiple, variable ontologies – looking through the kaleidoscope

Eighth, the doctrine of reflexivity means that the 'socio-technical cartographer' of controversies (Venturini 2010) can be reflexive about research concepts, potential biases, and his or her role in coproducing the object of enquiry. Accordingly, concepts of sustainability cannot be taken for granted: indeed, there may be multiple and shifting sustainabilities whose socio-material constitution must be traced. The same, of course, goes for notions such as wind power(s), market(s), quality/-ies, innovation(s), and science(s). This openness to the malleability and contested nature of things relates to the notion of variable and 'multiple ontologies' (identities) (Callon 1991; Mol 1999), namely that things as we know them may change and shift over time, and that they are situated in particular contexts. Such a variable ontology of entities and their mutual relatedness in the assemblages they co-constitute mean that when one entity shifts the entire assemblage/configuration shifts as well. As in a kaleidoscope, we see an ever-changing pattern as the cell is rotated, causing the materials to be set in motion.

Showing the universe from an algorithm – from the lateral perspective

Ninth, the Anthropology of Markets offers a lateral perspective; that is, an Anthropology of Markets-based account using the principles of ANT tends to tell stories that 'erode the distinction between the macro- and micro-social' (Law 1994:17). This is the principle that applies when this study traces software algorithms. Whilst these may seem to be innocuous micro-actors, this book will show how the network assemblage around wind turbines and software algorithms is entangled in macro-actors such as the Chinese state, and institutions, policies, and politics of the electrical power sector; and also how algorithms affect the emerging socio-technical assemblage around wind power. This makes the spatial and hierarchical – structural distinction between micro and macro superfluous. Networks around software algorithms are thus entangled in, and entangling, networks around wind power development and the Chinese power sector. This means that, as a prerequisite, it is necessary to acknowledge how changes in one assemblage have implications on the others.

As networks/socio-technical assemblages around wind turbines, software, wind power, and electrical power are inherently enmeshed, it becomes possible to tell a broad story about Chinese greening of electrical power, Chinese catch-up, and the economic transformation sector by focusing on what might seem to be small and innocent actors, such as algorithms. And so, just as the wind turbine cannot function or be understood without an understanding of its constituent components, this book traces controversies around different turbine components, displaying their interconnectedness and how it becomes possible to 'see the universe in an algorithm'. Or, as MacKenzie (2003) put it, it becomes possible to show 'an equation and its world'. Figure 2.1 illustrates how this book looks at entangled socio-technical

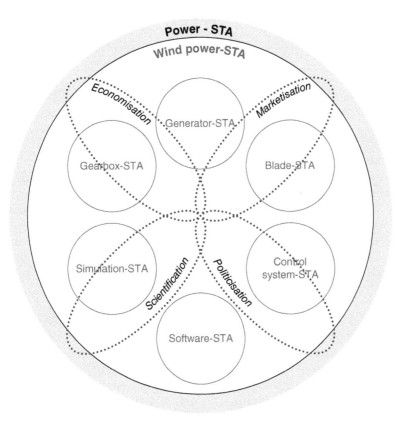

Figure 2.1 Entangled socio-technical assemblages in processes of marketisation, economisation, scientification, and politicisation.

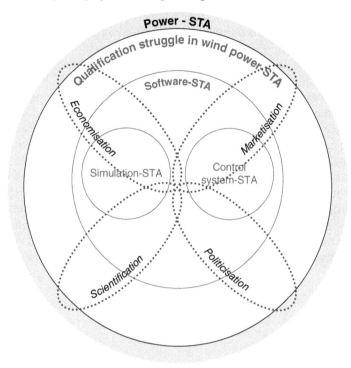

Figure 2.2 Zooming in on the socio-technical assemblage around software.

assemblages (STAs) around electrical power (constituting a 'Power-STA') and around wind power development ('Wind power-STA'), which in turn entangle and are entangled by socio-technical assemblages around various turbine components (e.g. generator-STA, blade-STA, gearbox-STA, software-STA, control system-STA, and simulation tool-STA).

In this mesh, Ambiguous Winds of Change zooms in on the assemblage around software, in particular assemblages around control systems and simulation tools (Figure 2.2)[10].

Expanding STS by stretching the boundaries of a 'modest sociology'

Finally, the Anthropology of Markets represents a so-called 'modest sociology' and 'weak' programme, which uses stories and empirical detail to provide an account of the singularity, specificity, and situatedness of the specific event of marketisation, rather than providing a 'strong narrative' of causalities and generalisation (Fraser 2010; Law 2004; Venturini 2010; Yaneva 2012). This reflects the Anthropology of Markets' philosophical roots in the micro-relational, processual, and reflexive lens of American pragmatism, and in particular Dewey's theory of valuation (e.g. Dewey 1915,

1927; Dewey cf. Hutter & Stark 2015; Whitehead 1978). What we should then investigate, through a 'methodological situationalism' (Hutter & Stark 2015:3), is the dissonance created by the trials of valuation over the framing of wind power. That is, we should trace how sites of valuation and moments of dispute and contention change and transform both the object of investigation and the identities of actors involved (Hutter & Stark 2015:2–3), as different, and often contested and/or conflicting, values are being associated with wind power.

The Anthropology of Markets' 'radical' programme of anti-reductionism (Fraser 2010; Law 1994, 2004; Stengers 2011; Venturini 2010) entails a focus on detail rather than broad sweeping generalisations. Indeed, when it comes to Sino-foreign supply chain relations, it seems that they often tend to unravel as soon as they have been forged, instead of solidifying into stabilised hierarchies or what may often be generalised into 'institutions'. A high degree of instability (overflowing) makes generalisation difficult, however, as we need to see when and how assemblages unravel, and when and how they do not. This makes a relational and processual lens, rather than a structural lens, particularly helpful and relevant when examining Chinese marketisation of wind power development. Meanwhile, this volume is positioned in a somewhat hybrid space between the specific and practice-based account of the constructivist Anthropology of Markets' lens and the claim for a broader account of Chinese marketisation, as it pictures a broader narrative of Chinese contested and experimental greening emerging from the algorithmic account of Sino-foreign relations around software in wind turbines. In this hybrid space there is an ambiguous yet fruitful area between the general and specific, an area that recognises there is merit to the identification of systems, institutions, and structures as long as one does not overlook the arduous socio-material work of forging and maintaining them. This volume therefore attempts to 'dare greatly', as it extends the findings from the algorithmic controversy mapping to a much broader account of Chinese contested wind power development.

Drawing up the inventory for mapping controversies in Chinese wind power development

Whilst the Anthropology of Markets is here proposed as a fruitful prism through which to enquire into Chinese wind power development, it does not provide much guidance about how to do it. Here, some of the analytic strategies applied are outlined.

One of the main principles of the adopted constructivist perspective implies that the researcher should strive to remain as open as possible when deciding which actors and entities are relevant for the analysis. This is based on the methodological premise of ANT that the researcher should always strive to 'follow the actor' (Latour 2005), as they emerge one by one during ethnographic fieldwork aimed at mapping a socio-technical assemblage. Instead of exercising censorship (Callon 1991:144) in a marketisation account,

> [T]here is no standard list. Part of the analysis would involve drawing up an inventory for each and every case. (Caliskan & Callon 2010b:8)

In marketisation, a host of different actors are likely to be involved, including state services, firms, consumers, economists, think tanks, the international monetary or financial institutions, experts, and regulatory or standardisation agencies (Caliskan & Callon 2010b:8). Yet, using an explorative research approach, the decision to trace software algorithms by 'disassembling' the turbine was not set in stone at the outset. Instead, whilst the decision to follow core technologies was reached relatively early in the research process (as it was predicted to produce more controversy), the focus on software algorithms and other components only emerged gradually through the eight or nine months of ethnographic fieldwork in China, as actors talked about their critical role in wind power development, turbine quality, and Sino-foreign supply chain relations. The focus on algorithms renders the present study a case of a particular moment when algorithms have become important tamers (framing devices) of uncertainty in wind power deployment globally, and increasingly so in China.

The controversy study is based on an extensive amount of primary and secondary data. The primary data consists of findings from 108 semi-structured interviews conducted during doctoral and post-doctoral fieldwork primarily in China (e.g. Beijing, Shanghai, Chengdu, Hangzhou, Zhangbei, Ningbo, Chongqing) and, to a lesser extent, in Denmark, Germany,[11] and the USA. The main bulk of interviews were carried out in Chinese (Mandarin), English, and Danish between 2010 and 2013. Follow-up interviews were conducted from 2015 to 2018. Interviews have been conducted with wind turbine manufacturers, component suppliers, universities and research institutes, industry associations, relevant ministries, Transmission System Operators (TSOs), design and consulting companies, with Sino-foreign joint ventures, government advisors, renewable energy think-tanks, certification bodies, test laboratories, agents/brokers (industrial spies), and finance institutions, and also includes observations and notes from conference proceedings. Whenever possible, company interviews were conducted with innovation managers, R&D directors and engineers, directors, general and managing directors, vice-presidents, chief executive officers, policy advisors, diplomats and state officials, political and technical experts and scientists, software designers, international business managers, sales managers, and chief strategists, amounting to 60 different organisations, approximately half of which are Chinese and half are 'Western'. The interviews took between 30 minutes and three hours. The actors that were critical in the configuration of China's wind power development assemblage were noted, while coding of the transcribed (verbatim) interview material, which amounted to 934 single-spaced pages, also helped in the decision on which actors to follow, as well as detecting themes and issues that would potentially form controversies around them (refer to *Appendix I*: Overview of types of collected data; *Appendix II*: Overview of coding procedures; *Appendix III*: Overview of interviews).[12] Abiding by the doctrine of critical reflexivity, the themes and codes were revised again and again, being checked against the prevalence of their presence in the data.

Attendance at scientific and industrial conferences and workshops since 2011 has also formed part of the empirical data material, as well as observations in research institutions and wind turbine factories, laboratories, test facilities, and R&D departments in China and abroad.[13] Data thus also consists of comprehensive field notes and a field diary, including reflections before and after interviews as well as reflections on participant observations.[14] Finally, the controversy study is also based on a vast mass of secondary (and tertiary) data. For the most part this stems from a substantial review of news, policies and five-year plans, industry reports, statistics – often in Chinese (Mandarin). In addition, data includes engineering textbooks, brochures, and hand-drawn pictures of wind turbines, power systems, software algorithms, electromagnetic waves, and so on.[15]

Engaging with sensitive issues in China

A precautionary note on conducting fieldwork in China should be added here. Some of the collected data was deemed 'sensitive' or 'controversial' by my respondents. Even issues that may not seem sensitive in a non-Chinese context might be deemed sensitive (i.e., controversial) in China, for example because many of the respondents were part of, or relying on, the Party cadre system. Such a high level of sensitivity and the associated need to anonymise data is a prevalent concern in the field of China Studies (Heimer & Thøgersen, 2006; Gorm Hansen 2017). The sensitive nature of data collection requires a constant balancing act, being always observant of almost invisible signs in body language (eye movements, etc.) as indications of whether or not the limit had been reached or sometimes even inadvertently crossed, and in particular being attentive to Chinese counter-reactions, such as non-action (*wúwéi*, 无为); that is, understanding what an incomplete answer to a question might mean. Accordingly, and to protect respondents, all interviews have been anonymised (Heimer & Thøgersen 2006). Indeed, with borderline 'sensitive issues', for example those related to the power sector, interpersonal relations (*guānxì*, 关系), and corruption, part of the fieldwork has seemed like undercover detective work, as I 'snowballed' myself through the Chinese wind power sector until a degree of saturation was reached. In this process, the ability to conduct interviews in Chinese (Mandarin) and to approach potential contacts through email correspondence in Chinese, as well as a prior knowledge of Chinese culture, played a vital role in building trust with respondents, and ultimately in constructing personal relations with them. Chinese contacts and relationships constituted obligatory passage points for enrolling otherwise inaccessible actors from SOEs and diplomats, for example, and to gain insights into otherwise hidden changes in rules and policies. Such new market intelligence is seldom to be found officially, but is often only accessible through ubiquitous 'Chinese whispers', which in turn must be checked as much as possible.

The level of sensitivity required has also been reflected in the way that it has sometimes been impossible to be allowed to decide independently whom to talk with. For instance, when conducting interviews during a field trip to China with a researcher group under the Sino-Danish Center for Education and Research (SDC), everything had, without prior agreement, been settled in advance by the Chinese collaboration partners without any chance to select which companies and people to talk to, and with interviews being translated through an interpreter. Sometimes, there have even been indications of being spied upon, as well as attempts to recruit the researcher as a guanxi agent, to assist in the work of maintaining relations with government officials, Party cadres, SOEs, and foreign companies. Indeed, some details may have been lost in translation during some interviews, and potentially also lost through the sensitivities of the spider's web of enmeshed state–business actors.

A sense of metaphors – and making sense through metaphors: the role of electromagnetic waves

Another precautionary note on mapping controversies in China refers to the process of rendering this algorithmic and kaleidoscopic story, and the doctrine of 'just observing a controversy' (Venturini 2010:6). On many occasions troubles have been encountered owing to an extensive amount of data and many potential storylines that interweave. Indeed, whilst the 'adventurous [research] journey' has been marked by both 'curiosity and jouissance' (Serres & Whitehead in Jensen 2010:12), 'mapping controversies' in China has often felt 'like wandering in a maze with a twine of threads to follow' (Venturini 2010:6). To make sense of the data, inspiration has at times been found in metaphors. In the process of plotting the story, consolation was found early on in Eco's (1983) notion of the highest and most refined form of the crime plot, namely constituting the story as a mystery, or a so-called rhizomatic maze whose structure is relational (Eco 1983:253). Closely related is Deleuze and Guattari's (1980) notion of a 'rhizome', with its entangled and endless net of roots under the earth, and Yaneva's (2012) notion of a 'meshwork', which constitutes 'a tightly knitted net' or mesh of entanglements (Yaneva 2012:2). These all helped in the process of sense-making, as did Venturini's (2010) notion of simultaneously fluid and solid volcanic 'magma' to denote the nature of 'controversy'. Such metaphors have been helpful as they allow us to embrace stories where there is not just one storyline, one conclusion, or one villain or hero, but rather multiple fractals, beginnings, and potential endings (Eco 1983:252; Kirkegaard 2014). Other metaphors that were employed by respondents in the field have inspired this research: for example, the 'Chinese spider's web' of enmeshed state actors in the social-ist market economy and the role of agents/brokers (or industrial spies), as well as human body analogies (e.g. central nervous system, spine, and brain) that explain the role of control systems and algorithms in the wind turbine.

However, there has been one metaphor that has persisted throughout, emerging and growing in many forms and guises: it relates to electromag-netism and its wave-like behaviour. In *Ambiguous Winds of Change*, this metaphor is used to illustrate particular phases in Chinese wind power development, as well as a particularly experimental and potentially disrup-tive mode of wind power marketisation in China, as introduced below, and as unfolded and illustrated further in Chapters Four and Nine.

Physically, electromagnetic waves imply a movement of energy and lie at the very foundation of all modern electrical power systems that transfer energy from fossil fuels or renewable sources to consumers. This energy is most commonly transferred by using alternating current (AC) electric-ity, which transmits energy via the electromagnetic fields that surround the wires, cables, and overhead lines that carry the electrical energy to where it is used. Electromagnetic waves are the common theme on the research journey through the key components of controversy in the wind turbine and the power system in each of the book's chapters; by following the electrical waves, so to speak. However, the metaphor is also used to explain more than controversies and the primary engineering purpose of a wind turbine to produce electrical power. Appropriately, the electrical wave concept also carries analogies that relate to the overarching theme of this book; that is, issues of *transformation* (the conversion of one form of energy to another), *dynamics* (the fast-changing interactions of electri-cal waves), *change* (the use of new or unfamiliar types of generation), and *disruption* (the threat to the essential balance in the power system). The metaphor is used as an analogy for the volatile oscillations in dif-ferent phases of Chinese wind power development (as reflected at its cli-max in the 'turbine wave attack', conjuring up an image of spectacular force, strength, speed, and power), but also to denote (potentially) specific Chinese characteristics of fragmented wind power governance. We will now look more closely at these properties.

Electromagnetic waves, interference, tipping points, disruption, and stalemate

Before diving further into the different meanings of the metaphor, it is nec-essary to understand the various characteristics of electromagnetic waves. Physically, electromagnetic waves comprise electric and magnetic fields. Always existing together, they form a multidimensional electromagnetic

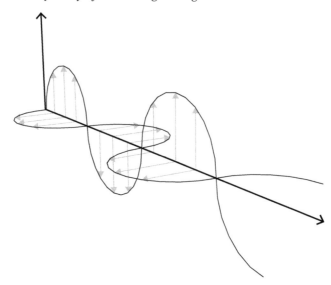

Figure 2.3 Metaphor of electromagnetic waves for controversy mapping.

field, characterised by electromagnetic waves that propagate/oscillate simultaneously in two dimensions (Figure 2.3), causing mutual interference.

Waves of the same type (whether electromagnetic, water, or sound) exhibit a fascinating property: they combine to produce a new wave, having hidden properties of the old waves but with, perhaps, very different consequences. A wave also has a periodicity: it repeats itself. Two waves rising and falling at the same time are referred to as 'in phase'. If they oscillate at different times then they are 'out of phase'. Let us focus on the three-phase electrical grid system: the backbone of the modern power system. A power genera-tor produces three phases of electricity. Each phase has its electrical wave exactly 120° out of phase with the next, and each phase delivers its power along its own wire. The beauty of this system is that if the loads are balanced on each of the phases, then the principle of combination of waves means that when the three wires come together, then all three waves cancel each other out and there is no need for a return wire back to the generator. If the loads are not equal on each of the phases, however, then the waves will not fully cancel each other out and there is a risk that the balance of the grid will be disrupted. Overall, grid stability depends on the balancing logic of the entire system, which – on closer inspection – depends on the constructive interference of waves:

Like the three-phase power system, the metaphor centres on the combin-ing of different waves and makes use of their characteristics, as follows:

• A strong centrally controlled system wave ('system frequency signal') may set the timing for the whole system.

- Waves in phase may combine and produce a stronger signal. Waves that are somewhat out of phase may also combine, but the result may not look like any of the individual waves. A number of smaller but very different frequency waves can affect the main wave, if there are many of them and they are sufficiently out of phase. This we refer to as 'constructive interference'.
- Waves may also combine when they are fully out of phase and can cancel each other out. But underneath, all the constituent waves are still active and propagating. This is called 'destructive interference'. This stalemate can be broken by an intervention that changes the system properties.
- If the result of a combination of waves hits the system's 'resonant frequency', then oscillations can be set up that can grow in amplitude and destruction until they threaten the collapse of the whole system. The rapidly increasing oscillation can be brought under control by an intervention that changes the system properties and thus the resonant frequency.
- The change needed to go from stalemate to collapse can be small: we will call this the 'tipping point' (inspired by Nicholson 2002).

Thus, whilst we can envision vertical wave action as the actions and transformative changes produced through interference with other waves, we can also think of the horizontal wave motion as the fluctuating controversies unfolding in Chinese wind power development marketisation, as these also change and interfere. This is in step with the notion that controversies are part of the process, not to be separated, sometimes negative and sometimes positive, but rendering co-creation over time. Like the electric and magnetic fields, the transformative changes cause controversies, and the controversies cause transformation. And so it is within this electromagnetic field (this 'space' or 'site') that multiple entangled controversies are unfolding and overlapping, themselves constituting oscillating waves and subject to constructive and destructive interference. Indeed, much like the interaction of electromagnetic fields, with both attraction and repulsion being contained in the same field, the volatile and multidimensional electromagnetic field of Chinese wind power development marketisation renders the controversies, as they unfold, highly entangled and overlapping, making it difficult if not impossible to disentangle them, and resulting in ubiquitous overflowing.

An electromagnetic metaphor for fragmented wind power development

At the same time, electromagnetism has within it the notion of the potential to charge, as well as power and the ability to raise tension – thus being an analogue to China's politicised marketisation. Accordingly, the metaphor of electromagnetic waves not only fits the object of enquiry – the wave-like property of the AC electricity produced from wind power, and the different phases of Chinese wind power development and the controversies they stir up – but also the context of enquiry: China itself. The oscillations of the Chinese government between centralised intervention and decentralised fragmentation are also very wave-like. The metaphor, as will be shown, can therefore be applied not only to an understanding of wind power and wind power development in China through its different phases ('waves'), but it can also shed light on Chinese fragmented authoritarianism and what and how this conveys marketisation of wind power development with its par- ticular 'Chinese characteristics': the oscillating movements in Chinese wind power development reflect the oscillating movements between a strong cen- trally controlled system and a looser locally controlled system.

This investigation has identified three phases in the marketisation of wind power development in China (explored further in Chapters Four and Nine where the metaphor is further unfolded), which all seem to be characterised by state-endorsed actors engaging in pragmatic experimentalism. Like the combining and interference of uncoordinated waves, this carries the risk of repeatedly advancing towards a tipping point, until the developments stand at the brink of collapse either through out-of-control constructive oscilla- tions or stalemate through destructive interference. Astute intervention,

---

Box 2.1

The story of electromagnetism and two old friends

Electromagnetism was first detected by the Danish chemist and physicist – and romanticist poet - Hans Christian Ørsted (1777–1851) in 1820, in discov- ering that electric currents create magnetic fields. To Ørsted, the discovery of the connection between electricity and magnetism was not just related to the technical perspectives and horizons opening up, but first and foremost a confirmation of the proposition of nature as an organically or cosmically connected whole (Gjesing 2013:19–20). As a universal romanticist, he crossed scientific borders and sought to let them create a synergistic outcome. The famous Danish fairytale poet Hans Christian Andersen (1805–1975) was a close friend of Hans Christian Ørsted, and in their talks, walks, and mail cor- respondence, they also shared views on nature, physics, electromagnetism, poetry, and metaphysics. In Andersen's writings, he discusses how it becomes possible to trace an entire 'fairytale world', a universe, just by looking at what unfolds in the microscope. In one of Andersen's such transformative fairy tales, 'A Drop of Water' [Vanddraaben'] (1847/1848) (Andersen 2003; Gjesing 2013), which was dedicated to H. C. Ørsted, Andersen allows 'a peek into a hidden and invisible reality, present just under the surface of the visible realm, but seen clearly through the microscope. What the microscope magnified is a world inside out' (Sanders 2017:102). In another fairytale, Andersen uses the issue of electromagnetism, which he has discussed with his friend Ørsted, as a foundation for a story about 'The Great Sea-Serpent' (1871) under the sea, namely reflecting the brave new world of continent-connecting electromag- netic telegraph cables [Den Store Soeslange'] (Andersen 1971).

though, just on the edge of destruction, seems to harvest the synergistic effects and leapfrogging possibilities for disruptive catch-up and upgrading. This bears witness to successive phases of threatened destabilisation and stalemate, and to the fragility, ambiguity and agile governance that is enabling China to upgrade and catch up through and in spite of marketisation that is on the brink of collapse.

Therefore, the metaphor applies to what are conventionally treated as micro-, meso-, and macro-level accounts (of wind power, industrial development/phases, and Chinese governance), providing a lateral story of entangled levels. Yet, rather than used to depict a specific trajectory in some path-dependent pattern or account of evolutionary orthogenesis, the metaphor is used to depict fragile and ambiguous stages/phases where development happens through constructive or destructive interference, ultimately being driven towards a delicate tipping point where everything is open and debatable. And so the metaphor is employed to account for potentiality – the ambiguous space where everything and anything is possible, a space of inherent instability, vulnerability, and fragility. It depicts a story of moments of contestations, of chance, and a space ripe with improvisation and experimentation, where chance and plan come together in a new whole.

In this account, whilst they are deployed to provide more certainty, algorithms paradoxically prove to be operating on a deeper level, often providing more ambiguity than certainty, and raising new concerns as they, themselves, are often the very source of overflowing and controversy. The metaphor can help to depict the constant tension between attempts to control (frame) the physical wind through centralised control, control systems, simulation tools, and algorithms, and the inherent inability to do so completely – in alignment with the notion of overflowing as the norm rather than framing as the norm. Indeed, the metaphor helps us enquire into the political space where algorithms try to control and tame the stochastically fluctuating (and oscillating) wind – the struggle for perfect framing, risk minimisation, and taking power over the random and stochastic wind – through probabilistic models and calculations, and the vain Don Quixote-like battle to do so.

An engineering metaphor as a new thread of life

Following the Danish fairytale writer Hans Christian Andersen, who saw electromagnetism as a potential thread of life in new comedy plays, fairy tales, and novels, this book uses electromagnetic waves as the thread of life, to account for Chinese experimental and disruptive wind power development marketisation, which is marked by great uncertainty and power struggles (see Box 2.1).[16] The inability to frame and disentangle actors and controversy completely is what conveys a specific Chinese 'flavour' to wind power development marketisation – one which is more 'political'. And so, just as the wind turbine cannot function or be understood without an understanding of its constituent components, this study traces enmeshed controversies that are configured around various turbine and grid components, displaying their interconnectedness and how it becomes possible to see the universe in an algorithm, unveiling the hybridity of things where markets, society, politics, science, technology, and nature are mixed. As an overall story of power, in physical and socio-political terms this study charts an ethnographic journey through the power field of the wind turbine, its algorithms, and the physical and socio-political electrical power network of Chinese wind power development.

Structure of book

With the engineering metaphor in hand, this book is structured as follows.

In Chapter Three, an empirical context and background to understand market reforms in China's power sector and upgrading and innovation in the country's wind turbine industry, as depicted in China Studies, is provided. Indirectly, this also provides a brief literature review for China Studies, showing how it has dealt with such issues. The chapter concludes with an outline of a relational gap in the extant literature, proposing a pragmatist tunnel to STS that can contribute not only to China Studies, but also to STS and New Economic Sociology more broadly. This concludes Part I of the book, followed by Part II's multifaceted and rhizomatic 'controversy study' of China's wind power development, diving into five entangled 'sites of controversy' in Chapters Four to Eight, each following different actors/ entities. This is illustrated in Table 2.1.

Chapter Four follows the ongoing qualification struggle of the Chinese marketisation of wind power development. This is done through a historical overview of the development of China's wind power sector, focusing on dynamics of requalification during the quality crisis and the turn to quality. Looking at the fundamental commodity, electricity, whose flow is traced through the vital components of the turbine and into the grid, the

Table 2.1 Mapped sites of controversy in PART II

PART II	Controversy study	Actors followed
First site of controversy	Access to wind power deployment	Following wind's qualification over three phases
Second site of controversy	Access to the electricity grid	Following colliding forces of the wind and grid
Third site of controversy	Access to money and relations in the Chinese 'spider's web'	Following (relations around) money: liquidity and debt chains
Fourth site of controversy	Access to intellectual property rights (IPRs)	Following control system algorithms
Fifth site of controversy	Access to standards and certificates	Following aeroelastic codes in simulation tools

chapter calls upon its essential trait, that of an electromagnetic wave, to explain the qualification struggle.

In turn, Chapter Five traverses the electromagnetic field out of the turbine, through the wind farm cabling, in and out of the sub-station, and to where the cabling meets the public grid. It is here that the book undertakes a controversy mapping to explore access to the power grid, depicting a struggle between coal and wind as it follows the fluctuating forces of the wind and observes the constitution of the state-owned grid to be 'hostile' to wind power. The cost of energy, the way it is calculated and the implications of support mechanisms are also explored. This provides a somewhat more conventional look at the contestation between fossil fuels and renewable energy in the 'Coal Kingdom' of China, which is marked by socio-materially grounded power struggles and vested interests. By following concerns about access to the grid, the analysis traces electromagnetic interaction at the grid connection and reveals a story of grid strength, voltage rises, points of instability, and voltage collapse, but also around cost calculations and support mechanisms. This constitutes a socio-materially hostile environment for wind power, and ultimately – through high curtailment rates – threatens to destabilise its framing as 'environmentally sustainable'.

In turn, Chapter Six enquires into controversies over access to government funding and interpersonal relations (*guānxi*) by following the money, specifically by focusing on liquidity and debt chains. Starting where the money originates, we follow the electromagnetic energy from the turbine as it flows into the precision instrument of the electricity meter, which uses the principle of electromagnetic induction to count the energy produced (megawatt hours). Once the energy is counted, the numbers find their way to the utility company, where formulae are employed to convert them into Chinese *yuan* (*renminbi*), based on various parameters that include the tariff subsidies set by central policies. These numbers, which are now separated from electrical energy and exist only on the utility company's computer screen, are crucial in assessing the ability to earn money from and loan money to the next wind project. In doing so, Chapter Six enquires into Chinese wind power development marketisation by diving into debt chains during a consolidation phase taking place in the wake of the 'quality crisis' in Chinese wind power, mapping the de- and reconfiguring of Sino-foreign supply chain relations around control systems as a liquidity and credit crisis hits the sector. This sheds light on the Chinese spider's web of closely entangled state–business relations, 'common pockets', and interpersonal relations (*guānxi*) in the state-controlled power sector. At the same time, the spider's web constitution of the sector reveals itself as inherently enmeshed in the contested 'system problem' (the system is not a 'pure market economy'), which threatens to stifle innovation and competition, and to destabilise wind power's framing as economically and even politically sustainable.

Chapters Seven and Eight map two algorithmic controversy studies, which follow control system algorithms and aeroelastic codes in simulation tools as they produce power struggles over IPRs and certification and standardisation. In Chapter Seven we return to the turbine and specifically the generator, where precise control of the rotor's electromagnetic field is essential to the turbine's proper and efficient operation. The control system that is tasked to manage the generator is one of many control systems (blade pitch angle, yaw drive, power output, etc.) that all have to function together and are monitored by the turbine's overall management system: the supervisory control system. The chapter then focuses on how the quality crisis and potential turn to quality have engendered multiple struggles in Sino-foreign customer–supplier relations over access to IPRs in control system core algorithms.

Chapter Eight moves along from the electromagnetic fields of the generator and traces the power back through the drive-train, the gearbox, and ultimately out to the rotor. The journey takes us to the design phase of this assemblage of components, before operation and before manufacture. Existing only in the memory of high-performance computers, the turbine's design is put through its paces using highly complex simulation tools that test all corners of its operational envelope. These tools, and the standards they are based upon, are the essential backbone that enable the design, test, and certification of a turbine that will be sold on the international market. The chapter then looks at a controversy study regarding the certification and standardisation of the core technology of simulation tools that are used in the design of new wind turbines, and the dominant qualification of 'quality by algorithm'. With the entangled controversies over China's attempt to abide by international standards but also to develop its own indigenous standards, software algorithms in simulation tools emerge as anything but mundane, benign, and innocent, but rather highly political. And so, as a metaphor, the five sites of controversy are depicted as enmeshed multidimensional electromagnetic waves, in Figure 2.4.

Ascending again to the nacelle house to gain a panoramic view after having traced controversy after controversy in detail, Part III concludes with the findings and reflects on broader implications. Chapter Nine discusses the findings and shows how an Anthropology of Markets' lens – by allowing the analysis to move into the algorithmic machine room of the wind turbine and traverse the electromagnetic waves – can contribute to and extend China Studies, as well as STS. Last, before crawling down the turbine tower and stepping outside, Chapter Ten discusses the broader implications of the findings, discussing implications for the literature on Varieties of Capitalism, for industrial upgrading, and for value chain governance, and sketches out a future research agenda – traversing boundaries between relational and structural accounts through a 'pragmatic tunnel' – within New Economic Sociology more broadly (also see Chapter Three).

And so, having rendered an overview of the unique analytical strategy that this work brings to bear – contributing to China Studies at the same time as it transcends the conventionally 'modest sociology' of the Anthropology of Markets and ANT, as laid out in much more detail in Chapters Three, Nine,

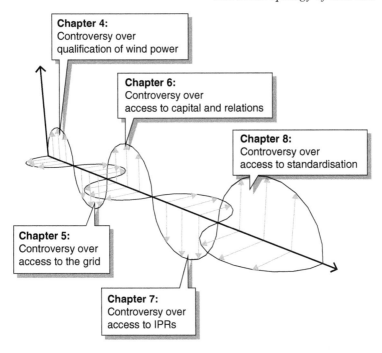

Figure 2.4 Electromagnetic waves to map five sites of controversy.

and Ten – it is time to set the empirical context for the controversy study and how it has been narrated in the vast field of China Studies. Chapter Three continues the journey, traversing the electromagnetic waves of wind power development with its 'Chinese characteristics' in mind.

Notes

1. Apart from drawing on the marketisation lens of the Anthropology of Markets and its emerging 'performativity programme' (Caliskan & Callon 2009, 2010a, 2010b), as well as on ANT, the book draws inspiration from the sociology of associations (Garud, Gehman & Karnøe 2010; Latour 2005a) and the underlying 'pragmatics of valuation' with roots in American pragmatism (Dewey 1915, 1939; Elias 1978; Whitehead 1978).
2. Latour's 1992 article, titled 'Where are the missing masses: Sociology of a few mundane artefacts', reintroduced the material actors into the centre of analysis.
3. For the specific type of socio-technical assemblage in marketisation, the notion of market STAs (mSTAs) has been proposed (Caliskan & Callon 2010b:22).
4. Whereas the concept of distributed agency has been applied to the invention of new goods, this study applies the notion to the invention of market sectors. The notion of distributed agency has been developed to counter the individual/ opportunity entrepreneurial model of innovation where the conception is that entrepreneurial agency is individual and strategic; instead, 'entrepreneurship can be fruitfully analyzed as a process of collective exploration'. (Doganova 2009:38). Along the same lines, Akrich, Callon & Latour (2002:191) display a

collective, non-linear theory of technological innovation as a matter of translation with heterogeneous actors mobilised into 'the art of interessement'.

5. This study looks at narratives, discourses, and rhetoric as narrative, discursive, or rhetoric tools/devices, as they do things through their socio-material constitution; that is, they can qualify and frame, severing links of emerging socio-technical assemblages. Hereby, this study takes a constructivist approach rather than a social constructivist, sensemaking, and/or institutionalisation approach to discourses or narratives (e.g. Czarniawska 2008; Phillips, Lawrence & Hardy 2004).

6. For instance the European Union Winter Package's proposal of a new market design (the market design initiative, MDI), which advocates for liberalisation as a matter of one-price electricity markets and consumers at the centre of markets. The proposal is endorsed by some, but regarded as market utopia and impossible owing to physics and economic theory by others (Hancher & Winters 2017; personal communication 2018).

7. Framing is both cognitive and physical in nature (Callon 1998:249) and works by establishing 'a boundary [a frame against the outside world] within which interactions – the significance and content of which are self-evident to the protagonists – take place more or less independently of their surrounding context' (Goffman 1971 in Callon 1998:249).

8. Overflowing denotes unexpected side-effects, which in mainstream economics would be coined as positive or negative externalities (Callon 1998:16–17; also see Coase 1960, 1988 for a definition of externalities). Overflowing may destabilise the framing temporarily, but when (temporarily) internalised, the overflowing is contained, and the framing can be restored. Contrary to mainstream economics in which 'framing' (i.e. assigning a more or less stable means of valuation) is the norm, ANT assumes that overflows are the norm (Callon 1998:23).

9. Framings work to blackbox as they exclude and bracket out some associations, and in doing so simplify and pacify the many potential associations that can be attributed to a thing. Framing as a matter of blackboxing enables a market assemblage, for instance, to be 'performed' (come into being) as framing – via the employment of various calculative framing devices – makes actors into 'calculative agents' that can perform 'calculative agencies' (Callon 1986b:28–34), calculating the value(s) of the good. Meanwhile, in STS (including ANT), blackboxes are always critical objects of enquiry. Whilst appropriating 'the engineers' term blackbox, a term describing a predictable input–output device, something the inner workings of which need not be known for it to be used', STS works to help 'open the blackbox' (Sismondo 2010:120), so to speak, showing how S&T, amongst other things, but also technologies, economics, algorithms, and so on 'produce black boxes, or facts and artifacts that are taken for granted' (Sismondo 2010:120), as well as showing how these blackboxed framings may produce contestation, and are thus not just mundane, innocent objectified 'matters of fact', but rather 'matters of concern' (contested 'things') up for negotiation and contestation (Latour 2005b).

10. Due to limitations in the visual tools applied, a 'disclaimer' to some of the book's figures must be made (figures 2.1, 2.2, 3.1, 9.1), as they seem to render a two-dimensional and static picture of the socio-technical assemblages rather than four-dimensional (including a sense of temporal dynamics). Two-dimensional figures tend to separate things into levels and layers, with some circles and brackets seeming 'larger' than others. Again, in a constructivist, lateral, and symmetrical lens, none of these layers should be taken for granted. Thus, while some circles are depicted as visually larger, this is not meant to entail that they are more powerful or important than others.

This is instead a matter of empirical investigation. Lastly, for practical reasons, many circles and brackets seem to be separated; yet, the reader of the figures should take into account how these different circles often tend to overlap, being entangled by and entangling each other.

11. Of these 108 interviews, 37 were conducted in collaboration with others under a larger research project on the role of global innovation networks (GINs) in wind power, funded by the SDC, in particular, with Stine Haakonsson, associate professor at Copenhagen Business School, and to a lesser extent, Jørgen Lindegaard Pedersen (Technical University of Denmark, Department of Management Engineering), Eleni Markou, Technical University of Denmark (Technical University of Denmark, Department of Wind Energy), and Kong Xinxin (Chinese Academy of Science & Technology for Development, CASTED, and MOST, China). In five of these interviews, the author was not participating in the interview, but has participated in preparation and analysis, and has been provided with the audio files and transcriptions. Six of the transcriptions were audio recordings of scientific presentations on wind power integration.
12. Interview quotes have been anonymised and translated from Chinese and Danish respectively to English.
13. Part of the data material also stems from an Asian Development Bank-sponsored trip to CEPRI's (China Electric Power Research Institute) then new wind farm test site facility (Zhangbei National Wind and Solar Energy Storage and Transmission Demonstration Project, including a trip to a wind farm in connection with a new test laboratory for grid connection of Chinese wind turbines). The trip was arranged for grid operators and wind farm developers, to learn about verification of grid performance.
14. During field trips, insights into Chinese and foreign component suppliers were gained, not only within the field of wind power, but also within other industries such as solar power. These interviews have served as background information, enabling an ongoing comparison between wind power and other (related) strategic or non-strategic industries, for example to cross-check whether or not the information on the wind power industry can be considered as unique to the industry, or whether there were more general trends of market construction across industries.
15. Throughout the book, central Chinese discourses and narratives (e.g. scientific development, indigenous innovation) mentioned both in Chinese plans and policies as well as interviews are also mentioned in Mandarin, along with selected Chinese key cultural notions and interview quotes to provide a better understanding of the proliferation of certain discourses and rhetoric.
16. This study hereby moves the object of enquiry of electromagnetic waves above sea level: that is, other studies have used metaphors that configure around electromagnetism under the sea. Not only Hans Christian Andersen, but also Starosielski's (2015) ethnographic study of 'the undersea network' of seamless and insulated fibre-optic cables carrying information between continents in the global information economy are worth mentioning.

References

Akrich, M., Callon, M. & Latour, B., 2002, 'The Key to Success in Innovation, Part I: The Art of Interessement', *International Journal of Innovation Management* 6(2), 187–206.
Andersen, H. C., 2003, 'Vanddraaben' ['The Drop of Water'], *Andersens samlede vaerker, Eventyr og historier I: 1830–1850*, Gyldendal, Copenhagen.

Andrews-Speed, P., 2012, *The Governance of Energy in China. Transition to a Low-Carbon Economy*, Palgrave Macmillan, Basingstoke.

Beckert, J. & Zafirovski, M., 2011, *International Encyclopedia of Economic Sociology*, Taylor and Francis/Routledge, London.

Blanchet, V. & Depeyre, C., 2016, 'Exploring the Shaping of Markets through Controversies: Methodological Propositions for Macromarketing Studies', *Journal of Macromarketing* 36(1), 41–53.

Breslau, D., 2013, 'Designing a Market-Like Entity: Economics in the Politics of Market Formation', *Social Studies of Science* 43(60), 829–851.

Caliskan, K. & Callon, M., 2009, 'Economization, Part 1: Shifting Attention from the Economy towards Processes of Economization', *Economy and Society* 38(3), 369–398.

Caliskan, K. & Callon, M., 2010a, 'Economization: New Directions in the Social Studies of the Market', Draft paper, 1–59.

Caliskan, K. & Callon, M., 2010b, 'Economization, Part 2: a Research Programme for the Study of Markets', *Economy and Society* 39(1), 1–32.

Callon, M., 1986a, 'Some Elements of a Sociology of Translation: Domestication of the Scallops and the Fishermen of St. Brieuc Bay', in J. Law (ed.), *Power Action and Belief: A New Sociology of Knowledge?*, pp. 196–233, Routledge & Kegan Paul, London.

Callon, M., 1986b, 'The Sociology of an Actor-Network: The Case of the Electric Vehicle', in M. M. Callon, J. Law & A. Rip (eds.), *Mapping the Dynamics of Science and Technology*, pp. 19–34, Palgrave Macmillan, London.

Callon, M., 1991, 'Techno-Economic Networks and Irreversibility', in J. Law (ed.), *A Sociology of Monsters: Essays on Power, Technology and Domination*, pp. 132–161, Routledge, London.

Callon, M., ed., 1998, *Laws of the Markets*, Blackwell Publishers/The Sociological Review, Oxford.

Callon, M., 2007, 'An Essay on the Growing Contribution of Economic Markets to the Proliferation of the Social', *Theory, Culture & Society* 24(7–8), 139–163.

Callon, M., 2009, 'Civilizing Markets: Carbon Trading between *In Vitro* and *In Vivo* Experiments', *Accounting, Organizations and Society* 34(3–4), 535–548.

Callon, M., Lascoumes, P. & Barthe, Y., 2001, *Acting in an Uncertain World. An Essay on Technical Democracy*, transl. G. Burchell, MIT Press, Cambridge, MA.

Callon, M., Méadel, C. & Rabeharisoa, V., 2002, 'The Economy of Qualities', *Economy and Society* 31(2), 194–217.

CCCPC (Central Committee of the Communist Party of China), 2013, Decision on major issues concerning comprehensively deepening reforms, 13 November 2013, adopted at the close of the Third Plenary Session of the 18th CPC Central Committee, http://www.china.org.cn/china/third_plenary_session/2013-11/16/content_30620736.htm

Czarniawska, B., 2008, *Narratives in Social Science Research*, SAGE Publications, London.

Czarniawska, B., 2013, 'On Meshworks and Other Complications of Portraying Contemporary Organizing', *Managing Overflow*, Gothenburg Research Institute, GRI-report, 2013(3), http://hdl.handle.net/2077/34252.

Deleuze, G. & Guattari, F., 1980, 'Introduction: Rhizome', in G. Deleuze & F. Guattari (eds.), *A Thousand Plateaus. Capitalism and Schizophrenia*, pp. 3–28, Continuum International Publishing Group, London.

Dewey, J., 1915, 'The Logics of Judgements of Practice (Part I), *The Journal of Philosophy, Psychology and Scientific Methods* 14, 505–523.

Dewey, J., 1927, *The Public and its Problems*, Holt, Oxford.

Dewey, J., 1939, 'Theory of Valuation', *Philosophy of Science* 6(4), 490–491 (October), https://doi.org/10.1086/286595.

Dobbin, F. (ed.), 2004, *The New Economic Sociology – a Reader*, Princeton University Press, Princeton, NJ.

Doganova, L., 2009, 'Entrepreneurship as a Process of Collective Exploration', *Centre de Sociologie de l'Innovation*, Working paper, MINES ParisTech.

Eco, U., 1983, *Rosens navn*, Forum: Copenhagen.

Elias, N., 1978, *What is Sociology?*, Columbia University Press, New York.

Fraser, M., 2010, 'Facts, Ethics and Event', in C. B. Jensen & K. Rödje (eds.), *Deleuzian Intersections in Science, Technology and Anthropology*, pp. 57–82, Berghahn Press, New York.

Garud, R. & Gehman, J., 2012, 'Metatheoretical Perspectives on Sustainability Journeys: Evolutionary, Relational and Durational', *Research Policy* 41, 980–995.

Garud, R. & Karnøe, P., 2003, 'Bricolage versus Breakthrough: Distributed and Embedded Agency in Technology Entrepreneurship', *Research Policy* 32, 277–300.

Garud, R., Gehman, J. & Karnøe, P., 2010, 'Categorization by Association: Nuclear Technology and Emission Free Electricity', in W. D. Sine & R. J. David (eds.), *Institutions and Entrepreneurship, Research in the Sociology of Work* 21, Emerald Group Publishing Limited, pp. 51–93.

Gjesing, K. B., 2013, 'Ørsted og Andersen og guldalderens naturfilosofi' ['Oersted and Andersen and the Golden Age Philosophy of Nature'], *Kvant – tidsskrift for fysik og astronomi*, December, http://www.kvant.dk/upload/kv-2013-4/kv-2013-4-KBG-Oersted-Andersen.pdf.

Gorm Hansen, L. L., 2017, *Triggering Earthquakes in Science, Politics and Chinese Hydropower. A Controversy Study*, PhD thesis, Dept. of International Economics and Management, Asia Studies Centre, Copenhagen Business School.

Granovetter, M. S., 1985, 'Economic Action and Social Structure: The Problem of Embeddedness', *American Journal of Sociology* 91(3), 481–510.

Hancher, L. & Winters B. M., 2017, 'The EU Winter Package', Briefing Paper, *Allen & Overy LLP*, February.

Heimer, M. & Thøgersen, S., eds., 2006, *Doing Fieldwork in China*, NIAS Press, Copenhagen.

Hutter, M. & Stark, D., 2015, 'Pragmatist Perspectives on Valuation: An Introduction', in A. B. A. M., Hutter & D. Stark, *Moments of Valuation, Exploring Sites of Dissonance*, pp. 1–12, Oxford University Press, New York.

Jenle, R. P., 2015, *Engineering Markets for Control: Integrating Wind Power into the Danish Electricity System*, PhD thesis, Department of Organization, Copenhagen Business School.

Jenle, R. P. & Pallesen T., 2017, 'How Engineers Make Markets Organizing System Decarbonization', *Revue Francaise de sociologies*, International Edition 3(58), 375–397.

Jensen, C. B., 2010, 'Ontologies for Developing Things: Making Health Care Futures through Technology', *Transdisciplinary Studies* 3, Sense Publishers, Rotterdam.

Karnøe, P., 2013, 'Large Scale Wind Power Penetration in Denmark: Breaking Up and Remixing Politics, Technologies and Markets', *Revue de l'Energie* 611, 12–22.

Kirkegaard, P., 2014, 'OPCOP – eller EUROPA BLUES 2.0 – om Arne Dahls nye Eurokrimi-kvartet' ['OPCOP – or EUROPA BLUES 2.0 – on Arne Dahl's new quartet of Euro-Crime Stories'], *Standart* 3, September 2014.

Kurunmaki, L., Mennicken, A. & Miller, P., 2016, 'Quantifying, Economising, and Marketising: Democratising the social sphere?', *Sociologie du travail* 58, 390–402.

Latour, B., 1983, 'Give Me a Laboratory and I Will Move the World', in K. Knorr & M. Mullay (eds.), *Science Observed. Perspectives on the Social Study of Science*, pp. 141–170, Sage, Beverly Hills, CA.

Latour, B., 1987, *Science in Action. How to Follow Scientists and Engineers through Society*, Harvard University Press, Cambridge, MA.

Latour, B., 1992, 'Where are the Missing Masses?: Sociology of a Few Mundane Artefacts', in W. Bijker & J. Law (eds.), *Shaping Technology-Building Society*, pp. 225–259, MIT Press, Cambridge, MA.

Latour, B., 2004, 'Why Has Critique Run out of Steam? From Matters of Fact to Matters of Concern', *Critical Inquiry* 30, 225–248.

Latour, B., 2005a, *Reassembling the Social: An Introduction to Actor-Network-Theory*, Oxford University Press, New York.

Latour, B., 2005b, 'From Realpolitik to Dingpolitik or how to Make Things Public', in B. Latour & P. Wiebel (eds.), *Making Things Public: Atmospheres of Democracy*, MIT Press, Cambridge, MA.

Law, J., 1994, *Organizing Modernity: Social Ordering and Social Theory*, Blackwell, Oxford.

Law, J., 2003, 'Ordering and Obduracy', *Centre for Science Studies*, Lancaster University, Lancaster, http://www.lancaster.ac.uk/fass/sociology/research/publications/papers/law-ordering-and-obduracy.pdf.

Law, J., 2004, *After Method. Mess in Social Science Research*, Routledge, New York.

Law, J., 2009, 'Actor Network Theory and Material Semiotics', in B. S. Turner (ed.), *The New Blackwell Companion to Social Theory*, pp. 141–158, Blackwell Publishing, Oxford.

MacKenzie, D., 2003, 'An Equation and its Worlds: Bricolage, Exemplars, Disunity and Performativity in Financial Economics', *Social Studies of Science* 33(6), 831–868.

Mol, A., 1999, 'Ontological Politics. A Word and some Questions', in J. Law & J. Hassard (eds.), *Actor Network Theory and After*, pp. 74–88, Blackwell, Oxford.

Muniesa, F., 2015, 'Actor-Network Theory', in J. D. Wright (ed.), *The International Encyclopedia of Social and Behavioral Sciences*, 2nd edn., Elsevier, Oxford.

Nicholson, P., 2002, 'The Real Science of non-Hertzian Waves', viewed 8 February 2018, http://www.capturedlightning.com/frames/Non-Herzian_Waves.html.

Padgett, J. F. & Powell, W. W. (eds.), 2012, *The Emergence of Organizations and Markets*, Princeton University Press, Princeton, NJ.

Pallesen, T., 2016, 'Valuation Struggles over Pricing: Determining the Worth of Wind Power', *Journal of Cultural Economy* 9(6), 527–540.

Phillips, N., Lawrence, T. B. & Hardy, C., 2004, 'Discourse and Institutions', *Academy of Management Review* 29(4), 635–652.

Reuters, 2018, 'China plans first spot electricity trading as Beijing reforms power market', 20 April 2018, https://www.reuters.com/article/us-china-electricity/china-plans-first-spot-electricity-trading-as-beijing-reforms-power-market-idUSKBN1HR1LA.

Romig, C., 2018, 'Powering the Dragon: the rise of Chinese renewables', *Poyry/PEI (Power Engineering International)*, 22 August 2018, https://www.powerengineeringint.com/articles/2018/08/powering-the-dragon-the-rise-of-chinese-renewables.html.

Yaneva, A., 2012, *Mapping Controversies in Architecture*, Ashgate, Farnham.

Sanders, K., 2017, 'A Man of the World: Hans Christian Andersen', ch. 4 in (ed.) D. Ringgaard & M. R. Thomsen, *Danish Literature as World Literature, Literatures as World Literature*, pp. 91–114, Bloomsbury Academic, New York.

Silvast, A., 2017, 'Energy, Economics, and Performativity: Reviewing Theoretical Advances in Social Studies of Markets and Energy', *Energy Research & Social Science* 34, 4–12.

Sismondo, S., 2010, *An Introduction to Science and Technology Studies*, 2nd edn., Wiley-Blackwell, Hong Kong.

Smith, A., 1776, *The Wealth of Nations*, Strahan and Cadell, London.

Starosielski, N., 2015, *The Undersea Network*, Duke University Press: Durham, NC.

Stengers, I., 2005, 'Introductory Notes on an Ecology of Practices', *Cultural Studies Review* 11(1), 184–196.

Stengers, I., 2011, 'Comparison as a matter of concern', *Common Knowledge* 17(1), Symposium: Comparative Relativism.

Venturini, T., 2010, 'Diving in Magma: How to Explore Controversies with Actor-Network Theory', *Public Understanding of Science* 19(3), 258–273.

Windeurope, n.d., 'Improving Power Markets', Market Design & Networks, viewed 20 March 2018, https://windeurope.org/policy/topics/market-design-networks/.

Whitehead, A. N., 1978, *Process and Reality*, Free Press, New York.

3 Setting the scene – empirical background to prise open the blackbox of Chinese wind power development

Political and industrial processes in China cannot readily be understood without reference to indigenous Chinese concepts. Therefore, at the same time as rendering the controversy study more understandable by setting the empirical scene, Chapter Three offers a brief account of the existing field of contemporary China Studies. Whilst not rendering a full review of China Studies – an impossible endeavour – Chapter Three focuses on how the extant literature has looked at aspects of Chinese corporate sector development in general and the power sector and wind turbine industry in particular; that is, issues related to the present enquiry. Apart from rendering an empirical context for understanding today's China and China's position in wind power, this overview of the literature serves as a foundation for developing some of the key concepts developed in this volume, such as the notion of a pragmatics of experimental and fragmented marketisation with Chinese characteristics. Further, it sets the context for a critical review of what this book dubs a 'relational gap' in the extant literature, which leads to reflections on how an Anthropology of Markets lens can contribute to the field of China Studies, and beyond.

Muddling through with piecemeal and ambiguous restructuring in China's corporate sector

The Chinese Party-State has since the late 1970s, and in particular since the early 1990s, moved from a planned economy towards a so-called 'socialist market economy', distancing itself from Maoist state socialism and embracing an increased marketisation through liberalisation and privatisation (Jones & Zou 2017:745). This has been enacted through multiple rounds of corporate restructuring and administrative reform (Jones & Zou 2017; Mertha & Brødsgaard 2017) ever since Deng Xiaoping's Open Door Policy (1978), gaining pace up to and upon China's watershed accession to the World Trade Organization (WTO) in 2001, which marked China's entrance into global competition. As a result of corporate restructuring, and in order to improve the profitability and competitiveness of

China's often ailing SOEs, the number of SOEs has decreased over time, and a private (or non-state) sector has emerged. This has been accompanied by a relatively far-reaching relaxation of government control and central planning (McNally 2006).

At least on the surface, the corporate reforms have entailed a legalistic (but often only 'on the surface') move from what may be termed an insider-based corporate governance model typical of stakeholder capitalism, towards an outsider-based corporate governance model that is typical of shareholder capitalism (concepts that have been deployed e.g. by Mayer 1996 and Gilpin 2000, but not in relation to China). In other words, this has indicated part of what comparative political economy (the Varieties of Capitalism lens) would term a shift from a 'coordinated' to a 'liberal' market economy (eds. Hall & Soskice 2001). Meanwhile, beneath the surface, state control has been retained to a large extent, sometimes even in private firms (McNally 2007; Meyer & Lu 2004; Nolan 2004; Oi 2005; Tam 1999; Wei 2003; Witt 2010), blurring the boundaries between the state and the corporate sector (Meyer & Lu 2004).

This makes the label of privatisation in China somewhat 'misleading' (Walder 2011:22): China's corporate sector today is still made up of a plethora of state-owned, private, and 'hybrid' company forms, where the Chinese state retains the majority of shares even in restructured companies. In this way, the Chinese state has held onto its power over the corporate sector. In addition, the CPC still controls the appointment of CEOs and presidents for the most important and strategic SOEs through their particular systems for personnel, namely the *bianzhi* and (Soviet-based) *nomenklatura* systems that together play a decisive role 'in governing China at the central and the local level' (Brødsgaard 2017:39–40).[1] The *bianzhi* and *nomenklatura* systems make it possible to retain state control over SOEs, provincial governors, local and central officials in the Party, government cadres, and government officials through appointments and positioning of CPC cadres to key positions in companies (Brødsgaard 2002, 2017; Keister 2000; Oi 2005; Shambaugh 2013:13; Tang & Ward 2003). Further, the *bianzhi* and *nomenklatura* systems relate to the Pro-Growth Incentive System for Bureaucrats (Naughton 2017:10), which rewards officials for growth (of GDP and revenue) through incentives and plans, thus constituting a 'powerful instrument' for 'encouraging growth and indirectly promoting investment and high-profile development projects' (Naughton 2017:10). Over time, however, personal promotions have become based not exclusively on economic growth, but also by introducing vaguer standards, 'such as environmentally friendly development, social welfare and good governance' (Mertha & Brødsgaard 2017:2). In this way, with time, China's political leadership has assigned higher performance ratings for environment- and energy-related work and technological innovation, rather than just favouring GDP growth (Delman 2005; Mertha & Brødsgaard 2017; PWC 2013).

Beyond dualistic accounts of either/or

As a result of the legalistic approach to its own corporate reforms, China evades most conventional labels and has often been conceptualised as an idiosyncratic 'case *sui generis*' (e.g. McNally 2007), or as a 'hybrid' (Redding & Witt 2009); that is, engaging in 'hybridisation where institutions transferred from other contexts are adapted and reconfigured to China's existing institutional structure' (Redding & Witt 2009:390). Ten Brink (2013) has accordingly coined the somewhat paradoxical notion of Chinese 'state-permeated capitalism'. Conversely, rather than seeking to accommodate China to a Western-biased framework, the emerging literature stream of 'variegated capitalism' has sought to account for the multiple forms of capitalism with*in* China (Andrews-Speed 2012:123; Fligstein & Zhang 2010; Jessop 2011; Peck & Theodore 2007; Peck & Zhang 2013; Zhang & Peck 2014).

China's way of groping forward

With these somewhat counter-intuitive trends and transitions in China, a somewhat polarised debate has emerged over time in the extant literature between understanding China as either representing total state control or total autonomy. Critical of such a dualistic approach, Jones & Zou (2017) have put forward an alternative framework that can find evidence for both sides of the argument (Tunsjø 2013 and Norris 2016 in Jones & Zou 2017:744). That is, 'the party-state/SOE relationship is best conceptualised not in dichotomous, either/or terms (either state control or total autonomy), but as an evolving struggle between disparate actors within a fragmented, poorly coordinated governance structure' (Jones & Zou 2017:744). In this framework, China's ambiguous, state-led, and piecemeal restructuring reforms and iterative cycles of liberalisation are reflective of the Chinese state's, and of the CPC's, cautious nature (Jones & Zou 2017:743). China continues to be 'groping for a way forward', 'feeling pragmatically for the stones under-foot while crossing the river', in its economic transition towards 'socialism with Chinese characteristics' (Wedeman 2011; Goldstein 1996). At the same time, radical political reform is being avoided and CPC's control of the corporate sector is being retained (Breznitz & Murphree 2011:48; Brødsgaard 2017; Goldstein 1996; Heilmann 2016; Jones & Zou 2017; Nolan 2004). As explored below, overall China has experienced 'seemingly contradictory forces of increasing enterprise autonomy and continued central control that characterises the evolving relationship between business groups and the Party-state' (Brødsgaard 2017:40).

China's 'National Team'

A central ambition of the Chinese political leadership has been to build strong domestic (state-owned) companies that can compete internationally (Jones & Zou 2017; Nolan 2001). This has formed an integral part of China's corporate restructuring reforms. Since its accession to the WTO, China has established a 'National Team' of 111 'central SOEs', or 'National Champion' corporations: an enactment of the slogan of 'grasping the large' and 'letting go of the small' of the early 1990s. These large business group corporations were formed around former state industrial plants in China's strategic pillar industries or old ministries, such as armaments, electricity generation and distribution, oil, coal, chemicals, telecommunications, aviation, and shipping (Brødsgaard 2017; Jones & Zou 2017:747). The resulting multiplant corporations, include amongst others, China's major power generating companies and power grid companies. Many of these corporations are listed on the Fortune Global 500, and encompass many daughter companies within diverse fields of businesses (Brødsgaard 2017; Keister 1998; 2000; Lin & Milhaupt 2013; Nolan 2001).

Retaining state control through SASAC and increased SOE autonomy

Over time, and as an 'unintended consequence of economic reform and administrative restructuring in China', the emerging powerful state-owned business groups ('National Champions') have resulted in a new corporate elite of managers (Brødsgaard 2017:39). These managers have increasingly attained an unprecedented level of managerial independence from government agencies (Brødsgaard 2017:39). Indeed, China's state transformation processes have had implications for the Chinese Party-State's control over SOEs, leading to a weakening of state control (Jones & Zou 2017:744). This loss of control had already become an issue by 2003. As a move to rein in control, administrative reforms took place in 2003 through the establishment of the State Asset Supervision and Administration Council (SASAC), a body under the State Council, which was 'charged with exercising authority over China's largest SOEs on behalf of the State Council' (Brødsgaard 2017:41). As such, the SASAC acted as 'shareholder, not a direct owner, planner or manager. Its remit is to protect and enhance state asset values – to promote their profitability – not to achieve strategic or foreign-policy goals' (Gill & Reilly 2007:42 in Jones & Zou 2017:746). Despite the establishment of SASAC, though, these central SOEs have continued to act largely as autonomous actors, capable of accruing huge profits. This has been made possible, for instance, through accumulating unpaid rents for nationally owned land that was given cheaply or for free, unpaid leases for nationally owned resources (oil, gas, coal), cheap loans and credit from state-owned banks, and through fiscal subsidies from the government (Brødsgaard 2017:49). In addition, central SOEs have been removed 'from direct ministerial or CPC control, with managers becoming responsible to profit-seeking shareholders', and there has been the introduction of private-sector management techniques and partial privatisation through stock issues (Jones & Zou 2017:746). In 2007, the State Council stipulated that future central SOEs had to remit part of their profit to the government, but remittance levels are still relatively low (Naughton 2008 in Brødsgaard 2017:43). Overall, these various and ambiguous moves of both state control and SOE autonomy reflect the continuing and ongoing struggles in the relations between the Party-State and SOEs (Jones & Zou 2017:749). Despite President Xi Jinping's attempts to harness increased state control and efforts to fight corruption (Heilmann 2016), SOEs are often still only given soft(er) budget constraints owing to their extended social obligations. Moreover, the ongoing muddled relationships between state and commerce continue to make interpersonal connections and relations (*guānxi*) an essential aspect of conducting business in China. These connections are employed, for example, to access resources from government officials or to embed businesses within critical actors through a 'cultivation of trust and understanding in mutually beneficial connection, with an instrumental aim to promote cooperation and increase future benefits' (Chang 2011:318–319). Overall, the shifting state–society relations under continuing reform constitute China as 'a negotiated state' (Saich 2011:250–255).

Comprehensively deepening reforms – and the Chinese power sector

The reform processes have also had implications for China's electrical power sector, which is dominated by SASAC-administered SOEs. Commercialisation and liberalisation reforms within China's electrical power sector began back in the 1990s. As in other sectors, these reforms were marked by pragmatism and cautiousness, and continued state control. They culminated with the restructuring of the energy sector in 2002, when power generation was unbundled from transmission. This resulted in the previous China State Power Corporation being divided into two grid companies (the State Grid Corporation of China, 'State Grid', and China Southern Power Grid Corporation), five separate power generating companies (the so-called 'Big Five' utilities: Huaneng Group, Huadian Corporation, China Datang Corporation, Guodian Corporation, China Power Investment Group), plus a number of smaller generating companies (García 2013; Liu & Kokko 2010; Lema & Ruby 2007). This manner of unbundling is conventionally considered important in ensuring regulated, fair competition, and an orderly and open electricity market (Shi 2012; Meidan, Andrews-Speed & Xin 2009). Nevertheless, China's electrical power system – the grid companies – is still responsible both for power transmission and for distribution, acting as TSO and distribution system operator (DSO). Owned by Central Government, China's two national grid companies (TSO and DSO) and the 'Big Five' generating companies form part of the SASAC-administered 'National Team'. At the same time, and as part of the unbundling reforms in 2002, the powerful NDRC and its Energy Bureau were created at national and local levels (Korsnes 2014; Lema & Ruby 2007).

Further power sector reform attempts stopped in 2004, owing to internal power struggles and vested interests (Andrews-Speed 2012:82), and up until the recent pronouncement of an 'Energy Revolution' (CPC Central Committee and the State Council 2015; NEA 2015) there has been no further major restructuring in the energy sector. However, the Energy Revolution does indeed indicate new attempts at liberalisation, in alignment with the general and radical strategy paper on 'comprehensively deepening reforms' even in strategic sectors, which came out of the Third Plenary Session of the 18th CPC Central Committee in November 2013 (CCCPC 2013; Mertha & Brødsgaard 2017). The CPC strategy document further proclaimed the aim to reduce the government's role in market operations. Whilst it pushes for price reforms of, amongst other things, electricity, water, oil, and natural gas, the public utilities responsible for electricity generation and transmission are still constituted as a 'naturally monopolized' industry (CCCPC 2013). Despite these recent pushes for and/or attempts at market reform, the Chinese electrical sector has found itself uncomfortably stranded somewhere between 'the plan' and 'the market' (Andrews-Speed 2012:81–82), as moves towards liberalisation have been followed by the affirmation of state control (Meidan et al. 2009; Shi 2012) This may change with NEA's draft rules for competitive real-time electricity spot markets to be introduced through pilots in 2019 (Reuters 20 April 2018; Romig 22 August 2018).

So far, though, China's electrical power sector and electricity prices remain under state control, despite China's Energy Policy (2012) and CCCPC strategy of comprehensive reforms (2013) stating the need to reform and liberalise electricity prices (CCCPC 2013; Mertha & Brødsgaard 2017; The Information Office of the State Council 2012). Significantly, electrical power from renewable energy, or so-called 'new energy', such as wind power, is constituted as 'strategic' and is also marked by heavy state involvement, which bears witness to how the '[g]overnance of the energy sector is high-level politics in China' (Korsnes 2014:180). In wind power, as a result, even though the sector also has several private firms (with wind turbine manufacturers being among them), 'the Chinese state participates directly in the wind power sector in several ways, e.g. by commissioning wind power projects, operating wind farms, and producing equipment for the wind power industry' (Liu & Kokko 2010:5523).

Fragmented authoritarianism in the Chinese power sector

The incremental and incoherent reforms in Chinese corporate restructuring, and particularly those in the power sector, can to some degree be seen as an effect of China's so-called fragmented authoritarianism (e.g. Lieberthal & Lampton 1992; Lieberthal & Oksenberg 1988; Mertha 2009; Mertha & Brødsgaard 2017). This institutional characteristic of China often results in protracted bureaucratic bargaining processes and lax local implementation of centrally determined policies, aspects that are commonly observed in the power sector. As an 'admittedly unwieldy moniker' in China Studies

(Mertha & Brødsgaard 2017:3), that is, as a somewhat unmanageable and cumbersome nickname or informal label, the concept of fragmented authoritarianism explains the somewhat contradictory situation in China, where there can be 'fragmenting forces at play' at the same time as 'the Chinese polity is an authoritarian system held together by a strong Party-state' (Brødsgaard 2017:38).

Fragmentation in China's power sector can for example be seen in how, instead of having one Ministry of Energy to coordinate and take responsibility, China has 11 different ministry-level agencies that influence energy policy, often with colliding interests and policies (Brødsgaard 2017:42; Meidan et al. 2009:596–597 in Jones & Zou 2017:745)[2]. The authority of powerful business groups administered by SASAC further enhances fragmentation in policy-making (Brødsgaard 2017:42). It is no surprise, therefore, that the very notion of fragmented authoritarianism was founded on an empirically historical analysis of China's state-controlled power sector (the case of hydro-power) (Lieberthal 2004; Lieberthal & Oksenberg 1988).

Basically, the fragmented authoritarian nature of Chinese governance stems from the manner in which China is divided into crisscrossing jurisdictions both vertically and horizontally, segregating central bodies from local bodies and one bureaucratic body from another. This 'matrix muddle' of crisscrossing lines (*tiao*, 条) and pieces (*kuai*, 块) (Lieberthal 2004:186–188) exacerbates the power struggles and vested interests along both horizontal and vertical lines. It is also intertwined with the iron triangle of business–party–state relations (Mertha & Brødsgaard 2017), as there are multiple contending 'principals' with potentially very different goals (Jones & Zou 2017:749).

Vested interests in Chinese natural monopolies and integrated fragmentation

Vested interests are, in turn, particularly related to monopolies in China's key economic sectors, where only a few are allowed to dominate (Brødsgaard 2017:45). These monopoly players are supported by preferential loans from Chinese state banks and other hidden subsidies, and are marked by vested interests tied into the political system, for example through the *bianzhi* and *nomenklatura* systems (Brødsgaard 2002, 2017). With bargaining taking place at and between all levels, and during all phases of policy formulation and implementation (Mertha & Brødsgaard 2017:4), the Chinese polity is characterised by 'state fragmentation and decentralisation' at the same time as Chinese politics in other regards is being integrated through centralised, strong Party rule and government control (Pearson 2005 in Jones & Zou 2017:747). To account for these 'seemingly contradictory forces of increasing enterprise autonomy and continued central control', Brødsgaard (2017:40) has coined the notion of 'integrated fragmentation'.

Fragmentation as basis for successful portfolio approach
in electrical power development

Whilst fragmentation can lead to protracted bargaining and poor policy implementation, Cunningham (2010) argues that it has laid the foundation for China's historically successful 'portfolio approach' to energy governance. Here, energy firms have been treated as a 'portfolio of assets' where central state ownership and control can be strengthened during periods of energy surplus 'and weakened during periods of energy shortage' (Cunningham 2010:225). Such fragmentation has served as a central factor for China's success in being able to meet rapidly rising energy demands during China's economic growth since the beginning of the 1980s. Likewise, the wind power sector has been influenced by an oscillating movement between centralised and coordinated control versus decentralised fragmentation in planning and development (Korsnes 2014). The fragmented authoritarian nature of Chinese energy governance has thereby at times enabled the central government to shift gear flexibly when needed, changing between increased national control through planning and coordination and the decentralisation of control through delegating responsibility to a local level.

Ang (2016), in turn, has related this oscillating tension between centralisation and decentralisation to China's economic development, in underscoring how central direction 'underscores the role of top-down planning', while local improvisation 'champions the merits of bottom-up initiative', rendering Chinese development characterised by 'both divergence and connection' and 'directed improvisation' (Ang 2016:69, 66). On the one hand, China's wind power sector has been formally governed by mandatory planning, with contractual targets for energy production between central and local levels, and between state and industry, and regulatory implementation (Heilmann 2010:117–118). On the other hand, it has often been ambiguously steered by intendedly ambiguous national visions and expectations rather than directed through implementation details (Andrews-Speed 2012; Korsnes 2016). This has left open a creative space for local trial and error, such as the bottom-up processes for the rapid industrial build-up of manufacturing sectors, as witnessed in the wind power sector (Andrews-Speed 2012:65, 71).

Overall, even though fragmentation can act as a hindrance for the implementation of policies, it can simultaneously act as a productive force of innovation, for example by allowing provincial governments to experiment with new central policies before they are rolled out at a national level. Fragmentation in China's energy governance has consequently been coupled to prevalent notions in the literature of a particular mode of Chinese experimentalism, pragmatism, flexibility, agility, adaptability, creativity, and innovation (Ang 2016; Breznitz & Murphree 2011; Heilmann 2008, 2009, 2010, 2011; Heilmann & Perry 2011; Kirkegaard 2015; Korsnes 2014;

Mertha & Brødsgaard 2017; Oi & Goldstein 2018), constituting a particularly Chinese 'arts of the state' - building on Mazzucato (2013) - with a central role of government (Korsnes 2015). According to several Chinese scholars, it is these traits that have made China able to engage in 'adaptive institutional change' (Dimitrov 2013 in Oi & Goldstein 2018:5), rendering the Chinese polity its 'authoritarian resilience' (Oi & Goldstein 2018) even amid constant change and transformation.

Chinese experimentalism and structured uncertainty

This Chinese 'arts of the state', which is inherently linked to fragmented authoritarianism, can also be related to the notion of institutional 'structured uncertainty' (Breznitz & Murphree 2011; Mertha & Brødsgaard 2017), which denotes how the central state level brings structure and control with ambitious plans and visions, whilst uncertainty is conveyed by the often (intentional) lack of guidance for implementation, leaving space for local interpretation and experimentation. According to Breznitz & Murphree (2011), China's 'structured uncertainty' shows how China is governed through ambitious plans at the central level, whilst not laying out any details for implementation at the local level (Breznitz & Murphree 2011:38). Overall, though, state control has not been relinquished, but rather, state transformation has meant that control 'is being exercised in a way that permits enormous interpretive latitude' (Jones & Zou 2017:750), whilst sustaining organised top-down political rule (Mertha & Brødsgaard 2017:5). As an example, while the official goals and reforms of the Chinese leadership are scientific development and the creation of a Harmonious Socialist Society, 'the exact definition of these goals is uncertain; interpretations range from simple social stability to comprehensive redistributive justice' (Breznitz & Murphree 2011:48) and an increased focus on the environment (Christensen 2013; Fan 2006). In this way, Chinese structured uncertainty is linked to the country's fragmented authoritarianism in the sense that policy outcomes often bear little resemblance to the policy-makers' original intent, because of vested interests in which policy rationality is counter-acted by institutional actors that act in more self-interested, short-term, and parochial ways, thus undermining the policy (Mertha & Brødsgaard 2017:4–5).

One of the keys to understanding the adaptability of China's political economy over the past few decades may thereby lie in the unusual combination of extensive fragmented policy experimentation with long-term policy prioritisation – the latter an integral part of state capitalism (Amsden 2004; Evans 1995; Wade 2004). As a fragmented developmental party-state (Oi 1995:1132), China has engaged extensively in experimental foresighted tinkering (Heilmann 2010:125), which has made it possible for the Chinese political leadership to encourage actors to try out imaginative solutions to achieve defined tasks and to flexibly handle new challenges as they emerge during experimentation.

Industrial upgrading in a reformed era and Chinese authoritarian upgrading

This experimental governance is thus linked to China's aim to build new industries and upgrade innovative capabilities. Drawing on a notion that was coined to understand the political and economic modernisation in the Arab world, argues Heilmann, China's mode of economic governance represents a case of 'authoritarian upgrading' or 'techno-authoritarianism', which 'challenges traditional assumptions about the economic and institutional superiority of Western governance models' (Heilmann 2010:109). Along the same developmental lines, Ang (2016) argues that China's non-linear economic development is a result of coexisting and complementary forces of 'direction and improvisation' in Chinese governance (Ang 2016:69). According to Ang (2016), China has, paradoxically, been able to experience rapid yet disruptive and non-linear economic development through the exploitation of its weak and inconsistent institutions, as development takes place in a coevolutionary process of mutual adjustment between markets and (local and central) governments. Along somewhat the same lines, Wedeman (2011) has recounted Chinese transformation as happening in cascades at the edge of order and chaos (Wedeman 2011:69, 88).

China's Run of the Red Queen

Rather than focusing on China's experimental mode of governance, another strain of literature has focused on the learning and upgrading of the capabilities of the country's industries and companies. Looking at China in the context of increased global decomposition and modularisation of not only production, but also of innovation, Breznitz and Murphree (2011, 2013) argue that China has 'developed a remarkably profitable and sustainable model of innovation. This model makes China into a critical part of the world innovation system, but it does not rely on China excelling in cutting-edge novel-product R&D' (Breznitz & Murphree 2011:19). Thus, somewhat provocatively, it is argued that China's success hinges precisely on its ability to follow behind technology leaders and innovators, rather than to lead, which has made China a success in second-generation innovation, even though it does not match the official Party doctrine of scientific development. By making reference to the world of Lewis Carroll's (2001 in Breznitz & Murphree 2011) *Through the Looking-Glass*, China is thus argued to 'shine' by pursuing a strategy of 'keeping its industrial-production and service industries in perfect tandem with the technological frontier' (Breznitz & Murphree 2011:3), adopting a strategy similar to the 'Run of the Red Queen': The Red Queen has to run as fast as she can just to stay in the same place; that is, 'to remain at the cusp of the global technology frontier without actually advancing the frontier itself' (Breznitz & Murphree 2011:3). Accordingly, Nahm & Steinfeld (2014) argue that such strategy, has enabled

China to pursue the status of a 'scale-up nation', through specialisation and multidirectional interfirm learning as well as the unique simultaneous management of tempo, volume, and cost.

Limits to copying the South-East Asian Tigers?

Today's transformed context of geographically and organisationally decomposed industries and technologies has led various scholars within China Studies, and also the neighbouring fields of Economic Geography, Innovation Studies, Development Studies, Political Science, International Business, and Industry Studies, to discuss China's competitiveness in a spatial context of increased economic globalisation and the technological modularisation of industries. Against the backdrop of the experience of the so-called 'developmental states' – the South-East Asian Tigers – that succeeded in rapid industrialisation during the 1970s and 1980s, some scholars argue that the present era of spatial and vertical disintegration of production and innovation activities across the globe and China's accession to the WTO present more severe competitive challenges to the country (e.g. Steinfeld 2004; Nolan 2001). The South-East Asian Tigers were able to succeed through government intervention and developmental state policies with clearly defined long-term goals and implementation modes, together with the establishment of large conglomerates (as described in the literature on the East Asian 'developmental state', cf. Amsden 2004; Evans 1995; Wade 2004). Such protectionist strategy in China, however, has been argued to constitute a risky and largely obsolete strategy (Steinfeld 2004; Breznitz & Murphree 2011). Conversely, even though China cannot simply emulate the strategy of developmental states in South-East Asia, Nolan (2001) has argued that it needs to build exactly such national conglomerates (such as the 'National Team') in order to protect its competitiveness.

Mathews & Tan (2015) argue, in turn, that China has always stayed aloof from the neo-liberal economic policies professed by the so-called 'Washington Consensus' (Mathews & Tan 2015:146). Instead, China has 'pursued policies where the state acts as ultimate pilot, coordinator and agent of change, modelled pragmatically on the prior successful development experiences of Japan, Korea, Taiwan and Singapore' (Mathews & Tan 2015:146). China seems to have surpassed the successes of other developing countries by putting 'a change of energy paradigm at the very core of its development strategy' (Mathews & Tan 2015:146). The country seems to be achieving several goals, not only promoting alternative energy industries, establishing future export industries, building national infrastructure, and reducing energy dependence, but also promoting rural development and 'playing its role in reducing the risks of global warming' (Mathews & Tan 2015:146–147). Accordingly, China's renewable energy sector has been characterised as 'a matter of manufacturing policy' (Andrews-Speed 2012:183).

Economists and political scientists within China Studies, however, offer a much more bleak picture, cautioning that China may resemble Japan more than looking like the East Asian Tigers, as China is currently undergoing a transition from two-digit growth rates to a 'new normal' of growth in single-figures. They thus raise fears that China is facing a 'lost decade', as Japan did when recession and domestic debt hit the Japanese economy after years of rapid growth and development (Kroeber 2016; Naughton 2014:21). These doubts as to the long-term sustainability of China's economic development are related to China's investment-driven growth model, which has been supported by a financial sector dominated by Chinese state banks that have not been steered by financial risk (Kroeber 2016; Lardy 2016; Naughton 2014; Saich 2011), and thus working in a distinctively different manner compared to conventional, risk-averse, commercial banks. Driven more by broader national visions of development and supported by the State when facing debts (Kroeber 2016), China's banking sector has for many years allocated credit towards inefficient SOEs, while it has been difficult for faster growing and often more efficient private enterprises to obtain bank loans (Kroeber 2016; Lardy 2016; Naughton 2014, 2017). The result has been poorly performing loans and a rising domestic debt level. These issues, in turn, were accelerated with the stimulus package after the global financial crisis, during which local governments were mobilized to initiate infrastructure projects; state-owned banks to loan without restraint to those projects; and state-owned enterprises to undertake the business and construction work (Naughton 2009 in Naughton 2017:11).

While the Chinese government managed to steer China out of the global financial crisis, this came at a substantial cost, it is argued: the rushed nature of the stimulus program resulted in overcapacity as well as a vast share of the investments being 'wasted on useless projects, although we have no way of knowing how large that proportion is' (Naughton 2014:19). While former Premier Wen Jiabao already in 2007 'described China's economy as "unstable, unbalanced, un-coordinated, and unsustainable," the unprecedented dependency on state investment has only further unbalanced the economy' (Naughton 2014:19). Further, while the growth model worked well during a phase where a build-out of infrastructure was needed, the infrastructure framework is nearing completion and labour force dynamics have changed (with low-skill wages rising and a limited amount of new migrant workers). China's debt load (debt-to-GDP ratio) as well as China's unprecedented high rates of investment (around 48 per cent of GDP since 2009 more or less permanently) (Naughton 2014:19) are consequently argued to be unsustainable (Kroeber 2016; Naughton 2014), with local governments unable to service their debts (Naughton 2014:21). Hereby, it is argued, the growth model has reached – or is nearing – its limit, necessitating a credit squeeze and overall a comprehensive restructuring of the financial and corporate sectors, as well as a potential rethinking of the growth model. Yet, as credit is still flowing more or less freely and as such restructuring reforms have not yet been implemented (despite the establishment of SASAC and the State Council's 'Decision on Reforming the Investment System' (2004), amongst other things), China is facing a resulting high number of low-productivity or no-productivity projects and zombie firms that are neither dead nor alive (Naughton 2014:21; Kroeber 2016).

Industrial upgrading in China's wind turbine industry

The development of Chinese innovation capabilities in key technologies, essential equipment, and R&D is a critical factor in the development of the country's wind turbine industry. And as Mathews & Tan (2015) have argued, China may well be able to make renewable energy and low-carbon technologies 'synonymous with its own industrial revolution', simultaneously 'breaking the "carbon lock-in" that has delayed the energy revolution in other developed countries' (Mathews & Tan 2015:148), as well as moving beyond its current stage as the 'world's factory'.

While China aims to shift its strategy of scaling-up to a strategy of grading-up, and to shift from quantity and high pace to quality and precision (Nahm & Steinfeld 2014; Naughton 2010), some scholars are pessimistic. Some studies have argued that there are limits to upgrading and innovation from manufacturing as Chinese players are captured in low value-added activities (e.g. Brandt & Thun 2016; Dongsheng & Fujimoto 2004; Fuller 2016; Steinfeld 2004; Xiao, Tylecote & Liu 2013). This capture is attributed amongst other things to today's globalised, highly deverticalised supply chains that require new capabilities, increased modularity and technology intensity, lax IPR enforcement, poor corporate governance, and restrictive demand-side and supply-side policies (e.g. Brandt & Thun 2016:78; Dongsheng & Fujimoto 2004; Fuller 2016; Steinfeld 2004; Tylecote & Liu 2013).

Others, conversely, have offered a more optimistic outlook for Chinese 'innovative manufacturing', since 'there is more going on than meets the eye' in the 'battle at the bottom' of the global manufacturing sector, as noted by some of the same authors in an earlier publication (Brandt & Thun 2010:1571). Therefore, some authors argue that it is exactly through China's position within manufacturing, and its ability to link up with foreign resources, that it has been able to develop proprietary know-how, which extends beyond manufacturing (Nahm & Steinfeld 2014). That is, China is developing 'unique capabilities surrounding technology commercialization and manufacturing-related innovation', which are 'related to multidirectional, cross-border learning' (Nahm & Steinfeld 2014:288), and which can lead to innovative manufacturing through relational learning (Herrigel, Wittke & Voskamp 2013; Nahm & Steinfeld 2014).

In terms of the wind turbine manufacturing industry, there have also been debates about the degree of Chinese upgrading and catch-up (Gosens & Lu 2013; Korsnes 2016; Nahm & Steinfeld 2014). Developing a taxonomy for different variants of knowledge-intensive scale-up in China, Nahm & Steinfeld (2014) illustrate how China has been able to learn from manufacturing in different industries, such as the wind turbine industry, particularly by engaging with other (often foreign) enterprises that can 'complete the package' (Nahm & Steinfeld 2014). Along the same lines, Korsnes (2016) discusses the sustainability of China's offshore wind turbine industry and its quality issues, illustrating how customer–supplier relations have led to interactive learning in China's offshore wind power sector. Gosens & Lu (2013), in turn, have enquired into the issue of China's wind turbine manufacturing industry from a technological innovation systems (TIS) framework. In doing so, they explore China's ability as an emerging economy to move from a status of 'lagging' to 'leading' and to expand into global markets. The authors argue that the 'main challenge to foreign market expansion lies in reforming the domestic TIS to focus on turbine quality rather than cost reduction' (Gosens & Lu 2013:243).

Technological catch-up through integration into global production and innovation networks

Many of the above-mentioned studies align with those that have discussed limitations and opportunities for China to learn, upgrade and upscale, and even leapfrog, through integration into so-called technological, sectoral, regional, or national innovation systems (Binz et al. 2012; Gosens & Lu 2013, 2014; Gu & Lundvall 2006; Gu, Serger & Lundvall 2016), or into GVCs, global production networks, or GINs through collaborative interfirm networks and systems of learning and innovation (e.g. Barnard & Chaminade 2012; Cooke 2013; Ernst 2006, 2008; INGINEUS 2011; Klagge, Liu & Silva 2012; Lema, Berger & Schmitz 2013; Lema, Sagar & Zhou 2016; Lewis 2013; Parrilli, Nadvi & Yeung 2013; Silva & Klagge 2013). Indeed, global industries, including the wind turbine industry, are witnessing increased global integration, as both production and innovation processes are being geographically and organisationally decomposed (Haakonsson, Kirkegaard & Lema forthcoming), for example through the help of knowledge-intensive business service providers (KIBS) (Haakonsson, Kirkegaard & Lema forthcoming; Strambach 2001).

As a 'globally organized web of complex interactions between firms and non-firm organizations engaged in knowledge production related to and resulting in innovation' (Chaminade (2009) in Barnard & Chaminade 2012:2–3), GINs, or what other scholars have more or less interchangeably dubbed international networks for learning and innovation (Lewis 2013) and collaborative innovation networks (Chen et al. 2014), are claimed to play a crucial role in the development of China's wind industry (Lewis 2013:3). A study by Lema et al. (2013), which focuses on the manufacturing value chain (and not the deployment services chain) within wind turbine industry, illustrates how Chinese wind turbine manufacturers have modularised their supply chain, offering considerable cost and time reductions, something that has been achieved exactly by *not* going it alone in technology development, but engaging in cooperation with foreign partners (Lema et al. 2013:39, 44, 63). Chinese upgrading is thus increasingly being achieved not only through conventional technology transfer, but also by engaging in codevelopment and learning and innovation networks with foreign partners, which is in line with the general trend of globalising knowledge production. Chinese wind turbine manufacturers seek to upgrade their innovative capabilities and catchup with global technology leaders by tapping into foreign resources (Silva & Klagge 2013:1353). Conducting a case study on GINs in China's wind power industry, Silva & Klagge (2013) argue that leading Chinese wind turbine manufacturers are now 'trying a new approach which fits into the general trend of globalizing knowledge production through the development of global innovation networks' (Silva & Klagge 2013:1353).

Chinese linkage, leverage, and learning as a matter of upgrading in wind power?

The above knowledge-seeking approach adopted by Chinese multinational corporations (MNCs) is, according to Mathews (2002), typical of MNCs from emerging economies, as they have often adopted a so-called strategy of linkage, leverage, and learning (LLL strategy) (Mathews 2002, 2006). As an example, Nahm & Steinfeld (2014) illustrate how Chinese wind turbine manufacturers have been capable of building innovation capabilities from manufacturing in the wind turbine industry, for example by engaging in reverse design and the reengineering of someone else's existing product, and in making someone else's (new) product design come true (Nahm & Steinfeld 2014). Industrial upgrading, conceptualised as a somewhat linear movement in the global commodity chain (from assembly companies towards becoming original equipment manufacturers (OEMs), brand manufacturers, and finally design manufacturers (Gereffi 1999:51), or as a matter of process, product, functional, and chain- or intersectoral upgrading (Gereffi 2005; Humphrey & Schmitz 2002; Morrison, Pietrobelli & Rabellotti 2008), may thus be possible.

Value chain governance and norms of quality

The ability to achieve industrial upgrading in GVCs, however, is claimed to depend on the type of governance mode of the GVC in which the company finds itself (Humphrey & Schmitz, 2002:1017), for instance as some relations can be more or less captive or relational than others, signalling different degrees of mutual learning and upgrading potential. This can be predicted and determined based on the 'three Cs': supplier capabilities, knowledge codifiability, and transaction complexity (Gereffi, Humphrey & Sturgeon 2005). Overall, the governance of the GVC as a matter of coordinating customer–supplier relations – and basically to coordinate them through insourcing (hierarchy), outsourcing (market) or through hybrid network forms (captive, relational, modular) (Gereffi et al. 2005) – is here founded on the logic of cost minimisation and efficiency of transaction cost economics (Coase 1988; Williamson 1981). Another way to conceive of governance in GVCs has been to enquire into the discursive and normative governance of the value chain, as discourses produce rules, institutions, and norms, for example about what constitutes 'quality' – often inscribed into standards – which frame buyer–supplier relations (Gibbon & Ponte 2008; Ponte 2009; Ponte & Cheyns 2013).

Understanding Chinese firm-level innovation processes in a Chinese context

In general, the modes of development and innovation adopted by Chinese companies described here seem more open and less risk-averse than the innovation mode conventionally pursued by Western MNCs: Their innovation dogma for many years has been to keep core competencies in house as a matter of protection (Barney 1991; Gilson, Sabel & Scott 2008; Helper, MacDuffie & Sabel 2000; Koza & Lewin 1998; Peteraf 1993; Teece, Pisano & Shuen 1997). In contrast, as already explored, China has adopted an LLL strategy as it has to exploit its own resource deficiency to upgrade (Mathews 2002, 2006), which it has done largely by tapping into foreign resources, seemingly adopting ideas from an open innovation paradigm that is argued to induce radical innovation (eds. Chesbrough, Vanhaverbeke & West 2008). In addition, Chinese companies have displayed what may be dubbed a 'launch–test–improve' model (O'Connor 2006) of accelerated innovation in product development (Williamson & Yin 2014). Having pursued the 'Run of the Red Queen' strategy (Breznitz & Murphree 2011) by tapping into foreign resources, Chinese companies have been able to pursue a cost-out strategy, pushing down prices radically and (in the context we are exploring) potentially helping make 'wind power a more effective energy option for the world' (Lema et al. 2013:65). Meanwhile, at the same time as it poses a competitive challenge for Western companies, this process is also what sometimes leads to Chinese quality issues.

In sum, it is critical to understand, as argued by Korsnes (2015), that 'China is not copying an existing system, but attempting to create something independent' (Korsnes 2015:59). That is, a situational approach to understanding innovation, science, quality, technology, and industry development in China is needed (Gorm Hansen 2017; Kirkegaard 2015; Korsnes 2015, 2016). As 'technology [as well as science, innovation] is constructed, locally negotiated and concomitantly emergent with its environment' (Korsnes 2015:7), analyses must take into account its socio-material and political constitution, and also enquire into how technology, science, and innovation are debated, shifting, sometimes colliding, or converging. In particular, as China pursues an official strategy of indigenous innovation,

which marks its attempt at 'Chinesification', that is of making Chinese innovation and technology homebred and 'Chinesified' (Korsnes 2015:58), whilst
displaying colliding emphases on applied science versus basic research
(Cao 2004a, 2014; Gorm Hansen 2017), debates about what innovation and
technological and scientific development should look like can be expected.
Overall, we may be witnessing how the Chinese state adopts a relatively
more experimental (and risk-prone) mode of 'market construction' than we
have witnessed in 'the West', one which spurs 'innovation of new industrial
sectors'. This is, in turn, enhanced and co-constructed by the experimental
innovation practices of Chinese companies and research institutes at a tech-
nology/product-development level, while both processes are accelerated by
the underlying Chinese investment-driven 'growth model'.

Minding the gap in existing studies on China

In the above, several inherent paradoxes for the opposing movements and
pressures within China have been indicated: there are opposing trends
towards fragmentation or integration, or control and autonomy, opening up
to global competition or closing down to protect domestic companies, downgrading or upgrading, applied science versus basic research, and much more.
Overall, the China Studies literature, and neighbouring literatures such as
Industry Studies, Innovation Studies, New Institutional Theory, Political
Economy, Economics, and Economic Geography, have provided rich empirical insights into the inner workings of the Chinese Party-State and bureaucracy, into corporate restructuring in the power sector, and into industrial
upgrading and innovation in manufacturing industries – and in the wind turbine industry in particular. This has been done through historical accounts
of the bureaucratic structures of the policy-making apparatus at different
levels, state–business relationships, accounts of changes in the Chinese market, and restructuring reforms. In addition, in order to describe the institutional particularities of China, the extant literature has developed numerous
useful concepts and notions – in particular, those related to experimentalism, pragmatism, and fragmentation. Some of these are used and extended
in this book, for example to describe a potentially unique Chinese mode of
experimental and fragmented marketisation in wind power development.

Summing up, the extant China Studies literature and its neighbouring
literatures have provided rich insights into topographic spatial structure.
Yet while they have given us insights into structure, they tend to miss out
on ('micro'-) processes of relationship building, or 'the relational'. Indeed,
existing studies tend to be impoverished in terms of a relational, processual,
and socio-material lens that can create a dynamic lens for issues of genesis,
dynamics and agency. That is, existing work in the extensive field of contemporary China Studies has tended to focus on traditional forces and usual
suspects – governmental actors or formal entities and institutional and/or
bureaucratic structures. More than that, these entities, institutions, and

structures are often treated as generalised, blackboxed 'given entities' that exist a priori and do not need exploration in and by themselves regarding their emergence, dynamics, and agency. For instance, by segregating analysis into a hierarchical and/or spatial account of macro-level institutions, meso-level governance structures, and/or micro-level corporate structures, the accounts tend to become fairly rigid, static, and distant as actors are seen 'from without' at a relatively high level of spatial or institutional aggregation. Further, the structural, hierarchical, and/or institutional perspectives tend to engender a focus on stability rather than transformation and controversy, which hardly seems fitting when it comes to understanding the contested marketisation of wind power development in the Chinese spider's web. Even studies that enquire into vested interests tend to do it at some distance, and to offer a structural and generalising lens rather than providing an account of the situated socio-material grounding of these interests. Further, the Economic Geography literature, though offering a number of insightful studies concerning Chinese wind power development and the Chinese wind turbine industry's integration into GVCs and GINs (e.g. Klagge et al. 2012; Lema et al. 2013; Silva & Klagge 2013), does not enquire into the dynamics of the quality crisis and the potential turn to quality, or into potential socio-technical boundaries that link up or tap into foreign resources around core technologies, or into potential power struggles and dynamics of Sino-foreign customer–supplier (supply chain) relations. Rather, studies on GINs, for instance, have tended to identify their existence based on corporate locations (spatial lens) and contractual technology transfer (contractual/formal and structural lens); studies have been lacking that try to trace and understand the actual technology and science in play. The result is that the wind turbine industry is largely treated as a monolithic blackbox.

To be fair, though, it must be noted that it has not been the main ambition of the extant literature to account for such situated, socio-material 'micro'-processes or relations. Instead, it has a place in its own right despite not having as its goal a study of issues of process, relations, controversy, emergence, dynamics, or agency. This volume is not a critique or dismissal of the China Studies literature. Rather, acknowledging its vast contributions, the book relates to and builds on various of its concepts as well as on the valuable and prolific empirical insights it has brought to bear on the specifics of China's electrical power system and the wind turbine industry, all of which is relevant for our purposes here.

A call for cross-fertilisation of relational and structural accounts in New Economic Sociology

All these things aside, though, the argument is that we risk overlooking some of the relevant material actors and entities (and their agency) that are involved in China's greening, as well as overlooking some of the inherent struggles involved, all of which are relevant in shedding light on the Chinese wind miracle, quality crisis, and turn to quality. That is, somewhat para-doxically, by looking at structures as fixed entities and 'facts', there is an inherent risk of overlooking the socio-material relations (and controversies) that constitute these same structures and institutions. The somewhat provoc-ative and maybe even counter-intuitive suggestion is that, in order to actually see the micro-foundations of existing structures and institutions, we need to look away from them, instead diving deeper by decomposing the wind tur-bine into its constituent component technologies and tracing relationships around them. In the following study, we will delve into different sites of con-troversy, entangled around the wind turbine and wind power. At the same time, these sites of controversy within the socio-technical assemblage around wind power development are enmeshed in the power sector as well as being enmeshed with an assemblage around software, as visualised in Figure 3.1.

Meanwhile, it should also be noted that recently various voices in China Studies literature have called for a move towards more dynamic, localised, and adaptive approaches in order to understand China's combination of

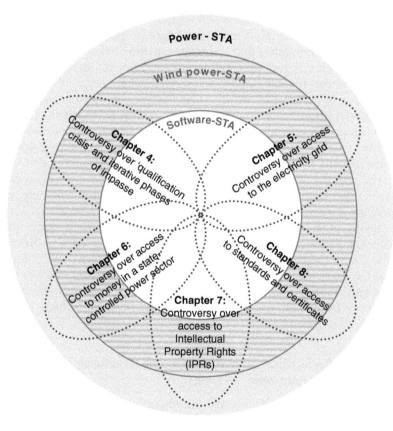

Figure 3.1 Mapping controversies over marketisation of wind power development in China.

central direction and local improvisation, and its resulting non-linear development (Ang 2016:69; Heilmann 2010). For instance, Mertha & Brødsgaard (2017:4) argue that a 'basic weakness' of the fragmented authoritarianism lens is to capture 'dynamics of autonomous social or political agents and organisations' (Mertha & Brødsgaard 2017:4), while others have argued for a more relational lens (Ang 2016; Heilmann 2010; Herrigel et al. 2013).

A notable and recent contribution to this debate is the budding conversation between constructivist studies within the S&T tradition and the China Studies literature (Gorm Hansen 2017; Greenhalgh 2005, 2008; Kirkegaard 2015, 2016, 2017; Korsnes 2015), as STS offers a reflexive and inherently relational lens. Kirkegaard (2015) has looked at Chinese wind power development in a contribution to the GIN literature within Economic Geography, arguing for a relational turn towards STS. Korsnes (2015) has explored Chinese renewable struggles in the offshore wind turbine industry through the lens of STS (Korsnes 2015) as has Gorm Hansen (2017), as she enquires into the scientific controversy unfolding over the development of hydropower in China and over the contested expertise employed around potentially human-induced earthquakes from hydropower dams. Other STS accounts on China have been conducted, though not with a focus on renewable energy. Instead, they have featured an empirical focus on medical science, for example illustrating how China's One Child policy was founded on missile science, owing to the computation power that allowed the prediction of demographic changes, which other scientists did not possess after the Cultural Revolution (Greenhalgh 2005, 2008).[3]

In sum, acknowledging the contributions and insights of both structural and more relational accounts, this study is not a manifest against structural accounts. Indeed, 'formal organizations, networks of actors and actor-networks, action nets and spontaneous organizing coexist – at the same time and in the same territory' (Czarniawska 2013:13). Rather, it calls for a more fruitful communication between the relational lens of STS, the structural accounts of China Studies, and large parts of New Economic Sociology. Such cross-fertilisation can help account for the processes of framing and overflowing, genesis, agency, dynamics, structure, and institutionalisation. In this way, the aim of this work is to take the developing conversation between China Studies and STS further, through a pioneering marketisation study and the method of controversy mapping. Doing so, it is hoped that it will be possible to trace some of the processes of forging the emerging and volatile relations of the socio-technical assemblage around wind power development, as well as the shifting content and quality of these relations.

Testing bridges and ready and equipped to map controversies

By offering the first ever constructivist marketisation study of China, the book argues that the coupling of STS and China Studies, and in particular a marketisation lens of the Anthropology of Markets, is an emerging and promising field, which can help bridge the gap and lend China Studies a more relational and processual lens that can shed light on market emergence, durability, and agency. Such a lens can hopefully render insights into how a quality crisis has influenced the quality of Sino-foreign relations in Chinese wind power, and how this has produced inherent controversies about the viability of the Chinese mode of experimental greening in this area.

In doing so, this work makes a reflexive 'pragmatic' move away from the foundational approach of China Studies and related literatures towards the relational perspective of STS. STS grew its foundational roots in American pragmatism, which begs an inherently relational and micro-processual lens (e.g. Dewey 1927; Elias 1978; Whitehead 1978), as it takes as its focus the mode of connecting/relating a nexus of entities (as laid out in Yaneva 2012:2). American pragmatist philosophy defines all things in terms of their relatedness, as they come together in an 'event' (Fraser 2010) for marketisation, for instance. One of the main contributions of this book is thus the indicative and pragmatic construction of a 'pragmatist tunnel' – through the use of the Anthropology of Markets – to shed light on Chinese greening, industrial upgrading, and technological catch-up (also see Kirkegaard 2015:82–87). This study begs us to 'dare greatly', testing new pragmatic tunnels that bridge the troubled waters of ontological and epistemological divides between STS and China Studies (and related literatures), to engage in the cross-fertilisation of perspectives.

More than extending China Studies, this research – through this pragmatic move – also bears affinities with New Economic Sociology, and in particular with that literature's emerging yet mounting interest in understanding issues pertaining to market genesis, dynamics, and (in)durability, as pointed out in Padgett & Powell (2012). In this volume, scholars call for accounts and perspectives that can shed light on 'how a play comes to be performed, or why this particular story is being staged instead of some other one', rather than resembling 'a play that begins with the second act, taking both plot and narrative as an accomplished fact' (Powell, Packalen & Whittington 2012: 434). In this way, the aim of this work is also to fill the relational gap in market studies within New Economic Sociology, namely by way of shedding light on some of the socio-material micro-foundations of how China has been able to create a wind power sector with unprecedented pace and scale, how this has involved power struggles and de- and reconfiguration of relations, and of the overall socio-technical assemblage around wind power development.

As in China Studies, the focus within market studies in New Economic Sociology has broadly tended to focus on institutions and structures, exemplified through studies on the role of social networks in the formation of the electricity sector (Granovetter & McGuire 1998), power structures of the oil- and coal-based economies (Mitchell 2011), and the institutional 'architecture of markets' (Fligstein 2001). Yet if we are to gain a richer insight into how certain effects and outcomes have been produced, on the ground, in Chinese wind power development marketisation, we must follow the processes as they unfold, instead of reporting the outcome after the fact, looking into their socio-material grounding and configuration.

Last, in addition to extending and contributing to China Studies and New Economic Sociology, this study also contributes, albeit more indirectly, to STS itself, and to Actor Network Theory and the Anthropology of Markets more specifically. This it does by offering a new and bolder paradigm: First and foremost, rather than restricting itself to a modest sociology, the book is much more ambitious, attempting to 'dare greatly' in terms of offering a fresh and unique perspective on how we can move from a narrow tracing of algorithms to a much broader account of Chinese development, providing (situated) generalisations and comparisons beyond the limitations of a 'modest sociology'. Second, this research extends marketisation studies by taking it to a non-Western controversial and paradoxical site for market studies: one where prices are fixed, where marketisation by its very nature is contested as it is entangled in a socialist context. This opens up to new ways to look at the multiple potential modes of marketisation.

The contributions, extensions, and bridging tunnels are further discussed after the controversy study in Chapters Nine and Ten, having completed the metaphorical journey through the wind turbine. Overall, then, the approach taken here is to build tunnels and bridges between fields and disciplines. The hope is to provide a situationally sensitive approach to understanding China's wind power 'miracle', and to comprehending China not as a monolithic structure of central communist planning, but rather as fragmented and experimentally pragmatic. And so, equipped with the necessary safety gear, it is time to put the Anthropology of Markets to work in practice, testing and stretching it, in a kaleidoscopic and algorithmic cartography of market controversy over Chinese wind power development, as we trace the relations around algorithms and other unforeseen actors in our exploratory journey through the wind turbine's electromagnetic universe.

Notes

1. A system and Latin word borrowed from the Soviet Union's state bureaucracy, the *nomenklatura* system implies the 'list of positions, arranged in order of seniority, including a description of the duties of each office' of political cadres, whilst the *bianzhi* translates as 'establishment of posts' (Brødsgaard 2002).
2. In early 2018, however, senior communist party leaders have revealed apparent government plans to establish a new Ministry of Energy, to replace the NEA (the latter reigning under the auspices of the NDRC). This is widely regarded as a sign of China's consolidation of its continued commitment to environmental protection and renewable energy (Mason & Lim, 8 March 2018).
3. Sismondo (2010), in turn, coming from China Studies, has laid out an overview of STS.

References

Amsden, A. H., 2004, *The Rise of 'The Rest': Challenges to the West from Late-Industrializing Economies*, Oxford University Press, New York.

Andrews-Speed, P., 2012, *The Governance of Energy in China. Transition to a Low-Carbon Economy*, Palgrave Macmillan, Basingstoke.

Ang, Y. Y., 2016, *How China Escaped the Poverty Trap*, Cornell University Press, New York.

Barnard, H., & Chaminade, C., 2012, 'Global Innovation Networks: Towards a Taxonomy'. *Circle*, 2011(4), Lund University.

Barney, J., 1991, 'Firm Resources and Sustained Competitive Advantage', *Journal of Management* 17(1), 99–120.

Binz, C., Truffer, B., Li, L., Shi, Y.J. & Lu, Y., 2012, 'Conceptualizing Leapfrogging with Spatially Coupled Innovation Systems: The Case of Onsite Wastewater Treatment in China', *Technological Forecasting and Social Change* 79(1), 155–171.

Brandt, L. & Thun, E., 2010, 'The Fight for the Middle: Upgrading, Competition, and Industrial Development in China', *World Development* 38(11), 1555–1574.

Brandt, L. & Thun, E., 2016, 'Constructing a Ladder for Growth: Policy, Markets, and Industrial Upgrading in China', *World Development* 80(C), 78–95.

Breznitz, D. & Murphree, M., 2011, *Run of the Red Queen: Government, Innovation, Globalization, and Economic Growth in China*, Yale University Press, New Haven, CT.

Brink, T., 2013, 'Paradoxes of Prosperity in China's New Capitalism', *Journal of Current Chinese Affairs* 42(4), 17–44.

Brødsgaard, K. E., 2002, 'Institutional Reform and the *Bianzhi* System in China', *The China Quarterly* 170, 361–386.

Brødsgaard, K. E., 2017, 'Fragmented authoritarianism' or 'integrated fragmentation', in K. E. Brødsgaard (ed.), *Chinese Politics as Fragmented Authoritarianism: Earthquakes, Energy and Environment*, pp. 38–55, Routledge, Abingdon.

Cao, C., 2004a, 'Chinese Science and the "Nobel Prize Complex"', *Minerva* 42, 151–172.

Cao, C., 2014, 'The Universal Values of Science and China's Nobel Prize Pursuit', *Minerva* 52, 141–160.

CCCPC (Central Committee of the Communist Party of China), 2013, Decision on major issues concerning comprehensively deepening reforms, 13 November 2013, adopted at the close of the Third Plenary Session of the 18th CPC Central Committee, http://www.china.org.cn/china/third_plenary_session/2013-11/16/content_30620736.htm.

Chang, K.-C., 2011, 'A Path to Understanding Guanxi in China's Transitional Economy: Variations on Network Behavior', *Sociological Theory* 29(4), 315–339.

Chen, Y., Rong, K., Xue, L. & Luo, L., 2014, 'Evolution of Collaborative Innovation Network in China's Wind Turbine Manufacturing Industry', *International Journal of Technology Management* 65(1/2/3/4), 262–299.

Chesbrough, H., Vanhaverbeke, W. & West, J. (eds.) (2008), *Open Innovation: Researching a New Paradigm*, Oxford University Press, New York.

Christensen, N. H., 2013, 'Shaping markets: A neoinstitutional analysis of the emerging organizational field of renewable energy in China', PhD thesis, Department of Business & Politics, Copenhagen Business School.

Coase, R. H., 1988, *The Firm, the Market and the Law*, University of Chicago Press, Chicago.

CPC (Communist Party of China) Central Committee and the State Council, 2015, 关于进一步深化电力体制改革的若干意见,中发(2015)9号文'全文 ['Several Opinions of the CPC Central Committee and the State Council on Further Deepening the Reform of the Electric Power System', No. 9 Text Full Text], 'Energy Revolution' ('Policy #9'/'Document No. 9'), 15 March 2015, http://www.ne21.com/news/show-64828.html.

Cooke, P., 2013, 'Global Production Networks and Global Innovation Networks: Stability Versus Growth', *European Planning Studies* 21(7), 1081–1094.

Cunningham, E. A., 2010, 'Energy governance: Fueling the miracle', in J. Fewsmith (ed.) *China Today, China Tomorrow. Domestic Politics, Economy, and Society*, pp. 223–258, Rowman & Littlefield Publishers, Plymouth.

Czarniawska, B., 2013, 'On Meshworks and other Complications of Portraying Contemporary Organizing', *Managing Overflow*, Gothenburg Research Institute, GRI-report, 2013(3), http://hdl.handle.net/2077/34252.

Delman, J., 2005, 'China's Party-State and the Private Business Sector: "Dog Wags Tail" or "Tail Wags Dog"?', *Norsk Geografisk Tidsskrift – Norwegian Journal of Geography* 59(3), 207–216.

Dewey, J., 1927, *The Public and its Problems*, Holt, Oxford.

Dimitrov, M., ed. 2013, *Why Communism Did Not Collapse: Understanding Authoritarian Regime Resilience in Asia and Europe*, Cambridge University Press, New York.

Dongsheng, G. & Fujimoto, T., 2004, 'Quasi-open Product Architecture and Technological Lock-in: An Exploratory Study on the Chinese Motorcycle Industry', *Annals of Business Administrative Science*, 3(2).

Elias, N., 1978, *What is Sociology?*, Columbia University Press, New York.

Ernst, D., 2006, 'Innovation Offshoring: Asia's Emerging Role in Global Innovation Networks', East-West Center Special Reports 10.

Ernst, D., 2008, 'Asia's 'Upgrading through Innovation' Strategies and Global Innovation Networks: An Extension of Sanjaya Lall's Research Agenda', *Transnational Corporations* 17(3), 31–57, United Nations.

Evans, P., 1995, *Embedded Autonomy: States and Industrial Transformation*, Princeton University Press, Princeton, NJ.

Fan, C. C., 2006, 'China's Eleventh Five-Year Plan (2006–2010): From "Getting Rich First" to "Common Prosperity"', *Eurasian Geography and Economics* 47(6), 708–723.

Fligstein N., 2001, *The Architecture of Markets: An Economic Sociology of Twenty-First Century Capitalist Societies*, Princeton University Press, Princeton, NJ.

Fligstein, N. & Zhang, J., 2010, 'A New Agenda for Research on the Trajectory of Chinese Capitalism', *Management and Organization Review* 7(1), 39–62.

Fuller, D., 2016, *Paper Tigers, Hidden Dragons, Firms and the Political Economy of China's Technological Development*, Oxford University Press, Oxford.

García, C., 2013, 'Policies and Institutions for Grid-Connected Renewable Energy: "Best Practice" and the case of China', *Governance: An International Journal of Policy, Administration, and Institutions* 26(1), 119–146.

Gereffi, G., 1999, 'International Trade and Industrial Upgrading in the Apparel Commodity Chain', *Journal of International Economics* 48(1), 37–70.

Gereffi, G., 2005, 'The Global Economy: Organization, Governance, and Development', in N. Smelser & R. Swedberg (eds.), pp. 160–182, *The Handbook of Economic Sociology*, Princeton University Press, Princeton, NJ.

Gereffi, G., Humphrey, J. & Sturgeon, T., 2005, 'The Governance of Global Value Chains', *Review of International Political Economy* 12(1), 78–104.

Gibbon, P. & Ponte, S., 2008, 'Global Value Chains: From Governance to Governmentality?', *Economy & Society* 37(3), 365–392.

Gill, B. & Reilly, J., 2007, 'The Tenuous Hold of China Inc. in Africa', *The Washington Quarterly* 30(3), 37–52.

Gilpin, R., 2000, 'National Systems of Political Economy', in R. Gilpin, *Global Political Economy*, pp. 148–195, Princeton University Press, Princeton, NJ.

Gilson, R. J., Sabel, C. F. & Scott, R., 2008, 'Contracting for Innovation: Vertical Disintegration and Interfirm Collaboration', *ECGI, Law Working Paper* 2008(118).

Goldstein, S. M., 1996, 'The Political Foundations of Incremental Reform', in A. Walder (ed.), *China's Transitional Economy*, pp. 143–169, Oxford University Press, Oxford.

Gorm Hansen, L. L., 2017, *Triggering Earthquakes in Science, Politics and Chinese Hydropower. A Controversy Study*, PhD thesis, Dept. of International Economics and Management, Asia Studies Centre, Copenhagen Business School.

Gosens, J. & Lu, Y., 2013, 'From Lagging to Leading? Technological Innovation Systems in Emerging Economies and the Case of Chinese Wind Power', *Energy Policy* 60, 234–250.

Gosens, J. & Lu, Y., 2014, 'Prospects for Global Market Expansion of China's Wind Turbine Manufacturing Industry', *Energy Policy*, 67, 301–318.

Granovetter, M. & McGuire, P., 1998, 'The Making of an Industry: Electricity in the United States', *The Sociological Review* 46(S1), 147–173, Special Issue: Sociological Review Monograph Series: Laws of the Markets, ed. M. Callon, May, https://doi.org/10.1111/j.1467-954X.1998.tb03473.x

Greenhalgh, S., 2005, 'Missile Science, Population Science: The Origins of China's One-Child Policy', *The China Quarterly* 182, 253–276.

Greenhalgh, S., 2008, *Just One Child: Science and Policy in Deng's China*, University of California Press, Berkeley and Los Angeles.

Gu, S. & Lundvall B.-Å., 2006, 'Policy Learning as a Key Process in the Transformation of the Chinese Innovation Systems, in B.-Å. Lundvall, Intarakumnerd, P. & Vang, J. (eds.), *Asia's Innovation Systems in Transition*, pp. 293–313, Edward Elgar, Cheltenham.

Gu, S., Serger, S. S. & Lundvall, B.-Å., 2016, 'China's Innovation System: Ten Years On', *Innovation* 18(4), 441–448, DOI: 10.1080/14479338.2016.1256215.

Haakonsson, S., Kirkegaard, J. K., & Lema, R. forthcoming, 'China's catch-up in wind power – a case study on decomposition of innovation', Sino-Danish Center for Education and Research, mimeo.

Hall, P. A. & Soskice, D. (eds.), 2001, *Varieties of Capitalism: The Institutional Foundations of Comparative Advantage*, Oxford University Press, Oxford.

Heilmann, S., 2008, 'From Local Experiments to National Policy: The Origins of China's Distinctive Policy Process', *The China Journal* 59, January.

Heilmann, S., 2009, 'Maximum Tinkering under Uncertainty: Unorthodox Lessons from China'. *Modern China* 35(4), 450–462.

Heilmann, S., 2010, 'Economic Governance: Authoritarian Upgrading and Innovative Potential', in J. Fewsmith (ed.), *China Today, China Tomorrow. Domestic Politics, Economy, and Society*, pp. 109–128, Rowman & Littlefield Publishers, Plymouth.

Heilmann, S., 2011, 'Policy-making through Experimentation: The Foundation of a Distinctive Policy Process', in S. Heilmann & E. J. Perry (eds.), *Mao's Invisible*

Hand: The Political Foundations of Adaptive Governance in China, pp. 62–101, 1st edn., vol. 17, Harvard University Asia Center, Cambridge, MA.

Heilmann, S., 2016, 'Introduction to China's Core Executive: Leadership Styles, Structures and Processes under Xi Jinping', in S. Heilmann & M. Stepan (eds.), *China's Core Executive Leadership Styles, Structures and Processes under Xi Jinping*, pp. 6–10, MERICS Paper, 1, June, https://www.merics.org/en/merics-analysis/papers-on-china/chinas-core-executive-leadership-styles-structures-and-processes-under-xi-jinping/.

Heilmann, S. & Perry, E. J. (eds.), 2011, *Mao's Invisible Hand: The Political Foundations of Adaptive Governance in China*, 1st ed., vol. 17, Harvard University Asia Center, Cambridge, MA.

Helper, S., MacDuffie, J. P. & Sabel, C., 2000, 'Pragmatic Collaborations: Advancing Knowledge While Controlling Opportunism', *Industrial and Corporate Change*, 9(2).

Herrigel, G., Wittke, V. & Voskamp, U., 2013, 'The Process of Chinese Manufacturing Upgrading: Transforming from Unilateral to Recursive Mutual Learning Relations', *Global Strategy Journal* 3, 109–125.

Humphrey, J. & Schmitz, H., 2002, 'How Does Insertion in Global Value Chains Affect Upgrading in Industrial Clusters?', *Regional Studies* 36(9), 1017–1027.

INGINEUS, 2011, *Project Final Report*, European Union, http://www.feemdeveloper.net/ingineus/userfiles/attach/20123131122294INGINEUS_finalreport.pdf.

Jessop, B., 2011, 'Rethinking the Diversity of Capitalism: Varieties of Capitalism, Variegated Capitalism, and the World Market', in G. Wood & C. Lane (eds.), *Capitalist Diversity and Diversity within Capitalism*, pp. 209–237, Routledge, London.

Jones, L & Zou, Y., 2017, 'Rethinking the Role of State-owned Enterprises in China's Rise, *New Political Economy* 22(6), 743–760.

Keister, L. A., 1998, 'Engineering Growth: Business Group Structure and Firm Performance in China's Transition Economy', *The American Journal of Sociology* 104(2), 404–440.

Keister, L. A., 2000, *Chinese Business Groups: The Structure and Impact of Interfirm Relations during Economic Development*, Oxford University Press, Hong Kong.

Kirkegaard, J. K., 2015, *Ambiguous Winds of Change – Or Fighting against Windmills in Chinese Wind Power: Mapping Controversies over a Potential Turn to Quality in Chinese Wind Power*, PhD thesis, Department of Business & Politics, Copenhagen Business School.

Kirkegaard, J. K., 2016, 'China's Experimental Pragmatics of 'Scientific Development' in Wind Power: Algorithmic Struggles over Software in Wind Turbines', *Copenhagen Journal of Asian Studies* 34(1), 5–24.

Klagge, B, Liu, Z. & Silva, P. C., 2012, 'Constructing China's Wind Energy Innovation System', *Energy Policy* 50, 370–382.

Korsnes, M., 2014, 'Fragmentation, Centralisation and Policy Learning: An Example from China's Wind Industry', *Journal of Current Chinese Affairs* 43(3), 175–205.

Korsnes, M., 2015, *Chinese Renewable Struggles: Innovation, the Arts of the State and Offshore Wind Technology*, PhD thesis, Department of Interdisciplinary Studies of Culture, Norwegian University of Science and Technology (NTNU).

Korsnes, M., 2016, 'Ambition and Ambiguity: Expectations and Imaginaries Developing Offshore Wind in China', *Technological Forecasting and Social Change* 107(June), 50–58.

Koza, P. M. & Lewin, A. Y., 1998, 'The Co-Evolution of Strategic Alliances', *Organization Science*, Special Issue: Managing Partnerships and Strategic Alliances 9(3), 255–264.

Kroeber, A. R., 2016, *China's Economy – What Everyone Needs to Know*, Oxford University Press, New York.

Lardy, N. R., 2016, 'The Changing Role of the Private Sector in China', Conference Volume.

Lema, A. & Ruby, K., 2007, 'Between Fragmented Authoritarianism and Policy Coordination: Creating a Chinese Market for Wind Energy', *Energy Policy* 35, 3879–3890.

Lema, R., Berger, A. & Schmitz, H., 2013, 'China's Impact on the Global Wind Power Industry', *Journal of Current Chinese Affairs* 42(1), 37–69.

Lema, R., Sagar, A. & Zhou, Y., 2016, 'Convergence or Divergence? Wind Power Innovation Paths in Europe and Asia', *Science and Public Policy* 43(3), 400–413.

Lewis, J. I., 2013, *Green Innovation in China. China's Wind Power Industry and the Global Transition to a Low-Carbon Economy*, Columbia University Press, New York.

Lieberthal, K., 2004, 'The Organization of Political Power and its Consequences: The View from the Outside', in K. Lieberthal, *Governing China: From Revolution through Reform*, pp. 171–205, 2nd edn., W.W. Norton & Co., New York.

Lieberthal, K. & Oksenberg, M. 1988, *Policy-Making in China: Leaders, Structures, and Processes*, Princeton University Press, Princeton, NJ.

Lieberthal, K. G. & Lampton, D., 1992, *Bureaucracy, Politics, and Decision-Making in Post-Mao China*, University of California Press, Berkeley, CA.

Lin, L.-W. & Milhaupt, C. J., 2013, 'We Are the (National) Champions: Understanding the Mechanisms of State Capitalism in China', *Stanford Law Review* 65, 697–760.

Liu, Y. & Kokko, A., 2010, 'Wind Power in China: Policy and Development Challenges', *Energy Policy* 38, 5520–5529.

McNally, C. A., 2006, 'Insinuations on China's Emergent Capitalism', East-West Center Working Paper, Politics, Governance, and Security Series No. 15, February 2006, https://www.eastwestcenter.org/system/tdf/private/PSwp015.pdf?file=1&type=node&id=32103.

McNally, C. A., 2007, 'China's Capitalist Transition: The Making of a New Variety of Capitalism', *Comparative Social Research* 24, 177–203.

Mason, J. & Lim, B. K. 2018, 'Exclusive: China plans to create energy ministry in government shake-up – sources', 8 March 2018, https://www.reuters.com/article/us-china-parliament-energy-exclusive/exclusive-china-plans-to-create-energy-ministry-in-government-shake-up-sources-idUSKCN1GK179.

Mathews, J. A., 2002, 'Competitive Advantages of the Latecomer Firm: A Resource-Based Account of Industrial Catchup Strategies', *Asia Pacific Journal of Management* 19, 467–488.

Mathews, J. A., 2006, 'Dragon Multinationals: New Players in 21st Century Globalization', *Asia Pacific Journal of Management* 23(1), 5–27.

Mathews, J. A. & Tan, H., 2015, *China's Renewable Energy Revolution*, Palgrave Macmillan, New York.

Mayer, C., 1996, Corporate Governance, Competition and Performance, *OECD Economic Studies* 27, 7–34.

Mazzucato, M., 2013, *The Entrepreneurial State: Debunking Public vs. Private Sector Myths*, Anthem Press, New York.

Meidan, M., Andrews-Speed, P. & Xin, M., 2009, 'Shaping China's Energy Policy: Actors and Processes', *Journal of Contemporary China* 18(61), 591–616.

Mertha, A., 2009, 'Fragmented Authoritarianism 2.0: Political Pluralization in the Chinese Policy Process', *The China Quarterly*, December, 995–1012.

Mertha, A. & Brødsgaard, K. E., 2017, 'Revisiting Chinese Authoritarianism in China's Central Energy Administration', in K. E. Brødsgaard (ed.), *Chinese Politics as Fragmented Authoritarianism: Earthquakes, Energy and Environment*, pp. 1–14, Routledge, Abingdon.

Meyer, M. & Lu, X., 2004, 'Managing Indefinite Boundaries: The Strategy and Structure of a Chinese Business Firm', *Management and Organization Review* 1(1), 57–86.

Mitchell, T., 2011, *Carbon Democracy: Political Power in the Age of Oil*, Vergo, London.

Morrison, A., Pietrobelli, C. & Rabellotti, R., 2008, 'Global Value Chains and Technological Capabilities: A Framework to Study Learning and Innovation in Developing Countries', *Oxford Development Studies* 36(1), 39–58.

Nahm, J. & Steinfeld, E. S., 2014, 'Scale-Up Nation: China's Specialization in Innovative Manufacturing', *World Development* 54, 288–300.

NEA (National Energy Administration) of the National Development and Reform Commission, 2015, 国家发展改革委国家能源局关于改善电力运行调节促进清洁能源多发满发的指导意见 发改运行[2015]518号 [The NEA of the NDRC's Guiding Opinions on Improving Electric Power Operation Regulations and Promoting the Reform of Full Release of Clean Energy Development and Operation, No. 518], September http://www.nea.gov.cn/2015-04/09/c_134136821.htm.

Naughton, B., 2008, 'SASAC and Rising Corporate Power in China', *China Leadership Monitor* 24.

Naughton, B., 2009, 'Understanding the Chinese Stimulus Package', *China Leadership Monitor* 28, http://www.hoover.org/research/understanding-chinese-stimuluspackage.

Naughton, B., 2010, 'Economic Growth: From High-Speed to High-Quality', in J. Fewsmith (ed.), *China Today, China Tomorrow. Domestic Politics, Economy, and Society*, pp. 71–90, Rowman & Littlefield Publishers, Plymouth.

Naughton, B., 2014, 'China's Economy: Complacency, Crisis & the Challenge of Reform', *Dædalus, the Journal of the American Academy of Arts & Sciences* 143(2), 14-25.

Naughton, B., 2017, 'Is China Socialist?', *Journal of Economic Perspectives* 31(1), 3-24.

Nolan, P., 2001, *China and the Global Economy: National Champions, Industrial Policy and the Big Business Revolution*, Palgrave, New York.

Nolan, P., 2004, *China at the Crossroads*, Wiley, Cambridge.

Norris, W. J., 2016, *Chinese Economic Statecraft: Commercial Actors, Grand Strategy, and State Control*, Cornell University Press, Ithaca, NY.

O'Connor, G. C., 2006, 'Open, Radical Innovation: Toward an Integrated Model in Large Established Firms', in H. Chesbrough, W. Vanhaverbeke & J. West (eds.), *Open Innovation. Researching a New Paradigm*, Oxford University Press, New York.

Oi, J. C., 1995, 'The Role of the Local State in China's Transitional Economy', *The China Quarterly*, Special Issue, 144, 1132–1149.

Oi, J. C., 2005, 'Patterns of Corporate Restructuring in China: Political Constraints on Privatisation', *The China Journal* 53, 115–136.

Oi, J. C. & Goldstein, S. M., 2018, 'Change within Continuity – Zouping County Government', pp. 3-27, in J. C. Oi & S. M. Goldstein, *Adaptive Governance in a Chinese County – Zouping Revisited*, Stanford University Press, Stanford, CA.

Padgett, J. F. & Powell, W. W. (eds.), 2012, *The Emergence of Organizations and Markets*, Princeton University Press, Princeton, NJ.

Parrilli, M. D., Nadvi, J. & Yeung, H. W.-C., 2013, 'Local and Regional Development in Global Value Chains, Production Networks and Innovation Networks: A Comparative Review and the Challenges for Future Research', *European Planning Studies* 21(7), 967–988.

Peck, J. & Zhang, J., 2013, 'A Variety of Capitalism ... with Chinese Characteristics?', *Journal of Economic Geography* 13, 357–396.

Peteraf, M. A., 1993, 'The Cornerstones of Competitive Advantage: A Resource-Based View', *Strategic Management Journal* 14(3), 179–191.

Ponte, S., 2009, 'Governing through Quality: Conventions and Supply Relations in the Value Chain for South African Wine', *European Society for Rural Sociology, Sociologia Ruralis* 49(3).

Peck, J. & Theodore, N., 2007, 'Variegated Capitalism', *Progress in Human Geography* 31(6), 731–772.

Ponte, S. & Cheyns, E., 2013, 'Voluntary Standards, Expert Knowledge and the Governance of Sustainability Networks', *Global Networks* 13(4), 459–477.

Powell, W. W., Packalen K. E. & Whittington, K. B., 2012, 'Organizational and Institutional Genesis: The Emergence of High-Tech Clusters in the Life Sciences', in J. Padgett & W. W. Powell (eds.), *The Emergence of Organizations and Markets*, pp. 434–465, Princeton University Press, Princeton, NJ.

PWC (PricewaterhouseCoopers), 2013, 'New Roadmap for Achieving the China Dream. Business and Economic Implications of the Third Plenary Session of the CPC's 18th Central Committee', viewed 20 March 2018, http://www.iberchina.org/files/china_plenum_pwc.pdf.

Redding, G. & Witt, M. A., 2009, 'China's Business System and its Future Trajectory', *Asia Pacific Journal of Management* 2, 381–399.

Reuters, 2018, 'China plans first spot electricity trading as Beijing reforms power market', 20 April 2018, https://www.reuters.com/article/us-china-electricity/china-plans-first-spot-electricity-trading-as-beijing-reforms-power-market-idUSKBN1HR1LA.

Romig, C., 2018, 'Powering the Dragon: the rise of Chinese renewables', *Poyry/PEI (Power Engineering International)*, 22 August 2018, https://www.powerengineeringint.com/articles/2018/08/powering-the-dragon-the-rise-of-chinese-renewables.html.

Saich, T., 2011, *Governance and Politics of China*, 3rd edn., Palgrave Macmillan, China.

Shambaugh, D., 2013, *China Goes Global*, Oxford University Press, New York.

Shi, Y., 2012, 'China's Power Sector Reform: Efforts, Dilemmas, and Prospect. Department of Industrial Economic Research', *The Development Research Center of the State Council of P.R. China*, Harvard Electricity Policy Group, Powerpoint presentation, 8–9 March 2012.

Silva, P. C. & Klagge, B., 2013, 'The Evolution of the Wind Industry and the Rise of Chinese Firms: From Industrial Policies to Global Innovation Networks', *European Planning Studies* 21(9), 1341–1356.

Sismondo, S., 2010, *An Introduction to Science and Technology Studies*, 2nd edn., Wiley-Blackwell, Hong Kong.

Steinfeld, E. S., 2004, 'China's Shallow Integration: Networked Production and the New Challenges for Late Industrialization', *World Development* 32(11), 1971–1987.

Strambach, S., 2001, 'Innovation Processes and the Role of Knowledge-Intensive Business Services (KIBS)', in K. Koschatzky, M. Kulicke & A. Zenker (eds.),

Innovation Networks. Technology, Innovation and Policy (Series of the Fraunhofer Institute for Systems and Innovation Research) 12, Physica, Heidelberg.

Tam, O. K., 1999, *The Development of Corporate Governance in China*, Edward Elgar, Cheltenham.

Tang, J. & Ward, A., 2003, *Inside the Enterprise. The Changing Face of Chinese Management*, Routledge, London.

Teece, D. J., Pisano, G. & Shuen, A., 1997, 'Dynamic Capabilities and Strategic Management', *Strategic Management Journal* 18(7), 509–533.

The Information Office of the State Council, *Energy Policy* 2012, 1st edn., 2012. October 2012, http://www.gov.cn/english/official/2012-10/24/content_2250497.htm.

Tunsjø, Ø., 2013, *Security and Profit in China's Energy Policy: Hedging against Risk*, Columbia University Press, New York.

Wade, R., 2004, *Governing the Market. Economic Theory and the Role of Government in East Asian Industrialization*, Princeton University Press, Princeton, NJ.

Walder, A. G., 2011, 'From Control to Ownership: China's Managerial Revolution', *Management and Organization Review* 7(1), 19–38.

Wedeman, A., 2011, 'Crossing the River by Feeling for Stones or Carried Across by the Current? The Transformation of the Chinese Automotive Sector', in S. Kennedy (ed.), *Beyond the Middle Kingdom. Comparative Perspectives on China's Capitalist Transformation*, Stanford University Press, Stanford, CA.

Wei, Y., 2003, *Comparative Corporate Governance – a Chinese Perspective*, Kluwer Law International, The Hague.

Whitehead, A. N., 1978, *Process and Reality*, Free Press, New York.

Williamson, O. E., 1981, 'The Economics of Organization: The Transaction Cost Approach', *The American Journal of Sociology* 87(3), 548–577.

Williamson, P. J. & Yin, E., 2014, 'Accelerated Innovation: The New Challenge from China', *MIT Sloan Management Review*, Research Feature, 23 April.

Witt, M. A., 2010, 'China: What Variety of Capitalism?', Working Paper, INSEAD.

Xiao, Y., Tylecote, A. & Liu, J., 2013, 'Why Not Greater Catch-up by Chinese Firms? The Impact of IPR, Corporate Governance and Technology Intensity on Late-Comer Strategies', *Research Policy* 42(3), 749–764.

Zhang, J. & Peck, J., 2014, 'Variegated Capitalism, Chinese Style: Regional Models, Multi-scalar Constructions', *Regional Studies*, DOI: 10.1080/00343404.2013.856514.

Part II

Controversy study - mapping five sites of controversy over Chinese wind power development

4   Qualification struggle in Chinese wind power – marketisation by advancing towards the brink of collapse?

Silently, I sit listening to the foreign wind power expert. We have talked for a long time this morning about the rapid and volatile development of China's wind turbine industry. Now he turns his attention to the current challenges that seem to be facing the sector. To do this, he refers back to the formative Renewable Energy Law (2005), which incentivised the scaling up of installed wind power capacity:

> *I found it a senseless policy back then – when the new wind power market started up around 2005 … a bad policy … because you use a lot of resources, arable land … eh, and grid, electricity grid in order to install some poor technology. But according to the Chinese experts, this was not a problem back then … they said, 'we have enough land, we will make sure to maintain them [the wind turbines], it will be okay'. They based this argument on a rationale of low production costs, that is, China will have a comparative advantage just by being cheaper. This was used to argue for not having to develop in technological terms. 'We can make do with the second-last [technology] generation.' Nevertheless, some Chinese experts were critical towards the lack of [certification] requirements and standards for wind farm design and wind turbine quality … But back then, the only thing that mattered, and the only thing really demanded in the Renewable Energy Law, was just megawatt … how much megawatt could be installed. Whether the turbine would be able to run, they didn't care. It was all about capacity [measured in megawatts or gigawatts], and nothing about productivity [measured in gigawatt hours].*

My respondent pauses. His account of the development of China's wind power industry takes a twist as he goes on with his story. He continues:

> *China has had all these agendas. They also had this industrial policy agenda with it, right, and that was quite obvious, and they didn't hide that either. [They are] more acknowledging that this was industrial policy.*

But whereas focus was previously on price and industrial growth in manufacturing,

> *this has [now] completely changed. They are gradually making it [quality] a priority in China. And they have moved fast to remedy the damages. Also, the rationale of having a lot of land for non-performing wind turbines has totally changed. Nobody talks like this anymore, due to all the quality issues that have emerged. They knew too little about it back then, and now they have learned their lesson ... the initial strategy resulted in enormous damages and accidents, very big damages and costs, and also conflicts, and everything ... So now the goal has changed, and the mantra is quality [...] What happened is that, after a while, they have decreased support, and they made it more difficult to meet the [certification] requirements, and then a consolidation is taking place between manufacturers. And this is what is happening now. I talked with a Chinese expert who predicted that it would take China ten years from around 2005 ... to reach this phase. So actually that fits pretty well with how it looks now. Already a while ago, they [the Chinese government] intervened with require-ments for the productivity of wind turbines and wind farms. And new restrictions keep coming all the time. (Interview with foreign research institute 2013)*

On my way home, I think about the development of China's wind power industry, and how the story of boom and bust in Chinese wind power as a matter of pure scale-up may be more complex than at first sight. Are winds of change blowing through Chinese wind power? And is the story of Chinese wind power – and of China – changing in ambiguous and maybe paradoxi-cal ways that we have not yet quite understood?

Later, I recall another talk I had earlier with an industry expert on the case of China and wind power. According to him, the development of China's market is a matter of foresight:

> *What is characteristic about China is that they always have some hidden plan. Nothing comes as a surprise for them. They have this idea about where they want to go, and they see everything in that light. And that's why they began with joint ventures [with foreign companies] ... they want to let someone in who doesn't run away with everything, but where some knowledge is transferred [...] It's about technology, it's also about management and know-how etc., and that's how they started out [...] It's learning and know-how and technology transfer and experimentation with some economic model compared to what they had before. That's simply ... they have had this perspective the entire time. (Interview with Chinese policy expert 2010)*

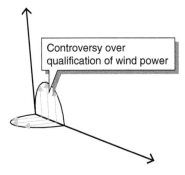

Figure 4.1 First site of controversy.

Pondering this hidden plan, I wonder how China's catch-up strategy will play out within core technologies, such as software, in the current qualification struggle that faces the country's emergent but fragile wind power development marketisation.

Embarking on a mapping of the first site of controversy, Chapter Four initially takes the fundamental commodity, electricity, whose flow can be traced through the vital components of the turbine and into the grid. The chapter calls upon electricity's essential trait, namely that of an electromagnetic wave, to explain the qualification struggle in Chinese wind power development and its entanglement in the undulating forces of Chinese fragmented authoritarianism (see Figure 4.1). What follows is a story that bears witness to three successive phases that accelerate or vary in speed, followed by stages that tip towards destabilisation and potential impasse. In this historical account, a 'qualification struggle' in China's socio-technical assemblage around wind power development is identified, as it has unfolded in the lead up to, during, and after the quality crisis.

- Phase 1 (1980–2002): incremental development and increasingly concerted efforts as industrial policy is scaled up; potential impasse of technology transfer dependency;
- Phase 2 (2003–2011): accelerated development through China's 'turbine wave attack'; instigating a potential impasse with the quality crisis;
- Phase 3 (2012–ongoing): upgrading through a flexible yet not yet fully realised turn to quality; potential impasse from struggles in Sino-foreign supply chain relations around core technologies[1].

It is always a simplification to demarcate temporally in phases. However, although the trends and traits of these different phases inevitably overlap, the point of such a demarcation is to make sense of how particular characteristics at certain points in time come together, producing a break with the previous assemblage to produce a new one. In general, whilst the passage of events in each of the three phases is marked by its own internal logic, each phase displays the characteristic patterns of self-inflicted disruption and in-built constraints. This has resulted in successive stages of venturing towards the brink of potential disruption and impasse.

Instead of leading to a complete collapse, though, the different stages at the brink of impasse have prompted flexible and creative (and sometimes radical) government intervention. These interventions have directed industry actors and the emergent socio-technical assemblage around wind power development to establish new ambitious visions. Curiously, and somewhat paradoxically, this has in turn enabled accelerated catching-up processes and learning through disruptive moves, on the overall path towards framing wind power as a reliable and sustainable renewable energy.

And so, like the electromagnetic fields of a wind turbine's three-phase generator, the three phases of Chinese wind power development have, metaphorically speaking, at times been able to synchronise (the wave forms being in phase with each other), resulting in strong constructive interference. At other times, though, the waves have been out of phase with each other and fighting against each other in destructive interference. As a metaphor for China's ability to catch up and engage in disruptive learning, the disruptive potentiality of the wave forms depict how China steers its wind power sector through oscillating moves of synchronisation (centralised control) and disruptive fragmentation (decentralisation).

Phase One (1980s–2002): incremental development – and increasingly concerted efforts

Phase One of China's emergent wind power sector started with the emergence of a Chinese wind turbine industry in the late 1980s, and was characterised by piecemeal and incremental experimentation, although this lacked the determination of whether or not to build up a domestic industrial supply chain or instead keep relying on technology transfer. The technology, industry, and innovation systems were relatively fragmented and modularised. Ultimately, however, efforts would come together in a more concerted manner as in-built limitations of the unconcerted efforts eventually started to reveal themselves, leading to more focused efforts to build up an indigenous wind turbine industry with home-grown equipment manufacturers. This was a phase marked by relatively fragmented technology and development.

The global context for Chinese wind power

Meanwhile, it is not possible to understand the progress in China's wind power development assemblage during this first phase without looking at the international context.

Early developments in the global wind power sector happened in the cradle of today's global wind turbine industry and were based in Europe, in particular in Denmark and Germany. Over time, though, the wind turbine industry has expanded globally and has become geographically widespread, to the USA and with large growth centres in Asia, particularly in China and India (Lewis 2007, 2013). In terms of technological R&D, development in Europe was largely driven by individual entrepreneurs and small firms that engaged in small-scale and scattered bricolage-like technological experimentation during the late 1970s and 1980s, when the budding roots of an industrial base for wind power started to emerge (Garud & Karnøe 2003; Karnøe & Garud 2012; Vestergaard, Brandstrup & Goddard 2004). In this period, innovation and knowledge transfer tended to take place between distributed industry actors in emerging industrial clusters and national innovation systems (Andersen & Drejer 2008; Bergek et al. 2008; Garud & Karnøe 2003; Kamp, Smits & Andriesse 2004; Karnøe & Garud 2012; Haakonsson, Kirkegaard & Lema forthcoming). In Denmark, for instance, the national test laboratory Risø – now a national wind energy research centre under the Department of Wind Energy at the Technical University of Denmark (DTU) – played a critical role in the interplay between wind turbine research and the construction of a nascent Danish wind turbine industry.

Later, as the global industry increasingly became 'big business' during the 1990s, and particularly so since the early 2000s, innovation became more and more systemised and formalised (and made confidential) (Haakonsson al. forthcoming). In particular, this happened with the inclusion of proprietary IPRs into multilateral legislation under the ramifications of the WTO in 1995 (TRIPS agreement, Trade-Related Aspects of Intellectual Property Rights) (Maskus 2002; WTO n.d.). An important technological shift, leading to more focus on research and innovation, happened in the mid-1990s when wind turbine designs started to shift from fixed speed to variable speed, which necessitated a certain degree of modularity of components owing to the complex and growing interdependencies between turbine components and between wind power generators and the grid (Hansen et al. 2004). This led to increased demands for better turbine and wind farm control, optimised design, and 'intelligence', and pushed the formalisation of RIS and TIS around wind power, the rise of mergers and acquisitions (M&As), and laid the foundation for the formation of today's mature, consolidated, globalised, and highly specialised and competitive wind turbine industry.

During this nascent period of the global industry, the efforts of China and other Asian countries in wind turbine technology and wind power development dawned, but only slowly. It was only in the 2000s with the global dispersal of production and innovation – that is, with the organisational and geographical decomposition and transformation of production and innovation activities – that China really appeared on the wind power scene (Haakonsson et al. forthcoming; interviews; Klagge, Liu & Silva 2012; Lema & Ruby 2007; Zhao, Wang & Wang 2012a). Western wind turbine manufacturers, component suppliers, design houses, and also so-called KIBS (Strambach 2001), which specialise in specific streams of knowledge within the sector, were all starting to increasingly localise their production and other selected activities in China, for example owing to the vast market potential there and the then comparatively low production prices. Along with this, emerging Chinese wind turbine manufacturers started to engage with foreign actors, whereby China could use the incipient GVC and innovation and learning networks around wind turbines to tap into foreign technology and knowledge resources (Haakonsson et al. forthcoming; Lema, Berger & Schmitz 2013; Lema, Iizuka & Walz 2015; Lema, Sagar & Zhou 2016).

China's piecemeal ascendance onto the wind power scene

China itself had already engaged in wind resource mapping in the 1980s, and there had also been some scant experimentation with wind turbines, both through foreign expert assistance, for example from Risø, and by sending Chinese electric power specialists to Europe to study the fundamentals of wind power engineering (interviews with research institutes, design houses, certification bodies, and wind turbine manufacturers 2011–2013). China's domestic experience in the 1980s was somewhat different from Europe's. The country's early adventures in wind power were a series of fragmented and scattered experimentations, plagued by indecisiveness and ambivalence as whether or not to make a coordinated and focused effort to create Chinese manufacturing capabilities in this area. Further, lacking the relevant experience, the first years were largely marked by investment in trials of small-scale grid-connected wind turbines, undertaken in the form of scientific research or state demonstration projects, with no commercial element. At this point, most financial support came from foreign grants, soft loans, and foreign aid, for example by attracting foreign experts to give advice or by sending Chinese engineers to Europe (interviews; Lema & Ruby 2007; Zhao et al. 2012a).

Meanwhile, as early as 1986, MOST had introduced the long-term National 863 high-tech development plan in order to meet the global challenges of technological competition by focusing on key scientific areas (e.g. energy), with the stated goal to reduce dependence on foreign technology (Ministry of Science and Technology, n.d.). However, it was only in the late 1990s that slightly more concerted efforts were made at building a Chinese wind turbine manufacturing industry. By 1996, the influential policy, the Ride the Wind Programme, promoted the formation of Sino-foreign joint ventures.[2] This was supplemented by other supportive financial instruments that assisted the buildup of an industrial basis and to attract foreign direct investments (FDI) and the localisation of foreign companies in China through economic incentives. For instance, lower import tariffs for renewable energy equipment were introduced, as was financial and regulatory support (e.g. investment and R&D subsidies, tax breaks, favourable pricing, and fixed tariffs) (Andrews-Speed 2012; Cherni & Kentish 2007; Fang, Li & Wang 2012; Klagge et al. 2012; Korsnes 2014; Lewis 2013; Lewis & Wiser 2007; Liu & Kokko 2010).

Together, these policies formed an integral part of the economisation of wind power, namely attributing a certain economic value to setting up business in China for foreign manufacturers, making it an attractive investment for potential investors. The above policies further mark China's renowned and notorious technology for market/trade market access for technology strategy: Intended to encourage manufacturing processes to be located in China through the preferential treatment of foreign companies, the underlying strategy was to encourage foreign manufacturers to locate there, with the intended side effect of spurring China's ability to learn and upgrade their capabilities by tapping into foreign technologies and innovation (Klagge et al. 2012). As expressed by a Chinese component manufacturer,

> your technology is an asset in your hand, you should take advantage of this asset, you should just find a good market, and China has a good market, and that is what I [Chinese supplier] want: to reap your technology in exchange for this market exchange. (Chinese diplomat 2013)

With increasingly coordinated policies on both the demand and the supply sides (such as the financial and regulatory support mentioned above), along with China's significant financial power and existing capabilities in heavy industry, a Chinese industrial base for wind power soon started to surface (Cherni & Kentish 2007; Lema & Ruby 2007; Lewis & Wiser 2007; Li 2010; Liu & Kokko 2010; Wang et al. 2011).

Attraction of foreign companies and technologies to build Chinese industrial base

The attraction of foreign technologies, FDI, and know-how has had a critical role in the construction of China's nascent wind turbine industry. Much of the knowledge about manufacturing wind turbines was gained through the acquisition of foreign design licences, imports of finished wind turbines and wind power technology, which formed the basis for extensive reverse engineering efforts and backward design of foreign design licences: a copy-catting strategy of reverse engineering and assimilation and absorption, so to speak (Chen, Rong, Xue & Luo 2014; Cherni & Kentish 2007; Klagge et al. 2012; Lema et al. 2013; Lema & Ruby 2007; Lewis 2007, 2013; Li 2010; MOST 2006; Nahm & Steinfeld 2014; Silva & Klagge 2013). A case in point was the Danish wind turbine manufacturer, NEG Micon (later merged into Vestas), which was the first foreign lead firm to enter the Chinese wind power market (doing so as early as in 1986), licensing its design directly to rival Chinese firms in the early days, before it came to understand the hidden dangers of this. The case of the German firm REpower is also an example of how several licences were sold to Chinese firms: In 1997 and 2001, REpower's predecessor, Jacobs Energie, licensed its design to the then insignificant Chinese wind turbine manufacturer Goldwind,[3] an emerging OEM. Goldwind was established as the first Chinese wind turbine manufacturer back in 1986 in China's north-westernmost Xinjiang Province. Today it is the world's largest wind turbine manufacturer (in terms of installed capacity) (Lewis 2013; Mathews 2016). And so, the stepping stones for the progression of China's wind turbine industry were laid out, by pragmatic experimentation with whether or not it was deemed worthwhile to invest in building a domestic manufacturing base or not.

At the brink of stalemate in Phase One: limitations of dependence on foreign technology

Whilst Phase One had so far succeeded in attracting foreign investments and technologies to China, the country's wind turbine industry was soon to feel some of the inbuilt limitations of this initial phase of industrial development, which created inertia and pushed development towards the brink of stalemate. In a market still dominated by foreign wind turbine manufacturers, and lacking a domestic supply chain, China's emerging wind turbine industry relied on comparatively expensive foreign component technologies. Further, lacking the long-term experience with developing wind power and wind turbines, the emerging manufacturers or OEMs (of which more or less only one would exist until 2005, namely Goldwind) would function more as pure-play assembly-companies, without the in-house capability to develop customised and optimised components themselves. These challenges were an indirect result of the copy-catting strategy of reverse engineering through absorption and assimilation – a strategy of technology transfer endorsed in Chinese policies and forming an integral part of the country's S&T strategy (e.g. MOST 2006; Interviews).[4] Another factor was the extensive fragmentation of authority between different bureaucracies and across national and local levels, which reflected an indecisive leadership. Entangled in China's particular 'matrix muddle' of fragmented authoritarianism, therefore, there was no clear consent as to wind power's role in the electrical power system, or whether or not China should seek to establish its own domestic industry or rely on turbine imports (Lema & Ruby 2007).

So, as the Chinese government procrastinated, the global wind turbine industry became increasingly 'big business' at the beginning of the 2000s. However, with China's accession to the WTO in 2001, and a heightened focus on sustainability and environmental and climate issues, as well as on harmonious, sustainable, and scientific development, wind power soon started to become a more strategic matter in China as well (Lewis 2013). More deliberate measures were going to be required if the Chinese were to be competitive and build up their own effective wind turbine industry. As Phase One drew to a close around 2002/2003, and as China's central government decided to break the relative deadlock and create a more coherent and coordinated policy for the wind power sector, a new and more concerted focus on establishing the industry was enhanced by the restructuring reform of the Chinese power sector in 2002. Apart from unbundling China's power sector into two state-controlled grid companies and the 'Big Five' generating companies, the powerful NDRC, and in particular its Energy Bureau, was established. This marked the dawn of a new era, as the NDRC would be responsible for taking on a more active role in coordinating the supply and demand for wind power and renewable energy in general, as a main component of the energy system (García 2013; Korsnes 2014; Lema & Ruby, 2007; Liu & Kokko 2010:5523; Yu et al. 2009).

Phase Two (2003–2011): China's 'turbine wave attack' – the explosive emergence of a Chinese supply chain

As wind power increasingly became big business during the early 2000s, with increasing interdependencies of technology and actors, and as China became more determined to build its own home-grown industry, the government intervened with a number of initiatives. First and foremost, the wind farm concession programme, which was introduced in 2003 and ran until 2009, helped to spur the development of large-scale wind farm development, with its guaranteed grid-connection tariff determined by a national tendering process and dependent on provincial wind resources (Li 2010:1159). In this government-led tendering system, which promoted rapid expansion in wind power development through its quantity-based system for the promotion of renewable energies (García 2013:130), wind farm developers were invited by the NDRC to bid for a concession to develop a given site that had been chosen by the government, assessed for good wind resources, and promised a fixed subsidy (García 2013; Korsnes 2014; Lema & Ruby 2007; Lewis & Wiser 2007; Wang et al. 2011:146; Zhao et al. 2012b).

The concession programme and local content requirements

The concession programme was the key element in a central decision to boost large-scale wind power development. It corresponded more or less with the time of the power sector reforms (2002), the introduction of the Party doctrine of scientific development (2003), and the notion of a sustainable Harmonious Socialist Society (2004), thus also reflecting the ambition to spur on local and indigenous (home-bred) manufacturing capabilities (García 2013:130). In this way, the concession programme marked a break with Phase One, as it tried to encourage less dependence on foreign companies and technologies through the requirement for indigenous manufacturing content. This local content requirement policy was introduced in 2003 (and tightened in 2005), and so at the start of the concession programme all tender bids were required to demonstrate a minimum of 50 per cent localisation. This had been raised to 70 per cent by 2005 to help encourage the development of a local industry, much to the discontent of foreign manufacturers who were unable to win concessions. There followed allegations from foreign companies and the WTO of unfair competition, which ultimately led to the abolition of the local content requirement in 2009. However, by then the regulation had fulfilled its original purpose, as most foreign manufacturers had already established local production in China and many of these had chosen to bring along their own key component suppliers to preserve their trust-based relational customer–supplier relations. This made it relatively easy for the Chinese government to remove the requirement (Cherni & Kentish 2007; Haakonsson & Kirkegaard 2016; Klagge et al. 2012; Lema & Ruby 2007; Lewis 2013; Lewis & Wiser 2007; Liu & Kokko 2010; Ru et al. 2012 Wang et al. 2011; Zhao et al. 2012b).

The kick-off of the Renewable Energy Law

Another influential government intervention during this phase was the Renewable Energy Law (Standing Committee of the National People's Congress (NPC) 2005). This is generally seen as the critical turning point for China's wind power sector, and the point at which installed capacity started to show unprecedented growth rates (Korsnes 2014; Li 2010; Yu, Ji, Zhang & Chen 2009; Wang et al. 2011; Zhao et al. 2012b). As expressed by a Chinese wind turbine manufacturer:

> What drives the growth is the Chinese policy. With the passage of the Renewable Energy Law. That was kind of a kick-off. (Interview with Chinese wind turbine manufacturer 2012)

The impact of the Renewable Energy Law comes from its 'unequivocal declaration of intent to promote renewable energy both as a part of the total energy mix and as an area of industrial and technological development' (Lema & Ruby 2007:3886). To support this declaration, a number of supportive incentive mechanisms were introduced, for instance 'a mandatory grid-connection system, national target system, cost-sharing scheme, and feed-in tariff scheme' (Standing Committee of the NPC 2005). Further, the Renewable Energy Law introduced the Renewable Energy Development Fund to support S&T development as well as to increase the localisation of manufacturing, with the underlying intent to spur the buildup of indigenous innovation capabilities in renewable energy (Cherni & Kentish 2007; Lema & Ruby 2007; Lewis 2013:68–69). In addition to spurring growth through quantitative targets, the Renewable Energy Law linked wind power development and other renewable energies discursively to the Chinese comprehensive notion of sustainable development, and emphasised its link to scientific development. Soon afterwards, as an increasingly comprehensive policy framework, with follow-up plans and programmes, emerged for the support of wind power and a Chinese wind turbine industry, China had finally decided what was up and what was down in wind power: it wanted its own indigenous wind turbine industry. And when China makes up its mind, rapid transformation is often bound to happen.

Rapid development in the Chinese wind turbine industry

The Renewable Energy Law's national target system for the development and utilisation of renewable energy set up a system whereby both mid- and long-term targets, in GW, for installed capacity of wind power were determined at central level by the energy authorities of the State Council. Soon afterwards, in 2007, quantity-based supply and demand schemes (mandatory market shares (MMS), and power purchase agreements (PPAs)) were introduced, which officially obliged transmission companies and local/provincial governments not only to provide each wind farm facility with a connection to the grid, but also to purchase all the renewable electricity produced (Bloomberg 2012:2; Cherni & Kentish 2007:3624; García 2013:132; Lema & Ruby 2007). This requirement was later reiterated in an edition of the Renewable Energy Law published in 2009. Overall, these measures were meant to create economic incentives for investments into the emerging socio-technical assemblage around wind power development.

And so, as money accordingly started to 'rush down the system very fast' (Interview with foreign control system supplier 2012), local governments and enterprises – 'stimulated from above' by government Five-Year Plans – were 'throwing themselves after the ball' as they competed against each other (Interview with foreign control system supplier 2012). As a result, and because the targets were not binding (García 2013:135) and did not specify a distribution system across provinces, targets were surpassed and adjusted upwards over and over again. For instance, the Medium- to Long-Term Plan for Renewable Energy (National Development and Reform Commission (NDRC) People's Republic of China 2007) set the initial target for wind power at 30 GW in 2020, but this was already met by 2010 and was quickly revised upwards to 100 GW (García 2013:135; Wang et al. 2011). A growth rate like this had never before been witnessed in the global history of renewable energy. China's installed wind power capacity was only 0.8 GW in 2004 but reached around 45 GW by 2010, making China the number one country in total installed capacity (since 2009), a top position it still holds with 188 megawatts (MW) installed by the end of 2017 (Andrews-Speed 2012; GWEC 2011, 2016, 2017a, 2017b; Klagge et al. 2012; Lema & Ruby 2007; Ru et al. 2012; Zhao et al. 2012a:223; Zhao et al. 2012b). This accelerated development happened in a period of global wind power development with high growth rates, but where 'a manufacturer that was competing on low turbine cost' had been missing. China filled this gap (Gosens & Lu 2013:247).

The emergence of a Chinese industrial supply chain

As wind power had rapidly become crucial in the manufacturing production chain of China's emerging renewable energy sector, there was a dramatic increase in the number of wind turbine manufacturers so that the rising demand for installed wind power capacity could be met (García 2013:137). Indeed, '[i]n practice, the government has induced policy experiments, which have set in motion some of the large state-owned enterprises (SOEs). These, in turn, have had an influence both locally and nationally, and have lobbied towards increased policy support for wind energy' (Korsnes 2014:196). To illustrate this, Goldwind was the only notable domestic wind turbine manufacturer until 2005.[5] However, by the end of 2007, there were around 40, and towards the end of 2008 there were between 70 and 80 companies operating in the sector. It was in 2006 that Chinese wind turbine manufacturers Sinovel and Envision were established; they were soon to gain significant market shares in China and globally. As expressed by an industry expert:

> China started ... as I remember it, around 2005, '06, or '07. And what did they do? They went out and bought some licences ... started producing some turbines or wind turbines from those drawings and explanations. And then they produced like crazy. (Interview with foreign wind turbine manufacturer 2013)

At the same time, the number of Chinese component suppliers rapidly increased and soon started to number in the hundreds, manufacturing – for example – blades, converters, control systems, bearings, and gearboxes (García 2013; Li 2010; Ru et al. 2012).

China sweet and sour – the bitter taste of 'unfair' competition

Owing to a preference for national companies, and in particular for SOEs, Chinese wind turbine manufacturers, wind farm developers, and power generating companies often beat foreign manufacturers in national bids, partly because of the local content requirement (also their lead was maintained after the requirement was abolished) and because of SOEs' ability to offer the lowest bids. This ability was partly the result of retaining a relatively large pool of Chinese and comparatively cheaper component suppliers (now less dependent on foreign expensive components), which led to heavy price competition. It was also a result of the legacy of obtaining foreign technology through licensing agreements, as this meant that many Chinese manufacturers had circumvented the high R&D costs inherent in developing new technology (Klagge et al. 2012:376). In addition, they had often adopted a modular approach to wind turbine technology, treating them largely as modules or LEGO bricks (Kirkegaard 2017) – that could be easily sourced from suppliers and then assembled, which allowed market- and price-based selection of suppliers and the squeezing of prices (Haakonsson & Kirkegaard 2016). Further, after winning the bid, the price was often adjusted and made more realistic.

As a result, whilst foreign wind turbine manufacturers, such as Vestas, Gamesa, Suzlon, and later General Electric and Siemens, had entered China in the hope of a promised 'land of honey and spinning turbines', foreign companies were soon to wake up to the concessions' 'overwhelming criterion to have low equipment prices …Which is not the cost of the 20 years but the costs up front, the CAPEX [Capital Expenditure]. […] We cannot compete on these' (Interview with foreign wind turbine manufacturer 2012). This way of focusing on 'very low price and very large installed capacity' but where 'nobody cares about twenty years of generating costs' stood in stark contrast to the Western companies' mode of competing, which was based on the optimised and lowest lifetime generating costs (the Levelised Cost of Energy, LCOE) measured in terms of the cost per GWh (Interviews with wind turbine manufacturer; government advisor; wind turbine industry association 2012, 2013).

As a consequence, as foreign wind turbine manufacturers were not able to compete on the up-front price of the turbine, the resulting competitive playing field 'was totally skewed – it had no resemblance of a competitive market' (Interview with foreign wind turbine manufacturer 2013). As 'a practical way of keeping foreign companies out of tendering, because we [foreign wind turbine manufacturers] could not compete in cost of megawatt' (i.e. installed capacity), there was 'one field over here with Chinese players, and a little bubble over here with foreign ones that were not competing' (Interview with foreign wind turbine manufacturer 2013). These new competitive conditions, in turn, made the Chinese market – and Sino-foreign supply chain relations – taste sourer than the foreign companies had envisioned. China, it was argued, played 'a nationalistic game' in which 'you really have to be smart to continue to make a good business here' (interview with foreign wind turbine manufacturer 2013). Creating an invisible boundary between what was considered fair and unfair competition during Phase Two, foreign manufacturers would sometimes argue that whilst,

> it is entirely fair to aim towards building up a sound industry, there has to be a balance. And I think that China may overstep that balance. I don't actually think they wanted to get rid of foreign companies, I never think it was their intention. (Interview with foreign wind turbine manufacturer 2013)

The accusation that China was 'tinkering with the balance', creating an 'unsound environment for foreign investment' was enhanced when, the 'market changed rapidly' (interview with foreign wind turbine manufacturer 2013), which happened when the industry was officially designated strategic in 2011 repealing all the original preferential treatment for foreign companies (interview with foreign wind turbine manufacturer 2013). In this way, whilst China had soon proved itself to be the 'world's factory' of wind turbines, Chinese 'powerful incumbent firms' seemed to have been 'able to entrench their positions and new players are either unable to enter the market or, if they succeed, tend to focus on maximising short-term profits rather than building sustainable businesses' (Andrews-Speed 2012:83). A balancing of the competitive space (or 'competing bubbles') was taking place.

Advancing towards the tipping point in Phase Two: the quality crisis

A picture of rapid growth in installed capacity, achieved successfully through a diversity of targeted incentives – and a broad financial push from the Chinese enormous fiscal stimulus package in response to the global financial crisis that pushed investments into infrastructure (Kroeber 2016; Lardy 2016; Naughton 2014) – and the creation of a Chinese wind turbine industry that gradually covered the entire supply chain, has been drawn, one in which wind power installations were overtaken by Chinese companies. With this ability to undercut Western manufacturers, it would seem that Chinese wind turbine manufacturers would be well placed to conquer the global market. However, they instead appeared to be running the risk of defeating themselves, or fighting against their own windmills in the domestic market. In about 2010 the wind turbine industry began to witness 'frequent reports of quality problems and technical difficulties of domestically manufactured wind turbines', such as fractures of blades and shafts, generator fires, gearbox ruptures and brake failures (Lian & Wu 2011 in Klagge et al. 2012:376). Whilst China had been able to engineer wind turbines at a much lower price than the least expensive models offered by their foreign competitors (Nahm & Steinfeld 2014), the central government's 'preference of industry creation, and hence quantity before quality' (Korsnes 2014:192) had created massive quality problems that resulted not only in component failures but also in poor performance and low capacity factors, an inability to connect to the grid, and even major accidents (Cherni & Kentish 2007; García 2013; Gosens & Lu 2014; Kirkegaard 2015; Klagge et al. 2012; Lewis & Wiser 2007; Li 2010; Yu et al. 2009). It became evident that many wind farms in China were, somewhat unsurprisingly, in hindsight at least, not generating the energy that was expected from wind farms of their installed capacity (Fang et al. 2012:353). The result of Phase Two was thereby a self-induced overheated wind power sector, with abundant overcapacity, quality issues, and increased competitive tension between Chinese and foreign industry actors, amongst other things. Some of these overflows are illustrated in the 'exploding wind turbine' in Figure 4.2.

Recalling the Chinese military metaphor of the 'human wave attack', China seemed to have produced its own 'turbine wave attack' in under five years. In this is mirrored a frontal attack of upscaling: flooding China not with infantry but with wind turbines (interview with Chinese government

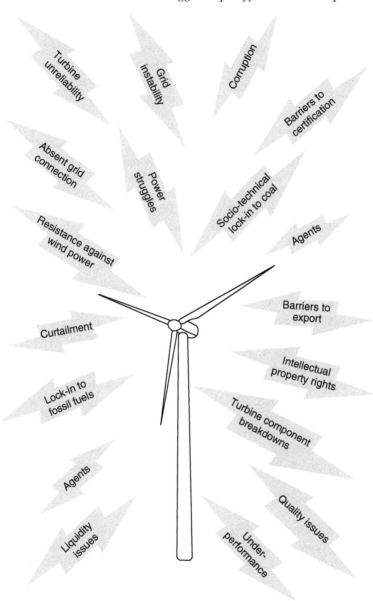

Figure 4.2 Examples of overflowing in wind power development.

advisor and wind industry association 2013). A marketquake shook the foundations of the wind power sector. Whilst Chinese companies had suc- ceeded in out-performing foreign wind turbine manufacturers in terms of the lowest price, and having become the largest wind power market in terms of installed capacity, the 'turbine wave attack' was soon to face a self-induced quality crisis, which would threaten the very survival of the entire market. As illustrated in Figure 4.2, the socio-technical assemblage around wind power development had produced extensive overflowing. Amongst the technological reasons for this emergent quality crisis were for instance the low quality of turbines, obsolete component technologies, poor control systems and poor turbine design, outdated wind farm control and management systems, and insufficient feasibility studies, resulting in poor geographical site selection and sub-optimal micro-siting of turbines, as well as a lack of targets for generated electricity (García 2013:137; Klagge et al. 2012:376). Meanwhile, one needs to look deeper to identify some of the underlying reasons why these quality issues had emerged with such speed, namely: preference for low prices squeezing out quality; targets for installed capacity; poor planning and fragmented coordination; and a lack of certification requirements. These are elaborated upon below.

Preference for low prices squeezing out quality

First, take the tendering processes for wind power development. These had continued to favour the lowest bid more or less exclusively, largely disregarding quality measures, such as a track record of efficiency, productivity, and reliability (García 2013:138; Korsnes 2014; Li 2010:1163; Liu & Kokko 2010:5524; Yu et al. 2009). This had led wind farm developers to intentionally underestimate the costs of wind farm development (e.g. for grid connection, turbine components) in their competition with other wind farm bidders, and ultimately to win the bid. If pushed far enough, this underestimation naturally leads to wind farm projects being unprofitable but, indirectly, it comes at the expense of wind turbine quality. To reduce capital costs, wind farm owners squeezed wind turbine manufacturers, and component suppliers, to lower the prices of their products. Ultimately, this resulted in a significant pressure on the manufacturing sector to produce poor-quality products (Li 2010; Liao et al. 2010; Yu et al. 2009):

> The low prices may impact the entire fledgling Chinese wind industry negatively as utilities may unduly pressurize wind turbine manufacturers to reduce costs, to offset the low concession. (Liao et al. 2010:1884)

The pressure on quality was further exacerbated by a financial support scheme (the feed-in tariff, FIT) that consistently did not cover the actual costs of developing wind power. In this context, only China's SOEs were able to survive, because of their relatively lax profit requirements, favourable loans from the state-owned banks, cheap access to land, and 'shared pockets' between business group members (interviews 2012, 2013; García 2013; Kirkegaard 2015; Korsnes 2014; Li 2010; Liu & Kokko 2010; Yu et al. 2009).[6] Meanwhile, the legacy of dependence on foreign licenses and the 'LEGO approach', and the squeezing of suppliers' prices, compromised quality, for example as manufacturers risked losing a systemic overview of the wind turbine's thousands of components. With a focus on building up an industrial base in Phase Two, Chinese wind turbine manufacturers had been satisfied to 'make do with the second-last generation' (Interview with foreign control system supplier 2013), reflecting the Chinese so-called 'Run of The Red Queen' strategy (Breznitz & Murphree 2011). This, however, also implied that Chinese wind turbine manufacturers and wind farm developers were soon to discover that they would sometimes have to rely on foreign components, even though they were more expensive, for the same reasons, in cases when quality was still part of the calculus. This was because of the deficit of experience of China's assembly firms, insufficient R&D investments, the lack of a substantial track record, insufficient proof of tested lifetime performance, and other quality-related features (García 2013:138–139). With only limited concern for becoming competitive in terms of quality,

> the most important thing was to let the industry try ... try produce some turbines. And then see whether any turbines would come out of that, and see whether any of them [wind turbine manufacturers] would become good at it. (Interview with foreign control system supplier 2013)

While the issue of 'unfair competition' had somewhat destabilised Sino-foreign customer–supplier relations, Chinese wind turbine manufacturers were often still heavily dependent on foreign design licenses and foreign core components when it came to core technologies. The reliance on foreign expertise had thus, to a large extent, come with a hidden price: Chinese manufacturers found they lacked an overview of the wind turbine's design and functioning. This not only had an impact on quality, but also restricted their ability to develop and manufacture indigenously designed wind turbines or turbine core components.

Targets for installed capacity

Another factor worthy of consideration is that the wind power targets that China set for itself can help to explain the squeeze on quality. Overall, targets for installed capacity created economic incentives for wind farm developers that were based on 'how many megawatt, how much capacity, that had to be installed' (Interview with foreign certification body/wind turbine manufacturer 2013). Focused exclusively on the installed capacity (measured in GW), plans and policies did not encourage or incentivise manufacturers or developers to ensure quality, as they 'didn't care whether they [the turbines] were running' to produce electricity (interview with Chinese think tank 2013), which is measured in GWh. As a result,

> they gave subsidies for the number of machines that came out of it. A totally mistaken strategy in my view. But that's how it was. And that

means that a host of companies – all more or less state-supported – started producing wind turbines, because now that was the thing. (Interview with foreign wind turbine manufacturer 2013)

In other words, there were no targets, or even minimum requirements, in the policies and plans for actually generating electricity, for operating at a decent efficiency, or even to be connected to the power grid (Kirkegaard 2015; Korsnes 2014). The manufacturing sector therefore started 'to produce poor quality products' (Li 2010; Yu et al. 2009:5224). As expressed by a foreign scientist,

they just wanted some capacity, but were not interested in whether any-thing [electricity] was generated. But that means … that may be a good strategy to get started, that you don't set up a lot of big barriers in the beginning. And it's obvious that this will result in some problems … these turbines are not very good at adapting to the grid. And in 2010 and '11, then you had some pretty large black-outs due to the voltage fluctuation. (Interview with foreign wind turbine manufacturer 2013)

Poor planning and fragmented coordination creating a 'free(riding)' local market

In addition, China's wind power sector had for many years been plagued by poor planning and fragmented coordination between the local and cen-tral levels, largely a result of Chinese fragmented authoritarianism (Lema & Ruby 2007). In practice, between 2003 and 2011 over 90 per cent of wind farms were approved by competing local governments and not by central government, with provincial governments being allowed to approve wind farm projects below 50 MW, where 'the rules of the game are much freer than for the larger wind farms' (Interview with foreign wind turbine manufacturer 2013). This implied that a lot of wind farms at exactly the size of 49.5 MW were installed often right next to each other, or one on either side of a provin-cial border, or next to a coal-fired power plant (García 2013; interviews; Jiang (ed.) 2011 in Korsnes 2014:187; Yu et al. 2009:5223), disregarding the ability of the grid to absorb the power. Further, decentralised control induced many provincial governments to go far 'beyond target, so that the wind power was not integrated into the system' (interview with Chinese think tank 2013):

Until recently, there was a rule that regional governments could approve wind farms themselves up to 50 MW without approval from the central government, whereas parks above 50 MW must go through an approval by the central government. It's sort of like a market controlled by Beijing, and then a free market. Of course, there's no such thing as a free market in a Chinese context, but it will simply be easier to get a project approval, if your project is below 50 MW – you don't have to go through Beijing. (Interview with foreign wind turbine manufacturer 2013)

Meanwhile, the adverse effect of fragmentation and decentralisation was overcapacity and curtailment. These effects had been further exacerbated by the way in which economic performance of local provinces in China functions as a 'principal yardstick for cadre evaluation under CPC's *nomenklatura* system and state administrative hierarchy' (McNally 2006:20). As a consequence, and since environmental targets have only later and gradually been introduced into cadre evaluation (Delman 2005; Mertha & Brødsgaard 2017; PWC 2013), local provincial officials in China were competing against each other in terms of economic growth, measured in GDP figures. Hence, provincial officials would primarily be concerned with the construction of a wind farm, as this could raise provincial GDP figures and create local employment, rather than being concerned with grid connection. That is, whether the wind turbines needed 'to be reinstalled, reinvested, retro-fitted' or not did not matter, 'because then it will again figure as 1,000 wind turbines, and thus increase provincial local GDP' (interview with foreign component supplier 2013).

Although wind farms are relatively quick to install, the extension of the grid and expansion of its capacity is expensive, requires significant coordination, and takes time (interview with Chinese think tank 2013). Therefore, the partial decentralisation of wind farm planning control combined with the lack of central coordination of grid capacity resulted in extensive overflowing, that is, with power curtailment of operational wind farms and, in the worst case, wind farms left without grid connections. Figure 4.3 shows that the national average curtailment rates have been a significant issue for many years. In some provinces such as Gansu, Xinjiang, and Jilin, curtailment rates have been extremely high; in Gansu nearing 50 percent of installed wind power capacity being affected in 2016 (Luo et al. 2018).

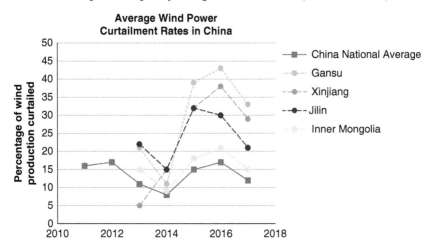

Figure 4.3 Average wind power curtailment rates in China 2010–2018.

Source: Luo et al. 2018.

In this way, China seems to have 'started out big ... And then you assume that there will be people to buy it all. You don't ask yourself: "What's the demand for this?"' (interview with foreign control system supplier 2012). Consequently, poor quality turbines and wind farm control, along with poor coordination between central and local levels, led to severe overcapacity and vast amounts of available wind power being downrated, or curtailed, and essentially wasted.

Together, these entangled and complicated issues – technically, structurally, and institutionally – eventually resulted in a rising number of grid-disconnected wind turbines, and underperforming wind turbines in terms of wind power generation and average annual wind utilisation (Li et al. 2012 in Korsnes 2014:186). Increasingly, new installed capacity was not followed by corresponding increases in the actual electricity energy generated from wind power (Li, Li & Feng 2014; Yang, Patino-Echeverri & Yang 2012), and anecdotal evidence and multiple industry reports indicated that around 30 per cent of installed capacity often remained dormant ('idle'), 'while the other 70% may be operating with minimal efficiency' (García 2013:129). It is widely acknowledged that between one-third and one-fourth of Chinese wind farms were dormant or underperforming in the period 2010–2012, with a grid connection rate at 75 per cent or below (Bloomberg 2012; Fang et al., 2012; Li et al. 2014; Yang et al. 2012; Zhao et al. 2012a:222). Still to this day, curtailment rates in China are high, at around 17 per cent across China in 2016 (GWEC 2017a:13, GWEC 2018:40). And so, combined with Chinese fragmented authoritarianism in Chinese wind power governance (Lema & Ruby 2007; Korsnes 2014), the 'lack of incentive to ensure long-term electricity generation permeates the whole industry chain from component suppliers to local governments approving wind farms, SOEs investing in the wind farms and grid utilities managing the wind farms' (Korsnes 2014:196).

Lacking certification requirements

Last, the emerging quality issue derives from the quality control aspect: certification. At the time, China had no certification requirements and was only starting to build up an accreditation, certification, testing, and standardisation system for wind power. The inability to demonstrate compliance with a standard of quality also started to have implications for the ability of Chinese wind turbine manufacturers to export to advanced markets, owing to 'little confidence in turbine quality, despite the rapid increase in sales' (Yu et al. 2009:5224). In this way, '[e]ven the perception of poor quality can severely limit market growth' (Lewis 2013:42), and exports accordingly remained meagre throughout Phase Two, as Chinese wind turbines were 'perceived as less reliable and of lower quality' (interview with Chinese wind turbine manufacturer 2012).

An emergent marketquake threatening to undermine the emerging assemblage around wind power development?

It seems, therefore, that China's quest for rapid growth came at the expense of quality (Korsnes 2014:196). Ultimately, the way in which China seemed to have wasted enormous resources mobilised questions about the very nature of Chinese industrial development. Indeed, the diminishing effectiveness of each GW being installed steadily gave credence to the question whether wind power was actually 'sustainable' in comprehensive developmental terms, that is, not only in economic, social, and environmental terms, but also in political and developmental terms of prospects for technological and scientific upgrading and catchup. Soon, market actors, such as wind farm developers, grid companies, and power generating companies, started to doubt the viability of continuing their investments in the emerging Chinese wind power market. Indeed, before allowing further wind power penetration, even grid companies started 'demanding that larger [higher] requirements are put forth, for higher quality' (interview with foreign research institute 2013).

China's 'turbine wave attack' appeared to have come with its own in-built, or self-inflicted, disruptive self-defeating consequences; a Trojan Horse effect, so to speak. Having engaged in market experimentation on a large scale, there seemed to be an imminent threat of a significant (potentially self-undermining) disruption, a volcanic marketquake, which could potentially unravel the entire assemblage. In particular, the 'price' of the marketquake was manifested in terms of the lack of a systemic overview of the integrated nature of wind turbine components and how their optimal design can increase efficiency, output, and assist in alleviating curtailment pressures, giving rise to a qualification crisis.

Phase Three (2012–2018): a flexible potential turn to quality

One might have thought that the quality crisis would entail the beginning of the end of China's wind power adventure. But time and history has proved this wrong. Indeed, the story is alive and well, and arguably in better shape than before. How did China manage to manoeuvre through the quality crisis? Once again, it was through radical government interventions during Phase Three, when the sector was redirected, manoeuvred, and steered back onto a path that, in effect, represents a seemingly determined 'turn to quality', since 'Beijing needs to take control' (Interview with foreign wind turbine manufacturer 2013):

> now they are finally putting in standards and requirements for a higher quality. Standards and requirements for other [things] than just installing gigawatts into the ground. (Interview with foreign wind turbine manufacturer 2013)

And so the third phase has been marked by attempts to fine tune the technology, dealing with risk and uncertainty through enhanced emphasis on R&D and basic research into certification and standardisation, to upgrade core technologies, indigenous design and control, and catch up in algorithmic intelligence. This push for scientific development has been promoted by a variety of new means – policies, plans, standards, targets, and regulations – issued by central government, primarily since 2010–2012 when the quality crisis was largest, instantiating an imminent and potential 'turn to quality' (Kirkegaard 2015). The strengthened focus on quality has since then been reiterated in China's 13th Five-Year-Plan (2016–2020) and the imminent Energy Revolution (2015), where focus is shifted from capacity expansion towards quality and efficiency. Indeed, new winds may be blowing in the world of Chinese wind power. In the following, some of the main interventions are presented, including the introduction of stricter standards and certification requirements; targets for generated electricity; enhanced incentives; centralisation of control and planning; media openness; and upgrading core technologies.

Introduction of standards and certification requirements

In terms of government interventions to requalify wind power as 'reliable' and 'sustainable', one of the first central government actions to raise quality and to address the use of relatively outdated technologies was the introduction of industrial and technical standards. For instance, in early 2010 the Ministry of Industry and Information Technology (MIIT) released a draft circular on Wind Power Equipment Manufacturing Industry Access Standards (Lewis 2013:57). These standards aimed to 'promote the optimization and upgrading of the industrial structure of the wind power equipment manufacturing industry, enhance enterprises' technical innovation, improve product quality, [and] restrict the introduction of redundant technology', and to 'guide the industry's healthy development" (MIIT in Lewis 2013:57). The next action was to qualify those manufacturers who could benefit from the 2011 classification, whereby wind power was listed as an industry under 'encouraged development'. In the Guideline Catalogue for Industrial Restructuring issued by the NDRC, wind power was eligible for preferential treatment, and now these preferential policies were restricted to companies producing wind turbines with a 2.5 MW capacity or higher (Lewis 2013).

According to the People's Daily Online (11 May 2011), these restrictions were predicted to lead to significant changes in the industry, pushing for higher quality and more qualified manufacturers, because as of 2011 no more than ten of China's approximately 80 wind turbine manufacturers were able to meet the certification requirements and new standards. In addition, 18 new technical standards were issued by the NEA (under the auspices of the NDRC), also in 2011, to improve the regulation of technology development in the sector, and to improve grid connection through new grid codes and forecasting systems (Lewis 2013:58, 74). Grid codes ensure that generating equipment such as wind turbines that are connected to the grid operate to a minimum standard and behave so as to help maintain grid stability. An example of this is through the requirement for a so-called low-voltage ride-through (LVRT) technology, which ensures that wind turbines stay connected to the grid without tripping even while the grid experiences short voltage dips (Li 2010:1161). Significantly, China did not have a grid code until 2011 (Basit, Hansen & Margaris 2013). With the myr-iads of new, smaller, and inexperienced wind turbine manufacturers, which had emerged since the Renewable Energy Law in 2005, the stricter stand-ards aimed to 'facilitate consolidation within the country's wind turbine manufacturing sector' (Renewableenergyworld.com 22 September 2011). With further and tighter standards for turbine quality introduced again as recently as October 2014, it is increasingly acknowledged that Chinese wind power is turning its attention away from quantity and towards quality (Bindslev 2014; Elers 2014; interviews; Li 2015).

Targets for generated electricity and means to reduce curtailment

Second, China's plans and policy instruments gradually moved from targets purely focused on capacity installations (GW) towards targets and instru-ments to ensure generated electricity (GWh) and to decrease curtailment. This is, for instance, seen in the introduction of more efficient FITs and supply and demand-related schemes, such as the Wind Power Technology Special Planning (2012) and the Notice on Integrating and Accommodating Wind Power (2013), introduced to overcome quality and curtailment issues. These latter interventions were partly a result of the supply-side and demand-side instruments (the MMAs and PPAs) of Phase Two, which had not con-sidered the hourly generation of electricity, but only encouraged installed capacity (García 2013:132; Lema & Ruby 2007:3888; Liu & Kokko 2010:5524; Wang et al. 2011:146). This had resulted in the poor implementation of pol-icies and lax compliance with requirements for grid connection. Further, as there were no penalties and/or lax enforcement of penalties for lack of implementation, grid companies, provincial governments, and power gen-erating companies seldom implemented these regulations as intended at the local level (Bloomberg 2012; Korsnes 2014; Lema & Ruby 2007:3888), reflecting the fragmented nature of Chinese energy governance.

To overcome these issues, China started to experiment with new means of ensuring both supply and demand for wind power by delegating respon-sibilities to the different actors involved, such as experimentation with a Renewable Portfolio Standard (RPS) around 2011–2012.[7] However, owing to political resistance and vested interests from power companies and grid cor-porations (Bloomberg 2012; interview with think tank 2016), the RPS has still (2018) not been implemented in the version first called for. Later, a draft regulation for Rules on Full Amount Purchase of Renewable Energy (2015) has been circulated to stakeholders for comments, suggesting the obligation of the TSO/grid operator to give renewable energy – both 'mandatorily purchased electricity and market based electricity' – priority access to the grid, and demanding the '"beneficiary' of the curtailment' (coal-fired plants) to compensate the affected wind farm operator (GWEC 2016:34; Song & Hong 2016). To solve the issue of curtailed wind energy, the Chinese government has further thrown 'three punches to tackle the problem' in 2016, for example by putting an emergency ban on new coal power construction, introducing new management rules to guarantee sale of renewable energy generation on the grid, and introducing consumption and generation targets for renewables (China Energy Storage Alliance 2016; Song & Hong 2016). These incentives come together with heavy investment in long-distance high voltage direct current (DC) transmission lines from north to south and east to west and will—alongside the Energy Revolution's competitive markets at wholesale and retail levels and the planned introduction of pilot spot electricity markets by 2019—work to reduce curtailment.

Enhanced support schemes and experimentation with appropriate price and support level

Third, energy pricing and financial support schemes, such as FITs, have been incrementally introduced, adjusted, and fine tuned, gradually covering the cost of wind power more fully, in order to ease the pressure on compromising wind turbine quality.

In Phase Two, during the concession rounds, nobody knew 'what is the reasonable cost for wind, because of the lack of experience by commercial projects' (interview with Chinese government adviser/Chinese wind industry association, 2013). Not knowing the 'appropriate' price or cost, the Chinese government experimented through the concession programme with finding ways to 'bring down the cost of generating wind electricity' (interview with Chinese government adviser and Chinese wind industry association 2013). Using price-setting 'as an experimental point for policy development' (Korsnes 2014:185), however, resulted in wind power prices being too low, and 'even lower than coal', since bidders 'only want to win the bid' (interview with Chinese government adviser and Chinese wind industry association 2013). Through consultations with the Chinese government, Chinese wind power experts eventually 'convince[d] the government [that this was] nonsense' (Interview with Chinese government adviser and Chinese wind industry association 2013), as low prices had led to unprofitable projects and poor-quality turbines. Over time, the Chinese government thus seems to have realised that

> 'it's better not to take the lowest price. Should be the average price, by all offered bidding prices, haha, that way should be better. Better than lower [lowest], but [still] not reasonable' (interview with Chinese government adviser and Chinese wind industry association 2013).

Over time, more criteria have been introduced to ensure quality, for example operational quality-related criteria such as availability rates and penalties for lost production (García 2013; Liao et al. 2010; Zhao et al. 2012a:228). From 2009, a fixed benchmark pricing (FIT) was eventually introduced by the NDRC, guaranteeing a (more) sufficient revenue by introducing a tariff that covered the cost plus a profit margin (Cherni & Kentish 2007; García 2013; Lewis & Wiser 2007; Zhao et al. 2012a:228;), and adjusted in accordance with regional differences in wind resources and engineering construction conditions (García 2013; Korsnes 2014; Wang et al. 2011; Zhao et al. 2012a:228). The FIT directly promotes generation (GWh) and not just installation (GW) for the wind farm's whole lifetime, thus constituting 'a big incentive for developers' to develop efficient wind farms (Interview with Chinese government adviser and wind industry association 2013): Thus, since wind farm developers will now only receive the FIT remuneration when electricity is actually fed into the grid, the FIT scheme in China has been instrumental in alleviating (though not entirely solving) the issue of curtailment and in raising quality. Overall, since the founding years, a host of fiscal and financial aids, preferential pricing policies, and tax rebates, as well as preferential loans, have been introduced to make investment in wind power attractive.

Centralisation of control and planning

The fourth indication that the political priority has changed over time is the oscillating movement between decentralisation and centralisation of approvals of new wind farm projects, since 'they [the Chinese government] said they want to take full control of the market. They don't want to accept this provincial free-riding ... the provincial free markets' (interview with foreign wind turbine manufacturer 2013): As wind turbine production was listed as an 'excess capacity sector' as early as August 2009 by the State Council, the Ministry of Land and Resources soon started to 'deny all applications for new wind turbine manufacturing facilities in an effort to slow down growth in the sector' (Lewis 2013:57). In 2011, the decision-making process was recalled by central government and all wind projects, including those below 50 MW, requiring wind turbine operators to obtain central approval from the NEA under the NDRC (Korsnes 2014; interviews). A Notice on Strengthening the Management of Wind Power Plant Grid Integration and Operation (2011) also required all wind farms to obtain approval from the central NEA in order to receive the FIT subsidy (Lewis 2013:74). As expressed by a foreign expert on wind power in China,

'I guess it was in '11 ... when administration practice was changed from the province approving wind farms below 50 MW ... then they made like a call-in decision, where they at least had to get in hearing at NEA. Above the 50 MW mark, it had been NEA always, which was supposed to approve of quite a lot of them... so they made this, kind of a decision to make a halt' (interview with Chinese think tank 2013).

Overall, the Chinese government seems to have oscillated between what can be termed decentralised fragmentation and centralised authority in order to reach development targets, in alignment with China's fragmented authoritarianism. That is, the decentralisation of authority was beneficial for the period of accelerated growth for the wind industry, while centralisation of authority in 2011 was aimed at slowing growth and consolidating the industry in a period of severe overcapacity (Korsnes 2014:196). This is reflected in how,

> [u]ntil 2011, China's wind industry saw a rapid expansion; yet, since 2011, there has been a slowdown. This slowdown is highly relevant for the governance of the wind sector; as coordination premised its rapid development in 2003, it was also coordination that led the expansion to a halt in 2011, by centralising the approval of new wind farms. (Korsnes 2014:186)

Overall, the Chinese marketisation of wind power development is experiencing alternating waves of consolidation and liberalisation (Jun He Bulletin 2013; Korsnes 2014; Pereira & Puertas 2013; Research Institute of Economy, Trade & Industry 2013).

Media openness

Fifth, the state-controlled media have gradually opened up, as they started to write articles on the quality issues within the Chinese wind power industry. Although the quality problems had emerged prior to the downturn in 2011, stories about them and the poorly functioning turbines were only permitted in the state-controlled Chinese media in 2011 (Korsnes 2014:188–189). Allowing the media to gradually highlight quality issues can be seen as a measure by the Chinese Party-State to steer growth in Chinese wind power, as the largely state-controlled media serve to either legitimise or delegitimise the wind turbine industry (Korsnes 2014:188–189).

Upgrading core technologies

Finally, the State Council and MOST issued the 12th Five-Year Plan for the Scientific and Technological Development of Wind Power in 2012. Although the Medium and Long-Term Plan for Renewable Energies (NDRC 2007) had already emphasised the desire for scientific and technological development of the renewable energy sector, it was only with the 12th Five-Year Plan that a dedicated scheme for the scientific and technological development of wind power was issued. It proclaims as its guiding ideology the Party doctrine of scientific development, and links up to the grand narrative of China's sustainable development towards a Harmonious Socialist Society. Emphasising the need to upgrade Chinese indigenous innovation capabilities within core wind power technologies, core technologies such as control system technologies and simulation tools for design and certification are constituted as critical for success in instigating a turn to quality, and for getting the industry back on track with more of a focus on innovation and quality (MOST 2012, s. 2, 1(2), 4, 2). The plan even goes so far as to problematise China's lack of indigenous intellectual property (IP) in regard to software tools for wind turbine design (MOST, s. 1, IV, 2(1a)), arguing how dependence on foreign design tools has been detrimental to China's capabilities in developing indigenous wind turbine design adapted to Chinese environmental conditions. The plan accordingly emphasises the need to reduce China's dependence on imports of foreign core technologies, such as design tools, as well as promoting the development of indigenous innovation capabilities within specific areas, including control systems, simulation software tools, certification, and standardisation, as well as furthering China's independent innovation through basic research into mathematics and aerodynamics and improving its wind power standardisation, testing, and certification system (MOST 2012, s. 2, 1(1), 2, 1(3), 2, 1(4)). With this, the plan is laid out for transforming China from a large wind power nation into a strong wind power nation, in order to ensure the healthy and sustainable development of the wind power industry.

Consolidating the wind turbine industry

The quality crisis and subsequent turn to quality—and subsequent industrial consolidation—were soon reflected in industry statistics. These had started to show falling rates in annual installed capacity, as depicted in Figure 4.4, in particular around 2010–2012 as the quality crisis hit.[8]

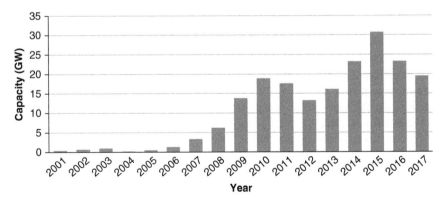

Figure 4.4 Annual installation capacities in China.

Source: GWEC 2015, 2016, 2017a, 2017b.

The oscillations in installations rates should be seen in a context of the quality crisis and turn to quality, but also in the broader global perspective, as much of these developments coincide with the global financial crisis that hit the world in 2008, and the Chinese response to this, that is, its economic stimulus package.

First, we see a big surge in wind power installations (and thus wind power investments) from 2008-2010. China's recovery from the global economic financial crisis was much faster than that of the rest of the world, largely owing to the Chinese government's resolute introduction of an economic stimulus package, which revived the economy through increased credit flow and investment in local projects, producing an increase in activity in the real (manufacturing) economy (Fewsmith 2010; Naughton 2010), such as wind power. Indeed, and somewhat paradoxically, it may hereby be argued that the stimulus package in response to the global financial coproduced the surge in wind power investments (along with other already described policy interventions), as well as coproduced the quality crisis in Chinese wind power.

The later dip in installations (around years 2010-2012) may in turn be attributed to the aftermath of the global financial crisis and inability to overcome this through the stimulus package. However, there are other more relevant reasons: first, a credit squeeze initiated by Chinese state-owned banks due to over-capacity issues following the marketquake and quality crisis contributed to industry consolidation (for more on this, refer to Chapter Six). Another possible reason for the decrease in installation rates was the reported poor administration and effectiveness of China's Renewable Energy Fund, which was introduced in the Renewable Energy Law and was supposed to cover the additional costs of wind power through a FIT subsidy, but was marked by delays (Qi 2013; interviews). Last, skewed competition between coal and wind for sufficient subsidies by means of electricity tariffs contributed to the dip (Ecobusiness 2014) as well as did the knock-on effect of the quality crisis and subsequent turn to quality: That is, the quality crisis impacted the level of investment, because '[t]he domestic manufacturing quality and unprofessional design of wind farms made most developers' financial returns unrealistic in the wind market' (Yu et al. 2009:5221), decreasing their interest in wind power investments (interviews). In other words, the quality crisis made the economisation of wind power development less attractive for investors, threatening the sector's marketisation. At the same time, the subsequent stricter requirements introduced by central government during the turn to quality – along with the credit squeeze - such as access standards, stricter control with wind farm planning and development at central level led to a consolidation of the entire industry, which soon stalled growth rates in the government-induced 'turn to quality'.

Overall, the installation rates fluctuate along with oscillating movements between decentralised and centralised control, marking how '[f]ragmentation in China's energy governance has allowed for a fast-growing wind turbine market' (Korsnes 2014:196). In other words, '[t]he government is indeed flexing all the muscles in its institutional body in order to navigate the development' (Korsnes 2014:196).

As China attempts to requalify wind power as sustainable in comprehensive terms by steering it towards quality, China may be argued to be moving from upscaling (through downgrading) to upgrading (through quality). Meanwhile, in doing so, it will undoubtedly redefine its relations with foreign companies, so much so that it has the potential to produce a path towards yet another (unintended) tipping point, if an attentive and pragmatic course is not steered.

Emerging Chinese Dragon multinationals in wind power

Despite – and because of – these dramatic developments, over time, Chinese wind turbine manufacturers and component suppliers have rapidly upgraded their capabilities with impressive pace. This has in particular been urged through the turn to quality. And so, within less than ten years, China has been able to move

> from having no turbine manufacturing experience to having the ability to manufacture complete, state-of-the-art wind turbine systems that are either already available or soon to be available on the global market. (Lewis 2013:166)

Assisted by consultancy companies, design houses, certification bodies, industry associations, and increasingly also service companies that support operations and maintenance, several Chinese wind turbine manufacturers have realised a series of rapid technological advances, such as producing larger turbines with higher capacities (up to 5 MW is now not uncommon) and variable speed, versions specifically for offshore installation, and also a host of patent applications (Klagge et al. 2012; Korsnes 2015; Lewis 2013; Ru et al. 2012). Further, the grid connection issues have forced market actors to develop new tools, resulting in an increasing stream of technological innovation coming from Chinese wind turbine manufacturers. Upgrading is also reflected, for example, in increased Chinese exports (though these are still relatively meagre), Chinese M&As of Western design firms, outward FDI (e.g. establishing innovation centres abroad), collaborative design and co-development programmes, and participation in the definition of standards (Silva & Klagge 2013:1353). By tapping into foreign resources, integrating into the emerging GINs in the wind turbine industry (Lewis 2013; Silva & Klagge 2013), Chinese wind turbine manufacturers have become what may be termed active 'system coplayers', or what Mathews (2016) and Mathews and Tan (2015) term 'Dragon Multi-Nationals'. And so 'China has been building a strong national wind turbine manufacturing capacity, alongside its buildup of wind farms. By the year 2015 there were five Chinese firms in the world's top ten wind turbine producers, with Goldwind emerging for the first time as the world's number #1 producer' (Mathews 2016:7).

The case of Goldwind is a particularly good example of the emergence of mutual learning through partnerships on an increasingly equal basis: In 2003, Goldwind engaged in a new design licensing agreement with the German wind turbine design company Vensys Energiesystems GmbH for a Vensys (direct-drive) 1.2 MW turbine (Lewis 2013). Following this collaboration in 2008, Goldwind acquired a 70 per cent direct stake in Vensys Energy (Klagge et al. 2012; Lewis 2013). In so doing, the company began to jointly develop several new wind turbine designs in partnership with Vensys (Lewis 2013). Further, Goldwind now has R&D facilities in both China and Germany and has built R&D capacity through collaborations with certification bodies, design houses, and universities in China and overseas (interviews 2011, 2012; Lewis 2013), and has engaged in a joint venture with Apple to supply clean energy to Apple's Chinese production partners (Ng 2016).[9] Another remarkable success story of rapid catch-up through the acquisition of innovation capabilities is the Chinese wind turbine manufacturer Envision, which was established in 2006 and has hired Western staff with expertise in wind power technology and software with the intention to focus on innovation, quality, and innovative software interfaces, in particular to ease the control of wind power development and integration for China's largely inexperienced wind farm developers. Envision has now established a Global Innovation Centre in Denmark, working on developing a two-bladed wind turbine, amongst other things (Envision.com, n.d.; interviews 2012, 2013).

Phase Three: advancing towards a new potential tipping point in the current turn to quality?

As China upgrades and catches up, Sino-foreign relations in the wind turbine industry are being reshuffled once more.

The turn to quality and the new capabilities of Chinese actors may produce possibilities for more mutual learning. In addition, with the introduction of more incentives to ensure the generation of electricity (GWh), a more equal playing field has emerged, which may eventually place foreign 'players into the same competitive space as the Chinese' (interview with foreign wind turbine manufacturer 2013), making foreign manufacturers more hopeful 'because all the value propositions that [a foreign wind turbine manufacturer] has can suddenly come back into play' (interview with foreign wind turbine manufacturer 2013). A collaborative space for common research, where 'both sides can win', is therefore potentially under construction, for instance in a mutual struggle to reducing the costs of energy to make wind power 'competitive' in the battle with fossil fuels (interview with foreign wind turbine manufacturer 2013).

Conversely, the strengthened ambitions and capabilities of the Chinese may induce more volatile Sino-foreign supply chain relations around core technologies, as a competitive arena is construed – in particular around software algorithms – making them highly political in a Chinese context.

When it comes to the more advanced and core designs and components, it is still often argued that Chinese wind turbine manufacturers lag behind (Klagge et al. 2012; Li 2010:1161). Even though several of them increasingly claim their designs are indigenously developed, according to foreign wind power experts (engineers and scientists), as well as several Chinese experts and industry actors, these designs often still rely on foreign core components, particularly critical control and design software tools (interviews). According to a foreign expert on wind turbine standardisation and certification in 2013, and in stark contrast to the official claims from China, 'there is [was] still not one single, completely Chinese indigenous design' (interview with foreign design house 2013).

Evidently, there are differing viewpoints on this issue, and it is worthy of further exploration in the following controversy studies. The same issue is raised as a matter of concern in various Chinese plans and policies, which problematise China's laggard status. For instance, China's Energy Policy (2012) problematises China's 'flimsy basis for independent innovation, backwardness in core technology, and dependence on imports for some key technologies and equipment' (The Information Office of the State Council 2012, s. VII, Accelerating Progress of Energy Technology). In turn, the 12th Five-Year-Plan for the Scientific and Technological Development of Wind Power (MOST & State Council 2012) construes China as a laggard in areas such as siting and design, intelligent forecasting systems, control and regulation, simulation software, and testing and standardisation. Moreover, China's weak background in independent innovation and core technologies combined with its historical dependence on key foreign technologies and equipment becomes a real matter of concern not only for wind power but also for China's sustainable scientific development. Along the same lines, the Medium- to Long-Term Plan for Science and Technology (2006–2020) raises as a matter of concern the strengthening of China's 'indigenous innovation capability, master core technologies in some critical areas, own proprietary intellectual property rights, and build a number of internationally competitive enterprises', in particular because 'core technologies cannot be purchased' (MOST 2006, s. II(1)). The above reveals how a competitive space is being constructed between Chinese and foreign actors, currently entangled in a highly politicised space.

Core technologies in the midst of the battle

This competitive race in today's wind turbine industry has become all the more challenging, however, as the global industry has reached a stage of relative maturity and technological refinement. Over time, wind turbine designs have become increasingly complex. If one is to be able to compete in the global market, this means that it is no longer sufficient just to assemble components without the systemic overview of the optimal way in which the components operate together. At the same time, this very design complexity has largely become invisible, or hidden, to the outsider's eye. Indeed, the keys to a modern turbine's competitive design lie hidden in software codes, algorithms, and in calculations performed by software simulations, most of them proprietary and locked behind IPRs and encrypted technical locks. Further key aspects are inherent in the quality definitions of international standards. Thus, the spotlight of international competition has fallen upon these core technologies, constituting algorithmic quality: wind turbine control systems, wind farm control systems, simulation tools for advanced designs, and other intelligent algorithmic tools such as for wind forecasting. In other words, as wind turbines have become increasingly intelligent or computer controlled, the R&D for modern wind turbines has been 'focused on continued design improvements to increase the resilience and the efficiency of the turbines, as well as on improved power electronics that facilitate smoother integration with the power grid' (Lewis 2013:28). Or, as expressed by a wind turbine engineer (aerodynamicist):

> there are two ways to differentiate your company and technology, that is, through the blades [i.e. aeroelastic codes in the blade simulation tools] and the main control algorithm. (Interview with foreign research institute 2012)

Indeed, a competitive game is constructed around the ability to tame the potentially disruptive forces of the wind through algorithms. This is highlighted in the current turn to quality, where Chinese wind turbine manufacturers have increasingly realised the need to buy or develop proper algorithmic quality components indigenously. Paradoxically, China's current turn to quality may bear within it the seeds of a self-undermining disruption and stalemate. That is, whilst it is still reliant on the close interaction between Chinese and foreign actors, on Sino-foreign joint development or cooperative R&D programmes, and on technology and knowledge transfer in particular in regard to core technologies, China's aim to free itself from dependence on others may destabilise the very Sino-foreign collaborative relations on which it still relies, creating volatile dynamics of simultaneous collaboration and competition.

How these dynamics play out, as the roles and positions are continuously shifting, negotiated, and contested along with China's increasing indigenous capabilities, is likely to have a significant impact not only on China's turn to quality and the configuration of the emerging socio-technical assemblage around wind power development, but also on China's potential green rise. Indeed, whilst there is potential for mutual learning and upgrading, China may – again – risk pushing development to the brink of a new self-inflicted tipping point. Nothing can yet be said for certain about the outcome of this, but by enquiring into how these relations are currently playing out can help shed light on some of the inherent dynamics and controversies over China's green rise, and the inherent power struggles as China emerges as a global green leader.

Opening the blackbox of the wind turbine

Summing up, while it seems that China has been able to steer the wind turbine industry away from a self-disruptive quality crisis that threatened to
destabilise the emerging assemblage around wind power development in
Phase Two, the current turn to quality in Phase Three has the potential to
tip over into self-inflicted disruption and stalemate as trials of strength over
access to 'critical' core technologies may disrupt the fragile Sino-foreign
competitive–collaborative supply chain relations on which the Chinese
wind power sector still relies. Therefore, all three phases have seen the system nudging towards the tipping point of collapse:

- First, there was extensive dependence of Chinese assembly companies
  on foreign suppliers owing to the lack of a domestic supply chain and
  the legacy of technology transfer in Phase One;
- Second, a Chinese quality crisis was born out of an incessant focus on
  installation rate and scale – the marketquake – rather than ensuring the
  quality of installations. This took place in Phase Two, leading to a quality crisis that threatened to unsettle the entire marketisation process;
- Third, potentially disruptive power struggles between Chinese and foreign players are taking place during the current turn to quality in Phase
  Three, as core technologies such as control and design software tools
  have been constituted as critical to frame wind power as sustainable.

(Refer to Table 4.1 where the three phases are summarised.)

To understand these intertwined phases, and the underlying rationale for
China's fragmented mode of governing the emerging socio-technical assemblage around wind power development, it requires an appreciation of the
socio-material nature of this area. That is, we need to open the blackbox
of the wind turbine and encompassing power grid to understand how the
current turn to quality has taken place along with a gradual realisation of
the socio-technical work and intricate algorithmic interdependencies that
are entailed in developing a wind turbine that can perform according to
international standards and without disrupting the power grid.

In the first two phases of wind power development marketisation in China,
the wind turbine was still treated largely as a blackbox. However, reliance
on foreign core component suppliers along with a lack of experience with
and insight into the socio-technical assemblage of the object of exchange
produced a variety of quality issues over time. Not only that, the quality
issues have threatened to destabilise the framing of China's wind power sector as 'sustainable' in Chinese comprehensive developmental terms. In turn,
Chinese market actors have increasingly come to realise the socio-material
nature of wind power and wind turbines and the various calculative tools
required to convert the wind into a valued and marketable investment
object. A central part of this realisation has been pushed by elements of

Table 4.1 Main traits of three phases of Chinese wind power development

	1980s–2002	2003–2011	2012–now
Phase	1	2	3
Characteristics	Fragmented unconcerted experimentation	Concerted development, but fragmented, decentralised coordination and planning	Consolidation and centralising control, 'turn to quality'
Accomplishments: Catch-up & upscaling/upgrading Balancing at the brink of collapse/overflowing	Attraction of FDI, foreign technology competencies Dependence on foreign expensive component technologies and turbine designs, 'assembly-companies'	Foundation of domestic industrial base and supply chain 'Quality crisis' from: • Targets for installed capacity • Price- and scale focus • Lack of certification requirements • LEGO-approach and dependence on foreign core technologies • Fragmented uncoordinated planning	Development of R&D and certification capabilities Fragility of Sino-foreign business relations around core technologies potentially undermining emerging learning networks
Radical government interventions	(Ride the Wind Programme, Program 861)	⇒ Power sector reform ⇒ Concession programme ⇒ Renewable Energy Law ⇒ Medium- to Long-Term Plan for Scientific & Technological Development (2006-2020)	⇒ Potential turn to quality through 1. GWh measures 2. standards and certification 3. pricing and support mechanisms 4. centralisation of planning 5. media 6. focus on indigenous innovation in core technologies, particularly software

Wind's qualification	Wind qualified as a matter of industrial policy; technology-for-market	Wind qualified as a matter of upscaling; industrial policy	Wind qualified as a matter of upgrading potential – wind needs to be qualified as sustainable through scientific development
Sino-foreign supply-chain relations	Attraction of foreign companies; joint ventures; localisation policies (e.g. local content requirements)	Localisation and preference of Chinese companies in tenders; Chinese assembly/LEGO-companies still dependent on foreign companies' core technologies	Chinese new wind turbine manufacturers with increasing design capabilities; fragile competitive-collaborative customer-supplier relations around core technologies
Industrial/technological development	Actors relatively fragmented, technology functional but basic	Increasing interdependencies of technology but also between actors	Fine-tuning and dealing with risk through science and technology; emphasis on certification, standardisation, and algorithms

aeroelasticity, mathematics, software, and other core technologies that have eventually objected to their neglect by claiming their own importance, for instance by producing underperforming turbines or overflowing into curtailed wind power. Indeed, the marketisation of wind power development is inherently linked to the economisation and politicisation of wind power, but also to scientification processes. What is witnessed is basically an emerging struggle to control and gain power over the risk and uncertainty of the stochastically fluctuating wind power through algorithms and other means.

The (c)overt industry agenda – and uncovering the Chinese 'laboratory'

The gradual realisation of the socio-technical nature of wind power has been part of a learning trajectory that, despite the extensive overflowing, has served the shifting agenda of the Chinese government well. That is, Chinese wind power development marketisation has been marked by many different, shifting, and sometimes colliding agendas along the way:

> Wind power development – that was industrial policy. In the beginning, it was about building an industry, and then within a number of years, China was meant to become competitive. Chinese industry experts were predicting that, within a certain number of years, based on the industrial base, China would be able to produce quality wind turbines. But quality was not the first step. That was not the important thing in the beginning. The most important was to make the industry try … to let them try out producing turbines. And then see if any turbines could come out of that, and find out who were getting good at it, while giving a lot of financial support at the same time. (interview with foreign research institute 2013)

The initial phase was thus a matter of letting the industry try things out, allowing 'a hundred flowers to bloom' (interview 2011),[10] this being made possible through China's 'entirely different [large] budget' than elsewhere – whilst intending that a maximum of a handful Chinese wind turbine manufacturers would survive in the long run. Indeed, it is argued that the overall intention was to only let a handful of wind turbine manufacturers survive in the long run. Accordingly, the Chinese government later 'close[d] the gate, then they impose stricter requirements, and then they are sorting out [the poor wind turbine manufacturers from the good ones]' (interview with foreign research institute 2013). This indicates a Chinese pragmatics of fragmented experimental marketisation in wind power development. Enabled by a Chinese political leadership that has been able to identify new relevant areas that are 'not really well developed', such as wind power, and to identify areas 'where we can become leaders', China has engaged in experimental and distributed agency of Chinese 'crowd-sourcing 2.0', so to speak, that could only have happened with the immense pools of state capital investment that only China can muster (interview with foreign control system supplier 2013). Meanwhile, the repeated advances that push the system towards the brink of self-inflicted disruption and potential stalemate indicate the delicate balancing act that the Chinese state has so far managed, muddling through with industrial development in Chinese wind power. Overall, and as will be further elaborated below, it seems that China has managed to develop a green industry through and in spite of the policy of permitting the onset of instability. This was expressed by a foreign wind turbine manufacturer:

> one of the things I've learned by studying China the last ten years is never to underestimate the capability of a Chinese company to learn from mistakes and move fast. I see them definitely being able to come up to world class level in the next three to five years. (Interview with foreign wind turbine manufacturer 2013)

And so the present study of marketisation becomes a laboratory study in its very own right: Chinese marketisation in wind power development seems one of the fastest and largest (laboratory) experiments with marketisation in history, as it has happened with unprecedented pace and scale, but also with repeated oscillating movements and space for extensive and unprecedented overflowing.

Reflections on the first site of controversy: the qualification struggle and marketisation through the interaction of oscillating waves

The site of controversy investigated here is one of the overarching qualification struggles in China's wind power development marketisation as the sustainability of wind power development in China is debated. We have moved alongside the wind turbine's generator, the component where the proper interaction of electromagnetic fields is crucial to producing the desired output power. In so doing, we have examined the disruptive interaction of the electromagnetic waves of China's three-phase wind power development trajectory. Now it is time to look closer at this potentially particular Chinese mode of 'marketisation at the brink of collapse', returning to the metaphor of electromagnetic waves, not to detect a certain 'general law' of (Chinese) marketisation, but rather to help detect and shed light on particular trends and potential particularities of Chinese wind power development marketisation.

Electromagnetic waves in Chinese wind power development marketisation

A wave-like oscillating movement has been evident in the above historical outline, one that swings between decentralised fragmentation and coordinated centralised planning, and between explosive growth and step-by-step trial and error.

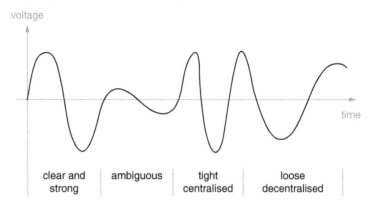

voltage

time

| clear and strong | ambiguous | tight centralised | loose decentralised |

Figure 4.5 Examples of various system frequency signals.

Metaphorically speaking, the Chinese Party-State seems to have issued a system frequency signal, a wave that sets the scene for wind power development at the onset of each phase; sometimes clear and strong, sometimes ambiguous and uncertain, but normally expressed through grand imaginary visions and ambiguous means of implementation (see Figure 4.5). This has, for example, been seen with the Renewable Energy Law, the introduction of support schemes, targets for installed power, and discourses and narratives on China's vision of a Harmonious Socialist Society through scientific development.

Thus, the Chinese socio-technical assemblage for wind power development has been mobilised through the government's mobilisation of a 'matter of concern' for the country's sustainable and scientific development, first with a focus to establish an industrial base, and later with a focus on the need 'to consolidate and to transition towards quality' (interview with foreign research institute 2013). Meanwhile, the 'system frequency signal' has varied in strength from loose decentralised control to tight centralised regulation (as indicated in Figure 4.5), indicating China's fragmented authoritarian and experimental system. As decentralisation has brought with it a plethora of uncoordinated experimentation, it has at times tipped towards potential stalemate/impasse. Repeatedly, the Chinese State has engaged in astute intervention just at the edge of destruction, harvesting the synergistic effects and leapfrogging possibilities for disruptive catch-up and upgrading. The combining of these uncoordinated waves of pragmatic experimentalism illustrates the latent danger: it carries with it the risk of constructive interference oscillating out of control on the one hand, and destructive interference leading to stalemate and impasse on the other.

Meanwhile, to understand this process through the metaphor we must take a deeper look. In any electrical system, there will be various pieces of equipment and loads that generate different electromagnetic waveforms, and these waveforms intersect and combine in the system. If the waveforms are significantly different, then the resultant wave can be distorted and can potentially cause disruption to the system.

The metaphor sees the local authorities and wind power companies as generating these various waveforms. The rapid mobilisation of an emerging socio-technical assemblage around wind power development is therefore not just the result of top-down master discourses and policies (i.e. not just the 'system frequency signal'). Rather, it is a result of constant 'alignment of expectations, and visions of incumbent and upcoming actors' (Korsnes 2014:196), which have been mutually and flexibly realigned to emergent situations. It is the interpretation of the national plans and policies at the local level that gives rise to the various uncoordinated forms of pragmatic experimentalism in the development of wind power, giving room and space for local 'free market' forces, as most evident in the 'turbine wave attack', which almost seems like an attempt at allowing some imagined invisible hand of the market to let heterogeneous actors co-create a new industry. Indeed, this may seem to be a specifically Chinese mode of free market – whilst still ultimately under control, 'guided by intentional anticipation' (Heilmann 2008:18), whereby the Chinese government sets in motion processes that lead to much more profound change than originally envisioned (Wedeman 2011:69, 88). In this way, Chinese structured uncertainty (Breznitz & Murphree 2011) and fragmented 'decentralised experimentation' can give room to learning through direct practical experience (Heilmann 2008:2, 19). The result is a 'volatile yet productive combination of decentralized experimentation with ad hoc central interference, resulting in the selective integration of local experiences into national policy-making' (Heilmann 2008:29). These waves of local experimentalism of different heights (amplitude) and period (frequency) may intersect and combine to produce a resulting wave that shows progress and development, although the individual waves can no longer be discerned or disentangled (see Figure 4.6). As long as the individual waves are not too excessive then the system can cope and absorb the anomalies of their combination.

As the underlying fragmented and uncoordinated local activities may continue and tend to increase in intensity and diversity, however, there may be a risk that they 'go overboard' through excessive experimentalism that produces (un)intended externalities, potentially to a degree of destabilisation and self-disruption. Metaphorically, the waves of experimentation increase in amplitude, change frequency, and maybe even alter wave shape. The resulting combination of these waves now approaches the system resonant frequency (see Figure 4.7) with the risk that they now drive the system – such that the rapidly developing oscillations threaten to destabilise and disrupt the system to the point of destruction. They overflow.

At the same time, though, the accumulation of fragmented local activities may instead start to be counter-productive and lead to a potential stalemate. Metaphorically speaking, the waves shift phase and amplitude and suddenly, instead of interfering positively, they interfere negatively and begin

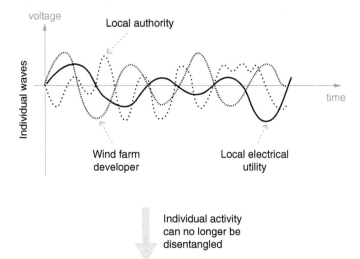

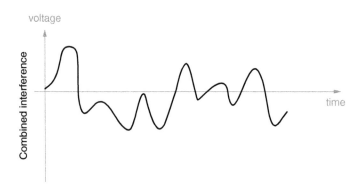

Figure 4.6 When individual waves interfere and combine.

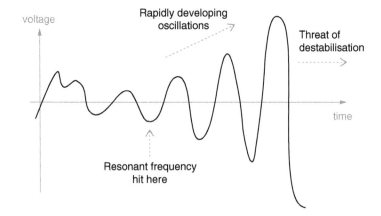

Figure 4.7 The risk of system destabilisation and overflowing.

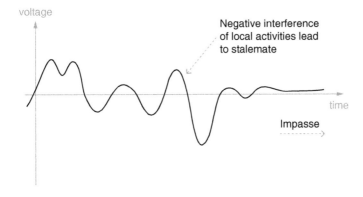

Figure 4.8 The risk of stalemate and impasse.

to cancel each other out (Figure 4.8). Development stalls, a barrier begins to be formed, and progress flounders. The excessive pragmatic experimentalism that has been allowed to continue has thus pushed the system towards instability of its own making. It stands now at the brink of self-inflicted disruption and stalemate. A delicate tipping point has been reached and the situation is finely balanced: one way and the system is driven out of control, and the other way the system stalls.

It is now, at the very brink of loss of control and potential disruption of impasse – but not before and not after – that the Chinese government may intervene to introduce changes to the system properties so that, metaphorically, its resonant frequency is altered and the waves of pragmatic experimentalism now combine so as to interfere constructively, thereby restoring stability (see Figure 4.9). It requires swift and agile action to do this, and at the right time – not too early or too late – otherwise there is a risk of contributing to the increasing growth of the oscillations, leading to further destructive interference and system collapse.

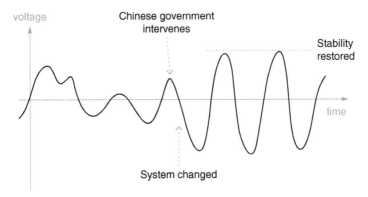

Figure 4.9 Radical and timely government intervention temporarily restores system stability.

It is in this way that the metaphor reflects the delicate balancing act that the Chinese Party-State faces in steering the development of new green industries through fragmented authoritarianism. The maximum learning is achieved when the 'mistakes' and 'failures' combine and threaten stability – that is, knowing when to refrain from intervention, and when radical intervention is timely: it is here where the best opportunities for learning and innovation are created. Looking at innovation as distributed amongst heterogeneous actors (such as in the 'turbine wave attack' strategy), with emergent agency, the 'mistakes' are not collective 'mistakes' but deliberately permitted collective experiments that open up for accelerated learning. As long as the intervention is swift and well timed, the ultimate destructive interference (collapse) is avoided. When succeeding in handling emergent 'crises' flexibly and agilely, the resulting combined wave amplitude – representing wind power development now at a higher level than before – shows how the potentially destructive goal of hitting the resonant frequency can lead to rapid learning and upgrading if flexibly governed. The volatile disruptions can lead to something constructive and positive. This provides a story of the paradoxical dynamics of Chinese experimental and fragmented marketisation. But the gamble is that the opposite may happen as well. It is a story of potentiality, ambiguity, and great volatility.

Whilst the self-inflicted quality crisis in Chinese wind power development marketisation was largely induced by a radical lack of government intervention, the government stepped in just in time, it seems, instigating radical change that could steer the turbine industry back towards a more sustainable path. These 'navigational skills' of the Chinese government (Korsnes 2014:196) have resulted in new learning, fine-tuning of policies and legislative measures, as well as price-setting and support levels. In the process, roles and positions, but also goals, have been redefined.

Potential particularities of Chinese wind power development marketisation

In sum, in the case of wind power development, China so far seems to be succeeding in marketisation through a pragmatic allowance of experimentalism, or through a distinctively Chinese mode of marketisation by pushing the system to the brink of disruption and impasse. Recalling the statement of a long-term expert on wind power in China (2013), it is the 'Chinese way' to learn from practice rather 'than learn from the theory or learn from imagination', which implies that China has been 'facing this problem [e.g. of curtailment], so it will force us to have the solutions. This is good' (interview with Chinese government advisor and wind industry association 2013). Meanwhile, others contest this positive framing of fragmentation, arguing that a lack of coordination is 'one of the main problems for China [...] That it's uncoordinated, what's going on, in relation to how much is actually happening' (interview with Chinese think tank 2013). Pace and scale in China makes the lack of 'a streamlined, coordinated planning' system (interview with Chinese think tank 2013) an overly critical and persistent issue.

In this way, the 'sustainability' of such fragmented and experimental pragmatics in mobilising a socio-technical assemblage around wind power development is being negotiated and contested. This fragmentation, along with the power sector's and wind power's 'political' constitution, renders Chinese wind power development marketisation with a specific flavour unique to China that will be explored in the next chapters. Indeed, in Chapter Five, a controversy is mapped over the contested access to the grid between wind and coal power, as curtailment and poor coordination in the power sector have adversely affected wind power's reputation. And so, getting out of the generator, leaving the three-phase electromagnetic field, an overarching controversy over the qualification struggle in Chinese wind power development has been traced, laying the foundation for the following four controversy studies that zoom in on different aspects of this qualification struggle. It is time to let the journey through the wind turbine continue.

Notes

1. Kirkegaard (2015, 2017) has made a temporal division of wind power development into three phases, namely phase one from the late 1980s to 2002 (the ascendance of China's OEMs, the second phase from 2003 to 2011 as the 'turbine wave attack' unfolded, and the third phase from 2012 as the flexible 'turn to quality' potentially occurs. This is the time division that this book is based on. With some similar findings, Li (2015) has made a temporal division of wind power development in China into an experimental phase (2000–2005), the take-off phase (2006–2010), and from quantity growth to quality growth (2011–present). Other previous studies have also referred to specific phases in China's wind turbine industry (e.g. Lema & Ruby 2007).
2. Joint ventures were the only way to enter the Chinese market, but from 2005 foreign wind turbine manufacturers started to establish wholly foreign owned enterprises (WFOEs) in China (Zhao et al. 2012b).
3. Xinjiang Goldwind Science & Technology and previously Xinjiang Wind Energy Company (XWEC).
4. For instance, as expressed in China's Medium and Long Term Development Plan for Science and Technology 2006–2020, '[i]ndigenous innovation refers to enhancing original innovation, integrated innovation, and re-innovation based on assimilation and absorption of imported technology, in order to improve our national innovation capability' (MOST 2006, s. II,1).
5. Windey has already a history of about 40 years and is thus one of the earliest Chinese wind turbine manufacturers, along with Goldwind. Along with Goldwind, Windey has had a comparably higher focus on R&D compared with most other Chinese wind turbine manufacturers (hereunder into control systems), but Windey remains smaller than Goldwind and some of China's newer wind turbine manufacturing companies.
6. Whilst Chinese SOEs were able to bid lowest and compete against foreign companies, often the actual price and cost level would be negotiated and settled afterwards, rendering the official bids rather a way to get a chair at the negotiation table (personal communication 2017).

7. In December 2012, a draft RPS was released by the Chinese NEA under the NDRC, with the aim to ensure that grid companies, generating companies, and provinces fulfil their obligations to generate, distribute, transmit, and buy the wind power generated (Bloomberg 2012; García 2013). The RPS thus specifically aimed at ensuring actual wind power generation, instead of 'boost[ing] project development further, but instead improve grid connection' (Bloomberg 2012). This was supposed to take place through the use of Renewable Energy Credits (REC) for generating electricity rather than just installing capacity.
8. As can be noted, a new oscillating wave, that is, a drop downwards, in annual installed capacity can be noted also in the years 2016 and 2017, which has been attributed to investment uncertainty owing to a planned discontinuation of the current support scheme, the FIT.
9. Goldwind's wholly owned subsidiary Beijing Tianrun New Energy Investment Co.
10. Originally, 'The Hundred Flowers Campaign' refers to Mao's policy of letting a hundred flowers bloom and the 'Hundred Flowers Movement' (1956–1957). During this period, the CPC encouraged its citizens to openly express their opinions of the Communist regime. However, after this brief period of liberalisation, Mao used this to oppress those who challenged the Communist regime by using force.

References

Andrews-Speed, P., 2012, *The Governance of Energy in China. Transition to a Low-Carbon Economy*, Palgrave Macmillan, Basingstoke.

Andersen, P. H. & Drejer, I., 2008, 'Systemic Innovation in a Distributed Network', *Strategic Organization* 6, 13–46.

Basit, A., Hansen, A. D. & Margaris, I. D., 2013, 'A Review of Grid Requirements for Wind Farm in Denmark and China', Technical University of Denmark.

Bergek, A., Jacobsson, S., Carlsson, B., Lindmark, S. & Rickne, A., 2008, 'Analyzing the Functional Dynamics of Technological Innovation Systems: A Scheme of Analysis', *Research Policy* 37, 407–429, doi:10.1016/j.respol.2007.12.003.

Bindslev, J. C., 2014, 'Nye skrappe møllekrav guld værd for Vestas i Kina' [New rigid turbine requirements are worth gold for Vestas in China], *Børsen*, 20 October, viewed 23 October 2014, http://borsen.dk/nyheder/virksomheder/artikel/1/292844/nye_skrappe_moellekrav_guld_vaerd_for_vestas_i_kina.html#ixzz3GrHK1ZmV.

Bloomberg New Energy Finance, 2012, 'Will China's New Renewable Portfolio Standard Boost Project Development?', *Renewable Energy: Research Note*, 11 May.

Breznitz, D. & Murphree, M., 2011, *Run of the Red Queen: Government, Innovation, Globalization, and Economic Growth in China*, Yale University Press, New Haven, CT.

Chen, Y., Rong, K., Xue, L. & Luo, L., 2014, 'Evolution of Collaborative Innovation Network in China's Wind Turbine Manufacturing Industry', *International Journal of Technology Management*, 65(1/2/3/4), 262–299.

Cherni, J. A. & Kentish, J., 2007, 'Renewable Energy Policy and Electricity Market Reforms in China', *Energy Policy* 35, 3616–3629.

China Energy Storage Alliance (CNESA), 2016, 'China Announces Renewables Quota, But is it Enough?', 8 March, http://en.cnesa.org/featured-stories/2016/3/8/china-renewables-quota.

People's Daily Online, 2011. 'China Fine-Tunes Wind Turbine Industry with New Guidelines', 11 May, http://english.peopledaily.com.cn/90001/90778/90857/7376036.html.

Delman, J., 2005, 'China's Party-State and the Private Business Sector: "Dog Wags Tail" or "Tail Wags Dog"?', *Norsk Geografisk Tidsskrift – Norwegian Journal of Geography* 59(3), 207–216.

EcoBusiness, 22 January 2014, 'China's Wind Power Sector Foresees a Recovery in 2014', viewed 30 January 2014, http://www.eco-business.com/news/chinas-wind-power-sector-foresees-recovery-2014/.

Elers, P., 2014, 'I Kina blæser der nye vinde' [In China new winds are blowing], *Børsen*, 19 September 2014, viewed 23 October 2014 http://borsen.dk/nyheder/avisen/artikel/11/93281/artikel.html#ixzz3GrFjXoDt.

Envision.com, n.d., *Envision*, http://www.envision-energy.com/wp-content/uploads/2017/12/Envision-Corporate.pdf.

Fang, Y., Li, J. & Wang, M., 2012, 'Development Policy for Non-Grid-Connected Wind Power in China: An Analysis Based on Institutional Change', *Energy Policy* 45, 350–358.

Fewsmith, J. (ed.), 2010, *China Today, China Tomorrow. Domestic Politics, Economy, and Society*, Rowman & Littlefield Publishers, Plymouth.

Garud, R. B. & Karnøe, P., 2003, 'Bricolage versus Breakthrough: Distributed and Embedded Agency in Technology Entrepreneurship', *Research Policy* 32, 277–300.

Gosens, J. & Lu, Y., 2013, 'From Lagging to Leading? Technological Innovation Systems in Emerging Economies and the Case of Chinese Wind Power', *Energy Policy* 60, 234–250.

Gosens, J. & Lu, Y., 2014, 'Prospects for Global Market Expansion of China's Wind Turbine Manufacturing Industry', *Energy Policy* 67, 301–318.

GWEC, 2011, 'Global Wind Report – Annual Market Update 2011', *Global Wind Energy Council*.

GWEC, 2016, 'Global Wind Energy Outlook 2016', *Global Wind Energy Council*.

GWEC 2017a, 'Global Wind Report – Annual Market Update 2016', *Global Wind Energy Council*.

GWEC 2017b, 'Global Wind Statistics 2017', 14 February 2017.

GWEC 2018, 'Global Wind Report – Annual Market Update 2017', *Global Wind Energy Council*.

Hansen, A. D., Iov, F., Blaabjerg, F. & Hansen, L. H., 2004, 'Review of Contemporary Wind Turbine Concepts and their Market Penetration', *Wind Engineering* 3, 247–263.

Haakonsson, S. & Kirkegaard, J. K., 2016, 'Configuration of Technology Networks in the Wind Turbine Industry. A Comparative Study of Technology Management Models in European and Chinese Lead Firms', *International Journal of Technology Management* 70(4), 281–299.

Haakonsson, S., Kirkegaard, J. K., & Lema, R. forthcoming, 'China's catch-up in wind power – a case study on decomposition of innovation', Sino-Danish Center for Education and Research, mimeo.

Heilmann, S., 2008, 'From Local Experiments to National Policy: The Origins of China's Distinctive Policy Process', *The China Journal* 59, 1–30.

García, C., 2013, 'Policies and Institutions for Grid-Connected Renewable Energy: "Best Practice" and the Case of China', *Governance: An International Journal of Policy, Administration, and Institutions* 26(1), 119–146.

Jiang, L. (ed.), 2011, Integrated Solution Strategies for Coordinated Wind Power and Grid Development – International Experience and China Practises, State Grid Energy Research Institute and Vestas Wind Technology (China) Co. Ltd, Beijing.

Jun He Bulletin, 6 June 2013, 'Administrative Law: Interpretation of 'Decision of the State Council on Cancelling and Delegating the Power of Approval of a Batch of Items Requiring Administrative Approval and Other Issues', http://www.junhe.com/images/ourpublications_en_img/jun_he_legal_2_update/43_20136131447534694.pdf.

Kamp, L., Smits, R. & Andriesse, C., 2004, 'Notions on Learning Applied to Wind Turbine Development in the Netherlands and Denmark', *Energy Policy* 32(14), 1625–1637.

Karnøe, P. & Garud, R. B., 2012, 'Path Creation: Co-creation of Heterogeneous Resources in the Emergence of the Danish Wind Turbine Cluster', *European Planning Studies* 20(5), 733–752.

Kirkegaard, J. K., 2015, *Ambiguous Winds of Change – Or Fighting against Windmills in Chinese Wind Power: Mapping Controversies over a Potential Turn to Quality in Chinese Wind Power*, PhD thesis, Department of Business & Politics, Copenhagen Business School.

Kirkegaard, J. K., 2017, 'Tackling Chinese Upgrading through Experimentalism and Pragmatism: The Case of China's Wind Turbine Industry', *Journal of Current Chinese Affairs* 46(2), 7–39.

Klagge, B, Liu, Z. & Silva, P. C., 2012, 'Constructing China's Wind Energy Innovation System', *Energy Policy* 50, 370–382.

Korsnes, M., 2014, 'Fragmentation, Centralisation and Policy Learning: An Example from China's Wind Industry', *Journal of Current Chinese Affairs* 43(3), 175–205.

Korsnes, M., 2015, *Chinese Renewable Struggles: Innovation, the Arts of the State and Offshore Wind Technology*, PhD thesis, Department of Interdisciplinary Studies of Culture, Norwegian University of Science and Technology (NTNU).

Kroeber, A. R., 2016, *China's Economy – What Everyone Needs to Know*, Oxford University Press, New York.

Lardy, N. R., 2016, 'The Changing Role of the Private Sector in China', Conference Volume.

Lema, A. & Ruby, K., 2007, 'Between Fragmented Authoritarianism and Policy Coordination: Creating a Chinese Market for Wind Energy', *Energy Policy* 35, 3879–3890.

Lema, R., Berger, A. & Schmitz, H., 2013, 'China's Impact on the Global Wind Power Industry', *Journal of Current Chinese Affairs* 42(1), 37–69.

Lema, R., Iizuka, M., & Walz, R., 2015, 'Introduction to Low-Carbon Innovation and Development: Insights and Future Challenges for Research', *Innovation and Development* 5(2), 173–187, http://doi.org/10.1080/2157930X.2015.1065096.

Lema, R., Sagar, A. & Zhou, Y., 2016, 'Convergence or Divergence? Wind Power Innovation Paths in Europe and Asia', *Science and Public Policy* 43(3), 400–413.

Lewis, J. I., 2007, 'Technology Acquisition and Innovation in the Developing World: Wind Turbine Development in China and India', *St. Comp. Int. Dev.* 42, 208–232.

Lewis, J. I., 2013, *Green Innovation in China. China's Wind Power Industry and the Global Transition to a Low-Carbon Economy*, Columbia University Press, New York.

Lewis, J. I. & Wiser, R. H., 2007, 'Fostering a Renewable Energy Technology Industry: An International Comparison of Wind Industry Policy Support Mechanisms', *Energy Policy* 35, 1844–1857.

Li, J., 2010, 'Decarbonising Power Generation in China – Is the Answer Blowing in the Wind?', *Renewable and Sustainable Energy Reviews* 14, 1154–1171.

Li, X., 2015, 'Decarbonizing China's Power System with Wind Power: the Past and the Future', *The Oxford Institute for Energy Studies*, January, OIES Paper, EL11.

Li, C.B., Li, P. & Feng, X., 2014, 'Analysis of Wind Power Generation Operation Management Risk in China', *Renewable Energy* 64, 26–275.

Liao, C., Jochem, E., Zhang, Y. & Farid, N. R., 2010, 'Wind Power Development and Policies in China', *Renewable Energy* 35, 1879–1886.

Liu, Y. & Kokko, A., 2010, 'Wind Power in China: Policy and Development Challenges', *Energy Policy* 38, 5520–5529.

Luo, G., Dan, E., Zhang, X. & Guo, Y., 2018, 'Why the Wind Curtailment of Northwest China Remains High', *MPDI Sustainability*, 10(2), 570, 1–26, https://doi.org/10.3390/su10020570.

McNally, C. A., 2006, 'Insinuations on China's Emergent Capitalism', *East-West Center Working Paper*, Politics, Governance, and Security Series, 15.

Maskus, K. E., 2002, 'Regulatory Standards in the WTO: Comparing Intellectual Property Rights with Competition Policy, Environmental Protection, and Core Labor Standards', *World Trade Review* 1(2), 135–152.

Mathews, J. A., 2016, 'China's Continuing Renewable Energy Revolution – Latest Trends in Electric Power Generation', *The Asia-Pacific Journal, Japan Focus* 14(17).

Mathews, J. A. & Tan, H., 2015, *China's Renewable Energy Revolution*, Palgrave Macmillan, New York.

Mertha, A. & Brødsgaard, K. E., 2017, 'Revisiting Chinese Authoritarianism in China's Central Energy Administration', in K. E. Brødsgaard (ed.), *Chinese Politics as Fragmented Authoritarianism: Earthquakes, Energy and Environment*, pp. 1–14, Routledge, Abingdon.

MOST (Ministry of Science and Technology of the People's Republic of China), n.d., 'National High-Tech R&D Program (863 Program)', S&T Programmes, http://www.most.gov.cn/eng/programmes1/.

MOST (Ministry of Science and Technology of the People's Republic of China), 2006, State Council, 国家中长期科学和技术发展规划纲要 (2006-2020) [National Outline for Medium and Long Term Science and Technology Development (2006-2020)], 9 February 2006, http://www.gov.cn/jrzg/2006-02/09/content_183787.htm.

MOST (Ministry of Science and Technology of the People's Republic of China), 2012, State Council, The Central People's Government of the People's Republic of China, 关于印发风力发电科技发展'十二五'专项规划的通知 ['The 12th Five-Year Plan for the Scientific and Technological Development of Wind Power], 国科发计,197 号, National Branch No. 197, 24 April 2012, http://www.most.gov.cn/fggw/zfwj/zfwj2012/201204/t20120424_93884.htm

Nahm, J. & Steinfeld, E. S., 2014, 'Scale-Up Nation: China's Specialization in Innovative Manufacturing', *World Development* 54, February, 288–300.

National Development and Reform Commission (NDRC) 2007, Medium- and Long-Term Development Plan for Renewable Energy in China, September. http://www.chinaenvironmentallaw.com/wp-content/uploads/2008/04/medium-and-long-term-development-plan-for-renewable-energy.pdf.

Naughton, B., 2010, 'Economic Growth: From High-Speed to High-Quality', in J. Fewsmith (ed.), *China Today, China Tomorrow. Domestic Politics, Economy, and Society*, pp. 71–90, Rowman & Littlefield Publishers, Plymouth.

Naughton, B., 2014, 'China's Economy: Complacency, Crisis & the Challenge of Reform', *Dædalus, the Journal of the American Academy of Arts & Sciences* 143(2), 14–25.

Ng, E., 2016, 'Wind Turbine Giant Goldwind in Power Joint Venture with Apple', *South China Morning Post*, 7 December 2016, http://www.scmp.com/business/companies/article/2052643/wind-turbine-giant-goldwind-power-joint-venture-apple.

Pereira, C. G. and Puertas, O., 2013, 'Decision on Abolishing and Delegating the Power of Approval of Several Items Requiring Administrative Approval China', lexology.com, 31 July, viewed 22 June 2014, http://www.lexology.com/library/detail.aspx?g=307b32e9-6921-41b8-8fad-94ea38125534.

PWC (PricewaterhouseCoopers), 2013, 'New Roadmap for Achieving the China Dream. Business and Economic Implications of the Third Plenary Session of the

CPC's 18th Central Committee', viewed 20 March 2018, http://www.iberchina.org/files/china_plenum_pwc.pdf.

Qi, W., 2013, 'How Debt is Weighing Down China's Wind Sector', Windpowermonthly, 16 April 2013, viewed 29 April 2013, http://www.windpowermonthly.com/article/1178534/analysis—debt-weighing-down-chinas-wind-sector.

Renewableenergyworld.com, 2011, 'China Releases Technical Standards for Wind Power Industry', 22 September, viewed 17 October 2001, http://www.renewableenergyworld.com/rea/news/article/2011/09/china-releases-technical-standards-for-wind-power-industry.

Research Institute of Economy, Trade & Industry (RIETI), 2013, 'Abolition of the Central government's Administrative Inspections and the Delegation of Authority to Local Governments', viewed 13 August 2014, http://www.rieti.go.jp/en/columns/a01_0381.html.

Ru, P., Zhi, Q., Zhang, F., Zhong, X., Li, J. & Su, J., 2012, 'Behind the Development of Technology: The Transition of Innovation Modes in China's Wind Turbine Manufacturing Industry', *Energy Policy* 32, 58–69.

Silva, P. C. & Klagge, B., 2013, 'The Evolution of the Wind Industry and the Rise of Chinese Firms: From Industrial Policies to Global Innovation Networks', *European Planning Studies* 21(9), 1341–1356.

Song, R. & Hong, M., 2016, 'China's 1-2-3 Punch to Tackle Wasted Renewable Energy', World Resources Institute, 27 April 2016, http://www.wri.org/blog/2016/04/chinas-1-2-3-punch-tackle-wasted-renewable-energy.

Standing Committee of the National People's Congress (NPC), 2005, Renewable Energy Law, 28 February 2005, http://www.npc.gov.cn/englishnpc/Law/2007-12/13/content_1384096.htm.

Strambach, S., 2001, 'Innovation Processes and the Role of Knowledge-Intensive Business Services (KIBS)', in K. Koschatzky, M. Kulicke & A. Zenker (eds.), *Innovation Networks. Technology, Innovation and Policy (Series of the Fraunhofer Institute for Systems and Innovation Research (ISI)) 12*, Physica, Heidelberg.

The Information Office of the State Council, Energy Policy 2012, First edition 2012. October 2012, http://www.gov.cn/english/official/2012-10/24/content_2250497.htm.

Vestergaard, J., Brandstrup, L. & Goddard, R. D., 2004, 'Industry Formation and State Intervention: The Case of the Wind Turbine Industry in Denmark and the United States', *Academy of International Business* (Southeast USA Chapter), Conference Proceedings, November 2004, pp. 329–340.

Wang, Q. Wen, F., Yang, A. & Huang, J., 2011, 'Cost Analysis and Pricing Policy of Wind Power in China', *Journal of Energy Engineering*, 137, 138–150.

WTO (World Trade Organization), n.d., 'Overview: the TRIPS Agreement', https://www.wto.org/english/tratop_e/trips_e/intel2_e.htm.

Yang, M., Patino-Echeverri, D. & Yang, F., 2012, 'Wind Power Generation in China: Understanding the Mismatch between Capacity and Generation', *Renewable Energy* 41, 145–151.

Yu, J., Ji, F., Zhang, L. & Chen, Y., 2009, 'An Over-Painted Oriental Arts: Evaluation of the Development of the Chinese Renewable Energy Market using the Wind Power Market as a Model', *Energy Policy* 37, 5221–5225.

Zhao, X., Wang, F. & Wang, M., 2012a, 'Large-Scale Utilization of Wind Power in China: Obstacles of Conflict between Market and Planning', *Energy Policy* 48, 222–232.

Zhao, Z., Ling, W., Zillante, G. & Zuo, J., 2012b, 'Comparative Assessment of Performance of Foreign and Local Wind Turbine Manufacturers in China', *Renewable Energy* 39, 424–432.

5 Controversy over access to the grid – making space for wind in the Chinese Kingdom of Coal

In the outskirts of Beijing on a full-blown Indian Summer day in 2013, I approach the end of my current field trip to China. The courteous, elderly Chinese gentleman, one of Chinese wind power's 'grand old men', wraps up the development of Chinese wind power development, and in particular the quality and related curtailment issues, in just a few breaths. What seemed like a riddle before suddenly stands in a new light, as he explains how the issues with curtailment have been for the best, as through a strategy of 'just doing it' China has accelerated problems. Doing so, it has been possible to 'learn from practice' rather than theorised imagination. This has speeded up disruptive learning. Later, a grid connection scientist experienced in China states, 'the outages in the grid system – for China it was a wake-up call'.

The riddle of Chinese wind power development begins to fall into its proper place. What seemed incomprehensible to me before starts to become clearer: the issues with curtailed wind power and missing grid connections may not only be a matter of poor coordination and planning, vested interests, and power struggles, but also an outcome of an experimental mode of development. Is what I am looking at here some of the particular 'Chinese characteristics' of the greening of the power sector, allowing quality issues to emerge, with vast amounts of wasted wind resources due to curtailment, all happening so that the sector can learn from it? However, how the story will end up remains a riddle to me. Will it become a story of China's 'fight against (own) windmills', producing a lock-in to fossil fuels, or will it be a story of an actual turn to quality in wind power that rescues the emerging wind power development marketisation in the power struggle between renewables and fossil fuels?

Diving into the risk of socio-material 'lock-in' to fossil fuels

The quality crisis described in Chapter Four suffered by the Chinese wind power sector did not come without warning and neither did it go unnoticed. Nor did it remain uncontested. On the contrary, it has produced such a severe disruption that the entire market was threatened, and it gave opponents of

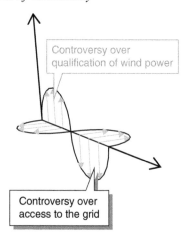

Figure 5.1 Second site of controversy.

wind energy such strong arguments against higher wind power penetration that they were difficult to refute. And so, as the journey continues, Chapter Five follows the electromagnetic field out of the turbine, through the wind farm cabling, into and out of the sub-station, and to where the cabling meets the public grid, conducting a controversy study over access to the power grid (see Figure 5.1). Zooming in on the electromagnetic interaction at the grid connection, a story of grid strength, voltage rises, curtailment, points of instability, and voltage collapse is revealed: a story of an unfolding competitive struggle between the powers of coal and wind to gain access to the electrical power grid at the very height of the quality crisis in Chinese wind power. This competitive space, in turn, has not just been configured around contested (in)flexibilities of the respective energy sources and the existing power grid, but, perhaps more opaquely, also around their contested costs. Overall, it is a story about how incumbent electrical grids, price and cost calculations, and support schemes are not neutral, but were originally designed to serve an electricity system based on centralised power plants with little technical flexibility (Tande & Jenkins 2003). This is what may come to constitute a socio-materially 'hostile environment' to wind power (Karnøe 2010, 2012, 2013). In the Chinese case, though, this hostile environment is entangled in China's fragmented authoritarianism and vested interests, which may further enhance the risk of socio-material carbon lock-in to fossil fuels (Mathews & Tan 2015; Callon 2007:140; Unruh 2000).

Coal as a stable base-load provider

Despite recent decreases in China's coal consumption, the electrical power system is still heavily dependent on coal (Mathews 2016; Mathews & Tan 2015). The green transformation of China's 'power system with

1000 GW of thermal generators, most of which are coal-fired, will be a huge effort [...] The reliance of the Chinese power sector on coal is and will therefore still be huge for years to come' (Göss 13 February 2017). China's power generation, transmission, and distribution system is namely dominated by large, centralised thermal (coal-based) power plants (owned and operated by electrical utilities such as China's 'Big Five') – a configuration similar to most of the world's conventional power systems today. Such systems, with a centralised generation system architecture, are based on a logic of maintaining system stability, which hinges on an operating principle of balancing power use/demand with power production/generation (Karnøe 2010). This balancing act is necessary because of the physical nature of electricity, namely the way in which electricity 'is a real time charge of electrons flowing at a constant frequency' (Karnøe 2010:223):

> The term real time refers to the fact that since there is no form of perfect storage for electricity, it must be consumed as it is produced to preserve the frequency or load balance. (Karnøe 2010:223).

In other words, as electricity – be it generated from coal, wind, hydro, solar – cannot yet be economically stored in amounts that are significant for national power systems, then operators are obliged to ensure that no more electricity is produced than can be consumed at any one point in time, reaching a cost optimum. This characteristic of 'real time interdependency of production and consumption' fundamentally separates electricity technology from other energy carriers, as the infrastructure cannot be separated from the consumption (Karnøe 2010:223). In turn, this implies that in a centralised power system such as China's, the main responsibility of the grid operator (or 'TSO', such as the China State Grid Corporation) is to maintain system stability through the instantaneous balancing of supply (generation) and demand (load) to keep the system frequency stable, and also to prevent power outages, which it does by 'buying reliability' (i.e. a known quantity of power) from large thermal power plants such as coal-fired power stations. Coal-fired power stations are therefore given a central role as base-load generators, as they are capable of providing a stable output (Interview with foreign wind turbine manufacturer 2013). In this way, coal-fired generation is conventionally perceived to be simple to manage and therefore 'really comforting to have' for the system operator (interview with Chinese think tank 2013), since they can use the large inertia of the thermal (coal-based) power plants to safely allow slow variations in the system frequency when load (demand) on the system varies. This means that, to a certain extent, power production can follow power demand and maintain the balance, which is critical to the system, through the balance-provider, the thermal power plant.

Contested operating logics – wind, the trouble-maker

As is evident from this, the classic perception of thermal coal power is that it ensures grid stability; that is, it forms the basis for balancing the power in a power system based on centralised power plants (Manwell, McGowan & Rogers 2010). A distributed power source like wind power, on the other hand, is associated with quite the opposite attribute because 'adding inter-mittent energy sources like wind to an existing configuration of electricity generation disrupts its smooth functioning' (Karnøe 2010:223). In China, wind power soon got the reputation of 'messing up the voltage' (Interview with foreign wind turbine manufacturer 2013) owing to its random nature; that is, the way that the wind fluctuates stochastically and intermittently. In particular, during the years of fragmented planning and rapid wind power deployment, the Chinese TSO, State Grid, started to complain that wind power was a nuisance, a source of grid instability. Wind was

> a trouble-maker and rubbish! Because when we need, we don't have. But when [we] don't need, there's too much. (Interview with Chinese govern-ment advisor and wind energy association 2013)

This framing of wind power as a trouble-maker is linked to the clashing of operating logics, namely between the conventional 'logic of balancing loads' versus the wind's 'logic of generating loads' (Karnøe 2010).[1]

With wind power suddenly being installed at rapid pace during the 'mar-ketquake', without being well planned and coordinated, the system was sud-denly faced with multiple loads that not only generated, but also did not contribute to, system balancing. In brief, wind power soon threatened the existing system's logic of balancing. In turn, this clash of operating logics (balancing versus generating) soon started to produce a power struggle of wind power's integration into and access to the electrical power grid. The issue – quite similar to that experienced by other countries with conventional centralised power systems – has been aggravated by the pace and scale of the quality crisis in Chinese wind power development. Poor quality control systems in turbines, for example, would not properly regulate the power factor, power production was not sufficiently managed owing to a lack of forecasting tools, or grid faults were not handled well owing to the lack of grid-friendly technologies such as LVRT (interviews). And so wind turbines themselves (for the most part asynchronous machines that, by design, may deviate from the system frequency) were starting to be framed as somewhat wayward when compared with conventional, precisely rotating, and syn-chronous generating machines such as used in coal-based power plants:

> wind turbines are NOT synchronous generators! They are asynchro-nous … an asynchronous machine swinging in a synchronous system. (Interview with foreign wind turbine manufacturer 2013)

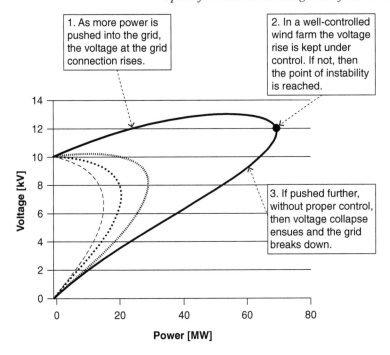

1. As more power is pushed into the grid, the voltage at the grid connection rises.

2. In a well-controlled wind farm the voltage rise is kept under control. If not, then the point of instability is reached.

3. If pushed further, without proper control, then voltage collapse ensues and the grid breaks down.

Figure 5.2 Wind power's potential to destabilise the grid.

In other words, wind power was soon being socio-materially constituted as an enemy to grid stability, with China's pre-existing conventional centralised power system configuration emerging as a 'hostile territory' for the adaptation to and integration of the fluctuating and intermittent wind power – in other words, wind power was not seen as 'fit' to the grid (Karnøe 2010:237). Figure 5.2 illustrates the precarious nature of wind power being fed into a weak grid which, if not properly controlled – with particular emphasis on the ability to control the rise in voltage with power penetration – can reach a point of instability, where a continued effort to push more wind power in will result in a grid collapse. It is, perhaps, little wonder that the Chinese grid was being constituted as a hostile territory to the penetration of poorly controlled wind power, and that grid operators were therefore reluctant to allow a troublemaker such as wind power to be integrated into the grid.

Lacking space in the power grid: curtailment

During the 'marketquake' of rapid wind power capacity instalments, vast amounts of wind power were connected to the grid in an uncoordinated fashion but with a notorious lack of investment in new grid extensions and reinforcements. This in turn soon engendered even further resistance against wind power from the regulator (the system operator/TSO/grid company), in particular as the quality crisis ensued. The resistance was further exacer-bated because until 2011 there were no Chinese grid codes for wind turbines (which, for instance, require LVRT technologies), which meant that they were unable to stay connected to the grid without tripping when the grid experienced short voltage dips. So the first challenge to finding space for wind power in the grid was the Chinese power grid itself. China's grid infra-structure has a reputation of being:

> very weak, very small (hěn ruò, hěn xiǎo, 很弱,很小). So when the wind farm is bigger and bigger, so integrating into the power grid ... the power grid cannot [absorb]. (Interview with Chinese wind turbine man-ufacturer 2012)

Of course, the reference to China's grid fragility has much to do with the geographical distribution of wind power in China, which is largely in the least populated areas ('the Three Norths'), whilst the major consumption (or load centres) are in the eastern coastal cities. If the grid is to supply these load centres, then the electricity from the wind farms in the north has to be transported over long distances, with significant amounts of wind power being wasted.[2] Then there is the challenge of the fragmented, uncoordinated planning of wind power development that took place during the years of rapid growth. Local governments often made speedy approvals of new wind farm projects on the one hand, without there being corresponding invest-ments in the power grid on the other hand, at the central level (Korsnes 2014:186; interviews). As expressed by a Chinese government advisor:

> We have more installed capacity, but the grid connection cannot be estab-lished this fast. At first, during the planning stage, the power grid company doesn't know where to develop wind, how much wind will be developed. So they cannot make their own grid connection plan. So the second one, also for big connection, the transmission line ... eh ... the feasibility study to approve the procedure and the cost of construction...the period of this [is] much longer than for wind. (Interview with Chinese government advi-sor and wind power association 2013)

Lastly, to add to all this, there were the combined challenges of inadequate technology, lack of experience, as well as lax enforcement of rules for grid integration, such as mandatory market shares (MMS) and power purchase agreements (PPAs)) introduced in 2007, which officially obliged TSOs and provincial governments not only to provide each wind farm facility with a connection to the grid, but also to purchase all the renewable electricity produced (interviews; García 2013:132; Lema & Ruby 2007) (also refer to Chapter Four). Both the general poor quality of the turbines during the years of extensive growth, and, in particular, the poor functioning of criti-cally important control technologies (at wind turbine and wind farm levels) and forecasting tools confronted the grid with unfamiliar power inputs. Introduce to this the inexperience of the TSO with the extensive stability work required to balance the power variations and control voltage stability, and it is perhaps not surprising that sections of the grid repeatedly tripped and were brought down by issues of instability. LVRT technology and the management of voltage stability, which were commonplace in most Western countries, were missing. As a result, and as we have already seen, the TSO started to frame wind power as disruptive and disturbing, unreliable, and non-controllable. Wind power added 'an extra chunk of uncertainty' which, amongst other things, required additional 'economic planning and guessing at tomorrow's load' (interview with foreign wind turbine manufacturer). This, in turn, resulted in the TSO being 'mathematically overconstrained' and faced with the uncertainty of forecasting in their work to manage voltage stability by the vital demands for balancing and forecasting wind power, exacerbated by connecting large chunks of wind power to the grid almost simultaneously (interview with foreign wind turbine manufacturer 2013).

The response from the TSO was inevitable: curtailment. In other words, literal overflowing - that is, curtailed (and 'lost') wind power – soon surfaced in vast amounts as the framing of the existing power grid could not contain it because of the lack of consideration of 'how to integrate all the wind. This has resulted in wind curtailment. A big concern. The capacity [its framing] of the grid has been exceeded' (interview with foreign wind turbine manufacturer 2013). The rapid rise in the level of wind power penetration had, in the eyes of the TSO, resulted in grid instability and they – when making a choice between wind and coal – had often decided that:

> the first thing they shut off is the wind power ... because the coal is cheaper and makes more money. So, if I were Chinese, I'd do the same thing. There's no question about that. (Interview with foreign control system supplier 2012)
>
> In this way, rather than curtailing or down-rating coal-fired thermal power plants, it was the grid-connected wind turbines, which are being curtailed because there's not enough space in the grid. That's simply the reason why! (Interview with foreign wind turbine supplier 2013)

The consequence was that the TSO would demand wind farms to disconnect from the grid, or down-rate their production (achieved by pitching the turbine's blades), even when the wind farm was able to produce more power.

The physical and institutional inflexibilities of the coal-based power system

The choice to curtail wind power and retain coal in the power system is, in turn, inextricably linked to the way in which coal power is framed not only as stable and reliable, but also as physically and institutionally inflexible, making it difficult to suddenly shut down or open up production in coal-fired plants. That is, the basis for constituting the coal-based power system as physically inflexible is that it takes a long time both to start up and shut down coal-fired power production to avoid thermally stressing critical components. This in turn does not provide a natural counterpart to variable wind power fluctuations. Conversely, wind farms can be flexibly turned on readily and can produce power right away – as long as the wind blows, that is. They can also be down-regulated (curtailed) or shut down just as easily. The penetration of large shares of stochastically fluctuating wind power during the marketquake in particular had not been handled well by an inert power system that is heavily dependent on inflexible coal-fired thermal power plants (interview with foreign wind turbine manufacturer 2013). At the same time as the power system is framed as having 'physical inflexibility', it is also marked by 'institutional flexibility' (interview with foreign wind turbine manufacturer 2013). The latter mainly refers to three things: the deficiency of a coordinated planning of wind farm development, the lack of flexibility in power pricing, and the absence of an institutionalised intra- and interprovincial market for power trading in the state-controlled and monopolised power sector (interviews 2012; 2013). Without an integrated interregional/-provincial trading system for electricity with flexible pricing, China lacks the ability to capitalise on power balancing possibilities (interview with foreign wind turbine manufacturer 2013). Another example of the missed opportunity to enhance power balancing possibility is the scant integration of wind power with hydropower (which constitutes China's largest renewable energy sector, apart from nuclear, and is categorised as a renewable energy source), which normally can serve as a balancing 'battery' for wind power, smoothing out periods of overproduction of wind power, and in turn minimising the issue of curtailment.

Overall, the socio-materially constituted physical and institutional inflexibilities are being framed as a barrier to integrating larger shares of wind power into the grid. In other words, they are 'tying China down by its own constraining ropes', some of which are regulative and institutional, while others are physical: 'China is doing all the right things, but being tied by itself' (interview with foreign wind turbine manufacturer 2013). It follows that the TSO would then see wind power as a nuisance, which reduces the grid manoeuvrability and increases the inflexibility, as the overflowing wind power cannot be traded across borders and must be wasted if it is not going to disrupt grid stability. In this way, as wind penetration had increased rapidly in the grid, and as the system had become mathematically overconstrained, 'the information is going up, options are going down' (interview with foreign wind turbine manufacturer 2013). There is thus no doubt that China's centralised and coal-based power system had turned out to be a hostile territory for volatile intermittent energy sources such as wind power; and wind power's framing as disruptive in the socio-technically inflexible power system produced extensive socio-material resistance against it, leading to high curtailment rates, which in turn spurred further arguments against the sustainability of wind power.

The politics of inflexibilities – and contested space(s) for wind power

We have seen how wind power has been framed as disruptive, and how the coal-based power system has been framed as both physically and institutionally inflexible. Yet this framing itself is also being contested and negotiated: 'there has always been uncertainty about the consumption of your [TSO's] load [energy production]' (interview with foreign wind turbine manufacturer 2013). This is a reference to the time prior to the introduction of wind power, when the power system was already plagued by uncertainty about loads (consumption) in the future. Wind power thus adds 'a little bit more of the same [uncertainty]' into the grid (interview with foreign wind turbine manufacturer 2013). Framed in this way, the issue of increasing wind power penetration is not so much about disruptive fluctuations, but about 'operations [and] commitment from the system operator [the grid companies]' to integrate larger shares of intermittent renewable energy sources into the system (interview with foreign wind turbine manufacturer 2013). This concerns, for instance, the enforcement of grid integration rules, as well as the adoption of tools, advanced control systems, and forecasting technologies, which can help increase grid operation flexibility through, amongst other things, better information. Thus, 'technology matters' both in the issue of grid flexibility, and in the matter of transforming wind farms into conventional power plants, which are controllable and predictable (interview with foreign wind turbine manufacturer 2013). In this way, and put provocatively,

> if somebody says that wind power screws up your voltage, it's a matter of bad planning and bad interconnection [...] and backwardness in technologies. (Interview with foreign wind turbine manufacturer 2013)

This reflects an underlying power struggle in the power sector. Indeed, as wind power takes up larger shares, and coal consumption is beginning to slow down, a zero-sum game is construed between wind power and coal: coal-fired power plants have no incentive to create space for increasing wind power penetration. The whole rationale that coal-fired power plants are 'delegated a quota to produce a certain amount of [gigawatt] hours on a yearly basis' means that coal fired power plants are politically, economically, as well as technically difficult, to shut down (interview with Chinese think tank 2013). Naturally, the coal-based power plants' primary basis of income is their energy production; they would therefore 'lose money' 'if they come under the quota, to which they have a right, and which they negotiate with the local government on a yearly basis' (interview with Chinese think tank 2013).

> This is a caution for policy people: Coal production versus wind production. Why would a coal producer reduce his production and earn less money to accommodate wind? ... He will say, 'it's not possible, I don't have flexibility'. (Interview with foreign wind turbine manufacturer 2013)

In this way, the resistance against wind power is thus also a matter of power struggles in China's electrical power sector, and not only a matter of poor planning, interconnection, and backwardness in technologies. This power struggle is further reflected in the lax enforcement and implementation of grid integration rules. The above points to the inherently political nature of the issue of wind power integration – and the many vested interests. The political constitution of the issue also implies that the argument '[t]hat coal is [physically and institutionally] inflexible is not written in stone!'. That is, the inflexibility is also a socio-materially construed issue, producing a political matter of concern: higher wind penetration into the grid is largely a matter of political will and determination to invest in grid expansion to create flexibility in the incumbent power system (e.g. through enforcement of grid integration rules) (interview with foreign wind turbine manufacturer 2013), along with a reallocation of quotas between wind and coal, as well as a matter of investment into an overall transition of the power system, from one based on centralised thermal power plants to a system with more distributed renewable energy. Accommodation of higher wind power penetration in other words requires a rethinking of the entire logic of the power system from one based on 'balancing passive loads' to one based on 'active load agency', and so gradually moving from what may be called a 'Grid 1.0' to 'Grid 2.0' (Karnøe 2012).[3] As trials of strength between wind and coal power started playing out, wind power soon started to gain numerous enemies amongst fossil fuel proponents who would

> still think that renewable energy cannot become a mainstream energy, that it cannot replace the traditional energy sources, chemical energy sources. They think they are nothing, that they are illusory, they think that within the next 50 years, 100 years, 200 years, we have to rely on coal, have to rely on oil, and the forces of this understanding are very strong. (Interview with Chinese certification body 2013)

Meanwhile, not only coal-fired power plants and the TSO were resisting wind power integration, but also local governments tended to prefer coal-fired plants, mainly because they were a good and stable source of provincial income and employment. In addition, they constituted a critical provider of affordable heating during the cold winter months (interview with Chinese think tank 2013).

In summary, the socio-materially founded associations of inflexibilities, lack of grid manoeuvrability, and wind power's disruptiveness had created a 'competitive space' between wind power and coal. This reflects how wind power's development is entangled in a fierce power struggle with coal, as a 'battle between the traditional power plant interests and the new technologies' unfolds (interview with Chinese think tank 2013). Put simply, 'that's what the battle [about wind power penetration] is about!': a struggle for wind power to gain access to the grid (interview with foreign wind turbine manufacturer 2013). At the same time, the above has indicated the socio-material grounding of vested interests against wind power in China's power sector, as these are founded in their physical and socio-material inflexibilities, the fluctuating electrons of wind power, colliding logics of the power system and wind power generation, but also entangled in institutional confines of the coal quota and China's fragmented system for energy governance.

The overflowing grid's curtailment rates at risk of delegitimising wind power

As the quality crisis in China's wind power sector ensued, these resistances against wind power did not bode well for China's greening of the electrical power sector. The issue of surging wind farm curtailment rates only exacerbated the issue, as this meant that the opportunity to produce sustainable energy was being lost: that is, 'curtailment – that's electricity not being used!', which made 'everybody in China crazy' and angry (interview with foreign wind turbine manufacturer 2013). This even started to destabilise wind power's framing as sustainable on a global scale, since 'the reputation of the whole industry suffers from it' (interview with foreign research institute 2013):

> It's completely insane. It's really worrying. In my world view, it's really worrying that they do it in this way. Because it destroys the reputation of wind power, right. [...] What do people think about wind power? People here [in Denmark], they taunt wind power when they read that 30 to 50 per cent of the wind turbines in China don't work, then they taunt us and say, 'what the heck is this about?' [...] And that damages the reputation of wind power. (Interview with foreign research institute 2013)

In this way, the curtailment rates – also coupled to underlying quality issues in the wind turbine industry during the quality crisis – started to produce even more resistance against wind power. And so, whilst most people agree that the environmental costs of wind power are less than coal power, the curtailment rates started producing concerns about this very 'fact', namely contesting the very framing of wind power's 'environmental sustainability" as curtailed wind power leads to consistently high coal-based power production alongside 'wasted' investments in wind farms. This can be reflected in a simple equation, which reads:

> Curtailed wind power = more pollution + more costs
> + less incentives for new wind power (Sandholt 2013).

Overall, China's wind power sector was facing potential delegitimisation as 'environmentally sustainable', as a result of the senseless policy of focusing on the quantity of turbines and installed capacity, rather than the quality and the amount of electricity actually generated, as well as a result of poor coordination and fragmented planning along with the socio-material constitution of the existing power system.

The global struggle to dissociate wind power from subsidisation – and contesting costs

Having looked at the struggle between wind and coal to find a place in an inflexible grid, we now turn to another front-line battle that has been taking place – and is still unfolding – between coal and wind, demarcating the front lines in the trial of strength: finding the 'true' cost and price of the energy they produce. Or, to put it another way, a battle unfolding around the issue of making wind power independent of subsidies, which, to a large extent, reflects how China's socio-technical assemblage around wind power development is inevitably entangled in the global pressure to reduce subsidies. Indeed, wind power's 'birth certificate' came with subsidies inscribed, so to speak, since wind power on a global scale has been introduced into existing electrical power systems, dominated by indirectly-subsidised fossil fuels, that are 'hostile' to wind power penetration. That is, attractive payment schemes (or, 'price-setting mechanisms' - oftentimes framed as support 'subsidies' such as 'Feed-in-Tariffs' (FIT)) - have proven essential to the mobilisation of socio-technical assemblages around wind power development on a global scale. This is due to the way in which wind power, as any new energy technology, faces challenges in terms of marketisation and funding because they do not offer any immediate economic benefit to their end-users. Instead, they often require reallocation of public funds due to the requirement for considerable funding of their development and infrastructure, which is often much more than what private investors alone can muster (Jacobsson & Bergek, 2004, p. 210; also see Kirkegaard, Caliskan & Karnøe forthcoming). Yet this economisation of wind power development has been heavily contested politically worldwide (Karnøe 2010), with questions asked about the economic sustainability and competitiveness of wind power. Currently, wind power in China is still reliant on subsidies, as it is elsewhere (but decreasingly so), and is thus being problematised as a 'political' product, rather than a 'real market product' in conventional neo-liberal arguments:

> So far, the wind industry is a policy product more than a real market product. The cost curve for wind energy is going down big time, but has still not reached the price of conventional energies. We [foreign wind turbine manufacturers] are aiming at making the [cost] curve steeper. This is done by reducing cost of production, installation, and service, and by increasing efficiency. (Interview with foreign wind turbine manufacturer 2012)

In this global struggle to reduce dependence on subsidies by reducing the cost of energy, there is much emphasis placed on core technologies that can increase the output of turbines or optimise their operation. Technologies such as wind turbine controllers and wind farm control systems are at the forefront here, together with forecasting and design tools, especially those that can optimise the integration of wind power into the power system and optimise the aero-dynamic design. These technologies have become increasingly constituted as 'critical'. This indicates how global competition in today's wind power sector is driven by seeking to reduce the levelised cost of energy (LCOE), a parameter which is fundamentally based on:

> how much electricity you can squeeze out of the wind. That's the first thing. The other thing is the cost of capital. (Interview with foreign wind turbine manufacturer 2013)

In essence, the LCOE provides a comparative measure of the cost of electricity generation. It is an economic assessment of the average cost of the energy produced by a power-generating asset, taking into account total initial investment costs and operational expenditure over its lifetime.

So here we have a battle line between wind power and coal (as well as other power sources) that is construed around the LCOE and the break even with conventional fossil fuel power sources. In China, and globally, the LCOE measure constitutes the central calculative device used in framing wind power as economically sustainable. It follows that leading wind turbine manufacturers consider that the next innovative breakthrough in the wind power sector will be when wind power breaks even with conventional energy. Such a 'revolution' would finally make it possible to associate wind power with 'real market prices' (interview with foreign wind turbine manufacturer 2013):

> I think the next breakthrough will be to bring down our costs of energy, where we can compete at market prices – when that happens – once the incremental breakthrough in technology has made the costs of energy so low that we can compete at market prices, we are going see a revolution again. And that is not going to happen tomorrow. (Interview with foreign wind turbine manufacturer 2013)

Such analyses of energy costs are, of course, also conducted in China, both in regard to wind power and coal power, and other sources of energy. Yet in China's coal-dependent power sector, it is

> very difficult for wind energy, also due to cheap coal. Wind turbines are still very expensive. But in the long term, wind turbines should still have the market. (Interview with Chinese ministry 2012)
>
> We are not like Denmark. We have many resources of coal. So it is difficult, when and how you decide to promote these new energy sectors,

since we have the low price [of] coal. (Interview with Chinese government advisor and wind industry association 2013)

This indicates the politically contentious issue of calculating comparative costs of energy, when entangled in China's legacy as a polluting yet growth-dependent 'Coal Kingdom'. Despite this, and to become framed as economically sustainable, that is, independent from subsidies in the competition with fossil fuels, the wind power sector is focusing on making stronger associations of economic viability and performance in order to construe wind power as a so-called real market product. To this end, research institutions and wind turbine manufacturers in China, and elsewhere, 'are putting a combined effort in bringing the wind industry out of a situation, where we need subsidies – and that's a global phenomenon' (interview with foreign wind turbine manufacturer 2012). The hope is that the resistance against wind power founded in arguments about subsidisation can be reduced. So far, however, it remains, but an aspiration, as:

> many [wind turbine manufacturers and farm developers] need government support. If in the future, the price of coal and conventional electricity keeps increasing, then wind energy will have a competitive advantage. Now manufacturers are dependent on direct support. (Interview with Chinese official 2013)

In this way, analyses, studies, and calculations of the costs and prices of energy are a very real part of the power struggle between wind power and coal, at the same time enmeshed in the political concern of the Chinese government and the CPC to ensure stable electricity prices in order to maintain social stability, whilst also ensuring that pollution levels do not reach unbearable levels. Accordingly, as expressed by a Chinese policy advisor, there should

> 'not [be] too much wind in China. Why? Because, it's still expensive' (interview with Chinese government advisor and wind industry association 2013).

The struggle to include 'real' costs in prices

The struggle goes further: Whilst opponents argue that wind power is economically unsustainable owing to the level of subsidies, wind power proponents attempt to counter these arguments by contesting how the 'real' costs of different sources of fossil fuel-based power are calculated and how they are included or excluded in prices. This feeds into the overall political discussion of subsidies. That is, since fossil fuel prices are 'not taking externalities [such as externalities from pollution and CO_2-emissions] into consideration', they do not account for 'what pollution has of extra costs' (interview with foreign wind turbine manufacturer 2012). Thus, as is the case in many places, power prices in China do not compensate for the negative externalities of fossil fuels (García 2013:140; Karnøe 2010). This means that the actual, but hidden, costs of fossil fuels are much higher than is reflected in the price of the electrical energy produced from them. In turn, this leads renewable energy proponents to argue that fossil fuels 'receive subsidies indirectly on the electricity price', creating a skewed and 'unequal market' (interview with foreign wind turbine manufacturer 2012):

> That's the big debate – because everyone is asking, when to get rid of subsidies [of wind power]. And nobody is talking about the enormous amount of subsidies going into fossil fuels – and the real cost of polluting with such things. So, it's a struggle. (Interview with foreign wind turbine manufacturer 2013)

As Chinese coal prices are still relatively low, improvements in wind turbine and wind farm performance to reduce the cost of energy are seen as key elements in improving the relative competitiveness of wind power, thus becoming independent of subsidies. Still, China's wind power sector is being supported through a FIT, but the Chinese government has now signalled an end to this by 2018. In part, this reflects the desire to reduce wind power's reliance on subsidies, but is also considered an indication of how the enormous increase in wind power capacity has raised the financial burden of the FIT to an unsustainable level for the Chinese economy (GWEC 2016), as well as an indication of how wind power has become more competitive with fossil fuels, and thus less dependent on support schemes.

Overall, socio-materially grounded prices and costs are being constituted as a politically sensitive issue - as are their underlying calculative devices and practices - with an effect on the framing and development of wind power. The above illustrates aspects of how valuation processes are political in nature, as we have seen how the very framing tools (e.g. FITs, LCOE) and their framings can become contested. Comparative cost and price calculations, as well as the selection of calculative devices – making coal and wind power more comparable in terms of costs (and subsidies) through the inclusion of the cost of hidden externalities – cannot be disassociated from politics, particularly in a coal-dominated yet fragmented power sector such as China's.

A greening energy future in lack of consensus? Vested interests and the environment revisited

In the politicised battle between wind and coal, negotiations and power struggles – and a lack of consensus – are taking shape along China's criss-crossing bureaucratic and administrative lines. Indeed, even within the China State Grid Corporation, which 'does not have a clear attitude towards wind' (interview with Chinese think tank 2013), there are diverse factional infights. Thus, despite resistance and conservativeness, thinking 'that the future is coal', 'there's nothing strange in the way that there's huge resistance in parts of the State Grid. And it's not surprising that some of them can see that in the longer run, well, yeah, of course we need to change this' (interview with Chinese think tank 2013). This in turn illustrates how, as soon as one starts to look closer, the structural and institutional view of fragmented authoritarianism, that 'where you stand depends on where you sit' (Allison 1971 as quoted in Gorm Hansen 2017:8), is not self-evident.

Reconciling the multiple and sometimes colliding agendas, targets, and ambitions across and within bureaucracies, and across and within central and local governments is needed for a smoother socio-material transition towards renewable energy in the power system. This, in itself, has been controversial because of the simultaneously 'fairly ambitious wind power plans, but also very ambitious coal expansion plans' (interview with Chinese think tank 2013). The lack of consensus across the decision-making silos on the future direction of China's future energy system, together with the uncoordinated planning, has thus not only produced barriers to the integration of wind power but also to the desired 'revolution of China's energy system' (that is, the Energy Revolution officially promulgated in 2015):

> So you think, asking whether it's a revolution of China's energy system? To reduce the use of coal, right? [...] Enhancing the use of renewable energy? This is the most fundamental issue, i.e. the awareness of renewable energy. [You ask,] do you think that in the future, like in Denmark, in Germany, there will be a reliance on renewable energy, and where not only 20, 30, 50, but 100 per cent should come from renewable energy sources? Originally, it was 20, then 30, then 50 per cent – like in Germany and Denmark now ... In a century, would the share rise to 100 per cent renewable energy? ... I think this is the most important direction. However, China's biggest problem is that there is no consensus on the structure of China's future energy system, there is no consensus, there is great resistance, from those engaged in traditional energy sources, like coal, nuclear, and those engaged in oil. (Interview with Chinese certification body 2013)

Despite such resistance and lack of consensus there are, however, increasing signs in the NEA of the NDRC of more focus on environmental protection in China's energy system, which has recently created the 'need [for] development of new energy' (Interview with Chinese official 2013). These signals of concerns for the 'environment' by the NEA indicate a remarkable shift in priorities and an indication of how environmental concerns may be coming back into the equation in China's wind power development marketisation, after having been largely left in the dark during the years of extensive growth when the primary concern was to build up a home-grown industrial base. Still, China's power sector is mostly a slow-moving actor, and no radical reforms are taking place overnight. Changes in China's power sector have thus been awaited for several years, if not decades, and in 2013 it was still difficult to find out how the State Grid is developing.

> Everybody talks about the State Grid having to develop. Everybody is talking about this Power Sector Reform [The Energy Revolution]. That's in the Five-Year Plans, it's in NEA's plan. And it's being mentioned at the Central Committee meeting, so something will happen, I think everybody is agreeing on that. But there's huge disagreement as to what is going to happen [...] But they try to articulate the necessity to change things in a somewhat 'harmless' way. 'It's not right now that things are going to change'. But at the same time you are thinking, 'if you can do something tomorrow, then let's try it, haha'. But the way that they are talking about it, it's by making it 'harmless". (Interview with Chinese think tank 2013)

This is a statement from early 2013. Today, after China embarked on its 'Energy Revolution' later on in 2013 and more concretely in 2015, China's energy system is eventually appearing to transform itself more confidently, and yet still only incrementally.

The imminent energy transition

China's government started adopting the idea of an energy transition, or energy revolution, in 2013, but it was not until 2015 when both the 13th Five-Year Plan (2016–2020) (National Development & Reform Commission 2016) was drafted in the run-up to the United Nations COP21 climate summit, and the so-called 'Document No. 9' was issued by the Communist Party of China's Central Committee and the State Council,[4] that the concept of an energy transition, or Energy Revolution, was actually carved out. The dawning of the long-awaited Energy Revolution signifies an aim to further deepen the power system reform, and marks a significant shift in Chinese energy policies with the goal to enhance renewable energy development and integration, by promoting distributed power generation, enhancing power generation dispatch, and enhancing the distribution and retail segments.

Apart from the introduction of stricter rules for grid integration and refined price-setting mechanisms[5] that will help reduce curtailment issues and the economisation and marketisation of wind power development (also see Chapter Four), this is to be done, for example, through the introduction of a wholesale electricity market and reforms and local experiments with the electricity pricing and trading system, as well as through a national carbon-trading market (Dupuy 2016; GWEC 2016:34–35; Ho, Wang & Yu 2017; interview with Chinese think tank 2016; Liu & Kong 2016; NEA/NDRC 2015a, 2015b, 2015c; Pollitt, Yang & Chen 2017; Romig 22 August 2018; Reuters 20 April 2018; State Council and the Central Committee of the Communist Party 2015). The Energy Revolution in turn hinges on an enhanced power infrastructure and thus also forms an integral part of China's ambitious One Belt One Road Initiative, which builds on the idea of revitalising the old Silk Road through an integrated energy net of power lines across China, connecting its neighbouring (and non-neighbouring) countries (Chung & Xu 2016). Together with the central government's attempts to curb the development of new coal power plants (Forsythe 2016) and strengthened emphasis on technological quality and energy efficiency 'to find ways to lower the cost of electricity generation and to further boost the competitiveness of the [wind turbine] manufacturing industry' (GWEC 2016:35), the Energy Revolution may imply that new winds are indeed blowing in Chinese wind power development.

Winds of change in Chinese wind power development – wind opponents becoming proponents

As China has embarked on its Energy Revolution, even 'stalwarts from the fossil fuel industry and not known to be supporters of the renewables industry' have started to signal a wish to move towards renewables (GWEC 2016:34). Thus, 'China is now on a path to permanently reducing its coal production and consumption, and coal imports, in favour of progressively greater reliance on green energy sources' (Mathews 2016:4). This signals a shift in attitudes among high-level government officials who now seem to want to promote a cleaner energy future for China. Many high-level government officials are concerned about the extreme air pollution in major cities, and express the desire to reduce air pollution and curb climate impacts (GWEC 2016:34).

In this way, by focusing on energy efficiency and system integration, the Energy Revolution marks a remarkable and much more concerted attempt to enhance the physical and institutional flexibility of the power system, in order to facilitate the development and absorption of more renewable energy (Dupuy 2016; interview with Chinese think tank 2016; Liu & Kong 2016). Again, these various trends also reflect that China's wind power sector is maturing, since the larger penetration rates have instantiated the move to create not only an investment market for wind turbines and wind power deployment, but also experiments with a nascent market for electricity pricing (interviews 2016).

And yet, since wind power development marketisation depends on multiple 'stakeholders', involving 'a lot of very powerful interests' (interview with Chinese think tank 2012) and vested interests across and within bureaucratic silos in China's remarkable matrix muddle, the country is likely to be muddling through its Energy Revolution for many years to come, as it is most likely not to be implemented without its own inherent power struggles as the 'battle between the traditional power plant interests and the new technologies' continues (interview with Chinese certification body 2013). Indeed, the transition to renewables is predicted to cause

> a ferocious scream. Everyone is calling, but the sound of the traditional forces [fossil fuels] are much greater than the forces engaged in renewable energy. (Interview with Chinese certification body 2013)

Despite the many colliding interests and agendas, the imminent Energy Revolution (and draft rules introducing spot electricity markets) indicates how the Chinese government has engaged in radical intervention, just in time when the wind power sector was facing a quality crisis, by installing frameworks for enhanced wind power integration, which may alleviate China's tendency to become socio-materially constrained, strangled, or tied by itself in terms of physical and institutional inflexibilities. Dependent on how the Energy Revolution is implemented, wind power may be reframed from a disruptive to a smooth, cost-efficient, and reliable energy source.

It seems, therefore, that the Chinese political leadership has realised with the Energy Revolution the need to circumvent high curtailment rates and the lack of a proper dispatching system. That is, it is not enough only to focus on generation (as was promoted during the first two phases of wind power development, namely through GW targets), but a functioning market assemblage necessitates the distribution and dispatch of wind power as well (as promoted by incentives to generate electricity, measured in GWh). This shift in calculative metrics (from GW to GWh) has necessitated an acknowledgement of the specific materiality of the object of exchange, namely wind power, and of the encompassing power system, as well as the comparative pricing (support) schemes for coal and wind. That is, to marketise wind power it must be integrated into the grid, which in turn requires the socio-material transformation and adaptation of the existing centralised power system (Grid 1.0), which – based on a logic of balancing the load – has been constituted as a hostile territory for wind power's logic of generating loads. Further, as calculative metrics are reconfigured, Sino-foreign supply-chain relations may also be reconfigured, for instance, as actors can come together competing on a more level playing field with remuneration based on energy (GWh) rather than installed capacity (GW). Moreover, they can join forces in common research programmes on system integration and on reducing the cost of energy, thus combining in a competitive fight with fossil fuels.

Reflections on second site of controversy: struggles over potential socio-material lock-in to fossil fuels

This chapter has shown how controversies in the transition to a sustainable energy system based on renewable energy, in China as elsewhere, are not just a matter of institutional or social factors but are also rooted in the very physical nature of the existing power system and the materiality of the object of exchange: the generated wind power from wind turbines. The analysis also indicates how two different, but linked, markets are being co-constructed in processes of economisation: the market of 'making wind a commodity' that can be integrated into the grid (i.e., the investment market for a wind power sector) without disrupting the grid's framing and without inducing extensive economic losses; and the still nascent market for electricity where the output from wind turbines is priced.

Chapter Five has traced how the socio-materially grounded framing of wind power as both disruptive and costly has created resistance to wind power amongst incumbent actors of the electrical power system, producing contestations over China's potential green turn and over any radical reforms of the power sector. The vested interests and political bargaining against wind power not only have roots in bureaucratic structures and China's high-level political arena for energy governance, but also have socio-material roots in the stochastically fluctuating electrons of wind power versus the stable and balancing factor of coal power. This has led to the substantive overflowing of the pre-existing grid's framing in terms of curtailment, in turn threatening the economisation and marketisation of wind power development, as wind power's framing as sustainable is destabilised. In addition, the vested interests and political bargaining against wind power are socio-materially grounded in the contested valuation of costs and prices - and their calculative devices and metrics - which are used to measure the comparative 'true' cost of energy of wind power and fossil fuels and to frame certain goods as 'true market' versus 'political' products. Participating in this socio-material power struggle of the assemblage around wind power development are, for example, the coal quota, local government contracts and incentive measures, physical and institutional flexibilities, electrons, electromagnetic waves, transmission lines, grid codes, vertical and horizontal lines of coordination, GW capacity targets, grid balancing practices, cost and price calculations, and forecasting tools. And so it is only by understanding the socio-technical nature of the specific commodity of exchange and of the specific encompassing system of exchange (grid system) that it becomes possible to understand the configuration of vested interests for or against wind power integration in China. Along the same lines, it is only by attending to the framing and valuation processes and the socio-material trials of strength in energy transitions to renewable energy that one can understand the contested nature of socio-technical sustainable transitions to renewable energy. It is here that this study indirectly extends not only to China Studies and its notion of fragmented authoritarianism (e.g. Lieberthal 2004), but also to the structural and institutional literature on 'sustainability transitions' and its linkage to 'innovation systems' (e.g. the multi-level perspective) (Geels 2007, 2011; Markard & Truffer 2008). That is, the relational and socio-material lens of the Anthropology of Markets has made it possible for the analysis to shed light on the socio-materially grounded contestations over the transitions to renwable energy.

Various scholars have also illustrated the inherent politics of energy and power markets in China and elsewhere (e.g. Andrews-Speed 2011; Jacobsson & Bergek 2004; Karnøe 2010; Mitchell 2011; Pallesen 2016), with some marketisation studies showing that adding 'intermittent energy sources like wind to an existing configuration of electricity generation disrupts its smooth functioning', producing negotiations over the value and worth of wind power

(Karnøe 2010:223). Indeed, processes of pacification, price-setting (and subsidisation), and overall valuation of wind power is seldom peaceful (Pallesen 2016). What arguably makes the integration of wind power into the power grid more politicised and sensitive in China is how the contestations over quotas, prices, costs, and subsidies, as well as over curtailment and integration, are entangled in a state-controlled and highly coal-dependent, politicised (and monopolised) power sector. China's transition to renewable energy is marked by politics and resistance as it is enmeshed in a power sector dominated by incumbent powerful state-owned business groups, state-controlled electricity prices, a strong coal-lobby, sunk costs in the coal-based power system, as well as in China's fragmented authoritarian planning system, where concerns for low electricity (and heating) prices are a main concern for the CPC in order to ensure social stability and retain a monopoly over political power. Accordingly, the chapter illustrates the potential risks in China of socio-material lock-in into fossil fuels (Unruh 2000; Callon 2007) – founded also in China's commitments to creating a fossil fuel system that is able to mine, drill, and transport huge quantities of energy (coal, oil, and gas) to serve China's fast-expanding manufacturing industry and economic growth (Mathews 2016). Meanwhile, what is also indicated here is how this materially hostile environment is not written in stone. Indeed, the imminent Energy Revolution may bear witness to the realisation of the need to reconfigure the power system to create better access for wind power penetration. And so, again, the Chinese government might succeed in intervening at exactly the right point in order to steer the Chinese wind power development assemblage back on track, embarking on its Long (Green) March, and muddling through towards a revolution in the energy system. And so, having looked at the struggle for access to feed power into the grid, we now continue on our journey by moving alongside the power flow and observing how the metering system converts the power flow into a money flow. In Chapter Six, this book's currency is no longer energy but money. We move onto computer screens with calculations of liquidity and creditworthiness that, as we will see, de- and reconfigure Sino-foreign supply chain relations in the consolidation phase that followed the marketquake.

Notes

1. Wind farms are generally located at the end of networks where loads (consumption) are traditionally placed; however, wind farms are not loads, they do not consume, but generate (hence the 'logic of generating loads').
2. As a response to this challenge, China State Grid has planned to invest RMB 600 billion (approx. USD 88 billion) into a 'highway network' of ultra-high-voltage (UHV) (1,300 kilovolts, both AC and DC) power transmission lines between 2009 and 2020, from north to south and west to east, to help the electrification and decarbonisation of China (energy seminar at Stanford University 2018).
3. Karnøe (2012) has described a power system with centralised power generation as a 'Grid 1.0' regime, which is steered by a load-balancing 'turning-up-and-down' logic (what he terms an 'Edison-Tesla configuration') where

consumers are generally passive in load balancing (Karnøe 2012:76). This is what the Chinese power system is like. This, in turn, is what produces a 'hostile territory' to wind power, as wind power is costly and disruptive to the model of generating and preserving load balance (Karnøe 2012:76). Meanwhile, argues Karnøe, the Grid 1.0 configuration is not set in stone. If transforming the grid system to a 'Grid 2.0', that is toward a 'volatility' logic instead, a new and less hostile system could be built with more wind power penetration, through the use of smart complementary generation, storage and consumption technologies, and new transmission lines (micro-grids) (Karnøe 2012:76).

4. Amongst its guiding principles, 'Document No. 9' launches 'Opinions on Clean Energy', to promote the usage and consumption of renewable energy. This includes many initiatives, for example, the comprehensive overall planning for annual energy balancing, the strengthening of daily operation regulations, procurement of sufficient ancillary services, as well as a strengthening of demand side management. Of particular importance, Document No. 9 emphasises the establishment of new mechanisms for distributed energy development (China Energy Storage Alliance 2015; Chung & Xu 2016).

5. For instance by introducing a distinction between expected and actual operational hours to the Chinese FIT, based on the curtailment rate. An investor has to secure that the generated electricity is accepted as a 'quota' by a local power operator, and in general has to have environmental permissions to build the wind power plant.

References

Andrews-Speed, P., 2012, *The Governance of Energy in China. Transition to a Low-Carbon Economy*, Palgrave Macmillan, Basingstoke.

Callon, M., 2007, 'An Essay on the Growing Contribution of Economic Markets to the Proliferation of the Social', *Theory, Culture & Society* 24(7–8), 139–163.

Chung, S.-w. W & Xu, Q., 2016, *China's Energy Policy from National and International Perspectives—The Energy Revolution and One Belt One Road Initiative*, City University of Hong Kong Press, Hong Kong.

Communist Party of China Central Committee and the State Council, 2015, 关于进一步深化电力体制改革的若干意见,中发(2015)9号文'全文 ['Several Opinions of the CPC Central Committee and the State Council on Further Deepening the Reform of the Electric Power System', No. 9 Text Full Text], 'Energy Revolution' ('*Policy #9*'/'Document No. 9'), 15 March 2015, http://www.ne21.com/news/show-64828.html.

Dupuy, M., 2016, 'China Power Sector Reform: Key Issues for the World's Largest Power Sector', *The Regulatory Assistance Program (RAP)*, March, viewed 8 December 2016, https://www.raponline.org/wp-content/uploads/2016/07/rap-dupuy-key-issues-china-power-sector-2016-march.pdf.

Forsythe, M., 2016, 'China Curbs Plans for More Coal-Fired Power Plants', *New York Times*, Energy & Environment, 25 April 2016.

García, C., 2013, 'Policies and Institutions for Grid-Connected Renewable Energy: "Best Practice" and the Case of China', *Governance: An International Journal of Policy, Administration, and Institutions* 26(1), 119–146.

Geels, F. W., 2007, 'Feelings of Discontent and the Promise of Middle Range Theory for STS: Examples from Technology Dynamics', *Science, Technology & Human Values* 32, 627–651.

Geels, F. W., 2011, 'The Multi-Level Perspective on Sustainability Transitions: Responses to Seven Criticisms', *Environmental Innovation and Societal Transitions* 1(1), 24–40.

Gorm Hansen, L. L., 2017, *Triggering Earthquakes in Science, Politics and Chinese Hydropower. A Controversy Study*, PhD thesis, Dept. of International Economics and Management, Asia Studies Centre, Copenhagen Business School.

Göss, S., 2017, 'China's Renewable Energy Revolution Continues on its Long March', *Energypost*, 13 February, http://energypost.eu/chinas-renewable-energy-revolution-continues-long-march/.

GWEC (Global Wind and Energy Council), 2016, 'Global Wind Report – Annual Market Update 2015', *Global Wind Energy Council.*

Ho, M. S., Wang, Z. & Yu, Z., 2017, 'China's Power Generation Dispatch', Resources for the Future (RFF Report), April 2017.

Jacobsson, S. & Bergek, A., 2004, 'Transforming the energy sector: the evolution of technological systems in renewable energy technology', *Industrial and Corporate Change* 13(5), 815–849.

Karnøe, P., 2010, 'Material Disruptions in Electricity Systems: Can Wind Power Fit in the Existing Electricity System?', in M. Akrich, Y. Barthe, F. Muniesa & P. Mustar (eds.), *Débordements: Mélanges Offerts à Michel Callon*, pp. 223–240, Transvalor – Presses de Mines, Paris.

Karnøe, P., 2012, 'How Disruptive is Wind Power? A Lesson from Denmark', *Debating Innovation* 2(3), 72–77.

Karnøe, P., 2013, 'Large Scale Wind Power Penetration in Denmark: Breaking Up and Remixing Politics, Technologies and Markets', *Revue de l'Energie* 611, 12–22.

Kirkegaard, J. K., Caliskan, K. & Karnøe, P., forthcoming, Comparative Marketization: Making Wind Power Investments attractive in Danish democracy, Chinese totalitarianism, and Turkish authoritarianism, presented in earlier versions at Copenhagen Business School, 6–8 July 2017, and at the International Market Studies Workshop, Copenhagen Business School, 6–8 June 2018, to be submitted in Organization Studies, mimeo.

Korsnes, M., 2014, 'Fragmentation, Centralisation and Policy Learning: An Example from China's Wind Industry', *Journal of Current Chinese Affairs* 43(3), 175–205.

Lema, A. & Ruby, K., 2007, 'Between Fragmented Authoritarianism and Policy Coordination: Creating a Chinese Market for Wind Energy', *Energy Policy* 35, 3879–3890.

Lieberthal, K., 2004, 'The Organization of Political Power and its Consequences: The View from the Outside', in K. Lieberthal, *Governing China: From Revolution through Reform*, pp. 171–205, 2nd edn., W. W. Norton & Co., New York.

Liu, X. & Kong, L., 2016, 'A New Chapter in China's Electricity Market Reform Energy Studies Institute', esi.nus.edu.sg, http://esi.nus.edu.sg/docs/default-source/esi-policy-briefs/a-new-chapter-in-china-s-electricity-market-reform.pdf.

Manwell, J. F., McGowan, J. G. & Rogers, A. L., 2010, *Wind Energy Explained: Theory, Design and Application*, 2nd edn., Wiley, Hoboken, NJ.

Markard, J. & Truffer, B., 2008, 'Technological Innovation Systems and the Multi-Level Perspective: Towards an Integrated Framework', *Research Policy* 37, 596–615.

Mason, J. & Lim, B. K. 2018, 'Exclusive: China plans to create energy ministry in government shake-up – sources', 8 March 2018, https://www.reuters.com/article/us-china-parliament-energy-exclusive/exclusive-china-plans-to-create-energyministry-in-government-shake-up-sources-idUSKCN1GK179.

Mathews, J. A., 2016, 'China's Continuing Renewable Energy Revolution – Latest Trends in Electric Power Generation', *The Asia-Pacific Journal, Japan Focus* 14(17).

Mathews, J. A. & Tan, H., 2015, *China's Renewable Energy Revolution*, Palgrave Macmillan, New York.

Mitchell, T., 2011, *Carbon Democracy: Political Power in the Age of Oil*, Vergo, London.

NEA/NDRC (New Energy Administration and National Development and Reform Commission), 2015a, 国能综新能〔2015〕177号, 国家能源局综合司关于进一步做好可再生能源发展'十三五'规划编制工作的指导意见 ['National energy system No. 177, Guidelines for the Comprehensive Division of the National Energy Administration on Further Completing the Preparation of the 'Thirteenth Five-Year Plan' for Renewable Energy Development'], 13 April, http://zfxxgk.nea.gov.cn/auto87/201504/t20150428_1911.htm

NEA/NDRC (New Energy Administration and National Development and Reform Commission), 2015b, 国家发展改革委 国家能源局关于改善电力运行调节促进清洁能源多发满发的指导意见 发改运行[2015]518号 [The NEA of the NDRC's Guiding Opinions on Improving Electric Power Operation Regulations and Promoting the Reform of Full Release of Clean Energy Development and Operation, No. 518], 4 September, http://www.nea.gov.cn/2015-04/09/c_134136821.htm.

NEA/NDRC (New Energy Administration and National Development and Reform Commission), 2015c, 国家发展改革委 国家能源局关于印发电力体制改革配套文件的通知, 发改经体[2015]2752号[NEA under NDRC issued a notice on the publication of supporting documents for power system reform, NDRC [2015] No. 2752], 30 November, http://www.nea.gov.cn/2015-11/30/c_134867851.htm.

NDRC (National Development and Reform Commission), 2016, The 13th Five-Year Plan for economic and social development of the People's Republic of China (2016–2020), transl. Central Committee of the Communist Party of China, Beijing, China, http://en.ndrc.gov.cn/newsrelease/201612/P020161207645765233498.pdf

Pallesen, T., 2016, 'Valuation Struggles over Pricing: Determining the Worth of Wind Power', *Journal of Cultural Economy* 9(6), 527–540.

Pollitt, M. G., Yang, C.-H. & Chen, H., 2017, 'Reforming the Chinese Electricity Supply Sector: Lessons from International Experience', *University of Cambridge, Energy Policy Research Group*, EPRG Working Paper 1704, Cambridge Working Paper in Economics 1713.

Romig, C., 2018, 'Powering the Dragon: the rise of Chinese renewables', *Poyry/PEI (Power Engineering International)*, 22 August 2018, https://www.powerengineeringint.com/articles/2018/08/powering-the-dragon-the-rise-of-chinese-renewables.html.

Reuters, 2018, 'China plans first spot electricity trading as Beijing reforms power market', 20 April 2018, https://www.reuters.com/article/us-china-electricity/china-plans-first-spot-electricity-trading-as-beijing-reforms-power-market-idUSKBN1HR1LA.

Sandholt, K., 2013, 'The Biggest Obstacle to Wind Power Development in China', *China Energy Viewpoint*, blog-post by K. Sandholt on energy policy in China, 27 January. Viewed 2 June 2014. http://www.sandholts.dk/?author=1&paged=2.

Tande, J. O. G., & Jenkins, N., 2003, 'Grid Integration of Wind Farms', *Wind Energy*, 6:281–295, DOI: 10.1002/we.91.

Unruh, G. C., 2000, 'Understanding Carbon Lock-In', *Energy Policy* 28(12), 1 October, 817–830.

6 Controversy over access to money in China's spider's web – diving into the 'system problem' of Chinese wind power development

As I find my foreign counterpart – the only other foreigner for miles, amongst Chinese children playing and kites flying in the blue sky around the Olympic City in Beijing – we soon find my favourite café in the area and sit down to have our coffee in a quiet, dark spot in the back of the room. I turn on the recorder and the talk takes off almost by itself. Although strangers, we have several things in common. Apart from being the only Westerners, we are both – me as a researcher and he as a control system supplier in the wind power field – struggling to understand exactly the same thing: The Chinese spider's web that seems to shape Chinese wind power development marketisation as well as Sino-foreign supply chain relations in it. Talking for a couple of hours, some of the components in the puzzle start to fall into their proper places. What he tells me is an intriguingly complex story of the challenges of trying to manage the thick mesh of the Chinese spider's web, denoting the tangled web of state-business *guānxì*, especially as the quality crisis has led to a turn to quality and an ensuing consolidation phase, which has overflowed into liquidity constraints and problems of gaining access to money in Sino-foreign supply chains. As he comes to the crux of the matter, and the increased need for Chinese agents to manage the turn to quality, he asks me to turn off my recorder. And then he continues.

Months later, I am on my bike to meet a long-time Chinese wind power expert and advisor, whom I've heard so much about. Sitting in the hotel lobby, I am beginning to suspect a point is missing in the algorithmic account materialising in my fieldwork in China as I dig into the Chinese 'spider's web'. And so it turns out that one of the missing bricks in the puzzle to understand the spider's web and the quality crisis in Chinese wind power development has been an account of the core issue of China's total industrial system, which has caused these quality crises to occur in the first place. According to him, the reason is that China is 'not a pure market economy ... and therefore you see overcapacity in many Chinese industries [...] In China everybody is competing for life on lower prices, and finally this led to damage ... so nobody is doing well. I think the market mechanism is not established yet.'

The Chinese gentleman explains: 'This is the problem ... it's also the "system problem" for China – you know, the state-owned enterprises.' It is his last comment in particular that stays with me as I leave the hotel lobby: 'But I'm worried about the basic system, it's not the driving force to improve.' And so, on my way back home I wonder if the particularity of the Chinese spider's web and the controversy over access to money is linked to an inherent controversy over China's system problem that may hinder a turn to quality.

Follow the money!

This investigation now delves into the third site of controversy in the marketisation of Chinese wind power development, continuing the wind power's journey from the turbine and into the grid, where the kilowatt-hours delivered mean money is earned, and where money means power. We thus venture into issues of earning potential, ability to raise loans, liquidity, and profits, of manufacturers and suppliers, as if traversing the interweaved and interfering electromagnetic waves of *guānxì* in the Chinese spider's web. In 'following the money', so to speak, the book focuses on the period of the quality crisis and consolidation phase (Phases Two and Three), periods which produced severe liquidity constraints in the supply chains of China's wind turbine industry, and which caused great volatility in Sino-foreign supply chain relations around control system technologies, in particular as struggles over access to money unfolded (see Figure 6.1).

What emerges through the rhizomatic account is both how Sino-foreign supply chain relations are deeply entangled in China's unfinished corporate restructuring process, which is likened to a spider's web, where the Chinese state infiltrates all relations in an opaque spider-like fashion, and the spider's web's entanglement in a Chinese system problem. It is this very system problem – namely the lack of a so-called 'pure market economy' – that has played a critical role in the creation of the quality crisis in the first place.

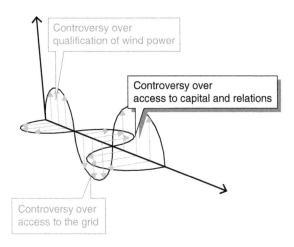

Figure 6.1 Third site of controversy.

This leads, as we will see, to the contestation over the very political sustainability of China's green marketisation with Chinese characteristics.

From being awash with money to radically squeezed for credit

With such entrenched accounts, it is first necessary to look back to how the marketquake was enabled in the first place, namely through large investments and high liquidity, and how the ensuing quality crisis then instigated a consolidation phase that put a credit squeeze on the entire wind power sector.

Overall, the marketquake was fundamentally enabled by China's considerable financial investments in wind power, supported amongst other things by the country's substantial investment funds (in particular after the economic stimulus package implemented in response to the global economic crisis in 2008) (Kroeber 2016; Lardy 2016; Naughton 2014), development banks, and a significant amount of international climate finance, facilitated by the Kyoto Protocol's Clean Development Mechanism (CDM).[1] Meanwhile, the vast amount of funding available soon produced a paradoxical problem of 'too much money!' in the industry (Interview with Chinese government advisor and wind industry association 2013). And so the high liquidity soon produced a virtual gold-rush that resulted in 'a lack of project evaluation behind credit decisions' (Korsnes 2014:193), overcapacity (Kroeber 2016; Lardy 2016; Naughton 2014), and resulting curtailment. It also led to a preference for underbidding SOEs in government-led bids, in an industry that was driven by quantity and price and 'not so much about the quality' (interview with Chinese component supplier 2012), as SOEs were able to offer comparably lower turbine prices through scale advantages and soft budget constraints (as discussed in Chapter Four). Meanwhile, as already mentioned, the result was soon a 'quality crisis' in the wind turbine industry.

Somewhat paradoxically, and again, the Chinese government had generated a problem to which it had to find a rapid resolution: that is, easy access to money had enabled the quality crisis to run (almost) out of control. As a reaction to the quality crisis and overcapacity issues, central government radically intervened. It did so to a large extent by strengthening the control of credit, so as to consolidate the industry, changing its tune entirely. In other words, now the state-controlled banks who, earlier, were not so risk-averse 'won't lend them [investors such as wind turbine manufacturers, wind farm developers, power generating companies] money, that's how it [the rapid growth] has been halted' (interview with foreign control system supplier 2012). Thus, this

> has been a way [of the Chinese Government] to stop the train. It was like saying, 'now we stop the money flows and regulate the banks, so they [wind turbine manufacturers, wind farm developers, generating companies, and others] cannot borrow money' (Interview with foreign control system supplier 2012)

A lack of profitability in projects and mounting debts in supply chains

Meanwhile, the halting of credit soon started to produce a new problem, namely one of debt chains and a reduction in liquidity in China's emerging socio-technical assemblage around wind power development.

Apart from suddenly lacking access to easy credit, investors in wind power had already found themselves squeezed in terms of insufficient remuneration for energy production, as the tariff was only equivalent to that received by thermal power plants. This problem of liquidity and inadequate profitability was exacerbated by the poor cross-provincial management of the Renewable Energy Fund from the Renewable Energy Law, whereby

> there have been years, where they [wind farm developers, power generating companies, wind turbine manufacturers] couldn't get the money out, and then they haven't been able to pay for the turbines. And then the banks have financed it, because they knew that the province was obliged to pay for it ... but that payment has just been pushed and pushed and pushed. (Interview with Chinese think tank 2013)

Lastly, investors also witnessed the unit costs of wind power generation increase because of the high curtailment rates. Together, these issues squeezed both power generating companies and wind farm developers financially, as they were losing the potential revenues from the power that was being curtailed and thus profit margins were under pressure (Bloomberg 2012:5; Qi 2013). In turn, the increasingly severe liquidity issues soon started to overflow into 'chain debts in the Chinese wind power industry' (Qi 2013), which severely restricted the industry during consolidation. Starting upstream and moving down through the value chain, first power generators, then wind farm developers, and eventually wind turbine manufacturers would each stop their 'own payments down the chain' (interview with foreign control system supplier 2012). Finally, because 'the government owes subsidies to wind farm developers, the developers owe payment to turbine manufacturers, and turbine makers owe payment to component suppliers', these chain debts developed throughout China's wind power sector (Qi 2013), squeezing the liquidity of the Chinese SOEs (interview with foreign control system supplier 2012). This issue of liquidity was in turn exacerbated by rising coal prices, at the same time as electricity prices had been stable, which meant that generating companies

> are actually losing money – at least they claim so – from producing electricity from coal. And then they have no money to pay for the wind turbines, they've got. And then they [the wind turbine component suppliers] don't get paid by [X or Y or Z, that is, Chinese wind turbine manufacturers]. You know them all. I'm just saying, they are all lacking money. (Interview with foreign control system supplier 2012)

The above indicates the required valuation work in terms of economisation that is needed for the marketisation of wind power development, transforming it into a profitable and attractive object for investment.

Follow relations around the (lack of) money!

By following the flow of money, or rather the sudden lack thereof, we have seen how China's assemblage around wind power development was, again, affected by oscillating movements between decentralisation and centralisation of state control – this time with a focus on how this affected credit, liquidity, and profitability, after the marketquake. We will now explore how these processes have de- and reconfigured relations between customers and suppliers, as chain debts started to mount. We are therefore diving into the Chinese spider's web of entangled state–business actors, all enmeshed in the Chinese contested 'system problem'.

The spider's web: China's business groups living in and out of each other's pockets

The Chinese SOEs, however, turned out to be highly resilient during the period of financial constraints because of their special status. Tied to other members in various business group structures, formally and informally, they tended to feel more or less secured by their mother company, their 'brothers' and 'sisters', and their so-called 'common pockets': it was 'no big deal whether the money is in one box or the other' (interview with foreign control system supplier 2012).

For instance, the case of Guodian United Power Corporation, which is one of the world's largest wind power companies, illustrates this: the power-generating company China Guodian Corporation. This is one of the 'Big Five' listed on the SASAC list of China's National Champions (State Asset Supervision and Administration Council) the case of one of the world's largest wind power companies, Guodian United Power Corporation, which is a daughter company of the the SASAC-listed (State Asset Supervision and Administration Council) power-generating National Champion company, China Guodian Corporation, that represents one of China's 'Big Five' power generating companies. (Korsnes 2014:190–191). One of Guodian's subsidiaries is the wind farm developer Longyuan Power, which is responsible for Guodian's renewable energy assets, which it manages through the wind turbine manufacturer Guodian United Power, wholly owned by China Guodian Corporation (Korsnes 2014:190–191). The result of this constellation is that, somewhat paradoxically, the supplier of wind turbines, Guodian United Power, in a manner of speaking sells turbines to itself, that is, to its own mother company and one of its subsidiaries. As a consequence of such intricate relations, most of the SOEs involved in wind power did not close 'down as the rest of us would maybe do', even when they had not received payments from their customer(s) for a while,

> because they say, 'the one who owes me, is my brother. I'll get them'. And they don't have a board of directors asking you, 'are you sure of that?!' (Interview with foreign control system supplier 2012)

Overall, China's large state-owned wind turbine manufacturers and wind farm developers are often influential companies, which benefit from their unique position as subsidiary of a parent company from a related industry, such as machinery and equipment manufacturing, and which often have direct links with electric power utilities (Korsnes 2014:190–191). Accordingly, when facing soft budget constraints these companies would often be prepared to sacrifice short-term profitability in order to win bids and secure projects (Chang 2011; Liu & Kokko 2010; Yu et al. 2009:5223). At the same time, though, they are not inherently interested in fighting for profits or market shares, as they have often already been guaranteed a certain annual market share by the state (interview with foreign control system supplier 2013). Furthermore, owing to their engagement in many diverse portfolio activities from across their business group, some of them have been able to turn away (sometimes temporarily) in times of financial turmoil from wind power deployment towards other business activities. In this way, state-owned generating companies would

> want to have … wind power, 'we have the new energy'. Haha. They want the reputation. Reputation's better than the profit, and at that time, coal power was still profitable. So the wind projects lose a little bit of money, [but] the coal power still has profit. So no problem. (Interview with Chinese government advisor and wind industry association 2013)

As a consequence, whilst newer and smaller private wind turbine manufacturers were starting to go bankrupt, the SOEs 'still do not want to give up' even though they were losing money (interview with Chinese component supplier 2012). The resilient nature of China's SOEs reflects the prevalence of soft budget constraints – a legacy of the 'iron rice bowl' due to the extended social obligations of SOEs in China's state-controlled electricity generation and equipment manufacturing sectors. These are not so much driven by profit maximisation but more by local objectives: employment, development of local industry, public control (or even ownership) over the power sector, tax revenue, and local growth rates (García 2013; Zhao, Wang & Wang 2012a:224). In this way, whilst Chinese market reforms have been aimed at restructuring the central redistribution system and the governance of SOEs, with the aim of making local governments and SOEs switch from 'soft budget constraints' to 'hard budgets' (Lin 2006 in Chang 2011:322), there is still a long way to go before this takes place in Chinese wind power development marketisation.

Strangled Sino-foreign customer–supplier relations during the consolidation phase

Whilst Chinese SOEs could ride the wave relatively comfortably, the story was quite different for foreign component suppliers because the mounting debts soon started to have an 'effect all the way down' to foreign sub-suppliers who were at the bottom of the debt chain:

> Chinese companies are linked closely together like in a chain. If the state-owned banks lack money, then the State Grid, the power gener-ating companies, the wind farm owners, and the wind turbine manu-facturers lack liquidity. And then, in the end, there is no money for the European suppliers. They need some money in order to be able to pay. (Interview with foreign control system supplier 2012)

In order to survive and not to be compelled to leave China altogether, for-eign companies in China supplying components, such as control systems, to Chinese state-owned wind turbine manufacturers have been forced to develop creative ways to face the dilemma of postponed payments from their customers. A typical Chinese customer would comment, "just relax, it [the payments] will come. Just keep staying the same, then everything will be fine" (interview with foreign control system supplier 2012). At the same time, this meant an intricate balancing act of walking on eggshells, keeping on good terms both with the Chinese customer and with the com-pany board of directors back home in Europe or the USA.

Riding the storm together

Foreign suppliers were soon to realise that their survival in China during the credit squeeze depended on the maintenance of their customer–supplier relationship, even when these very customers did not pay promptly, or at all. What happened was that Chinese turbine manufacturers convinced some of their foreign suppliers that 'we'll have to ride the storm together' (interview with foreign control system supplier 2012). This was coupled to the business group structure of the wind power sector, in that if one sup-plier stops a service or supply to a Chinese wind turbine manufacturer, it has direct implications not only for the relation between that wind turbine manufacturer and the wind farm developer, but eventually also with the mother company (generating company) and the grid company. Therefore, as the Chinese wind turbine manufacturer is dependent on a good relation-ship with its mother company, this hinging on providing timely and cheap service, foreign component suppliers

> can't just close down, because then [the Chinese wind farm developer] won't understand why the turbines are not running as they are sup-posed to, and then [Chinese state-owned wind turbine manufacturer]

says, 'that's those stupid people from [foreign component supplier]', and then we'll have a bad relationship with [the Chinese wind farm developer], and then we will be put down at the bottom of the [components] list. Out here you need to ride off the storm together. (Interview with foreign control system supplier 2012)

And then they [Chinese customers' keep an eye on you [foreign supplier]. They really keep an eye on you, how you behave ... and they reward you for it ... Because if you start to make trouble, then they will put you right back to the bottom of the [suppliers' list]. Then you will never get your money back, that's for sure. (Interview with foreign control system supplier 2012)

Whilst some foreign suppliers displayed total intolerance of this practice – resulting in a loss of market share and deteriorating customer relations, or in leaving China altogether – others attempted to display tolerance towards delayed payments. By 'treating the culprit nicely' (interview with foreign control system supplier 2012) and thereby 'acting somewhat as a bank, which offers credit to their Chinese customers', they aimed to show their understanding of how the Chinese wind power sector, and ultimately Chinese society, functions. Further, owing to the entangled nature of both smaller and larger SOEs in the power sector, who all have 'the same owners' (Interview with foreign control system supplier 2012), foreign suppliers were unable to identify the 'culprit', as these relations are

complex. There's a lot of common pockets and blurred boundaries. How to find out, who it is that doesn't pay [us] the money? ... For instance, when [Chinese wind turbine manufacturer] doesn't pay, then it's likely because [wind farm owner] doesn't pay, and then in the end it's because the State Grid and the state don't pay! (Interview with foreign control system supplier 2012)

As the money stopped flowing down the system, foreign suppliers found themselves in a dilemma, as they acknowledged that 'it's not their [the customer's/wind turbine manufacturer's] fault' that payments were delayed, but ultimately that of the Chinese government. Yet, as 'nobody can take the Chinese State to court', foreign suppliers felt compelled to stay on good terms with everybody in the chain to keep hold of their customer (interview with foreign control system supplier 2012):

That's actually wrong. Because they [the State; the wind farm owners] are the ones who are guilty, because they are the ones, who have not paid [a Chinese state-owned wind turbine manufacturer]. Well, it's ... actually, you support the one, who is the reason for the problem, right. Actually, we do that. And that's ... in terms of how we tackle this normally, then it's totally wrong. (Interview with foreign control system supplier 2012)

While some foreign suppliers chose to take a 'no tolerance' policy towards non-payment by customers, many continued to deliver their services as contracted (but just not new services) in order to 'keep on good terms with the [wind farm] owners'. If they discontinued their service, 'I've spoiled the relation that I wanted to keep, because then I have created a bad reputation in regard to service' (Interview with foreign control system supplier 2012).

Emergence of agents and 'go-betweens'

The second effect of the credit squeeze, as profits were dwindling and debts surged, was the emergence of a new kind of Chinese actor to smooth out the constrained relations between Chinese customers and foreign suppliers. The role of such an actor cannot be overemphasised. Doing business in Chinese wind power without a Chinese agent (or brokering service company) in between customer and supplier became increasingly impossible because the agent is 'often the cousin of some government official' and functions through his/her *guānxì* with government officials whom they can 'butter up' (interview with foreign control system supplier 2012). It is important to acknowledge that agents in China's consolidating wind power sector play various roles. First, they act as a 'buffer guarantee of future payment'. Second, they can help with 'nurturing the soil both politically and commercially' to get access to state-owned customers and supportive officials at the highest political level (interview with foreign control system supplier 2013). And third, they can assist in taking on some of the tasks that foreigners do not have the necessary resources to conduct, because 'we don't have the connections for that. We have the connections to those who have the connections. And that's what we have to exploit' (interview with foreign control system supplier 2012).

A buffer for non-payments

Considering the first function, that is, a buffer for non-payment of debts, an agent

> doesn't just need good relations, he also needs to have lots of money. He needs to be a buffer for the payment. Instead of waiting for the money for nine months, we'll get them in three months. So we reduced the risk. (Interview with foreign control system supplier 2013)

In addition to this buffer function, the agent works to ease the communication and negotiation processes. According to one agent, 'I know foreigners very well. I can translate Chinese needs and foreign needs, make them meet – not word by word. But making things work' (interview with Chinese agent 2013). In this way acting as a brokering 'lubricant' (interview with Chinese agent 2013), the agent assists the foreign companies who 'are just like a baby, and I'm like a mother for them, so I deliver the results for them' (interview with Chinese agent 2013). Helping communication between the Chinese customer and foreign supplier, the agent engages in an embedding form of *guānxì,* which is prevalent in Chinese business relations, as it promotes a 'cultivation of trust and understanding in mutually beneficial connection, with an instrumental aim to promote cooperation and increase future benefits' (Chang 2011:319).

Using agents to connect to others

The second activity ensures connections to customers, and supportive offi-cials' help to 'open up for a meeting with the right people' (interview with foreign control system supplier 2013). This is important for foreign compa-nies, since 'it's only the Chinese who actually know who's in charge' in China (interview with foreign control system supplier 2013). The construction of such *guānxì* and the use of agents is critical to the survival of foreign companies:

> I don't have the philosopher's stone, nobody has the philosopher's stone, but in my personal opinion, I think that the closer ties you can create, in relation to the customers that you work with, and the closer you can get to the top of the company ... now I'm talking about personal relations ... the closer you can get to the political top and developing this network ... then you can ... I don't dare to say to a Party member ... but that you come so close to the decision-makers, so they can see that a collaboration can give them something. In that case, I think that the risk of getting sidetracked both financially and technically becomes smaller for a Western partner. (Interview with foreign control system supplier 2013)

Establishing such relations with government officials and Party members requires that the agent is 'paid a few more percentages', in order that he can 'butter up' the relevant people (interviews with foreign control system sup-pliers 2012, 2013), acting as a hybrid middleman or an 'obligatory passage point' to get leverage on the relevant officials. In this way, some foreign sup-pliers have chosen to pay some 'extra dividends' for the services provided, whereas others have paid through investments in time and money to build trust and interpersonal relations (*guānxì*) (interviews with foreign control system suppliers 2012, 2013). With their contacts, agents

> really can do things ... it's not just empty talk, they can ... they can ... a lot of them really know some tricks, that's ... [...] they know some peo-ple and can tell them to buy this. (Interview with foreign control system supplier 2012)

Because of the entangled nature of SOEs in Chinese wind power, 'the better the network, the closer you'll be to the right decision-makers ... And having the right relations, I think that's the best form of security' against lacking or delayed payments (interview with foreign control system supplier 2013).

Thus, by 'knowing the right people', the agent plays a critical 'bridging' (or brokering) role (Burt 1992 in Chang 2011:318), which means that the *guānxì* is used to link groups that are otherwise not connected together, 'usually to benefit his or her own interests' (Burt 1992 in Chang 2011:318).

Agents as market intelligence

Third, exploiting an agent's relations so as to benefit from their market intelligence can help foreign suppliers tremendously in regard to knowing in advance 'where the market is moving' and 'what kind of regulations have been introduced, and what impact they have' (interview with foreign control system supplier 2012):

> They [Chinese state-owned wind turbine manufacturers/customers] would never tell us anything in the first place, I can guarantee you that. That kind of information – you won't get … what's … what market they are working in, and their … that part out here, that's one hundred per cent closed to us. That means that the requirements that park owners get from some grid company, a grid code, whatever … what they are basing that on, they won't tell us. We just get the specifications and then we must fulfil it. (Interview with foreign control system supplier 2012)

Much of the official market data in China is often not considered trustworthy or up to date, so foreign companies have felt the need to cultivate relations with agents in order to get access to unofficial market intelligence, which is critical 'to make sure that you understand what's going on. Many things take place behind the curtains here, and nobody can really see what's happening' (interview with foreign control system supplier 2012). In this way, by cultivating *guānxì*, or 'employing *guānxì* as strategy', foreign suppliers can reduce uncertainties concerning, amongst other things, resource allocation, information transmission, and market competition (Chang 2011:320). And so foreign suppliers are trying to reduce the uncertainty and complexity they experience in the Chinese wind power sector, in particular during the credit squeeze, 'by establishing relationships with local partners who can offer relevant information, advice, and support' (Boisot & Child 1999 in Chang 2011:328).

Outsourcing part of the spider's web – and relations as a source of agency

Overall, the agent functions as a critically important intermediary who links actors together, using their contacts but also through the help of material means, such as cigarettes, money, beer, wine, and Chinese strong rice wine liqueur (*baijiu*). The agent frequently handles the direct relationship himself and 'smokes the necessary cigarettes and drinks the proper amount of beer and wine' with the Chinese end customer (state-owned manufacturers, developers, and/or grid companies) and with the central and local government officials (interview with foreign control system supplier 2012). In this way, 'it's also a matter of outsourcing relations and the related drinking and smoking' (interview with foreign control system supplier 2013):

> It's crazy, crazy [the need for connections]. And the best ... the easiest way to do it is to outsource a bit of it, I think. And then use these 'go-betweens' [agents] who are around. (Interview with foreign control system supplier 2012)

The ability to construct relations with agents of foreign actors as well as an agent's ability to relate to officials have therefore emerged as a certain form of relational capital and a source of agency, as it makes it 'possible to do anything'. That is, if you have the right relations, 'everything is possible' (interview with foreign control system supplier 2012). According to one Chinese agent, 'the best relation with Chinese people is not just about business. In China, the law is one thing, but the law can be changed by a person, if you have the right relationship' (interview with foreign control system supplier 2013). As part of President Xi Jinping's ambitious strategy of Comprehensively Deepening Reforms (CCCPC 2013), China is undertaking comprehensive anti-corruption campaigns. Whilst *guānxì* sometimes may border on the edge of corruption, sometimes overstepping the boundary and sometimes not, it is evident that in wind power the market has 'turned more corrupt' during the consolidation phase and the ensuing credit squeeze (interview with foreign control system supplier 2013).

Transformation of relations – from cowboy hats and boots to building associations of trust

As liquidity issues started to affect Sino-foreign customer–supplier relations, the quality of their relations was also transformed over time. This reflected the changing capabilities of Chinese customers and the gradual move from a quality crisis to a turn to quality. This in turn reconfigured relations between Chinese customers and foreign component suppliers, as the industry was transformed from a sellers' market to a buyers' market (interview with foreign control system supplier 2012). Unsurprisingly, the effects were also felt in the relationship between the foreign component supplier and the head office back home.

Transforming a sellers' market to a buyers' market – taking off the cowboy hats and boots

In the initial growth phase of the Chinese turbine industry, around 2007, 'the wind market was a "sellers' market"' (interview with Chinese employee in foreign control system supplier 2012), which somehow made doing business 'way too easy, on our premises' (interview with foreign control system supplier 2012). In this context, foreign suppliers had no troubles finding customers, as Chinese SOEs

> just needed to install, install, and they were buying stuff like crazy ... the money, it was an awful lot of money, which were put into this wind turbine thing ... and there were no problems in terms of payments, well, the liquidity was incredibly high. (Interview with foreign control system supplier 2012)

Accordingly, at this stage there was neither the time nor the need to build associations of trust. Instead, 'it was just that the market was so big and demanding that they [the Chinese wind turbine manufacturers] were hungry for all this [foreign technology]', and with so many new wind farm installations, 'the Chinese customers required high-speed response' (interview with foreign control system supplier 2012):

> Because major wind turbine [manufacturers], they all ... some have the government relations ... so the Government wants efficiency ... they don't know the details ... 'I think in half a year or one year, you have to get this size'. Then all the guys below him just want to move fast, implement. The time schedule is important. (Interview with Chinese employee in foreign control system supplier 2012)

As a consequence of the rapid growth that ensued, Chinese buyers of control systems virtually did not know what they were getting; rather 'they just knew that it was a control system'. Nevertheless, contracts were signed 'without knowing what it was all about. It was so easy. You didn't have to sit down and try to understand'; on the contrary 'you just had to bring a piece of paper, and then they would sign. And we got the money' (interview with foreign control system supplier 2012). However, this way of doing business, 'with cowboy hats and boots on, and then moving ahead' (interview with foreign control system supplier 2012), could not last forever; and it had to change during the consolidation phase as the turn to quality set in. With the onset of the entangled quality and liquidity crises, the situation changed, and around the beginning of January 2012 'when it really hit', the sellers' market was transformed into a buyers' market (interview with foreign control system supplier 2012):

> It changed overnight, in January [2012]. I think so. There were some new initiatives from the government, some economic restrictions have been introduced for the wind power sector, which have meant that it's changing now. And then, I can sense that it's not so much about selling a product anymore, it's about selling a relation. (Interview with foreign control system supplier 2012)

Suddenly, foreign suppliers found themselves needing 'to sit down and think a bit. And you must talk with the Chinese, and need to teach them how to trust you' (interview with foreign control system supplier 2012). In this way, 'we are back to the things, which really trigger them [the Chinese]', that is, building *guānxì* through associations of trust' (interview with foreign control system supplier 2012). The industry thus started to function differently, as opposed to previously when

> you didn't have to sit down and try to build trust. Well, that's for sure what you need now. If the Chinese don't trust you, you can leave. I normally say it this way: you may have the best product, at the best price, but you cannot sell it, if you don't know the right people. (Interview with foreign control system supplier 2012)

Contracts (or working around them) – and moving towards guānxì

In the West, a traditional and well-understood means of establishing and stabilising collaborative relations – building trust – is through the use of formal agreements and contracts. In contrast, part of the process of trust-building in China often starts in working around contracts *after* they have been signed. Thus,

> when you sign a contract [in the West], it's certain, because according to Western culture, or let's say Danish culture, when he's signing a contract, he's very careful, each sentence, every word, so after signing the contract, he has great respect for this contract. (Interview with Chinese control system supplier 2013)

In China, however, a 'contract is not a contract in the classic understanding. Under the best of circumstances, it's a letter of intention, and that's it' (interview with foreign control system supplier 2012). Thus, a contract in China is 'only a piece of paper. Even though I have a signature here, but after I [can] change it … that's the difference' (interview with Chinese control system supplier 2013). Without a 'culture of the contract', the Chinese 'credit [reputation] system is based on the person, I only work with the people, I believe in' (interview with Chinese employee in foreign control system supplier 2012). What should be particularly emphasised here is that using such a Chinese pragmatic approach towards contracts is essential when entering into business relations with SOEs, who operate under 'special conditions':

> So that means that he's [Chinese SOE] not 100 per cent complying with the execution of the contract, and this is a big difference. Frankly, it's not just our clients, but in China all state-owned units, or all private Chinese companies are like this. There may be ten points in the contract, but there will not be full implementation of all of them. It's just about laying down

the supply and demand relations of the two sides, nothing more [...] We all know that there was too much in the contract, so it's nothing more than an establishment of a relationship between the supply and demand sides. (Interview with Chinese control system supplier 2013)

The result of subsequently working around the contract conditions as a pragmatic means by Chinese companies to establish relationships is that the conventional framing device – the contract – in the eyes of foreign suppliers is '[not] worth the paper it has been written on' (interview with foreign control system supplier 2013). To add to this post-contractual uncertainty for foreign actors, there is also a blurring of the expected roles: 'It's very strange, in China there is no clear boundary between business and personal relationships' (Interview with Chinese agent 2013).

Contestation over lacking respect

Overall, during the time of consolidation and the ensuing liquidity issues in China's wind power sector, relations based on trust and understanding started to become more highly valued. As Chinese actors were faced with liquidity issues, they started to contest the legalistic and formalistic approach to partnerships employed by many foreign suppliers. When foreign suppliers relied on a conservative 'to the letter' approach, this often resulted in the loss of Chinese customers. In order to win back their customers, foreign suppliers saw themselves being forced into 'trying another approach', to rebuild relations which had gone 'sour'. Rather than just being focused on obtaining signatures, it became necessary 'to have a talk and to hear what actually went wrong' (interview with foreign control system supplier 2012), in the realisation that 'we are making a serious mistake if we think that it [the contract] has got the same meaning [in China] as in the West' (interview with foreign control system supplier 2013):

> It's not so much about looking at the contract. It helps that you sit down together at the table. But it's more about building up trust, so they trust you and trust what you tell them. It takes time. Costs some money. Haha. But when that has been settled, and you have invested the time, then you can do anything. (Interview with foreign control system supplier 2012)

In changing strategy, it soon started to become apparent that one of the things that had gone wrong was a lack of understanding about the need for a Chinese agent during times of financial constraint. Whilst some foreign suppliers refused to engage with agents altogether, others saw that something was needed, even though they

> found it very difficult in the beginning when there was suddenly someone [...] It's not how we do things normally, it isn't! We don't want any

go-between … no … 'why is he there? What is he doing?' It's difficult to understand. 'And does he keep the money to himself, or what does he do?' It's … we just don't understand. (Interview with foreign control system supplier 2012)

In fact, many suppliers had an initial resistance to agents, and relations consequently became destabilised during the liquidity crisis. With this unwillingness from some foreign suppliers to accept the agent's role, some Chinese customers simply stopped their orders 'because we didn't want to pay the right people for their services, I'm totally sure that's why [we lost our customers]. And nothing else' (interview with foreign control system supplier 2012). This led to a straining of relationships, as

they just stop paying … yeah, but they think that they have been treated badly. And we think we have been treated badly. And then people stop talking. And that's the worst thing you can do. Especially out here. (Interview with foreign control system supplier 2012)

This demonstrates that there were additional layers to the account about the debt chains in Chinese wind power. The non-payment of invoices was not only due to the intricate 'common pockets' syndrome, but also the refusal to acknowledge the need for an agent in the first place. According to a Chinese agent,

in the beginning they [foreign suppliers] didn't want to have such a relation, to use these relations. But I think they cannot make business without it, as they will make so many mistakes. (Interview with Chinese agent 2013)

Gradually, though, through recognising the function of the agent and the need for building trust through *guānxi*, several foreign suppliers changed their strategy, working to reestablish the dialogue with their Chinese customers. This was often by accepting the introduction of an agent by the customer, which in turn resulted in the reenrolment of them as customers. Work had to continue in trying to repair the damage done to the relationship, as the refusal to recognise the need for agents was interpreted as a lack of respect for Chinese culture during the phase of rapid growth:

They [the Chinese] want that you as a Westerner understand Chinese business mentality. You need to understand China. You must act with respect, you must be honest. They may not be honest with you, but to a certain degree they are anyhow, because as soon as you get under their skin … under their skin, I think that the communication becomes much easier. I don't use as much time for negotiation, when the trust has been established. But it takes such a long time! (Interview with foreign control system supplier 2012)

Implications for relations between headquarters and subsidiary

It was, however, not just the relationships between the foreign supplier and customers in China that felt the impact of financial controversies: relations between the supplier subsidiaries in China and their headquarters back home were also strongly affected.

Chinese concern for a lack of understanding of Chinese culture

The first issue to arise relating to the lack of respect for local culture was that local Chinese employees in Danish subsidiaries became concerned that Danish headquarters displayed a lack of 'trust' (*xinren bu gou,* 信任不够), 'respect', and 'confidence' (interviews with Chinese and foreign employees in foreign control system suppliers 2012, 2013; interview with Chinese control system supplier 2013). Seen as a matter of 'arrogance', this was taken to constitute a 'common illness' (*tongbing,* 通病) in foreign companies (particularly Danish) (interview with Chinese control system supplier 2013; interview with Chinese agent 2013) operating in China:

> Yes, they [Danes] do not understand the Chinese market, but we [the local employees] have been ignored. So we feel very sorry, we lost to our competitors, especially in the Chinese market. [...] This regional culture [in China] is too diverse, but you should listen to the local managers in what to say. (Interview with Chinese employee in foreign control system supplier 2012)

As a result of not feeling 'respected' or 'listened to', Chinese employees in various subsidiaries started to feel 'lonely', 'very frustrated', and 'very angry' (interviews with Chinese employees in foreign companies 2012, 2013). As a reaction to this, the subsidiaries expressed the need for more Danish employees to make the move to China as long-term residents, in an effort to better understand the local culture. Accordingly, some foreign suppliers have also sought to reduce the complexity of relations between headquarters and subsidiaries, for example by sending expatriates to China for longer stays to control their affiliates and operations in China directly and to do 'a bit of undercover work':

> The headquarters doesn't understand what's going on out here [...] You know, well, that the week after we've returned home, then it's old knowledge we have got. It's no use [...] And that's actually what I try to do. [Trying to find out] what the hell is going on. (Interview with foreign control system supplier 2012)

Attempts to establish joint ventures – albeit (often) eventually unsuccessfully – have been another means whereby Danish and other foreign companies have tried to make it easier 'to do as the Romans' (using the

Chinese expression '*ruxiang suisu*' (入乡随俗), which literally translates as 'when entering the village, follow local customs') (interview with Chinese employee in foreign control system supplier 2012).

> In China it's easier to do as the Chinese, adapt and be flexible. But especially Danes find this very difficult. They should learn to 'do as the Romans'. A lot of foreigners are very bad at this, Danes and also others. Danes want to understand why and how things happen. Instead, I just tell them, 'you just follow me', but I don't provide the reason, just the results. That's very difficult for foreign people. (Interview with Chinese agent 2013)
>
> When you are not at work, you can consider yourself the king of your own world without a problem, but when you are working to get a market share in another market, I think you need to forget about your own identity. (Interview with Chinese employee in foreign control system supplier 2012)

As a further way to enhance trust, some foreign supply firms have started, to various degrees, to locate manufacturing, service, and even R&D activities in China in order to give subsidiaries more autonomy, because 'they are the ones who know the culture. Know the language. They are the ones who know all the nuances' (interview with foreign control system supplier 2013).

In these various experimental ways, relations have been, and are being, negotiated over time. Furthermore, as Chinese companies have acquired new capabilities, they no longer accept the 'student–teacher relation', but demand a more equal relationship of mutual learning and knowledge-sharing; 'that's the kind of respect that I think you must build up' (interview with foreign control system supplier 2013). Indeed, as expressed by a foreign control system supplier, 'we should never think that we can save the world with our own solutions' (2013).

Understanding the Chinese ball game and ongoing negotiations between subsidiary and headquarters

Over and above the need to stabilise relations with Chinese colleagues and customers, the second issue is one faced by many foreign employees working permanently or interchangeably between the home country and China: the maintaining of relations with their board of directors and management. This has become increasingly difficult in the stagnating and liquidity-constrained Chinese wind turbine industry:

> Had it been a Western company, then you'd say, then the collaboration would have stopped there [owing to a lack of payments], right, and our customer would probably have stopped his development, because he couldn't get funded … But it seems like the Chinese [companies]

somehow still have so much money that they can still pay their employees, so they are just continuing business [...] And production, sales, and
development and things like that, it's still running. And that's kind of
a strange schism to face, because how is that possible!? (Interview with
foreign control system supplier 2013)

So, with the argument that 'the moment your presence is gone, then you
are out of their [the Chinese customers'] conscience', foreign subsidiaries
in China have often tried to convince their headquarters that, in spite of
liquidity issues, it was necessary to continue working with *guānxì* as they
needed to be 'nurtured, nurtured, nurtured' on a constant basis (interview
with foreign control system supplier 2012). Understandably, this would
sometimes produce disputes with the headquarters as they demanded a halt
to the deliveries when payments were delayed:

> And then it gets even worse, as the Board [of Directors], of course, tells
> me that then we need to stop activities – you do that in Europe. Then
> my next challenge is that this is not possible. I need to be on friendly
> terms with them [the Chinese customer]. Otherwise, they will put me at
> the bottom of the list, and then I will be the last one to be paid. That's
> also what the state-owned companies do out here. They keep making
> sure that things run properly. Because they know that some day it will
> get better, and then it's good to have good friends. [...] That's almost
> the worst part – we cannot break them [the relations] – and that's why,
> I'm trying to kind of play by their rules. (Interview with foreign control
> system supplier 2012)

Somewhat paradoxically, subsidiaries experienced that 'our biggest challenge is when we have to report back to Denmark [...] it's *so* difficult!' (interview with foreign control system supplier 2013). That is, the headquarters
'does not get what's being said' or 'realise how difficult it is to do business
in China' because headquarters and subsidiary 'are so far from each other'
(interviews with foreign control system suppliers 2012, 2013). Finally, some
foreign salespeople and/or foreign managers in China have started to adopt
'several identities', using different names and business cards, for instance,
as they engage in relations with hybrid 'in-between' agents. Indeed, getting
to understand the Chinese spider's web requires people to lobby and to act
with 'secrecy', keeping 'their cards close to themselves' (interview with foreign control system supplier 2012).

The concept of quality modified by relations

Summing up the above, unstable and overflowing Sino-foreign relations
have been a consistent feature of the supply chain in China's wind power
sector, as it moved through a quality crisis and into the consolidation phase

that followed the quality crisis, and on towards the current turn to quality. The story uncovered indicates how quality is relationally constituted in China: Instead of being based on confidence in the quality of a product through legalities, technicalities, certificates, or formalities, the quality of wind turbines and their components in China has to a large extent rather been measured in terms of 'interpersonal relations' (*guānxì*). That is, 'when the Chinese buy things, it's not just about the quality, but also about price, service, and relations' (interview with foreign control system supplier 2012). In this way, there can be different processes of valuation:

> out here, having the best relation can justify that the product might not be the best [...] But on the other hand, it doesn't work either, if the product is too bad. But quality is something different in China. And it's related to relations. (Interview with foreign control system supplier 2012)

This spider's web-like nature of the Chinese wind power development assemblage leads some actors to argue that the potential turn to quality is hardly being implemented efficiently, specifically because of the allegedly 'corrupt governance structures' whereby SOEs are allowed to be inefficient. That is, several SOEs are managed by CEOs and directors who often aim for a political career within the Chinese communist *bianzhi* and *nomenklatura* systems, whereby the CPC can retain control through appointments of CPC cadres to key positions in companies (Brødsgaard 2002; interviews 2012, 2013; Keister 2000; Tang & Ward 2003). Directors are

> being appointed in the Party, and it's kind of an apprenticeship – to be director for a company is like an apprenticeship – and then they will become politicians. And that means, they are crappy leaders – it's [wind power] not their baby, right? (Interview with foreign control system supplier 2012)

This adds to the uncertainty over Chinese wind power development marketisation, with issues of, for example, protectionist industrial policies, bureaucracy, and corruption (Klagge, Liu & Silva 2012:376), which sometimes even result in 'fake shell' companies (interviews 2012, 2013). Overall, it seems evident that the Chinese state is infiltrating Chinese wind power development marketisation in multiple ways, often under the guise of various other roles and masks such as regulator, operator, wind farm developer, wind turbine manufacturer, as well as price-setter, manager, credit provider, and monitor through Party cadres and *nomenklatura* appointed in SOEs.

Problematising the Chinese 'system problem'

Having traced de- and reconfiguring supply chain relations around control systems – entangled in a Chinese spider's web – it should not be forgotten how these are inherently entangled in China's power sector and socialist market economy, which is marked by unfinished corporate sector reforms. Indeed, as Sino-foreign supply chain relations started to sour, an emerging controversy started to emerge over the very nature of China's corporate sector and over the protectionism of SOEs, which had allowed quality issues to emerge in the first place – a result largely of what is construed as China's 'system problem' of lacking market mechanisms:

> So this is the core issue of China's total industrial system. What caused this problem [of quality, curtailment, and overcapacity]? I think, it is caused by the lack of a pure market economy, and therefore you see China's overcapacity in many industries. You know, overproduction. [...] So if there are two [competitors/oligopolies, or even more competitors], competition will be better. But in China, it is often not a healthy competition making price competition better ... Instead the price is getting more and more whatever [lower]... In China we are all low price fighters, and this finally led to abuse [...] and everybody is doing bad. I think, it is because the market mechanism has not been established. (Interview with Chinese certification body 2013)
>
> This is the problem ... it's also the 'system problem' for China – you know, the state-owned enterprises. If you are a decision-maker, you are making the selection of the wind turbines dependent on the bidding ... when you select the lowest price of the turbine, and when you have the largest installed capacity. (Interview with Chinese government advisor and wind industry association 2013)

The 'system problem' – that is, China's 'quasi-market', state-directed political economy – is thus intricately linked to the surfacing issues of overcapacity, curtailment, poor quality, and lacking innovation. At the same time, the 'system problem' ultimately has roots in China's investment-driven 'growth model', which can be argued to have coproduced the 'turbine wave attack' in the first place, namely as Chinese state-owned (and -protected) and radically risk-prone banks and the "spider's web" constitution of the wind power sector, where 'everybody is state-owned, -financed, or -controlled' (interview with Chinese certification body 2013) has resulted in lacking financial prudence and interest in performance, in delivering electricity, or even in ensuring quality products and projects. That is, as companies 'are cross-financed, with common pockets' (interview with foreign control system supplier 2012), nobody 'care[s] about quality, and no authority is saying "this is good, this is bad [quality]"' (interview with Chinese certification body 2013). Particularly during the marketquake, SOEs had seldom 'cared about the cost', instead focusing on winning the bid, which is 'their achievement, their reputation', resulting in underbidding, 'making the project not profitable' (interview with Chinese government advisor and wind industry association 2013).

The result of quantitative installation targets was insufficient profitability of wind farm projects, low production availability and long-term performance, short operational lifetime, low up-front capital investments at the cost of much higher long-term generating costs, as well as other issues. Chinese turbines were accordingly built to last only around five years or so, rather than providing a guarantee period of 15 years and producing wind turbines that would bear the wear and tear (wind turbine fatigue) of 20–25 years of operation as in the West (interviews with foreign and Chinese wind turbine manufacturers and component suppliers; interview with government advisor and wind industry association 2013). That is, being driven by a growth imperative, they are not being 'responsible for the future, or for the turbine not working', SOEs would 'not [be] so worried about that [the quality]... but this is not only for wind, it's for everything' (interview with Chinese government advisor and wind energy association 2013). Together, these issues led to significant overcapacity and thus the financial insolvency of many wind farms (Zhao et al. 2012a:224), an issue not uncommon to other manufacturing industries in China (Rock & Toman 2015; Naughton 2014).

Overall, the above indicates China's lack of a 'pure market economy', with 'no driving force for manufacturers to improve their quality'. Meanwhile, the 'system problem' of a lacking 'market economy' in China is becoming problematised as a 'big trouble for the future' with repercussions for society and China (Interview with Chinese government advisor and wind power association 2013). The lack of this pure market economy means that in China the

> market is blind. I think under a mature market mechanism, players entering [the industry] are relatively smart, but under an immature market system, the players entering are very stupid [...] [It is] not the Chinese government's strategy, it's the result of China's entire economic system. That means that excess capacity is like the development of the survival of the fittest, which could contribute to good actors emerging to do the job. In China, however, people buy things in a market, which is not pure, so he will not buy the best, he will buy the cheapest, and therefore we don't have people to make any good products. (Interview with Chinese certification body 2013)

Therefore, what we may be witnessing is how China's fragmented experimentation in marketisation can risk spinning out of control if it is not flexibly handled. Indeed, 'the preference for low-quality, state-owned projects induced by government investment, is potentially destructive' (Korsnes 2014:193). Ultimately, this underlying controversy over the state-owned nature of the industry and the lack of impetus for quality and innovation could threaten the Chinese state's, and particular the CPC's, legitimacy, if not handled agilely, as it is becoming framed as a political problem.

The strong fist of the Chinese state

As a new political leadership under President Xi Jinping took over in 2013, there were signs that comprehensive liberalisation reforms would be implemented, with a proclaimed smaller role for the state owing to its commitment to comprehensively deepening reforms, along with a fight against corruption. Accordingly, China is proclaimed to generally pursue 'a market system that is uniform but open, orderly and competitive' (CCCPC 2013, III-Modern market system). Yet these liberalisation measures have been marked by inconsistent and selective implementation, only piecemeal and marginal restructuring in 'crucial yet politically sensitive areas such as deregulation of state-sector oligopolies'. This leaves a need for more transparency in debt management of the fiscal and banking systems, improved access for foreign investors, and the establishment of a level playing field for non-state market actors (Heilmann 2016:8).

Overall, as the Chinese government still seems to steer the energy, electricity, and – in particular – wind power development marketisation, it is still impossible to bracket actors into stable frames of either market or politics. Indeed, the state and politics seem to pervade everything. Despite attempts to move towards modern corporate governance, and disentangling 'the market' from government, the state seems ubiquitous (and even forms part of 'private' companies), though in several disguises. Entangled in China's ongoing capitalist transition, rather than reflecting the ideal type of external markets and arm's-length transactions, the Chinese state is heavily involved in the marketisation of wind power. In a Caijing article (24 March 2014) on the ongoing and partly stalled Chinese power sector reforms, the pervasive role of the political is also reflected. It is stated in the article that the Chinese government is currently in the process of shifting not only 'its old hand' (by reference to Adam Smith's (1776) 'invisible hand of the market'), but also the attached 'wrist', in order to be able to continue the stalled market-oriented reforms in the power sector. Somewhat paradoxically, the article leaves no doubt that the wrist is attached firmly to the arm and fist of the Chinese state, making the 'invisible hand' seem anything but; rather, it is very concrete and very visible (Caijing 24 March 2014), as evidenced in the above through the mesh of the spider's web, the system problem, and the oscillations between centralised intervention (or lack thereof) and decentralised local free-riding.

Reflections on third site of controversy: 'Chinese characteristics' of wind power development marketisation

In Chapter Six, some of the particular 'Chinese characteristics' of marketisation within wind power development have been traced: It maps a controversy unfolding over money in the liquidity-constrained wind power sector, and shows how this has impacted relations between foreign control system suppliers and Chinese (mostly state-owned) customers. In the controversy that has ensued over access to money, *guānxì* have been employed strategically as an obligatory passage point (Callon 1986) for entering the supply chain of the largely state-owned Chinese customers and for ensuring government support. That is, *guānxì* are employed strategically by companies to (re-)gain orders from wind turbine manufacturers, generating companies, and/or wind park owners. Whilst China Studies has dealt with issues around China's ongoing corporate restructuring and the role of *guānxì*, the Anthropology of Markets helps to shed light on the socio-material and temporal dynamics and agency of such relations. Indeed, in the Chinese assemblage around wind power development, the mobilisation of relations gives actors the power and ability to act, and thus have performative power because they can make different actors do things. At the same time, they are socio-materially and temporally constituted, for example through suppliers' lists and contracts, but more so by investments in time and money, and smoked cigarettes and drunken glasses of *baijiu* to build up associations of trust.

Overall, in the context of Chinese wind power development marketisation, quality becomes constituted as 'relational.' In turn, these relations are overly volatile and shift in nature and quality over time, de- and reconfiguring the wind power development assemblage. By tracing some of the transformative dynamics of 'the relational' in the marketisation of wind power, by following money and relations around them, this work indirectly sheds light on the negotiated nature of relations, positions, roles, prices, and identities of Chinese and foreign actors in this emerging assemblage. At the same time, this account maps a broader story of how the Chinese spider's web of ubiquitous state–business relations - enmeshed in a system problem of a lack of 'pure market economy' and of a prudent, risk-averse financial system, which is intricately entangled in China's 'growth model' - is being increasingly problematised. In turn, this may make wind power development politically unsustainable, as the wasted resources and focus on quantity over quality are contested and linked to the specific Chinese polity and socialist market economy. This tension is exposed particularly as the Chinese state increasingly seeks to move China towards sustainable, scientific development through an alleged move away from a (purely exclusive) focus on quantity, growth, and pace, towards higher impetus on quality and innovation. The Chinese government has to some extent intervened to meet concerns over SOEs and their lack of regard for profitability, such as through the establishment of SASAC in 2003 and the State Council's 'Decision on Reforming the Investment System' (2004) (Jones & Zou 2017:746). Further, there are evidently also differences between the operation of SOEs and private actors, with the latter focusing generally more on profitability, agility, quality, and innovation (interviews 2012, 2013). (Yet, still some private companies enjoy close relations with, and preferential treatment from, government relations, albeit often to a lesser degree). How these changes and differences will eventually play out only time will tell.

Having followed the electromagnetic energy flow from the wind turbine and into the grid, venturing into the financial and economic concerns over liquidity during and after the marketquake, travelling the electromagnetic waves of *guānxì* in the Chinese spider's web as a credit squeeze hit Chinese wind power development marketisation, Chapter Six has provided an overarching story of power: of power struggles over access to government *guānxì*, credits, and to a place on the suppliers' list of Chinese SOEs. Meanwhile, as Chinese actors have evidently asked for more respect in the supply chain, the de- and reconfiguring of Sino-foreign supply chain relations around control system technologies may also impact trials of strength over access to knowledge and control system core algorithms – an issue that is explored further in Chapter Seven.

Note

1. The CDM helped support around 80 per cent of wind farms in China during the period 2005–2012.

References

Boisot, M. & Child, J., 1999, 'Organizations as Adaptive Systems in Complex Environment: The Case of China', *Organization Science* 10, 237–52.

Bloomberg New Energy Finance, 2012, 'Will China's new Renewable Portfolio Standard Boost Project Development?', *Renewable Energy: Research Note*, 11 May.

Brødsgaard, K. E., 2002, 'Institutional Reform and the *Bianzhi* System in China', *The China Quarterly* 170, 361–386.

Burt, R., 1992, *Structural Holes: The Social Structure of Competition*, Harvard University Press, Cambridge, MA.

Caijing Magazine [财经], 2013, 电改试金石 [Stone-hard priceless advice for power reform), 24 March 2013, pp. 50–68, viewed hard copy 30 April 2013, available at http://magazine.caijing.com.cn/2013-03-24/112617256.html.

Callon, M., 1986, 'The sociology of an actor-network: The case of the electric vehicle', in M. M. Callon, J. Law & A. Rip (eds.), *Mapping the Dynamics of Science and Technology*, pp. 19–34, Palgrave Macmillan, London.

CCCPC (Central Committee of the Communist Party of China), 2013, Decision on major issues concerning comprehensively deepening reforms, 13 November 2013, adopted at the close of the Third Plenary Session of the 18th CPC Central Committee, http://www.china.org.cn/china/third_plenary_session/2013-11/16/content_30620736.htm

Chang, K.-C., 2011, 'A Path to Understanding Guanxi in China's Transitional Economy: Variations on Network Behavior', *Sociological Theory* 29(4), 315–339.

García, C., 2013, 'Policies and Institutions for Grid-Connected Renewable Energy: "Best Practice" and the Case of China', *Governance: An International Journal of Policy, Administration, and Institutions* 26(1), 119–146.

Heilmann, S., 2016, 'Introduction to China's Core Executive: Leadership Styles, Structures and Processes under Xi Jinping', in S. Heilmann & M. Stepan (eds.), *China's Core Executive Leadership Styles, Structures and Processes Under Xi Jinping*, pp. 6–10, MERICS Paper, 1, June, https://www.merics.org/en/merics-analysis/papers-on-china/chinas-core-executive-leadership-styles-structures-and-processes-under-xi-jinping/.

Jones, L & Zou, Y., 2017, 'Rethinking the Role of State-Owned Enterprises in China's Rise', *New Political Economy* 22(6), 743–760.

Keister, L. A., 2000, *Chinese Business Groups: The Structure and Impact of Interfirm Relations during Economic Development'*, Oxford University Press, Hong Kong.

Klagge, B, Liu, Z. & Silva, P. C., 2012, 'Constructing China's Wind Energy Innovation System', *Energy Policy* 50, 370–382.

Korsnes, M., 2014, 'Fragmentation, Centralisation and Policy Learning: An Example from China's Wind Industry', *Journal of Current Chinese Affairs* 43(3), 175–205.

Kroeber, A. R., 2016, *China's Economy – What Everyone Needs to Know*, Oxford University Press, New York.

Lardy, N. R., 2016, 'The Changing Role of the Private Sector in China', Conference Volume.

Liu, Y. & Kokko, A., 2010, 'Wind Power in China: Policy and Development Challenges', *Energy Policy* 38, 5520–5529.

Naughton, B., 2014, 'China's Economy: Complacency, Crisis & the Challenge of Reform', *Dædalus, the Journal of the American Academy of Arts & Sciences* 143(2), 14–25.

Qi, W., 2013, 'How debt is weighing down China's wind sector', Windpowermonthly, 16 April 2013, viewed 29 April 2013, http://www.windpowermonthly.com/article/1178534/analysis—debt-weighing-down-chinas-wind-sector.

Rock, M. T. & Toman, M. A. 2015, *China's Technological Catch-Up Strategy: Industrial Development, Energy Efficiency, and CO_2 Emissions*, Oxford University Press, New York.

Smith, A., 1776, *The Wealth of Nations*, Strahan and Cadell, London.

Tang, J. & Ward, A., 2003, *Inside the Enterprise. The Changing Face of Chinese Management*, Routledge, London.

Yu, J., Ji, F., Zhang, L. & Chen, Y., 2009, 'An Over-Painted Oriental Arts: Evaluation of the Development of the Chinese Renewable Energy Market using the Wind Power Market as a Model', *Energy Policy* 37, 5221–5225.

Zhao, X., Wang, F. & Wang, M., 2012a, 'Large-Scale Utilization of Wind Power in China: Obstacles of Conflict between Market and Planning', *Energy Policy* 48, 222–232.

7 Controversy over access to intellectual property rights for software algorithms

The meeting has been set up at short notice, a couple of days after the China Wind Power Conference 2012, which is held every autumn in grandiose settings on the outskirts of Beijing. During the conference this year, I wandered around the booths for several days, approaching and talking with dozens of people – European and Chinese wind turbine manufacturers, component suppliers, consultants, diplomats, researchers, agents and spies, experts, scientists, standard-setters, and everyone in-between. The hard work of introducing myself and my research has resulted in the swapping of dozens of business cards. While I have already written an introductory email to some of the people I have met in order to set up interviews, I have not yet reached a particular person on my seemingly endless contact list. However, someone has now written to me, keen to follow up on the brief talk we managed to have at the conference. It turns out that he is interested in learning more about my research.

As we sit down over a cup of coffee a few days later, my respondent says:

As I see it, now the second phase is coming, now that they have realised that it was too poor quality … it was cheap, the prices have been pushed all the way to the bottom, which has harmed the Western manufacturers, because they couldn't sell their turbines. They had decided that the price level per kilowatt had to be this low. But nobody can sell a quality turbine at that price. And then around one and a half years ago, the government went in and changed their standpoint. 'Okay, now we have to recognise that they are not good enough. They are not as they are supposed to be, so we have to do … focus on quality' … And that's actually the situation that we are witnessing now. So, two things could happen now. The first thing is that you continue buying licences in the West, and that you just continue looking at what the licence tells you. The other thing could be that you start paying what it costs to produce a quality turbine … Eh, I don't know whether that's the way they are going. I'm not sure. Because the Chinese want to do it themselves, just as the Danes want to do it themselves. What I think will happen is that they will focus more on [research and] development. They will focus more on innovation. They will focus more on leveraging knowledge. And start to understand what's going on. And start designing their own turbines. Personally, I think that's what will happen.

But what may this enhanced focus on innovation entail for Sino-foreign supply chain relations around core technologies? What is about to unfold is a story where the 'core technology' of control system software algorithms takes centre stage. While the software codes are sealed and protected in every possible way, Chinese customers 'try in every possible manner' to get access to these codes, my respondent reveals. Although none of his Chinese customers have succeeded yet, it is only a matter of time, and 'then the rest of us [foreign control system suppliers] have to quit, I'm sure', he says. Biking home from the café to my flat, I sense that the talk has set a direction for my journey through Chinese wind power development marketisation and the relations between Chinese and Western actors, one that is algorithmic in nature, and one which centres around IPRs to software codes as China transitions from a focus on quantity to quality.

The overflowing nature of intellectual property rights

In Chapter Seven, we delve deeper into the shifting quality of Sino-foreign customer–supplier relations as they unfold around the quality crisis and imminent turn to quality. This we do by focusing on Sino-foreign customer–supplier relations around the wind turbine's main supervisory control system, and in particular its proprietary algorithmic software, which represents one of the core technologies of a modern wind turbine because it regulates the turbine's performance and the algorithms that are implemented in it.

During the turn to quality, core technologies such as the supervisory controller have been framed as 'critical' to the requalification of wind power as sustainable in developmental terms, and overall to the realignment of wind power with the narrative of China's move towards sustainable and scientific development, due to its importance for wind turbine 'quality' and eased system integration. Therefore, this chapter takes us back on the journey through the wind turbine to the generator, where fine control is required over the electrical current that produces the generator's electromagnetic field. This fine adjustment is contained in a vital generator control algorithm and is kept under observation by the main supervisory controller.

The chapter then focuses on how the quality crisis and potential turn to quality has engendered multiple struggles over access to IPRs in proprietary control system software (see Figure 7.1). Whilst accounts of China and its lax enforcement of IPR have been given on many occasions, this volume sets the struggle over access to and possession of IPRs for control software and core algorithms into a context of increased strategic focus on indigenous innovation. As will be shown, whilst they are employed to frame and stabilise the ownership right to the software, IPRs turn out to have a propensity to overflow – entangled in a struggle over China's legacy of technology transfer – rendering the framing of goods through framing devices such as IPRs in a developmental context prone to controversy.

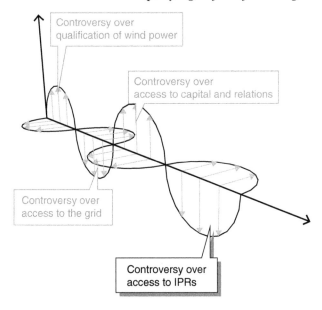

Figure 7.1 Fourth site of controversy.

The increasing strategic role of intellectual property rights in the wind turbine industry

China's emerging socio-technical market assemblage around wind power development has been founded largely on what has been termed a 'technology-for-market' policy (Lewis 2013:115), reflecting how technology transfer, often through the use of licensing agreements and joint venture partnerships, 'has always been the key priority in China's wind energy sector' (McGregor n.d:33). In turn, along with its greater integration into global processes, China has gradually come to the view that 'access to technology and information is critical for growth and that stronger IPRs can play an important role in providing that access' (Maskus 2002:146). One can also take a look at China's Medium- to Long-Term Plan for China's Scientific and Technological Development 2006–2020 (MOST 2006) to see how China now values the protection of IPRs and safeguarding of IPR owners as

> not only necessary for perfecting the nation's market economy system and promoting indigenous innovation, but also important for estab-lishing the nation's credibility and image in international cooperation. (MOST 2006, s. VIII, 4)

Whilst the above reflects a general trend in China, in particular since the country's accession to the WTO in 2001, the global wind power sector has also witnessed an increasing focus on IPRs, reflecting a trend towards a

greater protection of knowledge in general, and in the wind turbine industry in particular. In the international wind turbine industry's nascent stage,
knowledge-sharing was characterised by relatively free experience-based
learning and resourceful improvisation amongst various actors involved in
emerging national and sectoral 'innovation systems' (universities, research
institutions, companies, and policy-makers). However, as the global wind
turbine industry gradually consolidated and matured, the innovation process became more organised and closed (Haakonsson, Kirkegaard & Lema
forthcoming; Hendry & Harborne 2011). Thus, whilst an 'open source strategy' prevailed for the benefit of the whole system (Gregersen & Johnson
2009:26–27), since the turn of the century, patenting and other forms of
knowledge protection have taken centre stage, implying that innovation is
traded rather than shared in close collaborative arrangements (Haakonsson
et al. forthcoming).

The Agreement on Trade-Related Aspects of Intellectual Property Rights and China's accession to the WTO

These new developments in the global wind turbine industry reflect a more
general trend in the globalisation of markets. In 1995, IPRs were introduced
into global trade agreements with the overarching aim to further international trade and to encourage FDI and technology transfer through minimum standards for different forms of IPR regulation in WTO countries; that
is, through patents, copyrights, trademarks, and trade secrets (Maskus 2002;
Yang & Clarke 2005:549). This was enacted when the Agreement on Trade-
Related Aspects of Intellectual Property Rights (TRIPS) was signed under
the General Agreement on Tariffs and Trade (GATT), which has now
changed its name to the World Trade Organization (WTO). In this way,
IPRs became part of a regulatory standards framework, with 'obligations
of commercial policy that cannot be escaped' by WTO members (Maskus
2002:135). In turn, this means that firms that hold IPRs and which consider
investing in an R&D facility abroad, for example, will have to pay attention
to IPRs in that respective country, to ensure that its IPRs will be protected
(Mansfield 1994, 1995 in Maskus 2002).

Although China has been a member of the World Intellectual Property
Organisation (WIPO) since 1980, China only entered the WTO in 2001,
after 15 years of lengthy negotiations. Back then, characterised as a 'developing country', China fell under the obligation of the TRIPS agreement
to introduce and enforce IP protection of the same standard as developed
countries within a period of five years after accession. Since then, China
has accordingly ratified many IP-related international treaties and conventions, for example on trademarks, patents, and copyrights, working consistently on building an IPR system in accordance with the TRIPS agreement
(Bosworth & Yang 2000; McGregor n.d.; Wang 2004; Yang 2003; Yang &
Clarke 2005).

Lax intellectual property rights enforcement in China – also in wind power

Despite having built an IPR system within a relatively short time, on paper at least, China still suffers from a reputation of lax IPR enforcement, as well as from weak IPR regulation and implementation. Owing to widespread counterfeiting of almost all types of products in China, foreign companies in general consider IPR infringement an 'inevitable curse' of doing business in China (Bosworth & Yang 2000; Liu 2005; Wang 2004:253; Yang, Sonmez & Bosworth 2004:459; Zimmerman & Chaudhry 2009:309). Therefore, they often express concerns about bringing their 'crown jewels', or core technologies, to China, as they risk seeing their own technology coming back at them from Chinese competitors (McGregor n.d.:7). Overall, China's technology-for-market strategy in wind power has often been framed as a matter of Chinese wind turbine manufacturers being intent on reaping foreign technologies, for example through licensing agreements and joint ventures with Chinese partners:

> You know, when China is not able to do something, then they want to, you know, work on the foreign companies, to come here and you can get a better treat[ment], and we will reap your technology, ha ha! (Interview with Chinese diplomat 2012)

Whilst China acknowledges the importance of a stronger IPR system to enable the sustainable development of the Chinese wind turbine industry and to build indigenous innovation capabilities (MOST 2012) – to protect their own IPRs, to foster a culture of trust, and to build indigenous innovation capabilities – Western lead firms in the industry have become more cautious in their licensing strategy in China. This is reflected, for example, in how foreign lead firms, amongst other things, have scaled down or discontinued their licensing activities, as there have been multiple examples of IPR infringement (Lewis 2013; Riley & Vance 2012). Amongst industry actors it is argued that, as a consequence, foreign wind turbine manufacturers will actually become even more protective in China, with the result of 'stifling innovation collaboration in the country' (interview with foreign employee in Chinese wind turbine manufacturer 2012):

> I think a lot of companies are hesitant to come here to share knowledge, because China has not demonstrated the ability or desire to protect intellectual property. (Interview with foreign employee in Chinese wind turbine manufacturer 2012)

China's 'rule of man', 'rule by law' – and movements towards 'rule of law'

The issue of lax implementation and enforcement of IPRs, as well as a historically relatively weak R&D capacity, is often explained as emanating from China's cultural background, in both the Confucian tradition of 'rule of man' (*renzhi*, 人治) rather than 'rule of law' (*falü*, 法律), as well as in the communist so-called 'rule by law', which both tend to view IP as public property (Bosworth & Yang 2000:457; Chow 2002:339; Zimmerman & Chaudhry 2009; Zou 2006).

First, the 'rule of man' is founded in Confucian philosophy, where relationships are contextual, hierarchical, interpersonal, and reciprocal. In this context, obedience by the subject towards the ruler depends on the fulfilment by the ruler of his obligations, and not of a universally acknowledged set of rules. Hence, obedience to law owes more to informal constraints than formal law. Confucianism requires control of information, and a traditional Chinese belief is that inventions draw on past knowledge that belongs to all citizens (Chow 2002; Zimmerman & Chaudhry 2009:309). Consequently, '[t]he concept of IPR has always been at odds with the teachings of Confucianism' (O'Connor & Lowe 1996 in Bosworth & Yang 2000:457), partly because

> 'IPRs are government-sanctioned monopolies that seek to protect, by forbidding free copying, the 'original thought' of the IP-owner. On the other hand, Confucianism considers that learning takes place through copying and that imitation is a form of flattery' (O'Connor & Lowe 1996 in Bosworth & Yang 2000:457).

Second, in addition, Communist tradition views IP as public property (Bosworth & Yang 2000:453; Zimmerman & Chaudhry 2009). These socio-cultural and -political explanations are often employed as explanation for the alleged Chinese propensity to copy rather than innovate, which has also been the case in wind power:

> Why is innovation not so good in China? Cultural issue. IP is a problem. We are used to copying – we copy everything from the US...Facebook, Apple ... we lack the capabilities. It's a huge challenge. (Interview with Chinese control system supplier 2012)

Hence, whilst the TRIPS agreement is a reflection of the formal 'rule of law', as defined and set by 'the West', Chinese IPR enforcement seems influenced to a large extent by a tradition of the 'rule of man' and 'rule by law' instead. This produces anxiety that Chinese actors regard software as 'freeware', so to speak (interview with foreign and Chinese control system suppliers 2012, 2013).

Intellectual property rights and the role for technology transfer and innovation

To understand why the role of IPRs and lax IPR enforcement may produce controversy in Chinese wind power development marketisation, it is first necessary to take a step back to examine the different forms of IPRs, as well as how and why IPR protection in terms of software is particularly important but also ambiguous and controversial.

The importance of IPRs for international trade and technology transfer is linked to the way in which they grant a limited monopoly right to inventors. For example, through patent licensing agreements, a patent owner (the licensor) can license a patent to a licensee who is granted the right to make, use, sell, and/or import the claimed invention, in return for a royalty or other compensation (Kaya 2007:44). Evidently, this has been an extremely powerful mechanism for technology transfer to developing countries, and China's wind turbine industry is no exception. In addition to furthering international trade and technology transfer, IPRs are also generally perceived to encourage investment in R&D and innovation, since the inventor's guarantee of a monopoly right to the idea of the invention is secure for a certain period, and he/she will receive compensation for his/her investment. In this way, because IPRs minimise the risk of immediate copying by others, IPRs serve to ensure a return on investment and a recouping of development costs (Kaya 2007; Maskus 2002:144; Liebeskind 1996, 1997 in Spencer 2003:217). This rationale is also seen in the Chinese wind turbine industry:

> To me, patents are a complete pain … but to me, they are almost mandatory to innovation, because otherwise you have no business reason to innovate, because someone could just take it from you. (Interview with foreign employee in Chinese wind turbine manufacturer 2012)

Patents, copyrights, trademarks, and trade secrets

Overall, IPRs can take different forms. First, patents serve to protect technological inventions (as well as utility models and industrial designs) by giving exclusive rights to the inventor. In this way, a patent for technological inventions functions as a 'limited monopoly', which is granted by a national government to patent holders on their inventive ideas and typically lasts for 20 years (Kaya 2007:45, 51). Second, copyrights serve to protect original works (fixed in a tangible medium of expression), such as novels, films, and computer programs, by preventing people from copying or commercially exploiting them without the copyright owner's permission. The creator of an original work is thereby granted the exclusive rights to its use and distribution, effective during the creator's lifetime and a minimum of 50 years after his/her death (Kaya 2007). Third, an alternative IPR option to patents and copyrights is the trademark and trade secret. Trademarks make it possible to claim exclusive property of a product or service by use of a sign, which is capable of distinguishing the goods or services of one enterprise from those of other enterprises (Kaya 2007; WIPO n.d.). In turn, a trade secret is any confidential business information that provides an enterprise with a competitive edge. The unauthorised use of such information by persons other than the holder is regarded as IPR infringement. As the trade secret is kept intentionally confidential, for example through various technical means of literally 'blackboxing' (e.g. through encryption), the owner can enjoy unlimited monopoly rights on the invention without time limits. To keep the information on the trade secret confidential, non-disclosure agreements (NDAs) between the involved parties might be signed to prevent information leakages, such as breaches of confidentiality and corporate espionage (Kaya 2007; WIPO n.d.). Trade secrets are generally not protected by law in the same manner as trademarks or patents, and they are protected only as long as the secret is not disclosed. Thus, the key disadvantage of a trade secret is its vulnerability to reverse engineering and leakage (Kaya 2007).

Ambiguity of intellectual property rights with regard to software – on trade-offs between patents, copyrights, and trade secrets

When it comes to the specific case of software, additional complexity is added to the issue of IPRs, and to the choice of the most appropriate IPR mechanism. While there is international disagreement on the patentability of software, software companies are at the same time facing a strategic dilemma in their choice of software IPR. Indeed, while software invention requires considerable investment in time and money, it is easily copied, and how to further protect it remains a contentious issue within the TRIPS agreement (Kaya 2007).

Copyrights and patents are the two main IP forms under which computer software might be protected. However, software lies at the very borderline of copyrights and patents, which produces issues of ambiguity: whilst the TRIPS agreement places computer programmes under the copyright section, the question of whether or not computer programmes can be patented has not been definitively agreed. Instead, the issue is to be decided by the individual signatory countries. This discussion is basically founded in a debate on the 'common good' aspect of software. Opponents to software patents emphasise how software patents will limit competition and stifle software development and innovation, whilst those in favour of patent protection for computer software, in contrast, argue that it promotes investment in software development (Kaya 2007:44–46, 56). In addition to these ambiguities, the sensitive nature of software – that is, the way in which the valuable and costly codes can be easily copied if first they are revealed – actually often makes it safer to abstain from filing patents on software, since patenting requires software developers to make their codes publicly available. In the following, the trade-offs between patents, copyrights, and trade secrets that companies are facing, when choosing specific types of IPR protection of their software, are explored further.

The algorithmic nature of software – source and object codes and the choice of intellectual property protection

To understand the ambiguities in terms of how and whether software can and should be patented, in all the different countries and/or regions where it is traded, requires an appreciation of the material nature of a software code. Basically, computer software is 'an algorithm or a mathematical formula' inscribed in to a computer programme (Kaya 2007:64):

> An algorithm is a series of steps to solve a problem and a computer program is an implementation of that algorithm, which is like an implementation of the mathematical equation $E=mc^2$. (Kaya 2007:64)

In turn, as a mathematical formula, software code can be written in different classes of computer languages: source codes or machine/object code. The former is a higher level language than the latter, and one which more qualifies as an original expression (qualifying for copyrights), whilst the other qualifies more as a functional work of technology (qualifying for patents). Source codes are computer language instructions most frequently written and read by software programmers, and since these qualify as what may be termed an original expression, they automatically qualify for copyright protection. In turn, machine code basically consists of numeric codes (0s and 1s) that are readable by the computer, and which give the computer instructions on the functional tasks it performs. Owing to its functional work, machine code is by some argued to qualify better for patent protection (Kaya 2007). Meanwhile, whether it is advisable to patent a line of object code remains an ambiguous issue, as software infringement remains difficult to prove:

> It is possible to take out a patent on some software, but it is a bit tricky … it's easier with the hardware stuff, which is something that you can see. Where it's possible to see that somebody else has done the same [copied] … with software, it's very, very difficult to prove [the infringement of the newness of the invention]. (foreign control system supplier 2013)

Whilst the very material nature of the software code, and its functionality, has an impact on the ability to patent or not, there are several strategic trade-offs that companies need to take into account in their choice of the form of IPR protection. First and foremost, they must decide whether it is worth the money and time to file a patent application for software, or whether a copyright, which is automatic and free, is preferred (Kaya 2007). In addition, another more critical and sensitive difference between patents and copyrights is the way in which patents require a higher degree of openness as to the contents of the invention or the original work in order to obtain them. This in turn means that some companies decide to rely on non-legal means of IP protection such as trade secrets. These considerations are founded on the very material nature not only of software codes, but also of patents. That is, the contentious strategic choice of filing for a software patent or a copyright or of not using a legal means of IP protection at all is linked to the very materiality and the practices of the different means of IP protection. These considerations are outlined in the following sections.

'To lay open or not lay open, that is the question' – the tricky issue of patenting software algorithms

Considering the contentious issue of whether or not to file for a software patent, the crux of the matter lies in its very word: in the original Latin form, *'patere'* means 'to lay open'. The meaning of patent is in this sense basically a method of making something available for public inspection (Kaya 2007:45). Since the inventor filing for a patent must describe the invention in detail and make it public (Kaya 2007:51), a software inventor filing for a software patent must lay open the algorithms that are implemented in the software.

> This is evidently a risky business. Software is easily copied. Laying open the algorithms and software codes is thus a sensitive issue, as software companies have often spent considerable amounts of time and money in the development of new software. They therefore risk giving it away for nothing, and eroding the company's competitive advantage if filing for a software patent. Taking the case of companies developing software for control systems in China, for instance, we used forty years to develop it [the main control]. And all the others [foreign companies] have also done that' (foreign control system supplier 2012).

Consequently, most software developers for control systems in the wind turbine industry have not filed for patents on the software of their main control systems, neither in China, nor elsewhere:

> Sometimes it's actually better, when you talk about software, not to take out a patent on it, because then nobody can see it … because when you take out a patent, then you write … then you actually make … how … […] Then you write in details how it functions. Then you give it all away. Then it's actually better simply not to say anything about it. (Interview with foreign control system supplier 2013)

Meanwhile, patent regulations for software differ between countries, and patents have to be filed in each country respectively. While patents on software are widespread in the USA, for example, they are less common in the European Union (Kaya 2007:46), and in China only copyrights can be taken out on software (interviews).

Ambiguous protection of software through copyrights – the alternatives of trademarks and trade secrets

In contrast to patents, copyrights are free and automatic and do not require companies to lay open software codes, since copyrights do not require a formal application. The only thing required is that the work is fixed in a physical medium of expression. In this way, software, both the source code (in human readable form) and the object code (in machine-readable form), automatically qualify for copyright protection (Kaya 2007:44). As expressed by a Chinese wind turbine manufacturer involved in developing software indigenously:

> For our software modules, we don't give [access to] source codes to cus-tomers [...] That is our intellectual property rights [...] All the software modules we produce, we get copyright. (Interview with Chinese wind turbine manufacturer 2012)

However, copyright laws are ambiguous and only offer partial protection for software. That is, the scope of protection is limited compared to pat-ents. This is because of the way in which copyrights only offer protection against direct copying of an original expression, while the idea itself (or the procedures, methods of operations, or mathematical concepts) is not protected (Kaya 2007:44). In turn, the framing of 'original expression' is itself ambiguously defined, which leaves the decision between patents and copyrights contentious (Kaya 2007:57–58). Consequently, copyright protec-tion for machine code, which serves 'a utilitarian function which is tradi-tionally protected by patents (Kaya 2007:44), is not easily implemented as preventing others from writing code that has a similar function as long as they do not copy the code itself is not possible. That is, 'copyright cannot prevent second comers from recreating the same work or producing similar work using different expression' (Kaya 2007:44). Therefore, there is 'no copy-right infringement when a competitor uses the same idea in constructing his/her work provided that his/her creation is independent' (Kaya 2007:44). As an effective means of protection for the functional aspects of computer programmes is not readily available, competitors can, through reverse engi-neering and without access to the source code of the programme, imitate the programme's functional elements (Kaya 2007:50–51). In addition, copy-right protection in China is considered particularly weak (Zimmerman & Chaudhry 2009:309), owing to the tradition of 'rule of man' and 'rule by law'; this makes copyright a risky strategy.

As an alternative IPR option to patents and copyrights for software protection, trademarks and trade secrets may turn out to be the preferred option, even though they do not offer any strong legal protection. Only offering protection as long as it is not disclosed, the trade secret's key disad-vantage is its vulnerability to reverse engineering and leakage (Kaya 2007).

Controversy over intellectual property rights for algorithmic software

The above has outlined the contentious issue of IPRs – in China in general, and in regard to software particularly. We now focus on the role of IPRs for the supervisory controller hardware and software. Whilst control systems comprise both hardware (electronic hardware parts such as industrial programmable logic controllers (PLCs), converters, switches, and sensors) and software parts, the analysis looks in detail at the role of software, as industry actors frame the Chinese hardware, such as the control cabinet and its contents, as 'very standard', in contrast to 'the control software systems, which are core. [...] Software is key!' (interview with foreign control system supplier 2012).

The wind turbine's sub- and main controls – and the core algorithm

To understand how critical the main control system software is for a wind turbine's performance – and thus for the 'quality' of wind turbine technology – it is necessary to describe its function in the turbine.

A modern wind turbine comprises of many thousands of components, and many of them must be controlled (or regulated) for the proper, safe, and optimal functioning of the turbine, and to ensure its integration into the power grid according to the grid codes. However, the control is not all taken care of by one controller – there are many and various types of controllers that serve to ensure the efficient running of a group of components or a particular system. Many of these distributed sub-controllers take care of systems in various areas of the turbine, such as the blades, the generator, and the yaw system. One particularly critical distributed sub-control system is that which controls the pitch of the blades. These need to be regularly pitched in and out of the wind, so as to obtain maximum production as the wind speed changes. When the wind is blowing at above the rated speed, then the blades also pitch, but this time to ensure that the generator rated power is not exceeded and also to ensure the safe operation of the turbine.

Above all these sub-controllers sits a central supervisory controller (or main controller), which monitors all the sub-systems and gives the necessary commands so that the whole turbine produces the power that is expected in a safe and reliable way. The main controller communicates to the different units through communication protocols that allow a two-way exchange of data. To do all this, the main controller contains a software algorithm – a 'core algorithm' (interviews) – which encompasses the turbine's overall design principle; that is, the principle of how the components should operate together, and how and under which circumstances the blades should pitch. Containing the design principle, the main controller is generally considered not only the most critical and core part of the wind turbine's various control system technologies, but also of the wind turbine in general, because '[e]verything in the turbine needs to be controlled by the main control system [as it] makes the mechanics work [together]' (interview with foreign control system supplier 2012). Overall, the main controller is framed as

> the top component of the [turbine's] intelligence, whereas the others [sub-controls] are the 'slaves'. We [the main control] are the 'master'". (Interview with foreign control system supplier 2012)

Concerns about protecting the core algorithm – and Chinese interest in accessing the 'gold'

Owing to the advanced (and locked and protected) nature of the controller software, and owing to the requirement of extensive long-term experience for developing advanced control algorithms, the control system software is still the component where it is most difficult for Chinese manufacturers and research institutes to upgrade and catch up. However, as Chinese customers have gradually built up more indigenous capabilities, they have also gained more interest in gaining access to the core algorithms, in order to reduce their dependence on foreign suppliers (and their often more expensive component technologies), and thereby build indigenous innovation capabilities. This new ambition, however, has made customer–supplier negotiations around control software more difficult and contentious; for example, as Chinese customers have started to demand to 'get access to some source codes' (interviews with control system suppliers 2012, 2013) from foreign control system suppliers, requesting suppliers to reveal and lay open the IP of their 'gold', their software codes. This new and increasing interest in software algorithms on behalf of Chinese customers has caused concern for foreign software developers as they fear that their customers will leave them as soon as they have found a way to copy the software. According to this account, a Chinese customer will only have 'one interest [access to the core algorithm]. And as soon as he has got that, then he won't use us any more' (interview with foreign control system supplier 2013):

> I know the Chinese well enough to know that this [buying the controller] is not the only thing they want! (Interview with foreign control system supplier 2012)
> I am convinced that the moment you sell them a prototype [for a controller], they will disassemble it and start analysing what they can do to make this one. And they are working on that still, and they have not succeeded yet [although] they are trying hard anyhow. (Interview with foreign control system supplier 2012)

Owing to this critical nature of control systems, Western suppliers have been particularly concerned about protecting their core algorithm or the so-called 'spine' or 'brain' of the main controller, in particular in the light of

China's general eagerness regarding reengineering. Consequently, they have developed various means and methods of protecting it as a trade secret, in order that the Chinese customers 'cannot get into this system yet, but if they could ... they would like to ... then they would be able to install our software on another controller, on another system' (interview with foreign control system supplier 2012). In this way, control system software suppliers risk and fear 'losing their entire business' if another party gains access to their core algorithm, because the software would then be possible to transfer to another controller:

> Because ... when we talk controllers, then you also talk about software, and then you talk about source codes, and the source codes, that's our 'gold', I would say. (Interview with foreign control system supplier 2013)

Owing to these concerns, foreign control system suppliers have employed a host of more or less experimental means to protect the IPRs to their control systems and the software they use. Some of these traditional and non-traditional, as well as legal and non-legal, means are outlined below.

The legacy of technology licensing – the case of control system software in Chinese wind power

Traditionally, the main mode of protection has been through design licensing agreements.

Control system suppliers occasionally sell a software license directly to the Chinese wind turbine manufacturer. Typically, this grants permission to use one or more copies of the software in a way which, without a license agreement, would otherwise have constituted an infringement of the software owner's exclusive rights under copyright law. When licensed, the software will be under proprietary licenses (and not free or open source), implying that the end user is not allowed to distribute or copy the software to other wind turbine controllers and is bound by trade secrets in the form of NDAs (interviews).

However, the most frequently used method, at least traditionally and in alignment with the legacy of technology transfer in China's wind turbine industry, has been through the inscription of specific control systems into a turbine design license. That is, whilst a design license will contain provisions that allocate the rights, restrictions on the use of the turbine and its constituting components (e.g. in terms of geographical boundaries), liability, warranty, and responsibility to the different parties, the license agreement will entail a components list. Sometimes, this will also contain a list of recommended or obligatory suppliers, for example of control systems, which the Chinese licensor is then forced to buy for a specific number of wind turbines (interview with foreign control system supplier 2013). That is, while the licensor transfers drawings and specifications, for example, of the wind turbine and its component technology, the design license contains obligations for the licensor to buy and sell a certain number of wind turbines and pay royalties as a percentage of the sales. In this way, through licenses, control system suppliers will be formally protected by patents, copyrights, and/or trademarks, and will be able to receive a share of the royalties from the turbines that are sold. This type of technology transfer through inscription into design licences for a full wind turbine has often also been the case for a wind turbine's control systems and their software:

> In the case of a full technology transfer, the transfer typically comes with some IPR in the context of a license arrangement for either components or a full turbine in the context of a license arrangement for either components or a full turbine model to be manufactured locally. (Lewis 2013:110)

An example of this is the Chinese state-owned wind turbine manufacturer Dongfang Electric, which has agreed a manufacturing process license with the German company REpower. In this license contract, a number of conditions about technology transfer, learning, and rights to manufacture in accordance with the REpower design licence were signed. In addition, it involved a components list, which demanded Dongfang should use specific control system suppliers (interviews with Chinese wind turbine manufacturer 2013; interviews with foreign control system suppliers 2012, 2013).

The use of blackboxing locks of software codes

In addition to licenses, foreign control system companies have often adopted trade secrets as a way of protecting their IPRs to the software. In particular, the very spine of the system – that is, the main controller's core algorithm – is protected through various technical locks and encryption, which blackbox its contents, making it nearly impossible to copy:

> How it is technically protected, I don't know, I just know that it's protected and that's there's nothing they can do about it. (Interview with foreign control system supplier 2012)

Or, in other words, 'the very control part, the core [algorithm] we have closed, locked, and sealed in any possible way' (interview with foreign control system supplier 2012). Apart from this mode of using trade secrets, another way to protect the most vital core algorithms of the control system can be to sell parts of the object code, but not the source codes of the software itself. That is, fearing copying of the source codes, software developers for controllers 'normally just send this as a binary file [in object code]. And that's just some numbers of zeros and ones. You can't see what it is. That's what they got [in the initial phase of China's wind power development]' (interview with foreign control system supplier 2013).

Non-legal means of intellectual property protection

In addition to the above-mentioned legal means of IPR protection and technical blackboxing, software developers of controllers may consciously choose not to localise software R&D activities or the main algorithm in China in order to protect their IP. Instead, they only localise sales offices and/or establish offices there. Another strategy widely used to protect their 'crown jewels' – the core algorithms - is to only sell redesigns or make product improvements on older platforms, (interviews):

> This product that I am selling the source codes to, that is kind of old fashioned. In that way the potential damage [of IPR infringement] is limited. (Interview with foreign control system supplier 2013)

Others sequester their software algorithms abroad. This is based on the idea of 'dividing up the intellectual property part of the content and not having them in China' (Riley & Vance 2012). Finally, another non-legal form of IP protection is close trust-based personal relationships. As argued by a foreign actor,

> we have an NDA. We have the IPRs. And then again, we've got all that, but I think that when the light is turned off, I'd prefer having a close relationship. (Interview with foreign control system supplier 2013)

Despite these various legal and non-legal precautionary means for IPR protection, they do not always work as intended; instead they have tended to overflow, for example, leading to IPR infringement. A case in point is the infringement case between American control system producer American Superconductor (AMSC), which produces 'computer systems that serve as the electronic brains of wind turbines' (and its software affiliate Windtec) (Riley & Vance 2012), and the Chinese wind turbine manufacturer Sinovel, as explored briefly below.

Realising the power of core algorithms – and dealing with closed algorithms

Whilst we have focused relatively exclusively on the concerns of foreign control system suppliers up until now, Chapter Seven now delves into the perspective of Chinese actors with regard to accessing software algorithms after they have been protected through different means and locks.

Chinese wind turbine manufacturers are increasingly struggling to reduce their dependence on foreign suppliers and on wind turbine design licence suppliers. This struggle has been intensified with the turn to quality in Chinese wind power development marketisation. That is, the quality crisis has made visible the critical role of optimised control systems for ensuring the performance and reliability of wind turbines, and therein their quality. This can be claimed to reflect how Chinese actors have increasingly realised the need to comprehend the systemic interplay of the wind turbine's components, rather than relying on the initial 'LEGO-approach', to ensure its quality. That is, before understanding the systemic interplay of components, one cannot understand and master the development of the supervisory control system's core algorithm. This is thus constituted as an essential component for enabling a turn to quality in Chinese wind power, as well as to align with the Party doctrine of scientific development, and to frame wind power as sustainable again in comprehensive terms. The increased awareness of the critical role of control system software reflects a distinct shift from the initial phases of Chinese wind power development marketisation, during which Chinese customers would

> think the software is relatively unimportant, worthless. We don't focus on software, don't emphasise software. So we have to understand the idea of the Chinese customers, Chinese customers value the hard things, not soft things. (Interview with Chinese control system supplier 2012)

Evidently, whilst software was not treated as strategically important in the initial phases of wind power development by Chinese actors, this has changed over time, as the marketisation of wind power development has turned towards quality. Thus, Chinese manufacturers and others have only started relatively recently to pay attention to the main control software, not only because it is one of the most complex and advanced components, but also because it is a component that constitutes a relatively minor part of the whole cost of a turbine. That is, overall, Chinese companies started out by developing indigenous components that represented a relatively large share of the whole cost of a turbine, and components that were relatively easy to copy and develop (such as towers, brakes, gearboxes). Only later, as the quality crisis emerged did they realise the strategic and competitive importance of 'algorithmic quality' endowed by high quality control system software. Along with their enhanced capabilities, this led Chinese companies to shift focus away from upgrading in the more costly and 'easy' components towards the indigenous mastering of more challenging components such as blades and control system hardware and software in particular (interview with foreign control system supplier 2012).

The legacy of foreign licences – contested roles of the 'student' and the 'teacher'

The gradual realisation of the need to understand and optimise the functioning of the turbine, through the mastering of the core algorithm, evidently problematises China's legacy of dependence on foreign design licences, and as 'students who learned from a teacher' (interview with foreign control system supplier 2013). Today, Chinese wind turbine manufacturers 'have chosen to start designing their own turbines. So they are ready to design a new technology and to get independent from the old one' (interview with foreign control system supplier 2013). Further, with upgraded capabilities and heightened ambitions, Chinese customers will increasingly want to make changes in the software, so as to be able to adapt turbines to local environmental conditions. And this requires access to some of the source codes:

> All the software for the wind farm ... now the Chinese customer becomes more and more know about the industry ... so they have their own ideas. They say, why not we can ... because the low wind speed issue [in China making adjustments necessary] ... they want to talk to [control system supplier], they want to change, but [foreign control system supplier] says 'no'. We are ... I heard from the customer [Chinese wind farm developer]. (Interview with Chinese employee in foreign control system supplier 2012)

Striving to design their own wind turbines, Chinese manufacturers not only want to become independent from foreign design houses and consultancy firms 'who have sold them their license' (interview with foreign control system supplier 2013), but increasingly also want to develop their own indigenous control systems and 'to develop the software themselves' (interview with foreign control system supplier 2012), to 'get rid of them [control system suppliers]' (interview with foreign control system supplier 2012):

> They have produced the turbines based on a license, and that means that they have to pay for every turbine that they produce for that company. Of course they want to get out of that. So they want to develop their own turbines. That is what matters for Chinese turbines [...] Simply. That's what it's all about. They want that technology transferred. (Interview with foreign control system supplier 2013)

As Chinese customers are increasingly seeking independence from foreign technologies during the 'turn to quality', contracts (e.g. licensing agreements and NDAs) which have been employed as framing tools in customer–supplier relations have also become insufficient, since

> the Chinese are not as loyal to a components' list as in other countries. Well, it's written that there should be an [X]-controller and stuff like that. The Chinese look at it immediately and think: how can we get rid of this? (Interview with foreign control system supplier 2012)

This illustrates how Chinese wind turbine manufacturers have started to contest their role as the student and now want to redefine this 'inferior' position.

China sweet and sour – sweet relations gone sour: the double-edged sword of protection

As we have seen, foreign control system suppliers have been very protective of their software algorithms. Chinese customers have realised the critical role of the control system software algorithms and seen the need to master them. However, the very protection of software algorithms implemented to frame and modify the relations between foreign suppliers and Chinese customers has actually destabilised these very relations.

This is partly a consequence of how the IP barriers to algorithm access have often resulted in delays in the service that foreign control system suppliers' customers - Chinese wind turbine manufacturers - have been able to offer their Chinese customers, that is, the end user such as wind farm owners/developers and/or generating companies. Most commonly, the foreign control system supplier in China is not able to solve the technical issues experienced by their Chinese customer right away, as the control system supplier's software programmers are mostly, for security reasons, in the home country, far away and in a different time zone. Not sharing the codes with the Chinese control system subsidiary or with their Chinese customer (the wind turbine manufacturer), means that the Chinese end user (wind farm owner and/or generating company) experiences prolonged response times when technical issues occur and the local office is unable to assist with source code corrections (interviews 2012, 2013). From the perspective of the Chinese wind turbine manufacturer, such slow service creates a very bad impression in the mind of the wind farm owner and/or generating company. As customer-supplier relations with the end customer have soured over time, owing to the inflexibility and lack of access to software codes, some Chinese control system customers have attempted to shift their foreign suppliers. That is, Chinese wind turbine manufacturers are leaving their foreign control system suppliers in favour of another foreign or Chinese supplier that will better understand the nature of the Chinese supply chain and the need to be able to respond agilely to operational concerns of the Chinese end consumer (interviews):

> Their [control system] product and service is too expensive, they charge for everything, and very closed, not sharing anything. So the collaboration was closed. Apart from being closed, they are also too slow, their service is bad, and their control technology was old, not very fast and adaptable. (Interview with Chinese employee in foreign control system supplier 2013)

Another source of discontent and disruption of relations has been the reluctance of foreign control system suppliers to locate R&D activities in China owing to the fear of losing their IPRs. However, from the perspective of Chinese customers, investment in local design and adaptation to the customers' demands is important, which means that it is not satisfactory to keep R&D activities outside the Chinese market (interviews with foreign control system supplier 2012, 2013). Acknowledging that this has been a reason for discontent, some foreign control system suppliers have modified their strategy over time, for example by gradually locating their development activities in China to help stabilise relations with customers, and opening up some of the software to local key personnel. Other control system companies have likewise engaged in joint ventures with Chinese firms.

In this way, foreign control system companies have often been considered to be 'too tough on protection', making the hard protection of algorithms 'a double-edged sword' because it is also 'risky not to share anything' (interview with Chinese and foreign control system suppliers 2012). In short, with the improving capabilities and rising ambitions of Chinese wind turbine manufacturers, closed algorithms have created dissatisfaction amongst Chinese customers and have soured sweet relations.

Chinese (il)legal attempts at overcoming software protection

As relations started to increasingly sour, with Chinese ambitions and capabilities growing, and since it is nearly impossible to reengineer software algorithms when they are locked, there have been cases of illegal attempts to access core algorithms. A much-debated smoking gun example of IPR infringement and industrial espionage is that between the Chinese wind turbine manufacturer Sinovel – then the largest Chinese wind turbine manufacturer in China and globally, based on installed capacity, but now reportedly are close to being closed down – and AMSC. To protect its control system software, AMSC sequestered its software abroad, meaning that the control system software would supposedly sit on a secure server, inaccessible via the internet in order to prevent attacks from hackers (Riley & Vance 2012). Allegedly dissatisfied with its dependence on expensive AMSC controllers, and wanting to develop and adjust the software itself, Sinovel Wind Group Co. unexpectedly turned away shipments from its long-term supplier in 2011. The reason for this was soon revealed: it turned out that 'more than 1,000 Sinovel turbines by July' 2011, and many more since (Riley & Vance 2012), were

> running a stolen version of AMSC's software. Worse, the software revealed that Sinovel had complete access to AMSC's proprietary source code. In short, Sinovel didn't really need AMSC anymore. (Riley & Vance 2012)

Computer logs and messages have since proved that Sinovel blackmailed one of AMSC's employees, working at AMSC's research facility in Klagenfurt, Austria, to help China 'create software that could go on existing turbines as quickly as possible, using source code taken from AMSC's server in Austria' (Riley & Vance 2012). With this, Sinovel had 'succeeded in copying their [AMSC's] control concept like crazy' (Interview with foreign control system supplier 2012). With the stolen code, Sinovel was now able to adjust the software and make it fit any kind of controller, thereby reducing dependence on AMSC:

> They did not have the software. Or they had it, but they were not allowed to have it [...] And Windtec [AMSC's software company] said, you cannot get that. (Interview with foreign control system supplier 2012)

And so, borne out of discontent with their dependence on AMSC, Sinovel thus apparently attempted to make a Chinese power electronics company into the Chinese version of AMSC. The case was already being tried in a Beijing copyright infringement court case for stealing trade secrets in 2012, with the Klagenfurt employee pleading guilty and being sentenced to 12 months in jail (Hanna, et al. 24 January 2018 in Bloomberg.com; Riley & Vance 2012). However, the case was drawn out for many years owing to its sensitive nature and the way in which it would fundamentally be a trial against the Chinese state, owing to Sinovel's partial state ownership and close ties with the Chinese government. Eventually, Sinovel has been found guilty, not in China but in the USA, of 'orchestrating the theft in a rare criminal trade-secrets trial that has raised doubts over China's commitment to fighting infringement of intellectual property and corporate espionage' (Hanna et al. 24 January 2018 in Bloomberg.com).

Apart from disrupting customer–supplier relations, the case spurred outright controversy, as evidenced, for example, in trade relation tensions between the USA and China. There remains a great degree of uncertainty as to whether AMSC will be eventually compensated for how the theft of trade secrets on software code has dramatically decreased the value of AMSC's shares (Hanna et al. 24 January 2018 in Bloomberg.com). Overall, the controversy over contested algorithms seems to be entangled in wider international controversies over IPRs, industrial espionage as well as over China's upgrading and catch-up. Taking this case as an example of the international nature of the dispute can be seen in how the American Federal Bureau of Intelligence (FBI) was drawn into the investigation of the incident, and how Chinese spy agencies and buildings of the People's Liberation Army (PLA) are suspected to be involved, owing to China's 'far-reaching industrial espionage campaign by Chinese spy agencies' (Riley & Vance 2012):

> In terms of outright theft of intellectual property, there is growing evidence that China's intelligence agencies are involved, as attacks spread from hits on large technology companies to the hacking of startups and even law firms. (Riley & Vance 2012)

This case and ongoing Chinese attempts at opening source codes have over-all resulted in lacking trust in IPR enforcement in China. This, in turn, has repercussions for China's inclusion into the global 'innovation community' (interview with Chinese wind turbine manufacturer 2012):

> China is not received, they are not being full participants ... they are not even being allowed to be full participants in the innovation community, because people are proactively not including them, because, I'm nerv-ous about sending them things, like sharing my innovation, because I don't have confidence that they are going to be protected. (Interview with Chinese wind turbine manufacturer 2012)

On the other hand, whilst IPR infringement is illegal, some actors caution an understanding when it comes to Sinovel's supposed actions:

> If I were Sinovel, I would also have been angry due to that arrogant way of handling things [...] Actually, I can see it from Sinovel's side. And they just couldn't get access to anything [from AMSC], so it's under-standable that they did as they did. (Interview with foreign control sys-tem supplier 2012)

That is, as Chinese manufacturers have upgraded, they want 'to have their own strengths built up. Sooner or later you want this, you need to do this, so they try some ... try some change on these IPR issues, which irritates [AMSC]' (interview with Chinese wind turbine manufacturer 2012). In par-ticular, Chinese manufacturers aim to get access to the source codes (and not just the object code) in order to make adjustments themselves:

> Because they think that when they buy something, then they want to see it ... it's clear, then they want to be able to work on it [the codes] themselves [...] With object codes, they don't know what's inside the [black]box, but just hope that it works. That's how it [the object code] is. But we could sense that others ... nobody really wanted to buy any-thing unless they could get this. (Interview with foreign control system supplier 2013)

Reconfiguring relations between customers and suppliers

Overall, a shift in Sino-foreign customer–supplier relations is noted over time. In the initial phases of wind power development in China, Chinese wind turbine manufacturers did not request access to source codes. Instead, they were offered a complete package of hardware and software that was not customised. Over time, more customised and modularised control systems and even software algorithms were delivered, responding to Chinese rising demands and capabilities; for example not offering a full package of both hardware or software or a block of closed code, but only smaller selected software modules adapted to the Chinese context, which enables customers to make adaptations to programs themselves.

Therefore, a more or less constant request received by foreign control system suppliers in today's China is access to source codes. While imposing limits on sharing algorithms is critical to the survival of Western control system software suppliers, access to source codes is central to the upgrading being undertaken by Chinese wind turbine manufacturers. That is, knowledge of source codes can provide knowledge of how the wind turbine is regulated and knowledge of the interconnected nature of the myriads of turbine components, and thereby reduce dependence on foreign technologies despite the legacy based on foreign licences. Overall, a 'game of interests' is being construed, as both Chinese and foreign actors want their own voice: 'It's [like] two big animals wanting to dance together, haha, it's not easy to coordinate' (interview with Chinese official/diplomat 2012).

> These are the ultimate interests of the game, the reason why the Chinese companies ask the Danish companies to open the source codes. Chinese companies do not want their own control system controlled by others, they hope to change the ownership rights, to optimise [make adaptations to the codes]. (Interview with Chinese employee in foreign control system supplier 2013)

In this way, relations, positions, and relative roles have started to become contested and negotiated, as Chinese wind turbine manufacturers increasingly aspire to work on the codes themselves. As software algorithms have become the centre of contestation and negotiation, as well as the IPRs to them, relations between foreign control system suppliers and Chinese customers have also become negotiated and contested. In the following, we explore further the de- and reconfiguration of customer–supplier relations centered on software and IPRs.

'No pain, no gain', and separating the core from the non-core

Increasingly, some suppliers are acknowledging that a new 'competitive space' is opening up around source codes, realising that Chinese customers are often evaluating the quality of their control system suppliers in terms of how much they are willing to open up their source codes. This has led several foreign control system suppliers to experiment with how far into the control software's 'spine' or 'nervous system' they dare to go, that is, how far to open up without threatening their own existence. This strategy shows an appreciation of the Chinese customer's standpoint:

> We have to give something for free, free of charge, open the technology, some of the algorithms. [...] It is worthwhile to give. No pain,

no gain. If you give me more, then they [foreign suppliers] get more orders. (Interview with foreign control system supplier 2013)

As some foreign control system companies have decided to open up further, they have for example engaged in modularisation of their control system software, so their Chinese customers (wind turbine manufacturers), control system subsidiaries, and/or joint venture partners can provide faster service for the end customer. This modularisation 'makes it easier to control' what the Chinese partners get access to and what they do not gain access to (interview with foreign control system supplier). That is, through modularisation of software, foreign suppliers are able to safeguard, disentangle, and bracket the 'core' (the operational source code layer which connects to the other levels) from the 'non-core'. This allows them to open up the latter and sell selected software modules through exclusivity agreements with Chinese customers; these customers can then adapt the modules, resulting in higher customer satisfaction (interview with foreign control system supplier 2013). The ability to share openly, while protecting and blackboxing the most core elements, therefore becomes an important factor in holding on to Chinese customers:

> But when it comes to exactly this product [control system, including software], this is very attractive to them, because no one else has dared to open up the source code in such an extensive way as we have, and that's probably related to how the others can't protect theirs ... they cannot protect the most important. (Interview with foreign control system supplier 2012)

Renegotiating the algorithmic boundary

Meanwhile, the only way for foreign control system companies to differentiate themselves from competitors is often through the key algorithm and the degree of openness. This means that they are finding themselves in an ongoing struggle to discover the limits to how much can be shared without losing critical proprietary property, while at the same time maintaining or building new relations with Chinese customers. According to some foreign suppliers of control system software, they have now

> reached the limit, we are into the source code, where we ... the only thing we lack is to give them access to the central nervous system... [What] they are getting access to, that's all the different [sub-control systems], which are specific for the individual products, but the very main control, the core [algorithm] is protected. (Interview with foreign control system supplier 2012)
> It's pretty obvious, that they [Chinese customers] are expecting us to open up to all the knowledge that we've got. That's kind of the basic

assumption. That's a given. And that's one of the interesting tasks, I'd say, to find out how to do it without harming yourself, but at the same time making sure that they find it a reasonable partnership between customer and supplier. And that's a challenge. (Interview with foreign control system supplier 2013)

A rather radical example of opening up an algorithm has been the case of the Danish control system supplier Mita-Teknik A/S, who engaged in a partnership with Sinovel in 2012, right after Sinovel lost its control system supplier AMSC, and was thrown into an international IPR infringement case. While the two companies had had a collaborative relationship regarding technical development since 2008, a new strategic partnership was signed in 2012 whereby Mita-Teknik had the opportunity to change its former reputation as a closed and protective company, and to build new, or rebuild old, relations with Chinese customers:

> Mita-Teknik has made all data from the control system available to Sinovel, allowing the Chinese company's engineers to create unique solutions for their customers. (Wind Energy and Electrical Vehicle Review, 22 April 2012)

What has attracted notable interest in the media, as well as amongst industrial actors, is how under this agreement Sinovel allegedly 'owns the intellectual property rights to the modified and upgraded versions of the software and source code, as well as the right to use the initial version in all products the company produces' (Wind Energy and Electrical Vehicle Review, 22 April 2012; www.sinovel.com). Two companies having reached this kind of agreement illustrates how a constant negotiation over core algorithms – or over the algorithmic boundaries – is taking place in Chinese wind power development marketisation under the current turn to quality, which creates an ambiguous space of simultaneous collaboration and competition. As a matter of damage control, though, the source code delivered by Mita-Teknik is not the newest, but is built on an older platform and can still not be installed on a different controller without copyright infringement (because of technical locks). Therefore, 'a lot of them become disappointed because they find out that they won't be able to install the software on another controller' (interview with foreign control system supplier 2012).

Challenges for Chinese companies after gaining access to core algorithms

There is no doubt that some Chinese customers have gradually gained access to, and succeeded in making some adjustments to, the software in an operational wind turbine. Meanwhile, if they have not invested time and money in acquiring parts of the source code, they will still be dependent on the assistance of the control system software supplier for all minor and major adjustments that are made (interview with foreign control system supplier 2012). At the same time, even when they have acquired access to parts of the source code, such access requires a certain level of 'absorptive capacity', because 'if you don't know about it, then you don't know what to ask for' (interview with foreign control system supplier 2012). Sometimes, foreign control system suppliers even claim that they are uncertain whether their customers

> actually know what it is that they want. I'm not sure. Because, I'm not sure whether they know what it is that they are working with. (Interview with foreign control system supplier 2013)

To some degree, there is an indication that access to source codes has become framed as 'the mother of all solutions', even though this might not be the case (interview with foreign control system supplier 2013). Meanwhile, because some Chinese customers 'don't know what they can use it [the source codes] for', 'it's safe enough to sell it to them, because they don't know what they are doing' (interview with foreign control system supplier 2012). In addition, software codes can be full of errors and are generally in need of regular maintenance and updates, in order to keep the high-efficiency intelligent turbines running optimally. Therefore, 'if you don't understand how it's built, then it doesn't have any particular value' (interview with foreign control system supplier 2012).

Open it – and don't change a thing! On worthless codes and limits to absorption and reverse engineering

One of the main reasons for wanting access to the source codes is that this should make reengineering possible, so the turbine's control can be adjusted to the specific local ambient conditions.

> In [Chinese wind turbine manufacturer] we also want to do these kinds of things [reverse engineering]. For example, since the wind conditions for Chinese and foreign wind turbines are not the same, then we will only get sub-optimal results if we copy the European mature core algorithms. If we instead learn from the Danish experience combined with China's experience with reverse engineering, then we can get some unexpected results for China's real conditions. When these results are applied elsewhere, we can become very successful. (Interview with Chinese control system supplier 2012)

However, as it has turned out, Chinese customers have sometimes been unable to make changes to the acquired source codes. As expressed by a foreign control system supplier (2012; 2013), whilst some have engaged in risky (and often unsuccessful) 'guesswork' and 'trial and error, trial and error', many 'customers don't dare to do anything yet, haha [...] I actually think they were kind of overwhelmed by it [the software algorithms]'. The lack of courage to engage in the reengineering of source codes is in turn related to the potentiality of 'messing up everything' (interview with foreign control system supplier 2012), since one change in the codes will change the parameters for everything else. For instance, if the blades are made longer, this has implications for the loads on the tower, 'and then you have to put in some new parameters' (interview with foreign control system supplier 2013).

> This can give them a lot of other problems. They should ... there's a reason why we have built it [the software], as we have. And if they start changing a lot of the foundation, then it might all fall apart. Then it's kind of better first to build up some understanding of the different areas. I can be in doubt whether the Chinese have the insight and understanding for all of this ... and, in reality, maybe also lacking the kind of patience that is needed. (Interview with foreign control system supplier 2013)

In particular, and because the main control and the pitch control contain critical information on how to regulate the blades, the reengineering of source codes also requires knowledge of the aerodynamics of the turbine and of the aeroelastic design of the blades (interview with foreign research institute 2013). In this way, if there is a lack of knowledge, experience, and basic research about the aerodynamics lying behind the source codes, the 'critical' key source codes risk becoming 'worthless':

> In regard to the controller ... [...] if they don't understand the aeroelas-ticity ... then they can have all the source codes delivered that they want to [...] Well, the source code for the main control ... it takes into account the aeroelasticity of the wind turbine, and if you don't understand the basic behaviour of the turbine, then you don't know why [a control system supplier] has written the regulation code in this way ... so it is kind of a peculiar place to start out ... when they are attempting to gain knowledge, because they need to understand the turbine first. And maybe they don't. I don't know the Chinese ... but if you don't under-stand what a turbine is about, then you can't... (Interview with foreign research institute 2013)
>
> [This requires an] abstract way of thinking; you need to know what it [the coding] is based on [regulation principle]. One thing is to have some numbers delivered, which you must do your calculations on, and then you get a result. That's not how it's functioning. You need to know the dynamics. (Interview with foreign control system supplier 2012)

Evidently, the lack of understanding 'the reason behind it [the source code]' means that technology transfer through source codes only has value when matched with knowledge sharing and the experience to be able to absorb it, which takes investment in time and money for basic research. If one lacks long-term basic research into aerodynamics (and aeroelastic codes) contained in the source codes of the controller's core algorithm and simulation tools for turbine design, access to the 'source code is not of any use' (interview with foreign control system supplier 2013).

The last (and most difficult) mile – on construing a competitive game

In sum, a competitive struggle is developing around IPRs and software in core technologies between Chinese and foreign actors: Since 'it is one hundred per cent certain' that the Chinese will catch up and 'seize the market' (interview with foreign research institute 2013) – even despite temporary 'setbacks' – as Chinese actors are getting better 'step by step' but increasingly faster, foreign companies and research institutes are speeding up in terms of their own technological development in order to continue to stay 'a little bit better' (interview with foreign research institute 2013). That is, even though China still faces socio-material hindrances to rapid catch-up in the development of 'advanced' wind energy algorithms, this is not to say that China lacks the computational capacity and wit to do so. Rather, it is more a matter of China's shorter experience-span, a legacy of technology transfer resulting in sparse overview of the systemic interplay of components, as well as a fragmented innovation system with different scientists placed in disparate departments and localities, and a lack of basic research into the science behind component behaviour. Meanwhile, these hindrances are not fixed and are constantly being pushed, for example as Chinese companies engage in, or consider, the acquisition of control system companies and/or the hiring of foreign software experts. Consequently, apart from employing IPRs, foreign actors (companies and research institutions, sometimes in tight collaboration) are investing in the development of ever more intelligent solutions and elegant wind turbine designs in order to stay competitive with Chinese competitors in the current phase of wind power development where things are being measured in terms of their algorithmic quality, for example in terms of their control and design:

> We move forward rapidly and do everything we can to put aside resources for that [R&D]. But of course, they will find out something at some point, which can substitute for our system, but when we get to that, then [we will have developed something new, hopefully]. (Interview with foreign control system supplier 2012)

Whilst acknowledging that China will eventually catch up in these fields, because 'they are faster than us', China is 'still in the learning phase' (interview with foreign and Chinese control system suppliers 2012). Further, foreign research institutes and companies argue that 'the last mile is the most difficult one' for Chinese industry actors (interview with foreign control system supplier 2012). In particular, the complicated mathematics lying beneath the source codes takes time to learn:

> Luckily [for us], they [the Chinese customers/wind turbine manufacturers] have huge problems learning that. Well, it would surprise me if they could. How long have we had a prime time for the wind power industry out here? Five years. That they should have been able to learn this [in such a short time], which the rest of us have spent forty years to learn [would be surprising]... What we are good at in the West, and what they find a little more difficult out here, that is 'thinking outside the box' ... to see things from another perspective. Here they know how to calculate. If you have an equation [similar to an algorithm], they can solve it and get the right result. But you must know how to define the equation [algorithm]. (Interview with foreign control system supplier 2012)

This inability to 'define the equation/algorithm' is again being linked to China's educational and research system – with relative lack of focus on critical thinking and basic research – and China's legacy of copy-catting and reverse engineering, which has induced continued dependence on foreign design licenses and software technologies.

Problematising the assimilation and absorption strategy

The Medium- to Long-Term Development Plan for Science and Technology 2006–2020 (MOST 2006) links indigenous innovation to the strengthening of 'original innovation, integrated innovation, and re-innovation based on assimilation and absorption of imported technology, in order to improve our national innovation capability' (MOST 2006, s. II,1). In turn, 'the importation of technologies without emphasizing the assimilation, absorption and re-innovation is bound to weaken the nation's indigenous research and development capacity' (MOST 2006).

The above analysis has indicated potential socio-material barriers to leapfrogging and catching up around algorithmic source codes, despite attempts at assimilation, absorption, and reinnovation, as prescribed in the above quotes from the Medium- to Long-Term Development Plan for Science and Technology 2006–2020. These boundaries threaten to delegitimise China's technology for market strategy and associated assimilation and absorption strategy, which has formed an integral part of China's S&T strategy. In the 12th Five-Year-Plan for the Scientific and Technological Development of Wind Power (MOST 2012), for example, concerns over how Chinese wind turbines early on 'relied mainly on the introduction of foreign design techniques or on joint design with foreign agencies' are expressed, as China is still dependent on foreign core technologies owing to a lack of independent IPRs to indigenous advanced control system software or software tools for wind turbine design. Accordingly, improvements and indigenous IP within these areas are framed as critical to improving wind power equipment performance, 'and to protect the Chinese wind power industry's sustained, rapid, and steady growth' (MOST 2012, s. 2, 1(1), 2, 1(3)). In this way, the 'elixir' of indigenous innovation to realise 'the great renaissance of the Chinese nation' through 'innovation with Chinese characteristics' (McGregor 2009:3) sometimes overflows with a bitter taste:

> The 'Trade Market for Technology' policy didn't work as expected. They have spent more than 20 years to attract foreign companies and learn, but there is still not one single completely indigenously designed Chinese wind turbine. When there's some, the core technology, the software, is foreign. Or the capabilities have been bought, through M&A and foreign employees. (Interview with investment bank 2013)

So finally, the analysis has brought us round to (re)discovering that the root of the controversies over IPRs around software algorithms is founded in the concern for indigenous innovation as part of China's sustainable and scientific development in the current qualification struggle over wind power development.

Politicised relations around control system software and an emerging zero-sum game

Linked to China's ambitions of scientific development, the controversy unfolding around IPRs in Sino-foreign supply chains has become inherently political. And so,

> We have this discussion on source code. But it's the decision of the Government, that now they need to have their own IPR, that is to say ... they have to own the source code. (Interview with foreign control system supplier 2012)

Indeed, the issue of China's dependence on foreign IPRs is linked to a national narrative of China's victimisation by foreign patents. For instance, the Medium- to Long-Term Plan for the Scientific and Technological Development 2006–2020 argued that 'experience shows that developed countries are unwilling to transfer core technologies in China' (MOST 2006), at the same time as China's President, Xi Jinping, in a speech on Chinese innovation to Chinese scientists in 2014, stressed that China must strive towards making 'important breakthroughs in key technologies' and taking 'crucial technologies into our own hands' (Chinese Academy of Sciences, CAS, 2014). Along these lines, as President Xi Jinping has been quoted, '[s]cience and technology are the foundation of national strength and prosperity, and innovation is the soul of national advancement' (Buckley 2014).

Overall, the contentious nature of the issue of IPRs over source codes seems inherently related to its entanglement with broader contestations over IPRs and over China's innovation strategy and legacy of technology transfer, in which a competitive 'zero-sum game' between Chinese and foreign actors where actors are framed as either losers or winners, and not as mutual co-benefiters of interaction, is emerging. As expressed by a foreign China expert (2010):

> If you look at the Ministry of Science and Technology, MOST, and their thoughts on this, their Medium and Long Term Plan for ... the MLP [S&T 2006–2020], as it is called ... Well – if you read it closely, then ... where it really gets critical, that's regarding core technologies, and their analysis of this is ... that it's a zero-sum game: You cannot buy core technologies, you have to develop them yourself.

Reflections on fourth site of controversy – algorithmic controversy over intellectual property rights

In the analysis above, struggles over access to IPRs in control system source codes have been explored, together with some of the potential socio-technical algorithmic barriers to leapfrogging through reverse engineering that these have produced. In particular, while we witness some degree of upgrading in terms of control system hardware and software, catchup through leapfrogging has proved impossible in the case of the most critical control system software. It has hereby been revealed how the supposedly stabilising and pacifying framing tools of IPRs and algorithms that are meant to tame the wind by setting up boundaries of ownership and regulating the turbine's response to the forces of the wind have been anything but stabilising. Instead, IPRs have rather overflowed over and over again, producing highly fragile supply chain relations around control system software, producing unforeseen issues such as IPR infringement, dissatisfied customers, underperforming wind turbines, or wind power curtailment to reduce the risk of destabilising the grid, for example, as they confer ownership on specific entities to the exclusion of others.

By focusing on Sino-foreign customer–supplier relations around the core technology of control system software, and particularly around control system algorithms, this study has simultaneously uncovered an underlying story about contestations over China's S&T strategy of assimilation and absorption, and its focus on applied science over basic research, as the country's wind power development assemblage undergoes a contested transition from quantity to quality. Indeed, such a transition is neither smooth nor automatic. Meanwhile, the controversy mapping also displays contested roles and positions of actors in the supply chain, and how Chinese actors increasingly reject their position as dependent laggards, even if this also means that they may have to disregard the legal framing of IPRs. As identities, roles, and goals are shifting, the boundaries of ownership set by IPRs have become highly negotiable, with a resulting constant renegotiation over the algorithmic boundaries of sharing and opening source codes.

Overall, this book indicates the impossibility of setting up a straightforward division between the realm of technology and the realm of politics. How the role of IPRs of software algorithms in turn plays out in the issue of certification and standardisation is to be mapped in Chapter Eight, as we follow aeroelastic codes in critically important design simulation tools for wind turbine design, in which source codes for the main controller's regulation principle also play a role.

References

Bosworth, D. & Yang, D., 2000, 'Intellectual Property Law, Technology Flow and Licensing Opportunities in the People's Republic of China', *International Business Review* 9, 453–477.

Buckley, C., 2014, 'Xi Urges Greater Innovation in 'Core Technologies'', Sinosphere, *New York Times*, 10 June 2014, viewed 14 August 2014, http://sinosphere.blogs.nytimes.com/2014/06/10/xi-urges-greater-innovation-in-core-technologies/?_php=true&_type=blogs&_r=0.

Chinese Academy of Sciences, 2014, 'Xi urges independent innovation in science, technology', 10 June. http://english.cas.cn/resources/archive/news_archive/nu2014/201502/t20150217_140723.shtml.

Chow, G. C., 2002, *China's Economic Transformation*, Blackwell, Oxford.

Gregersen, B. & Johnson, B., 2009, 'A Policy Learning Perspective on Developing Sustainable Energy Technologies', *Argumenta Oeconomica* 2(23), 9–34.

Haakonsson, S., Kirkegaard, J. K., & Lema, R. forthcoming, 'China's catch-up in wind power – a case study on decomposition of innovation', Sino-Danish Center for Education and Research, mimeo.

Hanna, J., Smithe, C. & Martin, C., 2018, 'China's Sinovel Convicted in U.S. of Stealing Trade Secrets', Bloomberg.com, 24 January 2018, viewed 20 March 2018, https://www.bloomberg.com/news/articles/2018-01-24/chinese-firm-sinovel-convicted-in-u-s-of-trade-secret-theft.

Hendry, C. & Harborne, P., 2011, 'Changing the View of Wind Power Development: More than "Bricolage"', *Research Policy* 40(5), 778–789, https://doi.org/10.1016/j.respol.2011.03.001.

Kaya, T. A., 2007, 'Comparative Analysis of the Patentability of Computer Software Under the TRIPS Agreement: The U.S., The E.U., and Turkey', *Ankara Law Review* 4(1), 43–81.

Lewis, J. I., 2013, *Green Innovation in China. China's Wind Power Industry and the Global Transition to a Low-Carbon Economy*, Columbia University Press, New York.

Liebeskind, J. P., 1996, 'Knowledge, Strategy and the Theory of the Firm', *Strategic Management Journal*, Special Issue 17, 93–107.

Liebeskind, J. P., 1997, 'Keeping Organizational Secrets: Protective Institutional Mechanisms and their Costs', *Industrial and Corporate Change* 3, 623–663.

Liu, W., 2005, 'Intellectual Property Protection Related to Technology in China', *Technological Forecasting & Social Change* 72, 339–348.

Mansfield, E., 1994, 'Intellectual Property Protection, Foreign Direct Investment, and Technology Transfer', Discussion Paper 19, International Finance Corporation, Washington DC.

Mansfield, E., 1995, 'Intellectual Property Protection, Direct Investment, and Technology Transfer: Germany, Japan, and the United States', Discussion Paper 27, International Finance Corporation, Washington DC.

Maskus, K. E., 2002, 'Regulatory Standards in the WTO: Comparing Intellectual Property Rights with Competition Policy, Environmental Protection, and Core Labor Standards', *World Trade Review* 1(2), 135–152.

McGregor, J., n.d., 'China's Drive for "Indigenous Innovation". A Web of Industrial Policies', *APCO Worldwide, US Chamber of Commerce, Global Intellectual Property Centre*, Global Regulatory Cooperation Project, viewed 29 November 2014: https://www.uschamber.com/sites/default/files/documents/files/100728chinareport_0_0.pdf.

MOST (Ministry of Science and Technology of the People's Republic of China), 2006, State Council, 国家中长期科学和技术发展规划纲要(2006–2020) [National Outline for Medium and Long Term Science and Technology Development (2006–2020)], 9 February 2006, http://www.gov.cn/jrzg/2006-02/09/content_183787.htm.

MOST (Ministry of Science and Technology of the People's Republic of China), 2012, State Council, The Central People's Government of the People's Republic of China, 关于印发风力发电科技发展'十二五'专项规划的通知 ['The 12th Five-Year-Plan for the Scientific and Technological Development of Wind Power], 国科发计,197号, National Branch No. 197, 24 April 2012, http://www.most.gov.cn/fggw/zfwj/zfwj2012/201204/t20120424_93884.htm.

Riley, M. & Vance, A., 2012, 'Inside the Chinese Boom in Corporate Espionage', Bloomberg/Bizweek, 15 March 2012, viewed 15 May 2012, http://www.business-week.com/articles/2012-03-14/inside-the-chinese-boom-in-corporate-espionage.

Spencer, J. W., 2003, 'Firms' Knowledge-Sharing Strategies in the Global Innovation System: Empirical Evidence from the Flat Panel Display Industry', *Strategic Management Journal* 24, 217–233.

Wang, L., 2004, 'Intellectual Property Protection in China', *Library Review* 36(3), 253–261.

Wind Energy and Electrical Vehicle Review, 2012, 'Sinovel and Mita Teknik Join Forces in Wind Energy', 22 April, viewed 15 November 2012, http://www.evwind.es/2012/04/22/sinovel-and-mita-teknik-join-forces-in-wind-energy/18020.

WIPO (World Intellectual Property Organization), n.d. http://www.wipo.int/portal/en/index.html, viewed 30 March 2013.

Yang, D., 2003, 'The Development of Intellectual Property in China', *World Patent Information* 25, 131–142.

Yang, D., Sonmez, M. & Bosworth, D., 2004, 'Intellectual Property Abuses: How Should Multinationals Respond?', *Long Range Planning* 37, 459–475.

Yang, D. & Clarke, P., 2005, 'Globalisation and Intellectual Property Rights in China', *Technovation* 25(5), 545–555.

Zimmerman, A. & Chaudhry, P. E., 2009, 'Protecting Intellectual Property Rights: The Special Case of China', *Journal of Asia-Pacific Business* 10(4), 308–325.

Zou, K., 2006, 'Administrative Reform and Rule of Law in China', *The Copenhagen Journal of Asian Studies*, 24 April 2006.

8 Controversy over access to standards and certificates

On my way to one of my last interviews on this field trip, I wonder how the quality crisis and struggle to qualify wind power as 'sustainable' may play out in terms of testing, certification, and standardisation. My respondent – a foreign wind turbine manufacturer – gives me part of the answer. As it turns out, the qualification struggle does indeed also take place through standards.

> *And they [the Central Government] take control, because of the quality issues that we have seen. Simply – the market wasn't well run. […] Then Beijing needs to take control – and rightly so. And they should have done so a long time ago, because now they are finally putting in standards and requirements for a higher quality. Standards and requirements for other [things] than just [installing] megawatts into the ground, and that means that I am a bit hopeful again.*

Conversely, other foreign actors in China question this qualitative shift. That is, 'quality products are not the scope for the market right now. So there's no scope for foreign quality products. Maybe this will change, but I'm not sure it will – or at least it will take a long time.' Indeed, something new might be happening in China's emerging wind power sector and nascent software sector, but what and how remains somewhat of a riddle to me. As I board the plane home from Beijing, bound for Copenhagen, I wonder if the mapping of a potential, and controversial, turn to quality may also be a story of Chinese 'experimental green marketisation'. I cannot wait to write up the algorithmic story, so full of actors, relations, and controversies, and ripe with potential endings and new beginnings.

The overflowing nature of standards and certificates

Chapter Eight now takes the marketisation account into the fifth and final 'site of controversy'. We move out from the software of controllers and their codes and back to the machinery and hardware they regulate. In order for this regulation to be effective, the turbine needs to behave as designed, and

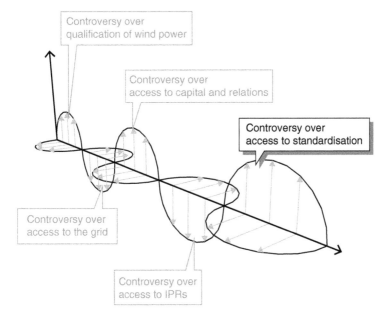

Controversy over qualification of wind power

Controversy over access to capital and relations

Controversy over access to standardisation

Controversy over access to the grid

Controversy over access to IPRs

Figure 8.1 Fifth site of controversy.

it is now the design we focus on. To be precise, it is the simulation tools and standards used for the design, optimisation, testing, and ultimately certification of a wind turbine that provide the arena for the fifth site of controversy.

Whilst standards and certification might sound rather boring, Chapter Eight proves this wrong. Diving into another algorithmic controversy over the issue of certification and standardisation in Chinese wind power development marketisation, which has intensified during the turn to quality, this research sheds light on another central, yet contested, component in China's innovation policy: international and domestic standards and certificates. What will be revealed is how potential socio-material obstacles and controversies in China's transition to renewable energy are not only founded in the country's institutional fragmentation and incoherence, but also in obstacles related to international standards and certifications, which 'may be hard to 'copy' (Andrews-Speed 2012:68) (see Figure 8.1).

China is striving not only to fulfil international standards but also to become a leader in the definition of new global standards, whilst at the same time developing indigenous, or 'Chinesified' (Korsnes 2015) domestic standards. The following thus maps a complicated account of China's 'two-track approach' (Ernst 2011a). In this enmeshed web of aspirations for international standardisation and indigenous (domestic) standards, Chapter Eight unfolds a story of the impact on Sino-foreign relations of the critical design software tools used for simulating and certifying turbines in accordance with international standards: the simulation tools and their aeroelastic codes. This story

Table 8.1 Entangled concerns in the struggle for catch-up in standardisation

	Main actors	Use simulation software & aeroelastic codes	Fulfil and lead international standards	Develop indigenous/domestic standards
Research and component design	Research institutions, universities and manufacturers	X	X	
Complete designs	Manufacturers, design houses and consultancies	X	X	X
Testing	Manufacturers and certification bodies	X		
Certification	Certification bodies	X	X	X

reveals a controversy over access to standards as well as an underlying controversy over the very right to qualify what is quality (and even science and innovation): a struggle over quality by algorithm. In so doing, entangled disputes between local practices of certification and standardisation, and over the universality of norms and conceptions of quality, are revealed. The account thereby spans and intersects international and domestic sites, but also traverses China's simultaneous and ongoing attempts to upgrade and catch up in design (research), in testing, and in its certification capabilities. The entanglement of concerns and involved main actors (e.g. manufacturers, research institutions, certification bodies) are indicated in Table 8.1.[1]

And so, as we trace a controversy over 'access to standards', this study delves further into the contested valuation processes of wind power development marketisation, once again revealing how supposedly stabilising and pacifying calculative framing devices such as these standards – just like IPRs – often tend to overflow.

Broadening ambitions in Chinese wind power out to the world

Before zooming in on Sino-foreign power struggles over software algorithms in relation to the issue of standardisation in China's emerging socio-technical assemblage around wind power development, it is necessary to take a step back, and to look at how China entered the wind power sector and wind turbine industry in the first place, and how the country's global ambitions have changed and expanded over time.

Gradual realisation of the power of standards and certification to realise Chinese export ambitions

China's original ambition for its emerging wind turbine industry was not for it to access and export to the international market, at least not at the outset.

Rather, with a huge potential domestic market, its first goal was to see if China could build its own indigenous industry. During the initial phases of Chinese wind power development marketisation, Chinese turbines were thus not required to be certified, as 'there were no requirements [back then] in China that they [wind turbines] had to be tested or certified or anything' (interview with foreign design company 2013).

As China later gradually embarked on standardisation attempts, its domestic standards were set intentionally low in order to make sure that domestic manufacturers could meet the standards and because 'quality products are not the scope for the market right now' (interview with foreign component supplier 2013). That is, as expressed by a Chinese certification body,

> When we set out to build a wind power industry, having in mind to develop this industry, that this was the future direction, China did not talk about it [i.e. certification and testing] ... that in order to move forward China's wind power industry ... But we also believed that standards, testing and certification were very important work, but at that time, we did not have our own industry, in 2003, right ... back then the industrial technology was still weak. (Interview with Chinese certification body 2013)

It was only later, after China ascended to the WTO in 2001,[2] and in particular when the quality crisis struck around 2010 with resulting overcapacity, that the export potential of Chinese wind turbines and the need to meet international standards to actually realise Chinese export ambitions, began to be considered more seriously.

With enhanced export ambitions, but suffering from an international reputation of relentlessly focussing on cost reduction rather than turbine quality, Chinese wind turbines manufacturers were soon to realise that if they 'ever wanted to get a chance to sell a turbine outside of China, then there was no other way than going through this [international certification]' (interview with foreign design company 2013) or through demonstration projects abroad (Gosens & Lu 2013:243). The overseas market was however still a completely different playing field, 'out of reach for most Chinese wind turbine[s] manufacturers, who are largely unfamiliar with international market rules and legal environments' (Qi 2011), and whose turbines were considered 'less reliable, lower quality, and less competitive' because 'they're not good [economic] performance' (interview with foreign employee in Chinese wind turbine manufacturer 2012). As expressed by a Chinese wind turbine manufacturer:

> You need some certification and also you need some track record ... that is a problem for us [...] We don't know the international market [...] For the European market, we need local research to develop the right standards for Europe in order to meet the requirements. (Interview with Chinese wind turbine manufacturer 2011)

Overall, with the quality crisis and overcapacity issues threatening the sustainability of the emerging socio-technical assemblage around wind power, the critical and strategic importance of certificates and standards was eventually realised around the time of the 'turn to quality', as the Chinese government was now

> putting in standards and requirements for a higher quality. Standards and requirements for other [things] than just [installing] megawatts into the ground, and that means that I am a bit hopeful again. (Interview with foreign wind turbine manufacturer 2012)

Aiming to frame wind power as reliable and technologically sustainable again, standards were in this way being positioned as strategic tools to reinstall the international reputation of Chinese wind turbines. This is seen, for example, in the Medium- to Long-Term Plan for Scientific and Technological Development (MOST 2006), which emphasises the need to upgrade in testing, certification and standardisation, e.g. through upgrading in critical simulation tools and aeroelastic codes.

What do standards do?

But why all the hassle with standards? Evidently, they can serve to act as powerful and excluding obligatory passage points; that is, construing a boundary or threshold level of quality whereby no products can cross international boundaries without meeting it. When products abide by the standards, the door is open to the international market. On the contrary, when products do not meet the standards, they may be prohibited from entering various markets. Indeed, in wind power,

> the market barriers they [the Chinese wind turbine manufacturers] are facing in terms of standards, in terms of all requirements, is actually quite extensive when you are entering from a Chinese setting into a developed market. You know, the standards in Denmark ... for 30 years ... are quite high, and you need to be able to prove that you can live up to those standards. (Interview with foreign wind turbine manufacturer 2012)

But how can standards hold so much power? Apart from promoting international trade by reducing risk, standards also operate by spurring innovation. These diverse roles of standards are briefly reflected upon below.

Promoting international trade by reducing risk – the role of type certificates in Chinese wind power

First, standards are powerful tools in furthering international trade, FDI, and technology licensing (Maskus 2002:144). Abiding by the definition, a standard functions 'as a rule for common and voluntary use, decided by one or several people or organisations' (Brunsson, Rasche & Seidl 2012:9). Through their provision for consensual rules, standards basically work to 'ensure the quality and safety of products, services and production processes' (Ernst 2013a:5). Within the wind turbine industry, turbine certification has expanded greatly over the last 25 years in general. That is,

> certification of wind farms, turbines or components is state-of-the-art and a must in most places around the world. Furthermore assessment to harmonised regulations is an active support of export and eases market entries. (Woebbeking 2010:1)

In particular as wind turbines have become larger, more technically advanced, and expensive, and as wind power provides an ever increasing share of the generation capacity of various national grids, standards have become more important, since larger wind turbines have also produced a more 'risk-infused business. With enormous up-front capital expenditures' (interview with foreign wind turbine manufacturer 2012). And so, '[r]isk perceived by financiers can also be reduced with quality certification for design and manufacturing practices' in the Chinese wind turbine industry (Gosens & Lu 2013:247). Overall, the technological and scientific development of the global wind power sector has converted risk and uncertainty into fields that need to be 'managed' (Power 2007 in Korsnes & Ryghaug 2017:751), in order that investors or creditors dare to invest, engaging in the economisation and marketisation of wind power development. Standards deliver this 'risk-management' through their provision of a harmonised means of measuring and comparing wind turbine performance. In other words, they provide a common 'ruler' of quality (Brunsson et al. 2012:4, 17–18; Fligstein 2001; Gibbon & Ponte 2008:8,15; Ponte 2009; Thévenot 2009:802). In the words of a Chinese certification body:

> A standard is used to detect a 'ruler'. It is to guide the foundation of your work, your basis for certified testing [...] Do you have a ruler? ... this job [of certification] could not be done without a ruler. (Chinese certification body 2013)

As a guarantee of confidence in the international market, and for establishing trust in products (Bowker & Star 1999; Brunsson et al. 2012; Star & Griesemer 1989 in Stark 2009; Thévenot 2009), standards have been seen as one of the institutional 'architectures' of markets (Fligstein 2001), since

> standard setting produces shared rules that guarantee that products will be compatible. This process facilitates exchange by making it more certain that products will work the way they are intended. (Fligstein 2001:35)

Therefore, certificates serve as a calculative framing device that serves to guarantee that the turbine has been designed and manufactured according to the appropriate design conditions and appointed standards, being assessed by an accreditation body. Furthermore, wind farm project certification can also serve to attest that the wind turbine will be installed, run, and maintained according to the demands of the design documents. Certificates thus provide an accredited guarantee of the investment that can be trusted (China Renewable Energy Scale-Up Program (CRESP) 2005:60; Vestas-China Wind Energy Association (CWEA) 2011). As a result, standards serve to reduce potential resistance against wind power from investors and TSOs/grid companies, as they 'are authority guarantee of products' quality, which are independent of both sides of supply and demand' (CRESP 2005:57).

How standards produce associations of trust

To understand in more detail how certificates and standards can produce such powerful associations of trust in the quality of a product, it is necessary to look deeper into their very socio-material constitution. Central to turbine type certification is that, when in alignment with international standards, the certificate provides tested – and accredited – proof and documentation of the turbine's power curve. This implies a certainty of output and thus economic performance. The certificate thus constitutes a warranty for the owner, as it offers 'a guarantee for the owner of the power curve, which again has a financial impact for the owner' (interview with foreign employee in Chinese wind turbine manufacturer 2012):

> If you can guarantee 99 per cent [of the power curve], that has a bigger impact on the operator's budget, than taking a little off the price [in the price negotiation of a wind turbine]. (Interview with foreign employee in Chinese wind turbine manufacturer 2012)

Apart from power curves as a guarantee of performance, standards and certificates also provide, amongst many other things, calculative metrics for availability and reliability. These refer to whether or not a turbine is suitable for operation and, therefore, capable of producing electricity and revenues for the owner (interview with foreign research institute 2013). Certification also provides an assurance of safety, as the certified turbine has proven that it has been 'constructed in a way that ensures that they don't fall down' – a concern which was very critical during the quality crisis (interview with foreign control system supplier 2013). Lastly, standards for the regulation of power output and power quality, as required in grid codes, provide proof of a turbine's ability to be connected to the grid without causing disruption, for example, during a grid fault.

Overall, this illustrates that the type certification of turbines can produce associations of quality by abiding to norms for technical and economic viability and sustainability. Hereby standards and certificates can work as pacifying framing devices, which ascribe associations to wind turbines of performance (e.g. calculated/simulated and proven/tested power curves and power output), safety, reliability (related to the downtimes/faults of wind turbines), and availability. Fundamentally what they do is construe associations of trust in a future profit margin, making the economisation and marketisation of wind power technologies possible as they blackbox the potential myriad cases of risk. Conversely, when turbines lack 'an international certification, nobody will finance it, and no local authorities will approve it' (interview with foreign employer in Chinese wind turbine manufacturer 2012).

Standards promoting innovation

Apart from their impact on international trade, standards are conventionally looked upon as 'the lifeblood of innovation in the global knowledge economy' (Ernst 2013b:9), spurring economic growth, productivity growth, and industrial development and independent innovation (Ernst 2013b; Wang et al. 2010). As China aspires to its ambition of scientific development and to realise a turn to quality in wind power, standards have become strategically important, since 'the development of technology also includes standardisation, so, that is to say, if future standardisation is made well, then it will also promote the development' (interview with Chinese certification body 2013). As expressed by a Chinese certification body:

> I think, if we can continue to implement this work, the quality of China's wind power equipment will be improved, it will play a big role. I think it is truly now a critical point [...] I think that in the future of China's industrial rise, we must do this part of the job [certification] well [...] And now I think that the standards, testing, and certification should precede the industry, because then you can drive the development of the industry. (Interview with Chinese certification body 2013)

Accordingly, to ensure WTO compliance, and to build indigenous innovation capabilities, MOST has been involved in the promotion of a Chinese certification and standardisation system. In particular, different reports issued by MOST in 2002 link the development of standards 'to building a harmonious society' through scientific development, marking the Chinese government's dawning focus on the role of standards in general, and in wind power particularly (Wang et al. 2010:5). Later, reports on China's standardisation strategy, together with various short-, medium- and long-term plans for the scientific and technical development programme in general, and in wind power specifically, have emphasised the strategic role of building a domestic testing, certification, and standardisation system. In tandem with this, these reports stress both the need to comply with international standards and also to develop Chinese indigenous standards (Ernst 2011a:20; Wang et al. 2010:7).

China's two-track approach

This two-track approach to a standardisation strategy – that is, the dual focus on both international and domestic/indigenous standards – indicates how China aims to transform itself from being a mere user of standards to taking the lead in creating international standards (Ernst 2011a:v). In an attempt to further transform itself from a catchup approach to an upgrading through innovation strategy (Ernst 2011a:v–vi), China considers its domestic innovative capacity

> to be the key to a sustainable transformation of its economy beyond the export-oriented 'global factory' model. To achieve this goal, China's government is very serious in its aspiration to move from being a mere standard-taker to become a co-shaper, and in some areas a lead shaper, of international standards. (Ernst 2011a:2)

Overall, as standards are positioned as a tool for indigenous innovation (Ernst 2011b:6), China has promoted 'homegrown', that is, 'indigenous' or 'Chinesified', standards, adjusted to the country's specific environmental conditions, and has also sought to influence international standards (Ernst 2011a, 2011b, 2013a; Wang et al. 2010). For instance, China has increasingly tried to adapt its wind turbines to the country's climate, where typhoons and low temperatures are common in particular regions, and there has therefore been the need to write Chinese indigenous standards. This renewed focus on developing indigenous standards reflects a realisation of how 'standards, testing, and certification also support technical progress of the industry, leading the development of the industry' (interview with Chinese certification body 2013). It also reflects the enhanced focus on the algorithmic (design) intelligence of wind turbines, and the enhanced need to lower risk owing to the increasing share of wind power in the national power grid.

The emerging international system for certified wind turbines – and the IEC 61400-1 standard

Accordingly, along with technological progress and the increasing role of wind power in national power grids, over the years, a complex of internationally harmonised standards

> has been developed gradually [at a global level] through the last ten years. It was [beginning] around the year 2000, I think. But it's only within the last five or six years that it has really played out. Before that, it was national standards. In the '80s and '90s, right, then there was a standard in Denmark, one in Germany, and one in the Netherlands. (Interview with foreign design house 2013)

The transition towards a framework for international standards has become gradually accepted, today working as 'de facto' rules, as it is recognised as much more convenient to have a common system to rely on, instead of multiple different national systems (interview with foreign certification body 2013). This means that most national systems attempt to abide by international standards, which are developed and monitored by the IEC, which deals with standards for all electrical, electronic, and related technologies. As certification procedures have been gradually harmonised across national boundaries, this at the same time means that, ideally, a certified turbine from another country will also be approved in other markets, as long as the level of standards is aligned. Accordingly, the international standard series for wind turbines, IEC 61400, has been under development since 1995 to harmonise various national standards, with the first issue of the international standard in 2001. Overall, the IEC 61400 is:

> a series of standards, which describes both…both how to certify it – that is, what is the certifying institution supposed to do, when they certify. And then there is a series of standards, which specify how you are supposed to document it technically, how you should calculate it and things like that…and how you should test this and this and that … So it's like an integrated system. (Interview with foreign certification body 2013)

In its current form, the standard comprises of 27 sections that cover various aspects of the turbine such as design requirements, acoustic noise measurements, and power quality measurements. Part 22 is dedicated to 'Conformity testing and certification', wherein it is described how testing is to be carried out to demonstrate conformity to the standard, what has to be documented, and how certification can be granted. With a certification according to IEC 61400 part 22, a turbine type has a guarantee that its performance has been documented and accredited to a respected international standard (IEC 61400 part 22, n.d.; IEC 2005).

Actors in the international standardisation system

In this integrated system of standardisation, testing, certification, and accreditation, a variety of actors are involved. First, the IEC itself has established a variety of different working groups, including members from, amongst others, domestic and international test laboratories, certification bodies, research institutions, wind turbine manufacturers, wind farm developers, design houses, component suppliers, and governmental agencies. Together, these actors negotiate the development of new and revised editions of the standard (Freudenreich & Frohböse 2010; interview with foreign design house 2013).

Second, and in accordance with international practice, national accreditation institutes are granted the right to accredit certifying institutions and test laboratories, according to a specific standard. Only a few internationally recognised certification bodies have been accredited to certify according to the IEC standards; for example, the merged companies Germanischer-Lloyd (GL) and Det Norske Veritas (DNV) – today constituting DNV GL - which together have acquired the consultancy company Garrad Hassan (GH), which has developed important software tools for certification such as the widely used simulation tool called 'Bladed'. The need for accredited third-party institutions is to ensure that the testing and certifying of turbines is kept separate from manufacturers and can thus be relied upon to be independent and rigorous when checking for compliance, thereby upholding the reputation of both the standard and the certification.

Third, certification bodies certify the turbines, ensuring compliance with IEC standards in terms of various safety and quality criteria for specific type certifications (Woebbeking 2010). As IEC standards are gradually being updated over the years, being published in several editions, certification schemes for assessment have been required to be updated and harmonised accordingly (Freudenreich & Frohböse 2010). Today, DNV GL has developed the most authoritative and widely used criterion for wind turbine system certification, namely the Germanischer Lloyd (GL) Guideline for the Certification of Wind Turbines, or the so-called GL 2010.

Fourth, in addition to certification bodies, test laboratories must be accredited to conduct accredited tests in accordance with IEC-standards (e.g. DEWI and DTU Wind Energy). Finally, certification involves the work of consultancy agencies that provide guidance to manufacturers that want to certify their products.

The establishment of a standardisation system with Chinese characteristics

China has been a member of the IEC since 1957, and the country has adopted the IEC wind turbine system certification system accordingly (CRESP 2005:59; Wang et al. 2010:2), although in 2005 there was still no full certification system for wind turbines in place. Nonetheless, China has upgraded its certification and standardisation capabilities, and today boasts a full accreditation, testing, certification, and standardisation system for wind turbines. Increasingly, the world is witnessing Chinese turbines receiving certificates from foreign certification bodies, including DNV GL and others, and even fulfilling the GL 2010-certification. The gradual buildup of capabilities within testing, certification, and standardisation has taken place within a relatively short time frame, often in collaboration with various international partners and programmes. For instance, the CRESP was sponsored by the World Bank and has provided expert advice to China on certification and standardisation (CRESP n.d.; Interviews; Worldbank n.d.). Having established a system for testing, certification, and standardisation, China is increasingly exporting turbines, often as demonstration projects, but increasingly complying 'with international [standards ... while] some are unique to China' (interview with Chinese certification body 2013). Further, China has become more actively engaged in the work of harmonising international standards, working in different IEC committees, seeing itself as an important core member of this harmonisation work, and with the aim to overcome the 'technical barriers to trade' created by different national standards:

> Actually, we follow principles in line with international standards in the whole testing process, believing that the wind power is a transnational and international industry. It must rely on free trade, we must rely on the cooperation between countries, so that global cooperation can develop soundly. That you cannot rest complacently on the laurels of certification, each country not being engaged with each other, that is not conducive to the development of global trade, so we should unify the world, which is a basic principle. (Interview with Chinese certification body 2013)

Evidently, China has raised its ambitions when it comes to certification and standardisation, and is intent on partaking in the formulation of international standards.

Central players in China's standardisation system

When China established its own domestic standardisation system, a variety of actors took up central roles in the marketisation of Chinese wind power. Placed under the General Administration of Quality Supervision, Inspection and Quarantine of China, the China National Certification and Accreditation Administration was founded in 2004 by the State Council to undertake accreditation of certification and test organisations and laboratories, in addition to accrediting the eligible certification organisations (CRESP 2005:56–57; Ernst 2011a). Other direct affiliates of the General Administration of Quality Supervision, Inspection and Quarantine of China are the China National Accreditation Service for Conformity Assessment, with authority to accredit certification agencies and test laboratories for wind power, and the Standardisation Administration of China, which is in charge of ensuring compatibility with, amongst others, the International Organization for Standardization (ISO) and IEC standards (Ernst 2011a:29).

The Chinese committee for standardisation in wind power is the National Wind Mechanic Standardization Technology Council, which is under the supervision of the National Standardisation Administration Committee (CRESP 2005:46; interviews). In turn, China boasts two domestic certification bureaus that are critical actors in the certification of turbines: China General Certification (CGC) and the China Classification Society. CGC, which is a Chinese certification body that was established for the certification of wind turbines in 2003, is the only Chinese certification centre that has been approved by China National Certification and Accreditation Administration to certify renewable energy equipment (CRESP 2005:57) and has relatively recently 'started to issue certificates for wind power equipment, which are recognized in a number of emerging economies' (CWEA 2012b in Gosens & Lu 2013:247). In this way, the CGC is responsible for testing products of wind turbine and component manufacturers, certifying the eligible wind turbine manufacturers, and allowing them to put certification marks on their products (CRESP 2005:57; cresp.org.cn; Wang et al. 2010).

The next set of actors is the various test laboratories in China. An example is the Chinese Academy of Sciences, which has a wind tunnel and a blade test centre (interviews). The China Electrical Power Research Institute, under the State Grid, works with standards for grid performance, and has different test laboratories connected to it. Finally, project developers and design institutes, consulting houses, and others can play an important role in the process of certification, in particular in advising wind turbine manufacturers and other industrial actors in how to comply with standards (Korsnes & Ryghaug 2017).

China's role as a 'laggard' in standardisation – and its problematisation

Even though China has succeeded in building a standardisation system within a very short time-frame, China is still considered a laggard by many foreigners, and even Chinese industry actors. The implication of this is that even though sometimes Chinese wind turbines have been certified in accordance with international standards, they are still not accepted abroad, or only in emerging economies. Instead they are required to recertify abroad, particularly in mature wind power countries, even though ideally the system should actually ensure that they are accepted directly (Interview with foreign design house 2013). There is evidently a lack of trust in China's standardisation and certification system. Indeed,

> [b]ecause developers and financiers around the world will likely scrutinize the performance of Chinese turbines in any market, it is imperative that these certificates hold similarly strict quality requirements as do established international certification organizations e.g., TUV [the German TÜV SÜD] or GL, if China wants to gain a foothold in advanced economy markets. (Gosens & Lu 2013:247)

The lack of confidence in Chinese certification is linked to China's relatively short track record in wind power and to the legacy of technology transfer and reliance on foreign design licences. This has meant that Chinese certification bodies have gradually attempted to align with imported foreign standards but have only relatively recently worked towards alignment with IEC standards (CRESP 2005; García 2013; interview with Chinese certification body 2013).

One further reason for the reluctance to accept Chinese wind turbines is that China does not fulfil the latest edition of the IEC 61400 standard, which has been published so far in three editions (Freudenreich & Frohböse 2010; IEC 2005; interview with foreign design house 2013). China is therefore considered one step behind the IEC standard (interview with foreign wind turbine manufacturer 2013; interview with foreign design house 2013). Consequently, Chinese turbines have been, and still are, often excluded from the most mature and developed wind power countries. Another challenge is that Chinese wind turbine manufacturers and wind farm developers have been accustomed to lax standard requirements in their domestic market. There are various reasons for this. To begin with, certification has de facto not been a requirement in China, and testing on a prototype was previously also not actually required. Instead certification has been accepted based on mere theoretical calculations and simulations of the design (García 2013:138-139; interviews 2012, 2013). That is, time-consuming and expensive full type certification has not been a requirement, and a simple design assessment has sufficed (interviews 2012, 2013). This means that, since it was possible to design, test, and sell turbines without an international certificate, Chinese companies had 'only considered getting a certificate from a European company if they wanted to export their turbines' (Korsnes & Ryghaug 2017:6). Last, whilst project certification is increasingly important in a European context to obtain insurance and government approval, and to attract finance, in China project certification is not required; instead, project risk is covered to a large extent by the government and government-affiliated agencies (Korsnes & Ryghaug 2017:4–5, 9).

Meanwhile, China's laggard-role has been problematised extensively in Chinese plans and policies. For instance, the 12th Five-Year-Plan for the Scientific and Technological Development of Wind Power (MOST 2012) raises the concern that the country remains reliant on foreign testing and design techniques; for example, to design blades and to simulate aerodynamics and loads. The plan thus argues that China must improve its capabilities for independent innovation, amongst other things, within research and innovative capabilities in turbine design, aerodynamics, basic research in mathematics, and the development of indigenous simulation tools. Further, recognising China's position as a relative latecomer, the plan further argues that its public testing system and wind power standards, testing, and certification system must be improved further (MOST 2012).

Algorithmic struggles around standardisation – tracing power struggles in the certification triangle

So far, Chapter Eight has outlined the context for China's path towards building a certification and standardisation process, discussing the IEC system and the overall implications of China's late arrival onto the international scene.

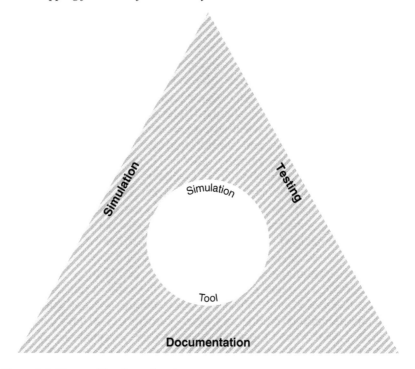

Figure 8.2 The certification triangle.

With the aim of shedding light on some of the inherent socio-technical struggles in China's effort to build its own capabilities for certification and standardisation during the imminent turn to quality, we now trace the certification procedure. Certification of a turbine design (or type certification) is the process of proving to an accreditation body that what has been calculated during the design phase can be tested and demonstrated to be correct. The 'certification triangle' outlined below – and visualised in Figure 8.2 – comprises iterative steps of 1) simulation/calculation, 2) testing, and 3) documentation, all of which are required to fulfil an IEC 61400 type certification.

The aim is to see that the prototype tests fit as well as possible the 1) simulations and calculations. When they do not align, the cause needs to be investigated, adjustments will then be made to the calculations/simulations, and 2) tests will be repeated. Finally, when thousands of test cases have been conducted, they will be 3) documented and accredited. Having gone through all three steps of the certification triangle, the turbine's structural and aerodynamic design is supposed to have been documented with respect to the tests on the turbine's loads, aerodynamics, and control (LAC). And yet, as will be discovered by tracing relations around the certification triangle, certification and standardisation is ripe with power struggles and contestations between Sino-foreign supply chain actors.

Step 1: developing a simulation software tool – a matter of loads, aerodynamics, and control

In the so-called 'certification triangle', an aeroelastic code for the modelling of the turbine's aerodynamic and structural design for the rotor and the tower must first be developed. On the basis of this, and on the generator and drivetrain characteristics, the turbine's performance can be simulated and the predicted power curve can then be calculated. The aeroelastic codes form the building blocks that model the behaviour of the turbine; for instance, how an aerofoil blade extracts power from the wind. It is programmed into the simulation software tool, which can then simulate the performance of the wind turbine design and, critically, the loads on the turbine.

The role of this step is to develop the optimal design performance, whilst at the same time ensuring that the structural design of the tower and foundations can transfer and withstand the loads from the aerodynamic forces on the rotor. It is, however, an iterative process: after having calculated how much power the turbine design will be able to produce, the different loads experienced by the various components need to be modelled, which are related to the control of the turbine, as well as to the aeroelasticity of the blades. The performance of the blades then changes under loading and so the power produced needs to be recalculated. To develop such code and the simulation programme software it employs involves the use of complex mathematics, together with principles of physics and engineering (Interview with foreign design house 2013):

> This turbine can be described mathematically, something about structural rigidities, how heavy it will be per metre, or something like that. And then the blades are normally described in terms of how the forces – the aerodynamic forces – how they are being influenced by the movement [e.g. the pitching] of the blades, right. And the movement of the blade and the wind coming in are giving like … all this you put into a model, where you have some numbers for this, and then you can put it into some software, some aeroelastic software, and then you can simulate it. (Interview with foreign research institute 2013)

If the aerodynamic loads from the forces of the wind on the turbine get too large, the blades or tower may suffer mechanical damage, which makes it critical to 'know how strong it should be, and you need to know the loads that will be put against it. You calculate that through a [software] programme. Well, in the good old days, it was easier, then it was more like just sticking your finger into the air' (interview with foreign design house 2013).

The quest towards an optimised performance–load ratio – the quest for optimised loads, aerodynamics, and control

As always in engineering design, there is a constant trade-off between increasing output and increasing the loads towards mechanical failure. What is crucial in wind turbine engineering, then, is the optimisation of the design to maximise the power production whilst managing the loads to keep within safety margins: the performance–load ratio. This is done through optimising the relations between the mechanical loads, the aerodynamic forces of the wind on the blade structure, and the specific turbine control regulation (LAC). With the overarching aim to raise the power output, a lot of aerodynamic research is currently going into the development of flexible elastic (non-rigid), lightweight blades used in combination with advanced regulation strategies (embedded in the main control system algorithms), as these together can increase the key performance–load ratio. The design trend is thus pivoted towards manufacturers' development of 'elegant' designs: slimmer towers, (aero)elastically optimised blade design, more active blade control, and a reduction of weight in the nacelle. Wind turbine manufacturers still, however, need to adhere to both national and international standards.

The result of all this optimisation is generally a bigger rotor on a precisely designed structure, a higher output (GWh produced), more stable integration with the power grid, and a lower more competitive cost of energy.

Certification in accordance with standards and the simulation tool

At the same time as manufacturers struggle and compete in terms of the most elegant design, Chinese certification bodies also strive to build capabilities for certifying in accordance with international standards as well as certifying and formulating domestic Chinese standards, as we are now moving towards certification in accordance with both international and national standards. A central component in this is the simulation software employed in the certification triangle during step 1: the mechanical load calculation tool, which simulates the mechanical loads on the turbine. The key algorithm of this is the aeroelastic code which embodies the behavior of the loads on the turbine from the wind, the aeroelastic design of the blades and, ultimately, their control.

So, and importantly, as well as simulating loading behaviour, the simulation model also contains the so-called regulation principle of the wind turbine's main controller, which was elaborated upon in Chapter Seven. That is, the aeroelastic code contains the core algorithm of the turbine's main control, as illustrated in Figure 8.3.

Owing to this close interplay between load simulation and the core algorithm of the turbine's control system, design houses, consultants, and others working with the development and certification of new turbine designs must know how the turbine is controlled, which means they must know about the contents of the supervisory main controller, and, critically, the blade pitch control. Fundamentally, these simulation tools are crucial to turbine design, in particular the aeroelastic codes, as they model the turbine, its control, performance, and safe operation. In turn they form the basis for an optimised and competitive turbine with reliable behaviour and known production qualities.

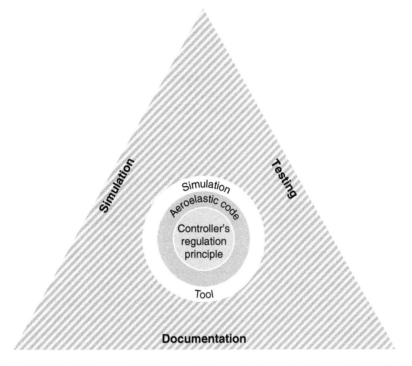

Figure 8.3 Simulation tool with controller's regulation principle – and aeroelastic code – at the crux.

Step 2: building a turbine prototype – testing and trimming the turbine

Once a simulation model has been developed that can reliably simulate the turbine, the second step of the triangle for the turbine manufacturer is to build and test a real turbine (a prototype) in order to find out whether the simulations agree with the actual in situ measurements of the loads, in production and in operation. In turn, 'if it doesn't work [as calculated/simulated], then you must re-enter the code and find out how things [work]' (interview with foreign design house 2013). But otherwise,

> You make some measurements [tests] and say, well, if the loads on the turbine fit your calculations, then it's actually good enough, and then it actually doesn't mean anything what the algorithms look like. You just try to compare those two situations [calculations versus testing]. (Interview with foreign design house 2013)

Sometimes, during this testing, it is discovered that the performance of the turbine can be improved, perhaps through a larger rotor and through changed regulation strategies of the control system. Continuous 'trimming' of the turbine takes place; that is, there are adjustments to the performance parameters in order to demonstrate the turbine's operational range. This applies not only to operation of the turbine under normal running conditions but also for various abnormal grid conditions or fault conditions. For all this to make sense, another set of software programmes must be employed to critically measure and analyse whether or not the turbine is actually performing optimally, or whether something should be adjusted. This use of independent software programs constitutes an essential 'external' check (validation), to critically assess the calculations made by the simulation tool originally used for the design.

Step 3: documentation for certification as basis for an accredited test

When all the physical testing has been completed, and the designers are satisfied that the turbine performs as designed and that the simulation tools correctly predict the turbine's behaviour and performance, the documentation for all this needs to be produced, thus moving to the next part of the certification triangle. A report is made that contains all the relevant design information (e.g. three-dimensional drawings of the blades, generator, and drivetrain), the design basis for structural design, the results of the load simulations, and the measurement data from the prototype tests. When completed by an accredited body, this finally constitutes a set of accredited measurements, which are needed for the certification of the turbine (interview with Chinese certification body 2013; interview with foreign research institute, 2013; interview with foreign design house 2013).

Having proven the turbine's structural and aerodynamic design, and demonstrated that the test measurements comply with the calculated simulations, the wind turbine design can be delivered to a certification agency, such as DNV GL, or CGC, for consideration for an accredited certification. The whole basis for the turbine design is thereby documented through drawings, specifications, calculations, simulations, and tests, all according to a standard. This is the last part of the certification triangle: the approval of the documentation.

> In order that the certifying authorities can certify, they must see documents demonstrating how we have done the calculations in the different systems, the likely faults. And those fault cases you must document according to the certification. They cannot approve it, if the turbine cannot sustain dangerous situations [...] And you must show simulations of how it will act in 100 years and all that – actually, it's quite complicated. (Interview with foreign design house 2012)

The critical role of simulation tools – HAWC2, Flex, and Bladed

Today, owing to the critical role of the simulation tools in the design and certification of new turbines, some international turbine manufacturers (e.g. Vestas) have established their own teams engaged with R&D on the issue of LAC. These teams use state-of-the-art simulation and design tools to opti-mise the operation of turbines in the constant trade-off between loads and production. Research institutions, such as the Wind Energy Department at the Technical University of Denmark, are also putting significant resources into the development of design tools, so-called optimisation tools, which here function as research tools rather than engineering tools. Well-renowned examples are Flex (models for wind turbine design) and HAWC2 (Horizontal Axis Wind turbine simulation Code 2nd generation, an aeroelastic code intended for calculating wind turbine response in time domain) (interviews with foreign research institute 2011, 2013). Through the HAWC2 tool,

> We are all the way down into the algorithm, we are all the way down into how everything is fitting together ... [...] and we know how it functions inside the stomach. And we also know how to use and apply it. So there-fore, we have much deeper knowledge than the users have. (Interview with foreign research institute 2013)

In addition to such research tools, there are commercially available simula-tion packages. For example, a load calculation tool developed and sold by Garrad Hassan (now DNV GL), under the name Bladed, has been instru-mental in turbine development in China's wind turbine industry, which, as we have seen, was established largely on foreign design licenses. Not having started out by developing indigenous turbine designs, virtually all Chinese wind turbine manufacturers, research institutes, and certification bodies made use of the Bladed tool during the formative years of the industry, and many are still using it today. Globally, Bladed has generally become 'the industry standard integrated software package for the design and certifi-cation of onshore and offshore turbines' (DNV GL n.d.; GL-garradhassan n.d.; Windpowerengineering n.d.). It should be noted that Bladed is a generic mechanical engineering tool, providing a well-developed user interface for commercial use, but, in contrast to the research tool HAWC2, it does not enable further research and development of the tool, because the core algorithms are locked (interviews with Chinese wind turbine man-ufacturers 2012, 2013; foreign control system suppliers 2012, 2013; foreign design house 2013).

Today's competition configuring around aeroelastic codes and algorithmic quality

Overall, today's intensified competition for producing optimised designs takes place against a background of standards for, and the certification of, wind turbine design. A key factor in this competition is the development and use of optimised aeroelastic tools and knowledge, which has basically become a 'parameter of competitiveness' (interview with foreign research institute 2013). The optimisation of the simulation tool's aeroelastic codes thus produces a competitive edge, separating the more advanced research institutions from the less advanced, and the more cutting-edge wind turbine manufacturers from the more mundane. In this regard, Western actors are frequently framed as 'superior', while Chinese actors are being framed as 'inferior'. For instance, aeroelastic analysis requires complex mathematical descriptions of both the dynamic and static behaviour of the blade, and the nature of these calculations is not contained in the standards. Instead, 'it's actually something, which is … it's not really described in the standards, how you do it … it's kind of a … it's a pretty tricky issue' (interview with foreign design house 2013). With a relatively long background in basic research into aeroelasticity, Western research institutes have pushed Western companies to move forward, trying

> all the time to push the boundaries of the possible [...] So we try to like put in an extra parameter all the time, putting as much knowledge into the system as possible. Because then you can produce larger turbines and stuff like that. (Interview with foreign research institute 2013)

Thus, the aeroelastic codes used in the simulation software and the source codes of the main controller are constituted as core to the ability to optimise the wind turbine's performance. Consequently, simulation tools and their algorithmic 'stomach' (interview with foreign research institute 2013) produce associations of algorithmic quality. In performing algorithmic quality ('quality by algorithm'), and assigning inferior and superior roles and positions to different actors (in terms of more or less advanced simulation tools), a competitive space is formed around these critical core algorithms and aeroelastic codes. In short, indigenously developed simulation tools help to produce associations of low cost energy, long-term performance, continuous development, and ongoing learning and upgrading:

> It might be that if you take a [foreign wind] turbine now and then a Chinese turbine at the side … it might be that the Chinese turbine is cheaper, but if they don't … if they don't generate any new knowledge by themselves, then the next generation of [foreign wind] turbines will have beaten this one in terms of cost of energy. And then they need to buy licenses from … so the only way they can make sure to have the lowest cost of energy, that's by staying some generations ahead. (Interview with foreign research institute 2013)

Further, and most importantly, because standards do not explain the hows of turbine design and development, they can also constitute a potential barrier to rapid upgrading and catchup for Chinese actors,

> because, first they [the standards] should be translated [...] Second, you have to understand these standards, and then also understand why they

have developed in that way, and why it is in this way … what principle is this based on. (Interview with Chinese certification body 2013)

Meanwhile, it is not possible to receive such written explanations (interview with Chinese certification body 2013) – instead, investments in basic research are required. As expressed by a foreign wind turbine manufacturer, while willingly providing assistance and recommendations for Chinese standards, 'when it comes to standards, that's where we start to become competitors again' (interview with foreign wind turbine manufacturer 2013).

Yet, as Chinese actors are so vigorously striving to upgrade and catch up with their development of simulation tools, the framing of inferior and superior actors should definitely not be taken for granted. This is well recognised by Western actors, who state that they must continuously 'develop and focus on development all the time … this is what is to keep us ahead' (interview with foreign research institute 2013); whilst at the same time most of them acknowledge that China will catch up completely sooner or later.

Blackboxes within blackboxes – entangled issues of certification and intellectual property rights, and complicated documentation

As has been shown, the algorithms of simulation tools are critical in the process of optimising and certifying new turbine designs. In the global competition for simulation tools, the core algorithms of commercial load calculation tools, such as Bladed, are locked. Thus, DNV GL's simulation tool Bladed is more like a blackbox, meaning that nobody actually knows how it calculates' (interview with foreign design house 2013). So, although customers can use the tool, they cannot see what it contains. It has

> some built-in standard routines, which Garrad-Hassan [now DNV GL] has built in; you have a pitch regulation, and then you have different things. And then there is a control regulation algorithm in Bladed. It is blackboxed. (Interview with foreign design house 2013)

Likewise, the algorithms of the HAWC2 and Flex are not open to others: 'they [the customers] don't know how it calculates. They don't. And that's actually, I would say, a core issue' (interview with foreign design house 2013). That is, a closed simulation tool 'involves some blackboxes', or even 'blackboxes within blackboxes' because the simulation tool's aeroelastic code also has 'the [main control] regulation built into it […] So that's the crux of the matter!' (interview with foreign design house 2013).

The consequence of this is that because the simulation tool contains the proprietary principles of the turbine's main controller and thus is often blackboxed through IPRs (and/or other means) (as described in

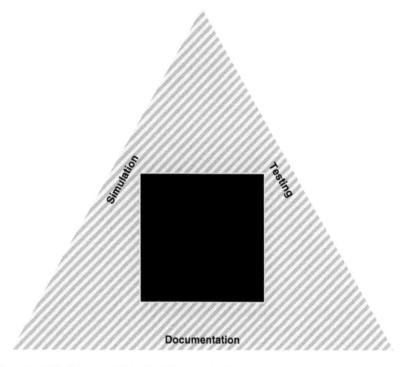

Figure 8.4 Blackboxes within blackboxes – locked aeroelastic codes with controller's regulation principle included.

Chapter Seven), as illustrated in Figure 8.4, there is an inherent risk of a customer's reliance on a closed simulation tool. This is almost inevitable without the customer having an indigenous simulation tool of their own.

As is becoming obvious, the matter of certification, testing, and standardisation is inextricably entangled in the topic of IPRs. A simulation tool is needed to obtain an accredited certification, whilst that same tool is often proprietary and protected, containing not only blackboxed aeroelastic codes, but also blackboxed control algorithms, which are protected by IPRs, trade secrets, technical locks, and encryption. This issue of blackboxes within blackboxes complicates the final step of the certification triangle: The documentation (step 3). That is,

> the aeroelastic code [being blackboxed] is one part. Then there is the other thing. Then they [Chinese wind turbine manufacturer] go to buy a main control from X [foreign control system supplier], and it contains an algorithm. How that algorithm functions in relation to the one in the simulation tool … That's actually … how can you actually document that? (Interview with foreign design house and international certification body 2013)

Since Chinese actors have been lacking an indigenously developed simulation tool, through which to conduct calculations in parallel with the commercial tool, it becomes impossible to test whether the simulations have any inbuilt mistakes. Instead, no such external validation check of potential mistakes in the codes can be made, as simulations with the same identical tool will evidently confirm (i.e., repeat) any potential miscalculations owing to the lack of external validation. This creates a further potential barrier to compliance with the IEC standards, which state that those who certify must make their own control calculations, simulating how the turbine functions with an independent control code (interview with foreign design house 2013).

Lack of basic research in aerodynamics and quality control – potential socio-technical barriers to reverse engineering

China's dependence on commercial simulation tools and their locked core algorithms is, in turn, entangled in China's legacy of using foreign design licenses – and a tradition of copying – to develop wind turbine technologies. In the initial years of building the Chinese wind power sector, the focus was evidently not on investments in the long-term basic research into aerodynamics and advancing aeroelastic codes. Consequently, 'although some Chinese actors are working with aerodynamics, they still need to develop an aeroelastic code' in contrast to 'other countries who have been occupied with wind power [and] have had research in this field, and have developed those codes themselves' over decades (interview with foreign design house 2013). Having followed a strategy of component technology sourcing, Chinese wind turbine manufacturers have thus risked losing the overview of the wind turbine, and its 'stomach', which is critical to optimising the overall turbine design and its performance.

The reliance on commercial, locked, simulation tools, such as Bladed, means that it is impossible to know whether it is the optimal tool to use or not. Software tools always contain a number of mistakes, but it is not possible to detect them or to change them without assistance from the simulation tool provider. That is, 'they can't change the code without asking [the foreign certification body]' for assistance (interview with foreign design house 2013). Thus, blackboxed algorithms can create socio-technical barriers to optimise turbine performance indigenously and conduct reverse engineering. When dependent on these commercial simulation tools, the adaptation of turbine designs to Chinese conditions consequently becomes difficult, because 'they can't adapt it ... if they encounter a problem' (interview with foreign research institute 2013). In addition, Bladed is generally not considered the most advanced code, or the best tool for optimisation or R&D: 'Bladed is an aeroelastic code. But not particularly advanced' (interview with foreign design house 2013). In this way, what Chinese actors get from Bladed is a 'kind of a standard package' for generic, common situations, 'but if you get into the more refined issues, then you have some weaknesses [in the code]' (interview control system supplier 2013). The same applies for the control system algorithm, which foreign control system suppliers have largely developed from other industries, in particular the marine industry, and only lately have been applied been to wind power. In this way, many control system suppliers are

> not experts on wind turbines. That means … what's the optimal algorithm? It's not X [foreign control system supplier] you should ask about this. They can develop an algorithm which works. (Interview with foreign design house 2013)

Somewhat paradoxically, the much-desired algorithmic source codes of the supervisory main control, risk becoming useless, as we witnessed in Chapter Seven, even when Chinese actors gain access to them, because these actors lack the systemic overview of the wind turbine's 'stomach':

> Well, I'd say, if they don't master this [the aeroelasticity inherent in the simulation tool for optimised turbine design], then I'd think that they cannot use that [main control's] source code for anything at all. (Interview with foreign control system supplier 2013)

The above reveals a number of potential socio-technical barriers to reverse engineering turbine designs.

Even though Chinese wind turbine manufacturers are increasingly acquiring foreign design houses and smaller wind turbine manufacturers, and receive assistance from advisory agencies and others, various industry actors tend to claim that the world still has not seen 'a proper Chinese design, which has been developed from the ground [and which] they have done properly, and where you can say that they have made it all from A to Z' (interview with foreign design house 2013). These barriers suggest that there is no easy way of leapfrogging in terms of developing indigenous wind turbine designs. This is particularly the case for today's modern advanced turbines, where creating certification capabilities is an immense task for the large turbines because of the increasingly strict quality requirements (interviews) and algorithmic intelligence.

Contesting accounts of Chinese algorithmic upgrading – transformative upgrading

But is this bleak picture the whole story about Chinese abilities to upgrade? No, evidently not.

There are multiple signs of Chinese transformative upgrading through disruptive learning, despite the socio-technical resistances and barriers. The ambition to meet and even set or lead international standards indicates the rising capabilities of Chinese wind turbine manufacturers, since 'you have to reach a certain stage, before you can actually manage internationally and start beginning to see an advantage [of standardisation]' (interview with foreign control system supplier 2013). Gradually realising the need for investment in long-term basic research, in particular into aerodynamics, China's certification bodies, universities, and research institutes have increasingly engaged in R&D of aeroelastic codes. And while Bladed may be closed, it has served as a basis for 'accumulating technological capabilities' (interview with Chinese certification body 2013), for example, as it has provided training courses by the 'knowledge-intensive business service provider' (Strambach 2001), such as Garrad Hassan/DNV GL. Further, even though Bladed is 'not open',

> it will have some interfaces, so we can make some development on the surface. We can use some programmes to help us to improve the software [and] if there is need to, they [Garrad Hassan] can provide some software support, but normally we will be able to do it ourselves now. (Interview with Chinese certification body 2013)

CGC has been working on improving their knowledge and developing the codes as they 'have to learn and learn' (interview with Chinese certification body 2013). In doing so, they have established technical teams dedicated to understanding and translating international standards and standard specifications, to conducting simulations and testing, and to developing and adapting standards to local conditions. One of the most difficult things in this work is to interpret and understand the meaning behind the standard specifications, which requires several years of studying for China as a 'new student':

> For us new 'students', so to say, it's very important, because we have to check with a lot of literature [...] Why is this, what is this principle, why should it be like this, right? (Interview with Chinese certification body 2013)

Although acknowledging their limits, increasingly Chinese actors are also trialling other simulation tools, for example Flex, as well as experimenting with developing their own indigenous codes. As eager students, Chinese wind turbine manufacturers are attempting more and more to reverse engineer software tools, since straight copycatting of international standards has proved insufficient. Accordingly, CGC is adopting different software tools for turbine design and claims to have gradually developed the simulation of control algorithms, and its own software (CGC 2013:9):

> That means we are also studying how to generate this typhoon model ... after hitting the blade, how much load it can bear from the wind? ... then we hope to develop a model of a typhoon and a typhoon simulation tool [replication tool with unknown outcome] ... Yes, an emulator

[replication tool with known outcome], which can guide the design of the typhoon blade that you want in the future. (Interview with Chinese certification body 2013)

Overall, Chinese actors have started to build indigenous capabilities for design as they engage in reverse engineering, when adapting turbine designs to typhoon conditions, for example. The adaptation of turbine design (and simulation tools) to local conditions thus 'forces you to be creative, there are no innovative people to give it to you, as others do not have these problems, isn't that right?' (interview with Chinese certification body 2013). The upgrading of capabilities in certification thus 'drives technological advancement of the entire industry'. Accordingly 'after doing this [work on revision of the standards], it will not only raise the quality of China's wind power equipment development, but also have a great role in promoting global development' (interview with Chinese certification body 2013).

De- and reconfiguration of collaborative relations around certification and standardisation

As has been examined above, there are different and colliding accounts of China's capability of transformative catch-up and upgrading. Evidently, China is contesting its role as inferior, and with increasing capabilities, 'things are getting better' in terms of being recognised in other countries:

> Owners in other countries say, we want the certification from GL [Germanischer Lloyd], not only from CGC. So they have to negotiate. Now things are getting better, because the basic is that CGC must conform to international standards, in order to certify...and your certification will be checked by all other certifications ... it's no problem. This is basic. The quality is first, second is to try to get more recognition from other organisations, yeah. (Interview with Chinese certification body 2013)

As Chinese actors strive to catch up and move towards writing their own indigenous standards, Sino-foreign relations are in turn being transformed, involving more 'learning from each other, promoting each other' (interview with Chinese certification body 2013). For instance, Chinese ideas for adapting standards seem to be increasingly and internationally recognised (interview with Chinese certification body 2013), and CGC is increasingly involved in different working groups within the IEC Wind Turbine Certification Advisory Committee (CGC 2013:17; interviews).

Despite the green shoots of recognition hinted at above, being included as equals in relationships is a continual struggle for Chinese actors. In the following, the negotiated roles and positions of Chinese and foreign actors, through which we can paint a controversy around the very right to define quality, are explored.

Contestations over exclusive international learning networks

Wind turbine development and certification is interdisciplinary by nature, and so particularly with aerodynamic research there exist a myriad of collaborative relations across the globe between different types of actors related to certification in the wind turbine industry. In mature wind power regions such as Europe and the USA, multiple 'formalised' and 'less formalised' collaborative relations have been established, for instance between developers of aeroelastic codes and their users. In these (often informal) collaborations, different actors engage in the work of comparing simulation codes and test measurements, since 'this is the only realistic way to verify the codes [of the simulation tool] and to improve them'; thus, it is only 'by working with those codes ... that's where you gain the understanding' (interview with foreign design house 2013). Likewise, with the main controller for a specific turbine design, wind turbine manufacturers and control system suppliers in Europe and the USA often engage in (in)formal collaborations. In addition, wind turbine manufacturers may ask test laboratories for assistance, when it comes to simulation tools and understanding why, for instance, the Flex or HAWC2 programmes are acting unexpectedly. However, it requires a considerable amount of knowledge and experience on behalf of the users to be able to ask research institutions and test laboratories 'informed questions':

> 'Some of the clever companies, the people ... they know ... they have a pretty good idea of what's going on inside and can ask some pretty clever questions about ... 'why – when they are running this ... why did it act like this?' [...] And then we [test laboratory/research institute] think, 'well, oops! We have to ask our developers', and then we have to say, 'well, that's a really good question, I'll go and check. I think you are right, it might be that in the future, in the next update ... or that the manual should be written a little more clearly, so you don't misunderstand ... why it acts like this, when you actually thought that that would be impossible' (interview with foreign research institute 2013).

In turn, these collaborative relations between the wind turbine manufacturers, control system suppliers, certification bodies, design houses, and/or test laboratories are often based on informal long-term personal trust-based connections, for example as wind turbine engineers often shift jobs within the sector. For instance,

> if you know these people who work in Garrad Hassan on a friendly level, you can make some suggestions, and then it's sometimes an advantage to speak Danish etc. If you have been playing together for a long time, you have some confidentiality. You can just call them, even in the evening, and get some support. And you can't do that if you sit

in China and get in contact with the service department of Garrad Hassan. (Interview with foreign employee in Chinese wind turbine manufacturer 2012)

In this way, 'knowing somebody' can help actors optimise codes, for example in Bladed, because 'of course it [Bladed] has its limitations. But then you can make some customer-specific changes, if you know somebody who knows somebody in GL [now DNV GL] (interview with foreign employee in Chinese wind turbine manufacturer 2012). In this 'dynamic international community [of learning within the wind turbine industry], research collaboration is very much like "give-and-take"' (interview with foreign design house 2013). In this way, when personal relations based on trust have been established, parts of the algorithmic source codes may be shared, which in turn enables code development and adjustments (interview with foreign design house 2013).

Exclusion from collaborations in the 'good international club'

Even though equal partnerships with Chinese actors included are increasingly emerging around certification and standardisation, these do not come uncontested. Indeed, Chinese actors have often faced barriers when attempting to join the international 'innermost research circles', as they still suffer from a framing of Chinese wind turbines as 'poor quality' and lacking algorithmic quality' owing to a 'lack of serious [basic] research in aeroelasticity'. As a consequence, the 'dynamic global research community' does not yet fully include China (interview with foreign design house 2013):

> 'The Chinese would very much like to join – how to put it … join the 'inner circle of the good international club'. They would love that, but then they must be able to give something. This thing about saying that we want to participate … but if they only think about what they can gain themselves, but not about how they could give something in return … in that respect, they are pretty poor partners' (interview with foreign design house 2013).

As Chinese actors are thus sometimes excluded from these collaborations, they have troubles, for instance, in gaining a deeper insight into the interplay between simulation tools and controller algorithms; instead, foreign control system suppliers and turbine designers have tended to collaborate directly, sometimes including research institutions and powerful certification bodies, but excluding Chinese wind turbine manufacturers. In this way, algorithms – being the framing tools they are – are evidently producing processes of inclusion and exclusion, overflowing into controversy. As such, they are transformed from innocent, supposedly mundane, calculative framing devices into destructive barriers, as they come to have an effect on the relations they de- and reconfigure.

Lost in the limbo of (lacking) recognition – inferiority and boundaries contested

The lack of trust also implies that CGC is often not regarded as being at the level of DNV GL, although it has been accredited as a certification body, which formally should qualify for international recognition. It is predicted that it will take years for China's young institutions such as CGC to gain full international recognition and trust outside China (interviews 2012, 2013), as Chinese certificates are still less acknowledged globally (Korsnes & Ryghaug 2017:5), owing to 'problems in being accepted at the same level as the well-known European institutions' (interview with foreign design house 2013). The lack of recognition implies that when China delivers certified and accredited calculations to European institutions to obtain European accredited certification, these calculations have sometimes not been accepted 'because when you do this kind of work, then there's always two parts ... the one thing is the formal [...] and then there's the second part: do you think that what you've got is okay?' (interview with foreign design house 2013).

> A lot of people were questioning it ... that is, a lot of people were not agreeing with ... because you [China] do not have any industry, the manufacturing industry is also very weak. When writing standards, they also think you [China] are just translating foreign standards. You don't have any people to make wind turbines, so how should you write standards? So there is still some resistance. (Interview with Chinese certification body 2013)
>
> We have made a lot of preparations for exporting, but there are some issues with the trust by foreign markets in Chinese certificates, they want to test them themselves. They don't trust [*Bu xiangxin*, 不相信]. This is a misunderstanding, we can do anything, so it is just an export barrier. It's protectionism, a trade barrier [*maoyi de tiaozhan*, 贸易的挑战]. There are also troubles with anti-dumping. (Interview with Chinese wind turbine manufacturer 2012)

Thus, lost in a limbo of lacking trust, the ideal of the certification system in which national accreditation institutions should mutually recognise each other, does not always function properly, or 'by the book', as Chinese actors are 'not being recognised' as they should be formally (interviews 2012, 2013). To overcome these exclusion mechanisms, time-consuming and expensive basic research in algorithms is considered a

> pre-requisite for the development of their own technologies, but also for being included in international networks in regard to these things [since] if they don't do research themselves and don't make anything,

which is relevant for others, then they won't get anything the other way. That's how it works. (Interview with foreign design house and former certification body 2013)

Meanwhile, as Chinese certification bodies and wind turbine manufacturers have increasingly managed to build capabilities and to experiment with development of indigenous simulation tools and aeroelastic codes, the role and position of Chinese actors as 'inferior partners' is increasingly contested. That is, Chinese certification bodies want

> to reach an equal status, like DNV and Germanischer-Lloyd [now DNV GL], right? [They] want to be internationally accredited. But I think that's the way towards the goal. The alternative is that the Chinese bring their turbines over here to DNV, make some agreements with DNV or Germanischer-Lloyd and have them certified. (Interview with foreign research institute 2013)

Thus, as Chinese capabilities are now 'fully in accordance with international standards, and we are participating in international exchanges of these international institutions', CGC argues that it has reached 'a platform to do something' (interview with Chinese certification body 2013), and thus has as 'their goal' achieving full international recognition, which is also expected to include them into global research networks (interview with foreign design house 2013). Indeed, Chinese actors are increasingly contesting framings of inferiority. And so, China aims to 'demand a bigger say in the rules and standards that govern global science and technology innovation' (President Xi Jinping in Buckley 2014), or, as expressed by a Chinese expert and advisor on S&T (2013),

> it is not okay that key technologies come from outside. We should control core technologies. China thinks in this way. But in the West, the MNCs [Multi-National Corporations] control the key technologies, often through standards.

China's dual track approach to standardisation engendering a 'standardisation war' - on entangled standards and IPRs

The above last quotes indicate how China's struggles for international recognition and inclusion into research circles, and its bumpy process of upgrading and catching up in standardisation and certification, is enmeshed in what may be dubbed a broader international, or even global, struggle, over standardisation, which, as it turns out, is entangled in a problem concerning IPRs and much more.

Inherently linked to the doctrine of scientific development, China's standardisation strategy is not only a matter of fulfilling international standards, but has become constituted as a 'two-track approach' (Ernst 2011a) as mentioned above: Rather than just staying abreast of international standards, and even leading the definition of new global standards, China at the same time seeks to develop its own indigenous, or 'Chinesified', domestic standards. China's political leadership does so by encouraging the development of domestic standards through a government-led, yet ambiguous and fragmented, approach to standardisation that does not resemble the so-called 'American-style' market-led, voluntary standards model (Ernst 2011b:2, 5). Rather than letting standards develop by competition, the Chinese 'government will continue to play an important role as a promoter, enabler, and coordinator of an integrated standards and innovation policy' (Ernst 2011a:1). Apart from developing indigenous standards for wind turbines adapted to typhoon conditions, for instance, China has also introduced a highly contested yet mandatory China Compulsory Certification (CCC) mark for safety approval of technological and industrial products (McGregor n.d:23) entering China.

Overall, China's dual-track approach to standardisation has produced thorny discussions of international trade and protectionism within the WTO, as its domestic standards are framed as 'trade weapons used to discriminate against' foreign products (McGregor n.d.:22). For instance, concerns have been raised that China's standardisation strategy (and its innovation policy) does not comply with WTO rules, since it is promoting the creation and application of national standards in the country, as opposed to using existing international standards. Accordingly, the issue of standards has even become coupled to China's listing of public government procurement for large infrastructural projects such as wind power ('the buy China plan'), as both are linked to concerns over protectionism (Ernst 2011a; interviews; McGregor 2011:19, 23). Further, the CCC mark has been framed as a tool of Chinese protectionism by foreign actors in China, and it has also produced fears of Chinese industrial espionage, particularly when it comes to software and encryption testing, as source code encryption keys are supposedly required to be shared when going through the CCC upon entry to the Chinese market (Ernst 2011a:37; interviews; McGregor n.d.:30).

Conversely, China largely sees their own strategy of domestic standards as a necessary means for survival after WTO accession constructed 'a policy vacuum', reducing former trade restrictions (licensing requirements, tariffs, and import quotas) (Ernst 2011a:4). And so, the promotion of Chinese indigenous standards is not only a matter of scientific development, but also a matter of reducing the 'control of foreign advanced countries over the PRC [People's Republic of China]', especially 'in the area of high and new technology' (Ernst 2011b:4) in a context of enhanced global competition, as well as a matter of managing the high costs of adopting international standards (Ernst 2013a).

In this way, '[t]he role of standardization, together with intellectual property rights and government procurement, are at the center of this conflict', only adding to already 'contentious disputes about exchange rates, trade, and foreign direct investment' (Ernst 2011b:1). That is, as standards increasingly include IPRs, standards, and their included IPRs, have become increasingly entangled, producing an increasingly hot topic, and spurring discussions of China's dependence on foreign technologies (and license fees), for example (Ernst 2011a; 2011b; Wang et al. 2010). Accordingly, China is now working 'within the international system' to include its technology in global standards, 'to strengthen its bargaining power and to reduce its exposure to high royalty fees', and with the 'long-term goal of creating patent-worthy technology essential to global standards' (Ernst 2011a:v). And so China continues its struggle for increased geopolitical influence 'to promote new sets of rules for international standardization, and hence to transform the international standards system itself' (Ernst 2011a:v). Overall, in the controversial 'competitive space' around standards and entangled IPRs, we are witnessing an emerging global 'standardisation war', which is entangling the issue of standardisation of wind turbines and China's dual-track approach, and in effect producing a 'hot topic in US-China economic relations' (Ernst 2011b:1).

The negotiated nature of standards and innovation – no such thing as 'the best algorithm' and the fight to define quality

Such contestation over standards is, however, nothing new in certification. Indeed, in the development of technical standards through the IEC, new standards and the development of new versions of existing standards are the very product of negotiation. This is, for instance, exemplified in the adoption of the third edition of the IEC 61400 standard, which has been met with a great degree of resistance (Freudenreich & Frohböse 2010). In this way, new standard formulations and the process of harmonising standards often constitute a contested issue, as different actors will strive to promote their own metrics and calculative devices, which is also seen in foreign companies and consultancies advising China on standardisation. The lack of consensus on standards and employed metrics makes it impossible to write into the standards *how* the simulations and testing should be conducted, as there is even disagreement within standard committees:

> In the standard ... there are some points ... I guess this is the critical point, that is, you have to do this and this. But not how one should do it. And this is also related to the fact that those people who make these [standards], they are researchers and some from industry etc., who sit in these committees. And to make a standard, they must agree that now you can do like this ... otherwise it cannot be included in the standard, right. And they aren't [agreeing]. And that means that as long as they don't agree [these] explanations cannot be included in the standard. (Interview with foreign design house 2013)

Despite such contestations, it can be claimed that today the international standardisation community around wind turbine certification has reached a consensus in terms of the goal of reaching algorithmic quality, and that the IEC 61400 standard can guarantee such quality by algorithm. That is, as the very compliance with a standard signifies that the turbine design has been optimised through the use of algorithms, and that a certain power curve can be documented and guaranteed, algorithms and aeroelastic codes in software tools have enormous agency and thus performative power: they can frame wind turbines as either good or bad, or as inferior or superior, as optimised and elegant, or mundane and inefficient.

Nevertheless, even the quality of algorithms underlying standards for wind turbine type certification is, by itself, negotiable, since there is no such thing as 'the best algorithm' (interview with foreign control system supplier 2012). This basically means that algorithmic quality is situational as 'there's no such thing as the best turbine'; instead, it depends on the situation: the project, terrain, wind conditions, and wind turbulence (interview with foreign wind turbine manufacturer 2012 foreign control system supplier 2012). As the criteria are open for interpretation in different contexts (Korsnes & Ryghaug 2017), standards, their metrics, and the calculative agencies they produce can become constituted as situational and debatable, and may produce a contestation over the 'universality of standards', as standards are contingent on local work and are not necessarily universal (Korsnes & Ryghaug 2017). A degree of scepticism towards foreign standards in China can thus be noted in its wind power sector (Korsnes & Ryghaug 2017). Whilst foreign certification agencies and advisory bodies try to sell their services for 'risk reduction', making the turbines and projects 'safer', European certificates have sometimes been rejected in China's offshore wind turbine industry:

> From a Chinese perspective, the European innovation strategy relating to offshore wind [and onshore] looks like over-engineered project development. This stands in contrast to the Chinese innovation strategy wherein taking risks is seen as a precondition for development. (Korsnes & Ryghaug 2017:10)

This Chinese scepticism is in turn founded in a collision between innovation practices, that is, between a relatively risk-averse regime of the IEC complex, or what by others in regard to technology entrepreneurship and innovation has been framed a model of 'improving, testing, launching' (O'Connor 2006), versus China's more risk-prone and experimental, less theorised mode of learning, or what has been framed a model 'launching, testing, improving' (O'Connor 2006). Indeed, in China, the relatively late introduction of certification requirements is argued to reflect a Chinese experimental and much less risk-averse innovation strategy. For instance, Chinese manufacturers tend to

> put the components faster into the turbines for example [...] Where we would instead have … if you take [foreign wind turbine manufacturer] for example, they do most of it in the laboratory. And they have a project

leader, and they calculate and make plans. Here – they don't make plans. They just jump into it, and then sometimes they make some mistakes. And then they re-adjust. So the time you would use on planning, you could use instead on ... learning from your mistakes. (Interview with foreign control system supplier 2012)

Again, and much as we have witnessed on a much greater scale than technology entrepreneurship, that is, in terms of China's seemingly experimental 'green marketisation', risk-taking in China tends to be seen as conducive to innovation rather than the opposite (Korsnes & Ryghaug 2017). This 'funny approach' is 'very different from ours [Europeans] and we simply don't get it. And it may be that they get something else out of it than we do, and that's interesting' (interview with foreign control system supplier 2013). Whilst some see the positive outcomes of China's 'just-do-it' approach, other (both Chinese and Western) actors argue that this approach is too risky and 'expensive – everybody hates retrofit, it makes everybody really angry. It's better to think ahead!' (interview with foreign wind turbine manufacturer 2013).

Underlying the controversy over standardisation and certification are colliding modes of measuring quality, of containing risk and uncertainty, and of conducting innovation, as well as between local practices and the universality of standards as international standards. Overall, as unfolded, and somewhat paradoxically, the pacification of goods through standards and certificates, as well as through algorithms, spurs controversy in and by itself. And so the framing devices of standards, IPRs, and algorithms that were meant to tame the uncertain power(s) of the wind, stabilising the framing of wind power as sustainable, are working at a deeper level, spurring ambiguity and uncertainty.

Reflections on fifth site of controversy: contesting quality by algorithm

In Chapter Eight, this study has delved into the framing of goods, that is, the framing of wind power as a sustainable renewable energy source and the work of pacifying it through the employment of standards and certificates. Through the lens of the Anthropology of Markets, standards and certificates possess agency, and they can attain a performative role, as they (temporarily) help reduce associations of risk and stabilise associations of quality, thereby taming the fluctuating and potentially disruptive forces of the wind, at least for a while. Yet, as China has faced socio-technical barriers to rapid catching up through leapfrogging in the arena of certification and standardisation, standards have paradoxically threatened to destabilise the framing of Chinese wind power as scientifically and technically sustainable.

This research displays the potentially controversial dynamics of the pacification of goods, namely as standards and other calculative devices, such as simulation tools and algorithms, become contested and overflow, owing to the way in which they produce contested mechanisms of both inclusion and exclusion. While standards ideally serve as pacifying calculative framing devices, which can make it possible to compare quality and deem certain turbines superior and others inferior, such framing is often to be 'brutally contradicted' (Callon 1986:25). In this way, whilst conventionally seen as critical architectures of market institutions, standards are not necessarily stabilising. The instability brought about by the standards examined here is, in turn, socio-materially grounded in the algorithms that lie beneath them. Indeed, in Chapter Eight, algorithms have revealed their second nature: far from being framing devices to prevent uncertainty and risk, they are themselves sources of ambiguity and uncertainty, and conduits of power struggles. This reflects how the pursuit of perfect framing is futile. This futility of perfect framing is even more evident as ambitions of meeting, developing, and leading international standards and of developing indigenous national standards intersect, entangled in China's ambition of achieving scientific development. It is equally the case when temporary socio-material barriers to international certification surface, founded in decades of Chinese reverse engineering, a politically planned and controlled research system, and a focus on fast industrial development through applied science over more long-term fundamental research with 'no immediate economic benefits' (Cao 2004:167). The fragility of framing through standards and algorithms is thus also intricately linked to how algorithms and standardisation and certification procedures entail, but mostly conceal, underlying and sometimes colliding modes of risk management and innovation practices. These differences are, for example, reflected when Chinese actors have used the identical simulation tool for cross-checking – something which has not necessarily entailed the conventionally required external validation – or when Chinese actors launch turbines onto the market without prior certification and qualification work or without abiding by the dominant qualification norm of 'quality by algorithm'. In other words, this investigation reveals how China's mode of experimental pragmatism in the marketisation of wind power development, now exemplified not only at the industrial development level, but also at the level of technology entrepreneurship, collides with the more risk-averse 'Western' innovation practices, which have set the framing for the overall certification triangle and standardisation community. Whilst not deeming any of the different innovation modes right or wrong, in particular as the risk-prone Chinese experimentalism has enabled Chinese disruptive learning, albeit bumpy and controversial, what is certain is that future research needs more situational approaches to understanding standardisation, innovation, and scientific practices on the ground, how they may differ, and how they form part of the marketisation processes.

Having uncovered and depicted the controversial site of certification and standardisation, this study has mapped an emerging negotiated, competitive space around standards, their calculative devices, and the agencies for calculation they construe. This space is, in turn, enmeshed in a wider international controversy over trade barriers and protectionism within the WTO as well as over China's goal of catchup, sustainable development and construction of a Harmonious Socialist Society through scientific development. This 'standardisation war' produces a 'hot situation' where 'everything becomes controversial' (Callon 1998:260), and where myriads of heterogeneous actors, such as standards, certificates, IPRs, government procurement regulations, FDI, experts, engineering expertise, scientific practices, trade weapons, mathematicians, software scientists, and aeroelastic codes in the marketisation of Chinese wind power development are assembled into a 'hybrid forum'. Indeed, Chinese wind power is entangled in the confrontation between simultaneous forces of interdependent markets characterised by extending boundaries and international organisations such as the WTO, and of forces of its own national protectionist 'community economy', together producing hybrid and evolving assemblages (Caliskan & Callon 2010a:42, 45) where innovation, standards, simulation tools, aeroelastic codes, and everything in between, become political.

Having revealed this second and paradoxical and ambiguous nature of standards, algorithms, simulation tools, and certification, we now leave the designer's domain of modelling and testing and make our way back to the operational machinery, that – even as these words are read – is producing the electromagnetic energy that we have been traversing and following during our algorithmic research journey. The journey is now coming to an end and now, as we metaphorically speaking find ourselves back in the nacelle house of the turbine, it is time to reflect and conclude on what we have found along the way in the controversy study.

Notes

1. Focusing on the increasing role of standardisation in Chinese wind power during the turn to quality, this study deals primarily with the role of wind turbine type certification (turbine design) in accordance with international standards under the IEC framework, as well as the emergence of a Chinese standardisation system, which both serve as so-called de facto technical standards, because they are adopted through consensus, sometimes expressed through industry committees of formal standards organisations. There exists both open, international, de facto, de jure, technical, type, project, and component standardisation and certification (CRESP 2005; Korsnes & Ryghaug 2016; Woebbeking 2010).
2. The WTO membership obliged China to establish a certification and standardisation system in alignment with the WTO Technical Barriers to Trade agreement (TBT) by which member states are obliged to accept the Code of Good Practice for Standardisation. And so, despite being a follower in terms of certification and standardisation, China has since then worked hard on building 'the skeleton for standardization strategy thinking' to make its standards meet the TBT (Wang, Wang & Hill 2010:3).

References

Andrews-Speed, P., 2012, *The Governance of Energy in China. Transition to a Low-Carbon Economy*, Palgrave Macmillan, Basingstoke.

Bowker, G. C. & Star, S. L., 1999, 'Some of the Trade in Analyzing Classification', in G. C. Bowker & S. L. Star (eds.), *Sorting Things Out*, MIT Press, Cambridge, MA.

Brunsson, N., Rasche, A. & Seidl, D., 2012, 'The Dynamics of Standardisation: Three Perspectives on Standards in Organisation Studies', *Organization Studies* 33(5–6), 613–632.

Buckley, C., 2014, 'Xi Urges Greater Innovation in "Core Technologies"', Sinosphere, *New York Times*, 10 June, viewed 14 August 2014, http://sinosphere.blogs.nytimes.com/2014/06/10/xi-urges-greater-innovation-in-core-technologies/?_php=true&_type=blogs&_r=0.

Callon, M., 1986, 'The Sociology of an Actor-Network: The Case of the Electric Vehicle', in M. M. Callon, J. Law & A. Rip (eds.), *Mapping the Dynamics of Science and Technology*, pp. 19–34, Palgrave Macmillan, London.

Caliskan, K. & Callon, M., 2010a, 'Economization: New Directions in the Social Studies of the Market', Draft paper, 1–59.

Cao, C., 2004, 'Chinese Science and the "Nobel Prize Complex"', *Minerva* 42, 151–172.

China General Certification (CGC), 2013, 'Wind Turbine Certification in China', viewed 20 November 2014, http://events.ciemat.es:8899/documents/36718/59272/CGCC-Wind+Turbine+Certification+in+China-Leijie+Chen.pdf/d0510b44-2bd9-4a7a-a9be-e2334654653b.

China Renewable Energy Scale-Up Program (CRESP), 2005, 'National Action Plan for China's Wind Power Industry Development', viewed 20 November 2014, http://www.cresp.org.cn/uploadfiles/89/253/NationalAction_EN.pdf.

CRESP, n.d., cresp.org.cn, 'China Renewable Energy Scale-up Program: Project Name: Establishment of Wind Turbine Certification Capabilities', viewed 20 July 2014, http://www.cresp.org.cn/english/content.asp?id=1465.

DNV GL, n.d., 'Bladed Wind Turbine Simulation Tool is Key for Optimizing your Turbine at Every Phase of its Design', viewed 15 March 2018, https://www.dnvgl.com/services/bladed-3775.

Ernst, D., 2011a, 'Toward Greater Pragmatism? China's Approach to Innovation and Standardization', Policy Brief 18, Study of Innovation and Technology in China, SITC.

Ernst, D., 2011b, 'Indigenous Innovation and Globalization. The Challenge for China's Standardization Strategy', joint publication of the UC Institute on Global Conflict and Cooperation and the East-West Center, 1–136, https://www.eastwestcenter.org/sites/default/files/private/ernstindigenousinnovation.pdf.

Ernst, D., 2013a, 'Standards, Innovation, and Latecomer Economic Development: A Conceptual Framework', *Economics Series* 134, East-West Center Working Papers.

Ernst, D., 2013b, *America's Voluntary Standards System: A 'Best Practice' Model for Innovation Policy?*, Economics Series, 128, East-West Center Working Papers.

Fligstein N., 2001, *The Architecture of Markets: An Economic Sociology of Twenty-First Century Capitalist Societies*, Princeton University Press, Princeton, NJ.

Freudenreich, K. & Frohböse, 2010, 'IEC 61400-1: 2005 ('edition 3') – Experiences', Germanischer Lloyd (GL) Industrial Services, presentation at DTU Wind Energy, January 2010.

García, C., 2013, 'Policies and Institutions for Grid-Connected Renewable Energy: "Best Practice" and the Case of China', *Governance: An International Journal of Policy, Administration, and Institutions* 26(1), 119–146.

Gibbon, P. & Ponte, S., 2008, 'Global Value Chains: From Governance to Governmentality?', *Economy & Society* 37(3), 365–392.

GL-garradhassan, n.d., http://www.gl-garradhassan.com/en/garrad-hassan.php, viewed 14 July 2014.

Gosens, J. & Lu, Y., 2013, 'From Lagging to Leading? Technological Innovation Systems in Emerging Economies and the Case of Chinese Wind Power', *Energy Policy* 60, 234–250.

IEC (International Electrotechnical Commission), 2005, 'International Standard. Wind Turbines – Part 1: Design Requirements', IEC 61400-1, 3rd edn., 2005–2008.

IEC (International Electrotechnical Commission), n.d., 'Online Collections, 61400 Part 22', viewed 20 March 2018, https://collections.iec.ch/std/series/iec61400-22%7Bed1.0%7Den. nsf/doc.xsp?open&documentId=7F38806C6BDA3194C1257CC90035D3F9.

Korsnes, M., 2015, *Chinese Renewable Struggles: Innovation, the Arts of the State and Offshore Wind Technology*, PhD thesis, Department of Interdisciplinary Studies of Culture, Norwegian University of S&T (NTNU).

Korsnes, M. & Ryghaug, M., 2017, 'With License to Build: Chinese Offshore Wind Firms Rejecting European Certificates', *Technology Analysis & Strategic Management* 29(7), 750–761.

McGregor, J., n.d., 'China's Drive for "Indigenous Innovation". A Web of Industrial Policies', *APCO Worldwide, US Chamber of Commerce, Global Intellectual Property Centre*, Global Regulatory Cooperation Project, viewed 29 November 2014: https:// www.uschamber.com/sites/default/files/documents/files/100728chinareport_0_0.pdf.

Maskus, K. E., 2002, 'Regulatory Standards in the WTO: Comparing Intellectual Property Rights with Competition Policy, Environmental Protection, and Core Labor Standards', *World Trade Review* 1(2), 135–152.

MOST (Ministry of Science and Technology of the People's Republic of China), 2006, State Council, 国家中长期科学和技术发展规划纲要 (2006-2020) [National Outline for Medium and Long Term Science and Technology Development (2006–2020)], 9 February 2006, http://www.gov.cn/jrzg/2006-02/09/content_183787.htm.

MOST (Ministry of Science and Technology of the People's Republic of China), 2012, State Council, The Central People's Government of the People's Republic of China, 关于印发风力发电科技发展'十二五'专项规划的通知 ['The 12th Five-Year-Plan for the Scientific and Technological Development of Wind Power], 国科发计,197号, National Branch No. 197, 24 April 2012, http://www.most.gov.cn/ fggw/zfwj/zfwj2012/201204/t20120424_93884.htm.

O'Connor, G. C., 2006, 'Open, Radical Innovation: Toward an Integrated Model in Large Established Firms', in H. Chesbrough, W. Vanhaverbeke & J. West (eds.), *Open Innovation. Researching a New Paradigm*, Oxford University Press, New York.

Ponte, S., 2009, 'Governing through Quality: Conventions and Supply Relations in the Value Chain for South African Wine', *European Society for Rural Sociology, Sociologia Ruralis* 49(3).

Qi, W. 2011, 'China's Wind manufacturing Industry set for High Capacity Boost', 10 May 2011, *Windpower Monthly*, https://www.windpowermonthly.com/ article/1068997/chinas-wind-manufacturing-industry-set-high-capacity-boost.

Stark, D., 2009, *The Sense of Dissonance. Accounts of Worth in Economic Life*, Princeton University Press, Princeton, NJ.

Strambach, S., 2001, 'Innovation Processes and the Role of Knowledge-Intensive Business Services (KIBS)', in K. Koschatzky, M. Kulicke & A. Zenker (eds.), *Innovation Networks. Technology, Innovation and Policy (Series of the Fraunhofer Institute for Systems and Innovation Research (ISI))* 12, Physica, Heidelberg.

Thévenot, L., 2009, 'Governing Life by Standards: A View from Engagements. Postscript to the Special Issue', *Social Studies of Science* 39(5), 793–813.

Vestas-CWEA (China Wind Energy Association), 2011, 'Wind Industry Evaluation Criteria in China. International Experiences and Recommendations' [中国风力发电评价体系。国际经验和建议。北京:中国出版社], on file with author (hard copy).

Wang, P., Wang, Y. & Hill, J., 2010, 'Standardization Strategy of China – Achievements and Challenges', *Economics Series* 107, East-West Center Working Papers.

Windpowerengineering, n.d., viewed 15 March 2018, https://www.windpowerengineering.com/electrical/gl-garrad-hassan-releases-new-version-of-bladed/.

Woebbeking, M., 2010, 'The forthcoming GL-Guideline for onshore Wind Energy – GL 2010', Germanischer Lloyd Industrial Services, Renewables Certification.

Worldbank, n.d., *China – Renewable Energy Scale-up Program (CRESP)*, viewed 14 July 2014, http://www.worldbank.org/projects/P067625/china-renewable-energy-scale-up-program-cresp?lang=en.

Part III

Conclusions and broader perspectives

9 Conclusions and reflections on Chinese marketisation of wind power development

> 'Only at the end of the trip does it make sense to credit the traveler with the courage and rationality necessary for its completion'
> (On the 'Serresean sea-journey' in Jensen 2010:12)

Having completed the trip into the algorithmic universe of the wind turbine, it is time to use that feature of a wind turbine that only those who ascend up to the nacelle are privileged with: the view from the nacelle's roof-top window. Chapter Nine gathers together the kaleidoscopic pictures from this study, to render a more panoramic overview. In its conclusion, this volume reflects and concludes upon the findings as well as upon how a lens of the Anthropology of Markets – by allowing the analysis to move into the algorithmic machine room of the wind turbine, and traversing the electromagnetic waves – can contribute to and extend not only China Studies, but also STS.

Brief summary of five sites of controversy

As a much broader story about China's specific mode of experimental marketisation, or what may be dubbed 'green marketisation with Chinese characteristics', has been rendered by the kaleidoscopic journey through the various components of the wind turbine, it is time to take stock of what was found on the research journey. This may be done by taking a look at the main findings from the five sites of controversy:

- Chapter Four moved alongside the wind turbine's generator and traversed disruptive electromagnetic waves of the three phases in wind power development. In this historical mapping of the arduous work of assembling a socio-technical assemblage around wind power development, with heterogeneous actors, a site of controversy over the overall valuation of wind power was depicted, as the analysis followed the 'qualification crisis'. China's emerging socio-technical market assemblage around wind power development has advanced though three distinct phases of industrial development. The first two phases allowed the sector to advance to the brink of a precarious tipping point towards disruption and potential stalemate, destabilising and restabilising the market assemblage around wind power development several times. In particular, with the ensuing quality crisis, wind power has ultimately (and paradoxically) been in danger of delegitimisation as unsustainable in comprehensive terms. At the edge of collapse, radical government intervention led on to a new stage of upgrading, namely through the instigation of a potential turn to quality. Wind turbine core technologies, and in particular software algorithms, were framed as critical to the relegitimisation of wind power, as they ascribe qualities of sustainability to wind power through associations of 'scientific development'. The critical nature of core technologies, in turn, produced fragile Sino-foreign supply chain relations around them that may again advance to the brink of a precarious tipping point towards potential disruption or stalemate.

• In Chapter Five the journey continued from the generator and followed the electromagnetic waves as they carried the power out of the turbine and into the electricity network. In doing so, the book delved into a controversy over access to the electrical power grid, enquiring into the risk of socio-technical lock-in to fossil fuels ensuing from the quality crisis. This unfolding power struggle in the power sector between the coal and wind power sectors over access to the electrical power grid was traced by following the emergent framings of wind power as disruptive and uneconomical, and of the power system as inflexible in terms of accepting wind power penetration, exacerbated by resulting high curtailment rates. The chapter explored how these socio-materially grounded framings, for instance produced by the balancing logic of China's coal-based power system and the fluctuating electrons of wind power, but also by skewed subsidies and cost and price calculations, constituted the pre-existing power system as socio-materially hostile to the accommodation of larger shares of wind power. This resistance in turn produced vested interests against wind power that are socio-materially grounded.

• Chapter Six, in turn, translated the power that was generated and fed into the grid into the revenue earned, and journeyed on into some of the financial calculations of liquidity, credits, and subsidies that co-constitute the emerging socio-technical wind power development assemblage. By following the money in a controversy over access to money and relations, the analysis moved further into the opaque relations of the Chinese spider's web. Deeply entwined in China's state-owned and state–controlled power sector, Sino-foreign supply chain relations around control system software have become severed as a consolidation phase unfolds in Chinese wind power upon the onset of the quality crisis, in turn coproducing an industrial liquidity crisis. The spider's web is one of many hybridities between the private sector and the state. In this intricate web of business and state actors, interpersonal relations (*guānxì*) and agents have gained high(er) importance. In turn, these *guānxì* have become constituted as a situational and relational Chinese form of quality, so that foreign control system suppliers struggle through the consolidation, unable to break up their customer relations even when payments are delayed or lacking. The result is transformed and volatile Sino-foreign supply-chain relations. The spider's web constitution of Chinese wind power development, in turn, is entangled in the country's system problem, that is, the issue of incomplete marketisation and the lack of a 'pure' market economy, which is problematised as a hindrance to innovation, quality, and scientific development, as well as in China's 'growth model' that – exacerbated by the government's stimulus package in response to the global financial crisis - has paradoxically contributed to the emergence of a quality crisis in the first place.

- Travelling back to the wind turbine and diving even deeper into its algorithmic universe, as core technologies such as control system software are constituted as critically important for the reframing of wind power as sustainable during the turn to quality, Chapter Seven mapped the controversy that is unfolding over core technologies such as control system software, and in particular over access to core algorithms and source codes in the main supervisory controller. Owing to the proprietary control system algorithms being securely protected, Sino-foreign customer–supplier relations have become highly disruptive and volatile, unravelling as soon as, or even before, they have been forged, as trials of strength over relative positions and roles in supply chain relations unfold.

- In Chapter Eight a controversy over access to standards was traced, as the analysis moved into an examination of the computer simulation tools and calculations used by certification bodies, test laboratories, standardisation organisations, and research institutions. Here, a struggle to qualify wind power as sustainable through the ascription of technological and scientific quality was revealed, in which entangled power struggles unfolded around the core technology of simulation tools and in particular their aeroelastic codes: over access to both IPRs and international standards, to international research networks, to the world market, and later also over the struggle to develop indigenous 'Chinesified' designs and standards. This enquiry into enmeshed controversies over both international and national standards revealed an inherent international standardisation war, over the very right to define what quality – and science – is, and over the very framing tools such as aeroelastic codes in simulation tools; and thus over whether or not the quality of wind turbines can or should be confined (only) to scientific notions of algorithmic quality (that is, 'quality by algorithm').

Overall, this study has depicted the Chinese marketisation of wind power development as a space of great volatility, fragility, and ambiguity where valuation is being constantly negotiated. Indeed, the valuation qualification (or framing) of wind power as sustainable – in economic, social, environmental, scientific, technological, political, and developmental terms – has been contested over and over again, to the brink of delegitimising the Chinese Party-State's industrial governance – and underlying growth model – of it.

In this study, nothing seems certain or stabilised, making it premature even to talk about stabilised and/or institutionalised marketisation processes for wind power development in China. Instead, the study in many ways demonstrates how 'the movement towards markets is by no means irreversible, other forms of economization can always be envisaged' (Caliskan & Callon 2010:23): This book has mapped a space of emergence and potentiality, where overflowing seems to occur even as soon as framing attempts have been instigated. Even calculative framing tools (IPRs, standards, algorithms, etc.) that are supposed to strengthen the framing through the calculations of value they enable, have overflowed, producing more controversy, and thus revealing the inherent fragility of framing attempts and their inherent power dynamics. In this way, wind power development marketisation in China constitutes a seemingly paradoxical situation of simultaneous solidity and liquidity where not just reconfiguration but also transformation remains a potentiality, and where the potential turn to quality may still be disrupted. Metaphorically speaking, while advancing repeatedly towards the brink of potential stalemate or disruption, China's emerging market assemblage resembles the fluid and solid magma erupting from a volcano, a metaphor which has been used to represent controversy (Venturini 2010). That is, in the context of Chinese wind power development marketisation, the explosive growth in installed capacity – instigated by a 'turbine wave attack' – can be claimed to have caused a 'marketquake' so immense that it has overflowed into erupting magma and volcanic shifts in tectonic plates (i.e., the de- and reconfiguring of relations), which have iteratively de- and reconfigured the entire assemblage, at times threatening to shake it to the extent that it will be pushed past the brink of collapse, with the risk of potentially leading to stalemate and 'destructive interference' (as depicted by the electromagnetic wave metaphor). Paradoxically, and as explored through the metaphor of electromagnetic waves, this extensive overflowing – a result largely of what this book, with inspiration from the field of contemporary China Studies, has dubbed a fragmented and pragmatically experimental mode of green marketisation with Chinese characteristics – is what has made it possible for the wind power development market assemblage to endure the quality crisis and for Chinese market actors to upgrade capabilities in innovative ways. China may thus have the potential to harness wind power by breaking the (electromagnetic) waves of its marketisation. Indeed, the country seems, in this case, at least for the moment to have succeeded in handling emergent crises flexibly and agilely, with the resulting combined wave amplitude having moved to a higher level than before. That is, China seems to have upgraded and caught up through moving the wave amplitude, namely by establishing the world's largest wind power sector with enhanced capabilities – increasingly so also in core technologies - despite certain socio-technical road-blocks on the way. There is, however, a note of caution to be struck because the strategy of market development, that is largely reminiscent of China's long-held, risk-prone, growth model, is characterised by great precariousness that, at least by some, might be considered 'too wasteful' in the long-run. The reason for caution may especially be relevant in technologically advanced sectors, and intricately interlinked sectors, such as the wind power and power sectors, as the potential 'failure' to steer the wind power market assemblage back on track may have broader repercussions for China's transition to renewable energy. So far, however, the account provided here is overall a hopeful one for China.

Unique insights from the Anthropology of Markets lens on China's 'wind power miracle'

This investigation set out with the intention of shedding light on some of the potential socio-material and algorithmic contestations over China's so-called 'wind power miracle'. To do so, it has conducted the first ever marketisation study of the country's still emergent socio-technical market assemblage around wind power development[1]. The marketisation lens – founded in the Anthropology of Markets, and here conducted through a five-site controversy study – has enabled a unique enquiry into how China's market for wind power development has emerged (genesis). Further, it has enabled an enquiry into how the emerging market has been maintained, transformed, and de- and restabilised over time, with iterative advances towards the brink of a tipping point between stalemate and disruption, culminating in a self-inflicted quality crisis and radical government intervention that have instantiated a potential turn to quality (dynamics). In turn, the analysis has illustrated how this disruptive mode of marketisation has de- and reconfigured Sino-foreign supply chain relations around core technologies – in particular software algorithms. As algorithms gain agency in their own right, they transform relationships and alliances around them, relationships and alliances that have become so fragile that they threaten to unravel almost as soon as they are forged (agency). This volatility and ambiguity of relations makes it hard to talk about stable institutionalised structures. Chinese wind power development marketisation in this way may take the notion of gales of 'creative destruction' to a whole new level (Schumpeter 1934).

Apart from noting these overall findings, it is worthwhile to reflect briefly on their unique nature, which may be enabled through the prism of the relational and processual lens of the Anthropology of Markets and the method of controversy mapping.

Tracing marketisation through algorithms – seeing the universe in an algorithm

This study has been able to provide a fascinatingly broad, while also kaleidoscopically and rhizomatically micro-algorithmic, story about China's green development of its electrical power sector through the specific case of wind power development. Unlike other more structural and/or spatial studies of China's development of a wind power sector and wind turbine industry, which conventionally focus on embedded institutions, state bureaucracies, corporations, financial institutions, value chain structures, or innovation networks or systems, as normally seen in China Studies (and the neighbouring fields of Economic Geography, Innovation Studies, International Business, Institutional Theory, or New Economic Sociology broadly), this book's multifaceted and lateral story has been provided by way of tracing socio-materially grounded relations and processes that have taken place around unexpected, and seemingly innocent and mundane, actors and entities, be they software algorithms, control systems, standards and certificates, coal quota, local government contracts and incentive measures, vertical and horizontal lines of coordination, GW targets, calculations of lifetime generating cost, grid inflexibilities, aeroelastic codes, source codes, IPRs, cost and price calculations, debt chains, and much more. Some of these are exemplified in Figure 9.1.

Through this unconventional methodological, theoretical, and analytical take on the marketisation of Chinese wind power development, the lateral and symmetrical analysis has gone to unforeseen places and involved unexpected (non-human) actors, which have seldom been part of conventional analysis. In doing so, the socio-technical wind power development assemblage has been revealed as a contested 'hybrid forum' with myriads of actors enrolled where 'facts and values have become entangled' (Callon 1998:260), for example over what is sustainable, quality, and even over what is constituting innovation and science. Evidently, Chinese wind power development marketisation has spurred and triggered the proliferation of multiple and heterogeneous new identities and unexpected groups that demand to be taken seriously, heard, and received (Callon 2007:158). This is for instance seen in how Chinese manufacturers and certification bodies continue to reject their own exclusion from international research circles or standardisation committees, or in how algorithms, power grids, control systems, or simulation tools emerge, making their existence felt as they demand to be recognised. Opening up the invisible world(s) of algorithms and their inherent codified equations, and mapping the controversies and relations that algorithms and other socio-material actors perform, this study has engaged ethnographically in tracing what algorithms 'do', that is, enquiring into how material actors co-perform and enact markets. By disassembling the wind turbine into its algorithmic components, we have reassembled the turbine and its socio-technical universe.

Not only that, but this work has also – by way of attending to often overlooked socio-material actors, and thus looking away from preconceived notions and concepts of institutional structures, market, economy, capitalism/socialism, innovation systems, GVCs, GINs, and so on, somewhat surprisingly been able to depict a much broader story about China's contested greening of the electrical power sector as well as about its negotiated

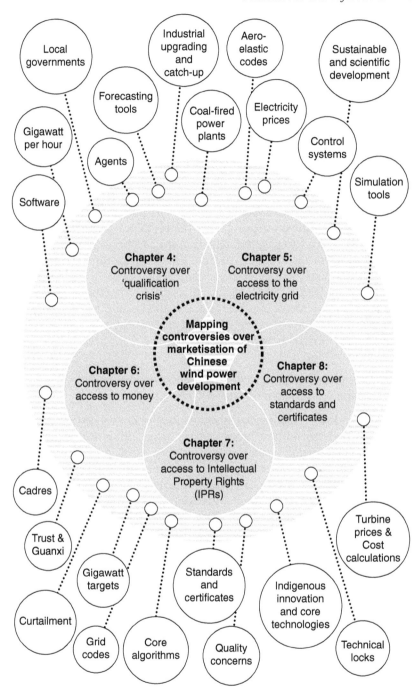

Figure 9.1 Examples of discovered actors in the socio-technical assemblage around wind power development.

socio-economic development, in particular revealing the contested nature of China's growth model as it plays out in China's wind turbine wave attack, and this very growth model's entanglement with the Chinese 'system problem' and the spider's web-like state–business relations. In this way, the study expands and transcends the boundaries of accounts conventionally construed around micro-, meso-, and macro-levels. The resulting lateral account has uncovered a story of the productive yet fragmented forces of China's experimental and pragmatic green development in this sector through wind power deployment, which at times has destabilised Sino-foreign supply chain relations. Moreover, indirectly, it has told the story of some of the various and entrenched paradoxes and dilemmas in China's transitional economy and the Party-State: That is, it has illustrated the contested legitimacy of China's mode of protectionism of SOEs, of state-led industrial policy spurred on by China's investment-driven (and risk-prone) pro-growth development model - along with only piecemeal reform of the corporate and electrical (and financial) power sectors – which, paradoxically, together have coproduced a potentially self-disruptive quality crisis and potential socio-material lock-in to fossil fuels. Indeed, it seems reasonable to suggest that the development of China's wind power sector in some regards would be bluntly framed a 'policy failure' by some, when considering the vast amounts of wasted resources, be they economic, environmental, or social.

Entanglements of Chinese wind power development marketisation – politicisation with a Chinese flavour

Wind power development marketisation in China has revealed itself as part and parcel not only of processes of politicisation, but also of economisation, scientification, and even what this book proposes under the term 'technification'. Indeed, the study reveals how, when you look at the marketisation of wind power development, it becomes impossible to distinguish the realms of markets, economics, politics, science, and technology (Caliskan & Callon 2009, 2010; Callon 2007:139). Whilst marketisation is known always to be inherently political, this study shows how its inherent politics comes with a certain Chinese flavour here, owing to the entanglement of Chinese fragmented authoritarianism and experimental, pragmatic governance as well as the politicised marketisation of a socialist market economy. Such a high degree of entanglement in politicisation can help explain the high propensity to overflow. The politicised nature, with a capital P, of all aspects of Chinese wind power development marketisation is summarised briefly below.

First, take the economisation of wind power development. As marketisation represents but one potential outcome of the broader and entangling processes of economisation, the underlying contested nature of wind power economisation – as discussed below - in a Chinese socialist context makes wind power marketisation inherently controversial.

Wind in and of itself has no intrinsic (monetary or non-monetary) value. Hence, to construe a market around it – producing wind power – requires that potential (corporate, scientific, financial, political) investors can see a potential economic value in it, that is, wind power must be economised for potential marketisation to take place. With no intrinsic value attached to it, the economisation of wind power development – making investments into an emerging market for wind power development attractive to potential (financial, corporate, political) investors – requires the 'pacification'/ stabilisation of wind power's framing as sustainable and worthwhile, e.g. in an economic, social, scientific, and/or political sense. Such pacification of the framing can e.g. be done through the use and adjustment of calculative devices and calculations such as GW- or GWh-based tendering criteria, support mechanisms and price-setting mechanisms, rules for grid integration, but also through IPRs, standards, credits, and quotas for renewable energy and coal, etc. The need for enhancing the framing of wind power as a sustainable investment good has in particular been critically needed during the unfolding qualification struggle that followed the quality crisis.

The controversy mapping has made visible some of the many contested valuation processes that are inherent to the economisation of wind power development in a Chinese context, for example as prices of wind turbines have been set artificially low as a matter of protectionism, as development hinges on continuous subsidisation (as in many other parts of the world a continuous issue of dispute), as cost calculations between wind power and fossil fuels are construed as skewed, and as curtailment and the quality crisis have created debt chains, wasted resources, and dwindling profits. Price struggles also exist between Chinese and foreign wind turbine manufacturers in government-led wind farm concessions. What makes the contestation over wind power economisation even more intense in the Chinese context, however, is the persistence of non-monetary valuations, such as the use of controversial relational *guānxi*, vested interests in the power sector that threaten to create a socio-technical lock-in to fossil fuels, SOE favouritism, and valuations based on developmental concerns for long-term national economic development and sustainable and scientific development rather than on concerns for corporate profits.

The above contestations over the economisation of wind power indicate the collision of different ways of valuing the potential worth(s) of wind power. That is, some things in Chinese wind power development are not valued (primarily) through 'market-based' economic prices, but are rather valued in developmental terms. At the same time they are enmeshed in the Chinese Party-State's struggle to retain political monopoly power, secure social stability through protection of state monopolies, and fight against pollution, amongst other factors. Entangled in a Chinese socialist market economy with limited price liberalisation and a great degree of state control, there is thus consistent contestation and negotiation over the very legitimacy of economising and marketising wind power in the first place. This, together with the concern for a transition to renewable energy, produces prices and subsidies that are highly contested and not based on premises of intersecting supply and demand curves, in a manner that is contrary to conventional neo-classical economics. Indeed, as eloquently demonstrated in various other marketisation studies in a non-Chinese context, prices are always inherently prosthetic (Caliskan & Callon 2009), socio-materially construed on the ground through market device prostheses and negotiations that must be put in place in order for valuation to take place.

Next, take scientification. Since sustainability in China is intricately linked to the CPC doctrine of scientific development, wind power development has been ascribed not only with economic value, but also with scientific (and developmental) value, as hopes of Chinese catch-up and upgrading are intricately associated with it. Scientification was not an integral part of marketisation in the first phase(s) of wind power development in China, but was much more driven by an industrial policy agenda and the construction of a manufacturing capacity, and a growth model supported by a very particular Chinese investment model. The imminent and ambiguous turn to quality has entailed a turn to science: with an ambition to ensure the 'scientific development' of wind power, we have witnessed an enhanced emphasis on the scientific expertise underlying wind turbine certification and the standardisation of new indigenous turbine designs, as well as on the development of indigenous IPRs in core technologies and the development of basic research capabilities, for example in software codes and mathematics (aerodynamics).

Such scientification of wind power development has in turn been pushed by China's increased integration into world markets and into GVCs and emerging GINs, as global competition in the wind turbine industry has recently, and increasingly, become centred around the turbine's algorithmic intelligence, because this is key to pushing down the cost of energy as well as to ensure optimised system integration. Meanwhile, such processes of scientification have also revealed themselves as inherently controversial and as producing power struggles, for instance as different modes of valuing scientific expertise, quality, risk and uncertainty, innovation practices, and agendas of applied science versus basic research are colliding. As wind turbines on a global scale have increasingly become valued according to their algorithmic quality, it may even be argued that marketisation in Chinese wind power development has also become entangled in processes of technification. This denotes how core technologies such as algorithmic software tools - construed as key to the pacification and taming of the uncontrollable and stochastically fluctuating forces of the wind - and Chinese indigenous innovation in these, can coproduce associations of algorithmic quality to wind turbines, thereby realigning it with the Party doctrine of sustainable development through 'scientific development'. Meanwhile, wind turbine technology and software tools and algorithms have become constituted as anything but benign, innocent, or mundane, but rather imbued with power struggles and 'big politics': That is, enmeshed for instance in the socio-material boundaries set up by IPRs and international standards, and a legacy of technology transfer and a focus on applied science, software tools and their calculative algorithms have become constitutive of (potential socio-material barriers to) the vision of a Harmonious Socialist Society through scientific development and indigenous innovation in core technologies. Accordingly, the calculative devices of software algorithms – meant to tame the wind by minimising risk and uncertainty – have somewhat paradoxically become objects of contestation, gaining agency as they de- and reconfigure Sino-foreign supply chain relations around them.

Overall, scientification and technification are inherently political processes, imbued with associations of China's developmental concerns for industrial upgrading. That is, scientific and technological research into the optimisation of software algorithms can help frame China's wind turbine industry as sustainable, coperforming/enacting the 'turn to quality' through a 'turn to (algorithmic) science'. Yet, whilst they serve to reduce uncertainty, scientific facts and algorithms often tend to produce even more uncertainty, for example as the emerging convention of 'quality by algorithm' is being contested. Underlying this is also a collision of modes by which science and innovation are practised: one is 'Western', more risk averse, controlled, theorised, and based on decades of basic research and applied science, while the other is 'Chinese', more experimental, and largely based on an impetus of applied science. As some of the inherent socio-material limitations to catchup through leapfrogging of this latter course have revealed themselves over time – as for instance seen in China's struggle to certify its wind turbines according to the highest global standards - we may be witnessing the reconfiguration and convergence of Chinese innovation practices and innovation policies.

A story of power and politics

Overall, this study has provided a study of power and politics, in both physical and socio-political terms, as we have traversed the electromagnetic waves of wind power and followed trials of strength over both seemingly minute and seemingly large and powerful actors.

Other studies within New Economic Sociology have also illustrated how (wind) power and electricity markets are imbued with power dynamics and politics (e.g. Granovetter & McGuire 1998; Mitchell 2011) and struggles over how to engineer the market most efficiently, as illustrated within the Anthropology of Markets (Jenle 2015; Jenle & Pallesen 2017; Karnøe 2010). Meanwhile, this book argues that the developmental and transitional context of China has made the marketisation of wind power market development politicised, sensitive, and controversial - and has created overflowing - on an unprecedented scale, and in particular has imbued it with a specific 'Chinese flavour'. Indeed, as the power sector in China is state led, there would never have been wind power development in the country, had it not been for the government's political decision to develop the industry in the first place.

Further, the very notion of marketising (and liberalising) wind power in a Chinese context is in itself a highly political – and unresolved – matter, as the Chinese socialist market economy is marked by fragmented authoritarianism, vested interests, protectionism, state control, and discursive party doctrines of Scientific Development. There are however indications of future liberalisation, through the planned introduction of spot markets for power trading.

This political configuration is the special flavour of Chinese wind power development marketisation that makes it a site of unprecedented ubiquitous overflowing as actions of framings, of assigning ownership, and of employed framing tools constantly instigate legal, ethical, scientific, or economic debates (Caliskan & Callon 2010:8), even over the very right to develop and catchup. Overall, the marketisation of wind power development is a matter of politics in all senses: there are big politics in the small, and vice versa. Everywhere politics is emerging: in the smallest algorithm, in a patent, in a contract, and in the price list for turbine components, as well as revealing itself in the future vision of a Harmonious Socialist Society, in certificates, and in the contractual handshake between Chinese and foreign manufacturers. Therefore, this study has shown how the 'big politics' of wind power development marketisation and Chinese greening can be traced just by looking at a software algorithm. Through the lens of the Anthropology of Markets, we have seen 'an equation and its world' (MacKenzie 2003). Or, likened to the notion of 'seeing a world in a grain of sand' (from William Blake's (1757–1827) poem 'Auguries of Innocence' (1963) in Warner 1976), the study has, in Latour's (2004) words, helped map 'the whole earth and heavens that have to be gathered' to hold one matter of concern, such as the marketisation of wind power development, or the sustainable green marketisation of China's electrical power sector, 'firmly in place' (Latour 2004:246). Indeed, it has been shown how this politicised power field has produced power struggles over algorithms, over wind power's access to the grid, and over access to money and government *guānxì*, standards, and IPRs.

By mapping controversies, and tracing algorithms and other seemingly mundane artefacts around the marketisation of wind power development in China, the wind and its marketisation is revealed as a (or multiple) politicised and negotiated 'matter(s) of concern' rather than a taken-for-granted 'matters of fact' (Latour 2004). Indeed, wind power, turbines, and algorithms come with their own politics, as power struggles unfold over their very definition and application. This renders this study a story of ubiquitous power struggles, or trials of strength, in the physical terms of wind power and also in socio-political terms. Thus, while abiding by the dictum of trying to stay 'sober with power' (Latour 2005:260), this study has revealed some of the politicised yet fragmented power struggles over the algorithmic taming of the wind, and over software tools for control and design - and the barriers they construct - entangled in global power struggles over IPRs and standardisation, and over the right to define what is 'proper' quality, science, and innovation. It has also shown power struggles between colliding priorities in the electrical power system between coal and wind as well as between vested interests of the state bureaucracy, all enmeshed in intricate state–business spider's web relations that de- and reconfigure Sino-foreign supply chain relations.

Developmental situation of China amidst colliding forces

Finally, the study has revealed how Chinese wind power development marketisation is inherently linked to the contradictory forces that the country is facing as a newly industrialised country (and 'emerging market') in a world of increasing globalisation, which produces colliding forces of 'opening up' and of 'closing down' (protectionism).[2] A good example of the former in this schism is China's accession to the WTO in 2001, recent attempts to become part of GVCs and GINs, and to fulfil, develop, and define international standards and IPRs. All these moves reflect processes of opening up, as China engages with the supposedly free circulation of people, knowledge, and technologies (e.g. software) (Caliskan & Callon 2010). Conversely, we witness nationalistic processes of 'closing down', such as the formation of China's 'National Team' and the establishment of SASAC, the discourse around indigenous innovation, and the introduction of local content requirements and national standards, which run counter to the global processes of opening up.

Whilst China's wind turbine industry would not have been where it is today without engagement in globally interdependent networks and in the trend towards supposedly more open innovation, the sector seems to face a dilemma: China is increasingly intent on becoming independent from foreign technologies; yet it still largely depends on fertile and equal relations with foreign actors when it comes to core technologies and basic research. In the ambiguous and paradoxical context of colliding forces and agendas of independence from and linking up to foreign actors, China is bound to maintain these relations, whilst they also seek to disrupt them. This paradox has made Sino-foreign supply chain relations overly fragile, in particular as the turn to quality has set in, because it creates simultaneous forces of competition and collaboration around core technologies. The dilemma is also felt acutely by the Chinese Party-State, and in particular the CPC, as it faces pressure to protect the country's SOEs and maintain their extended social obligations, on the one hand, and pressure to open up and engage more openly in GVCs and innovation networks on the other. Overall, this 'structural' dilemma produces many unforeseen and sometimes paradoxical effects, as well as processes both of fragmentation and centralised control and integration. What will happen as President Xi Jinping ensures his constitutional right to potential life-long presidency and favours control and centralisation over fragmentation is still uncertain, though, but this is clearly an important issue to follow in the years to come.

What this study's analysis then tells us is that China's processes of opening up and linking up are contested and negotiated in nature, and oftentimes counteracted by moves towards 'closing down'. It has also demonstrated that technologies such as software are not always circulating freely but may come with certain barriers and struggles. This renders the Chinese marketisation of wind power development a 'hot situation' (Callon 1998:60), in which there exists no stabilised consensus or knowledge base, but constant controversy. Meanwhile, as Chinese actors have upgraded capabilities and as a turn to quality takes place, there is a potential over time to create a more stable and even playing field of fair competition and mutual learning, as Chinese and foreign actors are increasingly competing based on similar criteria and harmonised means of measurement, such as energy (GWh) targets, standards and certificates, and IPRs. Such more 'level playing fields' may be further enhanced by the recent discursive move from indigenous innovation to open innovation, which is argued to work towards overcoming the latent political tensions in previous interpretations of indigenous innovation that have been seen as Chinese (c)overt protectionism.

Contributions

With all this in mind, it is now time to reflect on some of the contributions to China Studies and Science & Technology Studies of the present study, set in a Chinese context, from the pioneering perspective of the Anthropology of Markets.

Contributions to China studies

What the Anthropology of Markets brings to bear is a relational, lateral, and processual lens that brings more life to the relatively static and distant accounts of China Studies. In particular, by conducting the first ever marketisation study in China – through the event of wind power development – hitherto otherwise unseen socio-material struggles and micro-foundations in market construction and Chinese greening have been made visible. In doing so, higher fragility and volatility of relations than has otherwise been accounted for has been revealed.

In turn, the study's revelation of some of the socio-technical struggles inherent in such experimental pragmatics of marketisation, and in China's crisis-prone wind power sector, has been linked to an innovative experimental governance mode (Heilmann 2005, 2008, 2011) of Chinese market construction. This can be likened to a particularly Chinese 'arts of the state' (Korsnes 2015), where government interventions steer the industry forward flexibly by issuing ambiguous imaginations and expectations for the future (Korsnes 2015, 2016),[3] at the same time as industry actors learn from experimentation and from their failure. This illustrates the ambiguous simultaneity of 'direction and improvisation' in Chinese governance (Ang 2016:69). It is thus illustrated how failure in a Chinese context is not necessarily or exclusively a 'mistake', as long as it creates the opportunity for creative problem-solving, disruptive learning, and catch-up and leapfrogging. In this way, the thousands of disconnected wind turbines are in a Chinese perspective not always, and not necessarily, a failure, but a mode of accelerated learning and development. Linked to this pragmatic experimentalism are China's fragmented authoritarianism (Lieberthal 2004; Mertha 2009) and structured uncertainty (Breznitz & Murphree 2011; Mertha & Brødsgaard 2017): The experimentalism has largely been enabled through a fragmented mode of governance and China's investment-driven growth model where there is space for flexible interpretation of central policies at local levels, and where wind power development happens in oscillating movements back and forth between centralisation and decentralisation of central control, with authoritative intervention from the party centre tending to take place only 'during exceptional periods of crisis governance' (Heilmann 2016:7). Meanwhile, the volume also illustrates the contestation over what constitutes a 'failure'. That is, the 'contested failure' of wind power development in China is exposed, as the Chinese growth-driven development model has produced extensive overflowing in the case of a relatively high-tech sector such as wind power. Indeed, as the sustainability of this model is being contested, the book illustrates the need to take into account the specific socio-material and physical nature of the object of exchange (wind power) and the entangling pre-existing infrastructures (the power system) before assessing the applicability and viability of Chinese fragmented and experimental marketisation.

At the same time, this study illustrates, somewhat provocatively, that it is the experimentalism enabled through the paradoxical fragmented authoritarianism that helps to maintain a certain degree of balance, stability, and harmony in the longer run, whilst allowing for chaos in the short term. Contrary to some previous accounts of China as an authoritarian monolithic structure, this research enriches the literature by illustrating how it is through local experimentation, pragmatism, fragmentation, and disruption that stable harmony – a main priority all the way back to the divisionary Warring States period (475–221 BC), deeply embedded not only in the dogma of the CPC, but also in Confucian philosophy (Li 2006) – can be retained and innovation can happen. This is also what contributes to making the CPC, so far at least, capable of retaining political monopoly power, since space for local co-creation is retained to function as a sort of valve that releases part of the existing societal pressure from the public. Meanwhile, this study also indicates the delicate balancing act that the CPC must muster between control and fragmentation, the structural dilemmas that ensue, and the opening up to global competition and integration into GINs versus the protection of SOEs. Whilst a sub-theme in the Fragmented Authoritarianism literature relates to the paradoxical issue of authoritarian durability, resilience, and adaptability (e.g. Mertha & Brødsgaard 2017:10; Oi & Goldstein 2018), these studies have not inquired into how these dilemmas and paradoxes inherent to the Chinese Party-State's industrial governance play out in Sino-foreign supply chain relations in general or in the case of wind power development. This work helps to fill the gap.

By extension, some of the conflicting vested interests and agendas in this muddle matrix of China's fragmented authoritarianism have been revealed, for instance as the State Grid's attitude towards wind power penetration has shifted over time. More than this, the Anthropology of Markets lens has allowed the analysis to acknowledge the role of non-human actors in China's fragmented authoritarianism. For instance, the analysis has looked at the role of grid inflexibilities (deriving from construed institutional and physical constraints), protracted negotiations of an RPS, annually nego- tiated coal quotas and coal companies' resistance against wind power, Chinese undercover *guānxì*, the unexpected agency of software algorithms, and much more, all of which renders the vested interests in the power sector for and against wind power socio-materially grounded. Overall, the rela- tional, lateral, and socio-technical lens that this study brings to bear has indicated how - as one starts to look more closely, or as one takes the first step into the wind turbine nacelle and starts to trace relations around soft- ware algorithms - it is often virtually impossible to predict actions based purely on institutional and bureaucratic structures or position.

On a related note, the Chinese State's ubiquitous role in wind power development and in the power sector, and the constant yet protracted and contested marketisation and liberalisation of the sector, has revealed China neither as an ideal-type 'coordinated', nor as a 'liberal' political economy (cf. Hall & Soskice's (2001) Varieties of Capitalism paradigm). Indeed, some of the state-owned enterprises' propensity not to be governed (primarily) by profit or liquidity concerns, but rather by government *guānxì*, extended social obligations, and soft budget constraints fails to fit to a formal out- sider-based corporate governance model. On the other hand, consistent reforms of the corporate sector, including an extensive anti-corruption campaign enhanced under the current presidency of Xi Jinping, renders China's Variety of Capitalism anything but an ideal-type coordinated mar- ket economy governed by insider-based corporate governance norms. By illustrating, albeit to some extent indirectly, the simultaneous processes of liberalisation and protectionism, of opening up and closing down, this work aligns more with the variegated capitalism lens, which argues for the competitiveness of multiple types of capitalism within China (also includ- ing a more network/*guānxì* -based form of capitalism), arguing for a mode of capitalism that constitutes 'uneven development of globalizing but poly- morphic capitalism(s)' (Zhang & Peck 2014:5). At the same time, this study adds to these perspectives a socio-material lens: By enquiring into some of the socio-material struggles around wind power's qualification, some of the particular and situated 'Chinese characteristics' of Chinese marketi- sation of wind power development are revealed, such as the entanglement of Chinese greening in an ambiguous space and era of Chinese 'socialism' amidst increasingly globalised and geographically and organisationally decomposed production and innovation processes. Indeed, the account offered here stands in contrast to the conventionally more rigid and distant accounts given by institutional, structural, and hierarchical perspectives, such as the Variety of Capitalism lens, which – founded on an efficiency-based logic of transaction cost minimisation – assumes that institutional complementarities between political and economic realms will mutually converge and bind each other into path-dependent structures. In contrast, this book has uncovered China as a paradoxical site that lacks institutional complementarity, and disrupts emerging structures without making the entire assemblage around wind power development (or power of the CPC) entirely unravel. This has sometimes been coined through notions such as 'adaptive institutional change' (Dimitrov 2013 in Oi & Goldstein 2018:5) and 'authoritarian resilience' (Oi & Goldstein 2018) amid change and transformation. Therefore, this study has indirectly revealed how the fragmented and experimental characteristics of Chinese wind power development marketisation often make it impossible to bind relations into stable institutionalised structures or into stable governance structures, in turn making the notion of 'path-dependence' superfluous. This is because of China's unique and paradoxical state of being 'persistently uninstitutionalized' (Lieberthal 2004 in Breznitz & Murphree 2011:11), which, on the other hand, is what contributes to its resilience. In Chinese wind power development marketisation, different phases have been skewed towards one of the two extremes of either stabilisation or destabilisation, sometimes crystallising, albeit briefly, into configurations centred around quantity and GW targets, for instance, and at other times around quality and targets for GWh. What has been depicted is thus a constant process of solidification and disruption, of fragile institutionalisation and constant transformation. In this particular Chinese assemblage, new structures tend to be dissolved or reconfigured by radical new interventions (or by the radical neglect of intervention) by the Chinese political leadership, before they add up to path-dependent, complementary, stabilised, institutionalised structures. Meanwhile, this structured uncertainty is what has made it possible to establish new markets in an accelerated and innovative fashion, and to perform flexible change when needed, as well as what makes the Chinese configuration resilient despite its inherent volatility.

Summing up, this book argues that enhanced communication between China Studies and STS (and controversy studies and the Anthropology of Markets) is a promising field for future research. Although China Studies literature has not had as its primary objective the provision of a socio-material lens of relations and processes, the reflexive and socio-material lens of the Anthropology of Markets has proved itself a promising field for future situational studies of marketisation and industry formation, of Chinese greening, and of contested modes of valuing sustainability, innovation, quality, science, and expertise in China. Indeed, this study has shown the contested nature of these often blackboxed notions. Overall, future research in China

Studies would benefit from an enquiry into who has been given the power to invent the rules and conventions that define the standards which deem certain forms of quality, innovation, and sustainability in or out, who are given roles as followers and leaders (and by whom), but also by whom and through which tools the very target of the 'catching up' process has been defined.

Contributions to STS

More than contributing to China Studies, this study has – just by taking the marketisation lens to China – extended the Anthropology of Markets[4]. Treating the Chinese political regime as endogenous to marketisation, the book has opened up a whole new area of future marketisation studies in a developmental context. These future studies can help us to shed light on marketisation in non-Western, socialist, transitional contexts, where the movement towards markets has proved anything but irreversible, and where the fragmented authoritarian regime has proved to have a formative role in how marketisation in Chinese wind power development has so far taken place.

Indeed, by engaging in controversy mapping over wind power development marketisation, conducted by following algorithms amongst other things, this book has been able to tell a story of China's green transition to renewable energy, of Chinese experimental governance, and of socio-economic development as China transitions towards larger degrees of marketisation. By doing so, it has traversed the boundaries of conventional economic sociology and its embeddedness approach[5] as well as the 'weak programme' of STS and the modest sociology of Actor-Network Theory. Indeed, this study is very different from existing constructivist studies in that it simultaneously seeks to tell a much broader story about Chinese green marketisation by innovatively and myopically tracing relations around algorithms and other overlooked actors and entities[6].

Concluding comments on China's green transition in spite and because of experimental pragmatics of marketisation

At the outset, this study set out to look at the risk of fragmented experimentation spinning out of control, indicating how the Chinese crisis and response development can become contested, and providing the first ever marketisation study for China and specifically of Chinese wind power development.

The study illustrates how China has gradually moved from a focus on speedy low cost production and installed capacity towards quality and generated electricity. The book dubs this shift to be a potential turn to quality. Through this, a new strategic and more complex power game between Chinese and foreign actors has emerged, in which the dynamics of collaboration and competition coexist and collide. In these paradoxical relations, core technologies – in particular software tools and the algorithms therein – have become increasingly critical in China's struggle to qualify wind power as sustainable, as they are critical for the optimisation, design, and certification of wind turbines.

These unique findings have been achieved by focusing on five sites of controversy: the qualification struggle in Chinese wind power development, access to the electrical power grid, access to money, access to IPRs, and access to certificates and standards. By travelling through the wind turbine, both metaphorically speaking and in more literal terms, the study has rendered insights into issues of socio-technical market genesis, dynamics, and agency of marketisation.

In conclusion, this book confirms the hypothesis that China has been able to green its electrical power sector through wind power in spite of and because of its fragmented, experimental, and pragmatic mode of green marketisation. That is, China may, somewhat paradoxically, have been able to upgrade and upscale, and in some cases even catchup through leapfrogging, with unprecedented pace through and in spite of iterative advances towards a tipping point that threatens to produce stalemate and disruption, a course that the Chinese State has allowed to emerge. This is what constitutes China's mode of upgrading and catching up at the brink of collapse. By enquiring into how a socio-technical assemblage has been mobilised to invest time, energy, and money in wind power development, a Chinese pragmatic experimentation with developing new industries has been revealed. While it is China's fragmented pragmatics of green marketisation that have produced a quality crisis – threatening to delegitimise the marketisation process – it is the same pragmatics that are likely to enable the agile turn to quality and experimental learning, and the resulting disruptive moves of upgrading. In the turn to quality, algorithms have taken centre stage as a means of measuring quality and competitiveness. Meanwhile, whilst algorithms have been developed to raise certainty and reduce risk, taming the powerful forces of the wind, they have a hidden logic that tends to produce even more contestation and ambiguity rather than the reverse. This study illustrates how the disruptive development of wind power has produced highly volatile Sino-foreign supply chain relations around software tools, as well as how it has produced contestation over the underlying and risk-prone growth strategy underpinning the industry's trajectory, one which in the long-term may turn out to become 'too wasteful' in a technologically advanced sector such as wind power.

As an extended conclusion, but in theoretical terms, the constructivist analysis founded in the Anthropology of Markets and the method of mapping controversies has proved a productive and promising analytical strategy in terms of revealing some of the hidden socio-technical controversies over China's sustainable transition of its electrical power sector towards the higher integration of renewable energy. As an area of multiple entangled transitions – for example, from black to green, from coal to wind, from quantity, pace, and growth to quality and innovation, from manufacturing to innovation, from follower to leader, and from plan to market, Chinese wind power development marketisation is revealed as highly volatile and controversial, and thus inherently political. To account for such high volatility, the strategic role of technology and science, and how this can be constituted differently in different contexts (as can sustainability and quality), this book argues that the relational and processual socio-technical lens of the Anthropology of Markets can help provide new and valuable insights to China Studies. More than that, by moving the Anthropology of Markets to the socialist context of China, and extending the boundaries of sociology, this work also contributes to STS through its bold move towards making broader claims about Chinese greening based on a situated algorithmic controversy mapping. It also represents a first step towards moving forward the budding conversation between China Studies and STS forward through the first ever application of a lens of the Anthropology of Markets.

Whether the ambiguous winds of change that seem to blow over China's assemblage around wind power development will transform the Chinese market for wind power, and result in an actual, and substantial, shift in focus from price and quantity towards quality through S&T, remains to be seen, however. Indeed, the long-term comprehensive sustainability of China's fragmented and pragmatically experimental mode of green marketisation will only reveal itself over time. This is what ambiguity entails here. In this way, only over time may we learn whether or not the Chinese mode of learning from mistakes is a viable long-term sustainable strategy for development – for China itself, for related industries, or for other countries. Consequently, we are still to see if China may become a green leader for the world and a model for other newly industrialising countries and their transition to renewable energy. Indeed, as China muddles forward towards the 'new normal' of single-figure growth rates, we may soon be witnessing some of the (power, financial, corporate, science and other) reforms that have been called for as China transitions its development model for green(er) and more 'sustainable' growth. Rephrasing Cervantes, we may thus ask rhetorically whether China might (continue to) be fighting against (its own) windmills, or whether the seemingly self-disruptive behaviour may turn out to be a creative, pragmatic industrial policy that reshapes relations within the global wind turbine industry in the long run, enabling disruptive moves towards the Energy Revolution along the path of the 'Chinese Dream' of harmonious sustainable development.

Notes

1. However, although framed differently and for another audience, most of the research in this book is based on my doctoral research, which was also founded in the lens of the Anthropology of Markets (Kirkegaard 2015).
2. As has been described by Caliskan & Callon (2010), but not in relation to China and/or wind power.
3. Linked to Korsnes' argument is the STS-notion of socio-technical imaginaries, which has been promoted by Jasanoff & Kim (2015) to describe how

imaginaries of the future and future technology and science are deeply impli-
cated in producing collective visions of good and attainable futures, serving
as political instruments of legitimation. Another scholar emphasising the performative role of the future is Beckert (2016) – though not from an STS-lens - who
discusses the role of an (envisioned and imagined) future for enabling investment decisions and economic action in the present.
4. Kirkegaard & Caliskan (forthcoming) also discuss how the Anthropology of
Markets can benefit from taking the research program to a socialist context
such as the Chinese.
5. Building on the Anthropology of Markets, this study is founded on new STS-
based directions in social studies of the market within New Economic Sociology. This implies that the study shares both the appreciation of the valuable
insights offered by conventional New Economic Sociology and the critique
of New Economic Sociology that these new directions in market studies have
offered: New Economic Sociology has offered an insightful and fruitful critique of conventional economic discussions of the emergence of industrial
sectors for their focus on efficiency and equilibrium-thinking, as well as their
negligence of human agency. By showing that markets have to be marketised in
the first place, economic sociology has contributed with a better understanding
of how marketisation of a certain commodity relies on the dynamic mobilisation of a myriad of political, economic, engineering and entrepreneurial networks. However, whilst recognising these contributions, this study is critical of
the artificial boundary between 'society' and 'the economy' construed by New
Economic Sociology's institutional embeddedness lens (Granovetter 1998) (for
an elaborate outline, see Callon & Caliskan's (2009, 2010) critical review of
the embeddedness approach): Based in a Polanyian (2001) understanding of
the economy as enmeshed in (economic and non-economic) institutions, New
Economic Sociology treats the economy (and markets) and society as analytically separate, following an ideal-typical binary construct that separates the
'market' from its supposed exterior, the 'non-market' (also see Kirkegaard &
Caliskan forthcoming). With such construct, the economy (and markets) can be
conveniently treated as *embedded* in pre-existing social institutions (e.g. Granovetter & McGuire1998). Meanwhile, and following Mitchell (2002), this book
argues that the attempt of analysts to find the accurate location of the boundary between the market and its supposed exterior risks rendering the majority of economic encounters and institutional innovations empirically invisible
(also see Kirkegaard & Caliskan forthcoming). That is, instead of treating the
economy as embedded *a posteriori* into *a priori* existing social institutions, or
conceptualising the non-market as embedded in the market, new directions in
the study of markets have demonstrated what can be gained instead by dissolving the artificial boundary between the market and the non-market, instead
locating market exchange relations (marketisation) as analytically enmeshed
in larger processes of economisation, as well as in processes of politicisation
and scientification (Caliskan & Callon 2009; 2010; Callon, 2007; Kirkegaard &
Caliskan forthcoming; Kirkegaard, Caliskan & Karnøe forthcoming). Markets
and political economies are thus not to be treated as embedded in and exoge-
nous to social institutions. Instead, as economic and market processes cannot be
readily be separated from 'social' factors, or even from politics or science,
social institutions are endogenously co-configured by and co-configuring economic and market processes (Caliskan & Callon 2009, 2010; Kirkegaard &
Caliskan forthcoming; Kirkegaard et al. forthcoming). Accordingly, this study
sees the emerging socio-material market assemblage around wind power
development in China as co-configured by and co-configuring Chinese social

institutions, rather than being 'embedded' into and/or being (path-)-dependent on them. Apart from being critical of the artificial divide between the market and non-market, this study is namely also critical of how the embeddedness approach links up to canonical forms of path dependence (Martin 2010), as the lens of path dependence entails a risk of overlooking agency, and particularly of overlooking the potential heterogeneous socio-material agencies involved in bringing about markets. With New Economic Sociology's tendency to focus on social actors and stabilisation processes, strengthened by path-dependence, this study instead argues – along with new directions in the social studies of markets – for the need to focus on the socio-material constitution of markets, as well as for using a lens that can capture the inherent instability and contested nature of markets, their incessant need for maintenance, and their inevitable entanglement in processes of politicisation (Caliskan & Callon 2009, 2010).

6. Some might argue that such attempted 'panorama' view - rendering a more generalised overview of the findings - bears more resemblance to what STS, hereunder in particular ANT, criticises for promoting a faulty ideal of the 'panopticon' overview (that is, the Foucauldian (1995) notion of the panopticon to describe total control and surveillance in specific prison designs). Latour (2005), in particular, has criticised the ideal of the view of the panopticon lens, in that it tends to lead to over-generalisations, whilst lacking in empirical detail, thereby only rendering an illusionary coherence. In this study, the analysis has myopically traced the forging and dissolving of relations. Hereby, I argue that it still abides by Latour's ideal of the 'oligopticon' lens, which instead traces multiple spaces and sites (oligoptica) that 'do exactly the opposite of panoptica: they see much too little to feed the megalomania of the inspector [in the prison, or of the sociologist] or the paranoia of the inspected, but what they see, they see it well' (Latour 2005:181). Indeed, this volume aspires to the ideal of the oligopticon, in order to see things well, rather than assuming pre-existing social structures or hierarchies. Meanwhile, I argue that this does not exclude the need for and utility of attempting to bind things together to an overall narrative – in particular in a study like this which aims to cross-fertilise perspectives - which can point to certain, generalised patterns, as long as these identified patterns are grounded in the myopic tracing of socio-materially constituted and situated relations in the empirical material. In this way, the detected generalised patterns in this volume are still marked by the fragility and power of the many different relations that make up the whole.

References

Ang, Y. Y., 2016, *How China Escaped the Poverty Trap*, Cornell University Press, New York.

Beckert, J., 2016, *Imagined Futures, Fictional Expectations and Capitalist Dynamics*, Harvard University Press, Cambridge, MA.

Breznitz, D. & Murphree, M., 2011, *Run of the Red Queen: Government, Innovation, Globalization, and Economic Growth in China*, Yale University Press, New Haven, CT.

Caliskan, K. & Callon, M., 2009, 'Economization, Part 1: Shifting Attention from the Economy towards Processes of Economization', *Economy and Society* 38(3), 369–398.

Caliskan, K. & Callon, M., 2010, 'Economization, Part 2: a Research Programme for the Study of Markets', *Economy and Society* 39(1), 1–32.

Callon, M. (ed.), 1998, *Laws of the Markets,* Blackwell Publishers/The Sociological Review, Oxford.

Callon, M., 2007, 'An Essay on the Growing Contribution of Economic Markets to the Proliferation of the Social', *Theory, Culture & Society* 24(7–8), 139–163.

Dimitrov, M. (ed.), 2013, *Why Communism Did Not Collapse: Understanding Authoritarian Regime Resilience in Asia and Europe*, Cambridge University Press, New York.

Foucault, M., 1995, *Discipline and Punish: The Birth of the Prison*, Vintage Books, New York.

Granovetter, M. S., 1985, 'Economic Action and Social Structure: The Problem of Embeddedness', *American Journal of Sociology,* 91(3), pp. 481-510.

Granovetter, M. & McGuire, P., 1998, 'The Making of an Industry: Electricity in the United States', in M. Callon (ed.), *Laws of the Markets*, pp. 147–173, Blackwell Publishers/The Sociological Review, Oxford.

Hall, P. A. & Soskice, D. (eds.), 2001, 'An Introduction to Varieties of Capitalism', in Hall, P. A. & Soskice, D. (eds.), *Varieties of Capitalism: The Institutional Foundations of Comparative Advantage*, pp. 1–68, Oxford University Press, Oxford.

Heilmann, S., 2005, 'Regulatory Innovation by Leninist Means: Communist Party Supervision in China's Financial Industry', *The China Quarterly* 181, 1–21.

Heilmann, S., 2008, 'From Local Experiments to National Policy: The Origins of China's Distinctive Policy Process', *The China Journal* 59, 1–30.

Heilmann, S., 2011, 'Policy Making through Experimentation: The Foundation of a Distinctive Policy Process', in S. Heilmann & E. J. Perry (eds.), *Mao's Invisible Hand: The Political Foundations of Adaptive Governance in China*, pp. 62–101, Harvard Contemporary China Series, Harvard University Press, Cambridge, MA.

Heilmann, S., 2016, 'Introduction to China's Core Executive: Leadership Styles, Structures and Processes under Xi Jinping', in S. Heilmann & M. Stepan (eds.), *China's Core Executive Leadership Styles, Structures and Processes under Xi Jinping*, pp. 6–10, MERICS Paper, 1, June, https://www.merics.org/en/merics-analysis/papers-on-china/chinas-core-executive-leadership-styles-structures-and-processes-under-xi-jinping/.

Jasanoff, S. & Kim, S.-H. (ed.), 2015, *Dreamscapes of Modernity, Sociotechnical Imaginaries and the Fabrication of Power*, University of Chicago, Chicago.

Jenle, R. P., 2015, *Engineering Markets for Control: Integrating Wind Power into the Danish Electricity System*, PhD thesis, Department of Organization, Copenhagen Business School.

Jenle, R. P. & Pallesen T., 2017, 'How Engineers Make Markets Organizing System Decarbonization', *Revue Francaise de sociologies*, International Edition 3(58), 375–397.

Jensen, C. B., 2010, *Ontologies for Developing Things: Making Health Care Futures through Technology*, Transdisciplinary Studies 3, Sense Publishers, Rotterdam.

Karnøe, P., 2010, 'Material Disruptions in Electricity Systems: Can Wind Power Fit in the Existing Electricity System?', in M. Akrich, Y. Barthe, F. Muniesa & P. Mustar (eds.), *Débordements: Mélanges Offerts à Michel Callon*, pp. 223–240, Transvalor – Presses de Mines, Paris.

Kirkegaard, J. K., 2015, *Ambiguous Winds of Change – Or Fighting Against Windmills in Chinese Wind Power: Mapping Controversies over a Potential Turn to Quality in Chinese Wind Power*, PhD thesis, Dept. of Business & Politics, Copenhagen Business School

Kirkegaard, J. K., & Caliskan, K., forthcoming, When Socialists Marketize: The Case of Chinese Wind Power Market Experiments. Under peer review in *Journal of Cultural Economy, mimeo.*

Kirkegaard, J. K., Caliskan, K. & Karnøe, P., forthcoming, 'Comparative Marketization: Making Wind Power Investments attractive in Danish democracy, Chinese totalitarianism, and Turkish authoritarianism', presented in earlier versions at Copenhagen Business School, 6–8 July 2017, and at the International Market Studies Workshop, Copenhagen Business School, 6–8 June 2018, to be submitted in *Organization Studies, mimeo.*

Korsnes, M., 2015, *Chinese Renewable Struggles: Innovation, the Arts of the State and Offshore Wind Technology*, PhD thesis, Department of Interdisciplinary Studies of Culture, Norwegian University of Science and Technology (NTNU).

Korsnes, M., 2016, 'Ambition and Ambiguity: Expectations and Imaginaries Developing Offshore Wind in China', *Technological Forecasting and Social Change* 107(June), 50–58.

Latour, B., 2004, 'Why Has Critique Run out of Steam? From Matters of Fact to Matters of Concern', *Critical Inquiry* 30: 225–248.

Latour, B., 2005, *Reassembling the Social: An Introduction to Actor-Network-Theory*, Oxford University Press, New York.

Li, C., 2006, 'The Confucian Ideal of Harmony', *Philosophy East and West* 56(4), 583–603.

Lieberthal, K., 2004, 'The Organization of Political Power and its Consequences: The View from the Outside', in K. Lieberthal (ed.), *Governing China: From Revolution through Reform*, pp. 171–205, 2nd edn., W. W. Norton & Co., New York.

MacKenzie, D., 2003, 'An Equation and its Worlds: Bricolage, Exemplars, Disunity and Performativity in Financial Economics', *Social Studies of Science* 33(6), 831–868.

Martin, R., 2010, 'Rethinking Regional Path Dependence: Beyond Lock-in to Evolution', *The 2009 Roepke Lecture in Economic Geography*, 86(1), pp. 1-27.

Mertha, A., 2009, 'Fragmented Authoritarianism 2.0: Political Pluralization in the Chinese Policy Process', *The China Quarterly,* December, 995–1012.

Mertha, A. & Brødsgaard, K. E., 2017, 'Revisiting Chinese Authoritarianism in China's Central Energy Administration', in K. E. Brødsgaard (ed.), *Chinese Politics as Fragmented Authoritarianism: Earthquakes, Energy and Environment*, pp. 1–14, Routledge, Abingdon.

Mitchell, T. (2002) "The Market's Place" in T. Mitchell, *The Rule of Experts – Egypt, Techno-Politics, Modernity*, pp. 244-271, University of California Press, Berkeley.

Mitchell, T., 2011, *Carbon Democracy: Political Power in the Age of Oil*, Vergo, London.

Oi, J. C. & Goldstein, S. M., 2018, 'Change within continuity – Zouping County Government', pp. 3–27, in J. C. Oi & S. M. Goldstein, *Adaptive Governance in a Chinese County – Zouping Revisited*, Stanford University Press, Stanford, CA.

Polanyi, K., 2001, *The great transformation: The political and economic origins of our time*, 6th ed., Beacon Press, Boston, MA.

Schumpeter, J. A., 1934, *The Theory of Economic Development*, Harvard University Press, Cambridge, MA.

Venturini, T., 2010, 'Diving in Magma: How to Explore Controversies with Actor-Network Theory', *Public Understanding of Science* 19(3), 258–273.

Warner, J., 1976, 'Blake's "Auguries of Innocence"', *Colby Quarterly* 12(3), 126–138.

Zhang, J. & Peck, J., 2014, 'Variegated Capitalism, Chinese Style: Regional Models, Multi-Scalar Constructions', *Regional Studies*, DOI: 10.1080/00343404.2013.856514.

10 Broadening out perspectives and looking ahead

Before ending the research journey, Chapter Ten sheds light on some broader perspectives that the findings from this investigation have indirectly brought to bear on neighbouring literatures, in particular Economic Geography and New Economic Sociology.

Variable ontology and relational ambiguity and volatility in the supply chain

One of the most remarkable things in the case of Chinese wind power development marketisation has been how the identities, roles, and positions of customers and suppliers, and other actors – including for instance wind power itself, the grid, certification bodies, software algorithms, contracts, and IPRs – have revealed themselves as highly unstable, negotiable, and controversial, open to doubt or question (Callon 1991:141). This hybrid and ambiguous nature of agency and actor identity – or the 'variable ontology' (Callon 1991) or even 'multiple ontologies' (Mol 1999) of things – that has been revealed can help shed light on the relational volatility and ambiguity of the supply chain configuration around software tools, which has been depicted in the controversy study. Chinese actors have often strived for a new stepping stone that could lead to catchup as soon as, or even before, they have attained a new position, in order to redefine their role and identity in the supply chain. In this way, they have consistently redeemed and renegotiated their position and their right to upgrade and catch-up, sometimes redefining their attributed role and position as inferior or rejecting their role as excluded from access to core algorithms or international research circles, be it through legal and/or illegal means.

The variable and/or multiple ontology/-ies of actors is thus linked to how the goal of Chinese actors is being constantly redefined as they upgrade, and to the hybrid identity of deeply entwined state–business actors. That is, new goals, visions, and ambitions are constantly being produced, rendering Chinese wind power development marketisation a transformative and simultaneous collision of identities, roles, and (sometimes contradictory) directions. Such inherent role ambiguity has configured the supply chain as dependent on what may be termed paradoxical 'sustained contingent collaborations' rather than stabilised governance relations (Herrigel 2010:24), even in a more extreme form than before detected. In turn, and to repeat from Chapter Nine, this makes it hard, if not impossible, to talk about fixed structures, hierarchies, or path dependence from institutional embeddedness, in the case of Chinese wind power development marketisation, and lays the ground for the need to think of new innovative modes of collaboration and of contracting for innovation (Gilson, Sabel & Scott 2008; Helper, MacDuffie & Sabel 2000).

Upgrading through disruptive learning

The uncovering of fragile supply chain relations to some extent, and indirectly, sheds a new light on how China upgrades its capabilities through what may be termed disruptive learning in the global value chain for wind turbines.[1] That is, rather than upgrading in a linear fashion, China seems to, somewhat paradoxically, have been able to upgrade and upscale with unprecedented pace – and in some non-core technologies even catchup - through and in spite of taking development to the brink of tipping over into disruption. By upgrading at the brink of collapse, Chinese market actors have been forced to find creative and agile solutions, moving from being mere assembly companies to becoming manufacturers with an enhanced reputation, capable of more indigenous innovation. Examples of this are Envision and Goldwind. And so, by linking up with foreign actors and spurred on by sometimes radical government interventions (or radical lack thereof) – illustrating a radical ability for self-correction – China has mustered an imminent turn to quality through scientification and technification, which has allowed the country's emerging assemblage around wind power development to accelerate its move from 'upscaling by downgrading' towards 'upgrading by quality'.

Chinese upgrading as a matter of valuation in (dis)associational moves

By illustrating China's contested and negotiated move from upscaling by downgrading towards upgrading by quality, this study simultaneously opens up the issue of upgrading as a matter of valuation processes that work to qualify (frame) Chinese manufacturing products, such as wind turbines, through the socio-material production of associations (e.g. of quality, relations, scientific development, sustainability).

On the one hand, China has engaged in the requalification of wind power as sustainable through (partial) disassociation of wind power from poor quality, low prices, downgrading, and low tech. On the other hand, Chinese actors are also engaging in multiple associational moves, as they associate themselves with science, patents, IPRs, indigenous standards, and quality, in order to tap into global networks for research and innovation, or GINs (e.g. Ernst 2006; Silva & Klagge 2013), in associational '*guānxì*-like' moves.

By enquiring into these valuation processes, this research indirectly renders an account of some of the socio-technical processes and struggles of 'GIN*ing*', that is, the qualification processes to associate/frame Chinese wind power and Chinese actors as reliable and valuable collaboration partners to become associated with global research and innovation networks around proprietary core technologies. The book therefore provides a lens through which we can trace parts of the arduous socio-material work that the processes of building relations around core technologies between Chinese and foreign companies, certification bodies, and research institutions entails, and which with time may result in the emergence of 'GINs'. Meanwhile, by disassembling the wind turbine, and tracing the process of building and forging relations around core algorithms, the book indicates some of the existing socio-technical exclusion mechanisms and barriers to GIN integration and formation, and to industrial upgrading in the GVC, around the wind turbine's core technologies. That is, the analysis has showed how core algorithms tend to have (partially) resisted mobilisation into emerging GINs. It also displays how certain actors at times may be excluded from research collaborations owing to a lack of associations with algorithmic quality of Chinese wind power technology and science. In this way, future research should enquire further into the potential socio-material barriers to the strategy of LLL (Mathews 2002). Meanwhile, rather than arguing that these socio-technical barriers are insurmountable or permanent, this study argues that research should look into how such (temporary) barriers are socio-materially construed, how they are contested, and how they may be overcome. Indeed, the argument of this book is that China by and large has mustered the ability to upgrade, despite such temporary hindrances, through contestation, negotiation, associational moves, and consistent experimentation, this resulting in a bumpy trajectory of upgrading through 'disruptive learning'. At the same time, it illustrates how there are still limits to catch up in core technologies such as software algorithms in control systems and simulation tools, as there are socio-material boundaries to leap-frogging strategies such as copy-catting and reverse engineering, since core software technologies demand long-term investment in basic research.

The relational, processual, and lateral lens provided in this book is fundamentally different from the spatial lens of GINs (and the structural and hierarchical lens of GVCs) within Economic Geography, however, which tends to offer a somewhat externalised perspective at the meso-level, at the risk of overlooking the particular, and especially running the risk of overlooking the very process of relationship building ("the relational") that lies at the basis of emergent structures and constitutes the fabric of institutionalised hierarchies. That is, this study "looks away" from the structures, instead diving deeper, looking into the quality and shifting content of their underlying relations by disassembling the wind turbine into its component parts, rather than staying at the aggregate industry level, and treating the wind turbine as a black-boxed entity. By digging into and focusing on specific (core) components of the value chain, it has become possible to trace how socio-material relations around proprietary software algorithms in the GVC are forged and transformed, and to map struggles over attempts to integrate these into emerging GINs. And so, by zooming in on the meaty nature of these relations, their quality and flows of knowledge, actors, and how they are effects of framing struggles, it is indicated how core technologies such as software algorithms still tend to remain part of the GVC, being traded in customer-supplier relationships where the limits to knowledge transfer and co-creation are determined by foreign companies, and that still imminent processes of 'GINing' are inherently controversial. That is, while other less core components may readily have been 'GINed', and with less controversy, the book's more fine-grained account of processes of 'GINing' around specific (core) components reveals how these tend to stay in the value chain.

Contesting 'quality by algorithm'

While depicting upgrading as a matter of valuation processes, struggles over quality conventions have also been revealed. The book's enquiry into processes of wind power qualification has led to an examination of how an algorithmic understanding of quality has been promoted through standardisation and certification processes globally, and in Chinese wind power development marketisation in particular, as well as into how such a confined understanding of quality is being negotiated in Chinese marketisation. In this way, the study is related to studies that look at value chain governance as a matter of 'normalisation' (in Gibbon, Bair & Ponte 2008; Ponte 2009) and 'governmentality' (Gibbon & Ponte 2008): Through this lens, the construction of quality norms and conventions through standards is seen as a matter for value chain governance, steering, and power exertion. Meanwhile, even though these lenses (and the related field of 'economies of worth' (Boltanski & Thévenot 2006; Stark 2009; Thévenot 2009) acknowledge that quality standards produce a certain power dynamic'[2] and that there is an inherent politics to the measuring instruments employed for standardisation (Gibbon & Ponte 2008; Ponte 2009:241; Ponte & Cheyns 2013:461), this work extends these by illustrating how the fight over such quality conventions are not just socially constructed, but also inherently socio-materially constituted. That is, they involve non-human actors such as algorithms, aeroelastic codes, and simulation tools. In the analysis, it has been shown how certification and standardisation bodies, as well as powerful wind turbine manufacturers, design houses, and research institutions, have used standards as a means of excluding Chinese manufacturers who wish to enter the global market and want to become part of the emerging (in)formal global innovation and research network around optimised aeroelastic codes. In this way, this research contributes by capturing some of the micro-foundational and socio-technical contestations over such quality work (or work of qualification) through standardisation.

As Chinese wind turbine manufacturers have gradually learned from foreign customer–supplier relationships and upgraded capabilities, Chinese customers have started to contest the standards, for example by revolting against the internationally set standards: Chinese actors increasingly aim at setting international industrial standards themselves, and developing their own indigenous turbine designs and Chinesified standards – in what Korsnes (2015) would call engaging in 'Chinesification' – to gain more power in the value chain, and to even define and lead it. Overall, this indicates an ongoing power struggle for moving up the value chain, and for deeper and stronger integration into and control of GINs and GVCs.

What is more, the Anthropology of Markets lens has made it possible to trace the unfolding power struggles around aeroelastic codes, as well as around the very right to define quality as algorithmic. This is seen, for instance, in how Chinese human and non-human actors have objected to purely scientific and algorithmic understandings of quality as grounded in the certification triangle. For example, algorithms in simulation tools have not revealed themselves easily, at the same time as Chinese actors have sometimes objected to the purely algorithmic and scientific notion of quality, by proposing a more relational mode of valuing quality. This struggle over modes of valuing quality reveals an underlying struggle over colliding practices of innovation and science at the corporate level, namely of the classically 'Western' mode of certified and accredited test cases, documented evidence, theorisation and simulation, external validation, and of continuous optimisation of software algorithms to reduce risk and uncertainty, versus a Chinese experimental and more risk-prone mode of innovation. Meanwhile, there are indications that these colliding innovation practices are increasingly converging: as Western companies and research institutions increasingly realise that the ever more important role of simulations, certification, testing, and algorithmic refinement may ultimately end with the stifling of innovation, if taken to an extreme, some of them have started to look for ways in which to accelerate their mode of innovation. This entails for instance a look to China's 'launch, test, improve' model, in the consideration of a modified and less risk-prone model of 'discovery, incubation, and acceleration', which can serve to accelerate the traditionally Western risk-averse innovation model of 'improving, testing, launching' (O'Connor 2006; interviews). Conversely, as the qualification struggle continues to unfold in the marketisation of Chinese wind power development, and as some of the inherent socio-material boundaries to China's 'copy-catting' strategy and focus on utilitarian applied science over basic research have started to reveal themselves, Chinese companies may come to the realisation for the need of a less risk-prone innovation strategy than the 'launch-test-improve'-model, which has produced accelerated development but at high costs. Indeed, Chinese actors may be realising that an extension of the corporate-level 'launch-test-improve' model to the industrial level – enabled by a national-level growth model not driven by risk-aversity – has proven too wasteful, costly, and unsustainable in the long run. Reflecting a (potential) reshuffling of conventional modes of understanding learning as driven by 'exploration' or 'exploitation' (March 1991), the seeming convergence and reorganising of innovation modes illustrates an ongoing negotiation of the 'right balance' of risk-taking in innovation processes both at corporate and industry levels.

As a struggle over the very framing of what constitutes quality and over 'quality by algorithm' as imposed by Western companies and institutions unfolds, even the very framing tools applied have become contested. This reflects how valuation processes are often involving attempts by relatively more powerful actors 'to impose their valuations on others and consequently to impact strongly on the distribution of value' (Caliskan & Callon 2010:13, drawing on Bourdieu 2005 and Fligstein 2001). Indeed, whilst framing devices such as standards and certificates, as well as simulation algorithms, are supposed to pacify and stabilise a framing, they have rather in the case of Chinese wind power development marketisation tended to produce more overflowing and ambiguity. This is reflected in the ongoing qualification struggle where unsettled negotiations of the framing of the wind makes the very identity (ontology) of wind – and its generated power – variable and multiple (Blok 2013; Mol 1999). That is, we are witnessing the ontological politics of wind power, and the resulting many worths of wind power(s) in the specific site of China (mimicking Blok's (2013) notion of "many worths of nature(s)" (Blok, 2013: 3, 16). In this site, wind power has in many instances been framed through calculative devices such as algorithms, that is, what we may term 'quality by algorithm', yet, at least as many times, algorithms have objected to this qualification.

Opaque calculations of transaction costs in the coordination of governance relations

Industrial upgrading, in turn, has in the Economic Geography literature generally been treated as contingent on the specific type of governance mode of the GVC (or 'global commodity chain') (Gereffi 1994, 1999, 2005; Humphrey & Schmitz 2002; Morrison, Pietrobelli & Rabellotti 2008; Schmitz 2004:6). That is, prospects for local enterprises to upgrade are dependent on the type of GVC that they are tied into (Schmitz 2004:1), be they for instance hierarchical, captive, modular, relational, or market-based (Gereffi, Humphrey & Sturgeon 2005). Meanwhile, this volume has indirectly illustrated governance relations in the Chinese wind turbine value chain as anything but stable or predictable. In this way, the present study extends conventional accounts of value chain governance as a matter of dyadic coordination of customer–supplier relations based on a transaction-cost based calculus (Gereffi et al. 2005:82): The high fragility of governance relations – enmeshed in opaque state–business spider's web-like relations – renders a transaction cost-based efficiency rationale[3] relatively opaque, and not necessarily the most fulfilling explanation for value chain governance in China's wind turbine industry. Indeed, a purely economic rationale has often proved the least important factor in the present study, whilst other more relational or political factors have played a much more important role in the choice of customers and suppliers or in the choice to outsource or insource production.

Further, modes of coordinating governance relations in the value chain governance of Chinese and Western manufacturers seem to be, if not reversed, then converging. In the initial phase Chinese wind turbine manufacturers relied heavily on market-based transaction (outsourcing) and modular network governance, to squeeze cost and prices. Yet today they are moving towards more hierarchical coordination (insourcing) or relational coordination to lower long-term cost. That is, the long-term costs of outsourcing even core components has proved too high owing to the compromising of quality and the resulting lack of systemic overview of the wind turbine in-house. Conversely, Western wind turbine manufacturers in China are moving in the opposite direction as they seek to reduce the price level of their wind turbines to be able to compete. They have thus started to experiment more with the outsourcing of non-key components, moving from relational to more modular governance. In this way, Chinese and foreign wind turbine manufacturers have over time converged in terms of their governance mode (Haakonsson & Kirkegaard 2016).

A final reflection, then, on the issue of GVC governance. In this work, the account of governance has been twisted and reversed compared with more conventional accounts. First, value chain theory construes governance relations within a linear chain of dyadic relationships where the institutional context is largely overlooked. Meanwhile, the customer–supplier relation is hardly dyadic in the Chinese context of wind power. Rather – and at least – it is triadic, as the Chinese state will always partake in the transaction in either obvious or invisible ways (as will often unexpected actors such as software algorithms). Second, the power dynamics of the governance relation have been reversed in the present analysis. In value chain theory on governance, the supplier is primarily looked upon as the inferior and dependent party, whilst the buyer (or lead firm) is the one governing the chain. In this study, however, foreign suppliers of control systems, design licenses, or simulation tools, or what may be coined as knowledge-intensive business system (KIBS) providers (Haakonsson, Kirkegaard & Lema forthcoming), have taken the conventionally powerful role owing to their longer experience and higher level of capabilities, while it is the Chinese wind turbine manufacturer that for a long time has proved dependent on foreign supply of high-tech components.

Moving beyond rigid hierarchical accounts of chain constructs

By way of tracing micro-processes of relationship-building and of construing associations, this book has indirectly rendered an account of value chain governance as political, messy, variable, and self-disruptive, through experimental moves of trial and error and network relations. Hence, by looking away from the GIN or GVC construct in the study's analysis, and instead conducting a journey around critical core components, some of the micro-processual and micro-relational aspects of constructing and governing GINs and GVCs have been indirectly revealed. In what may be characterised as variegated and/or disruptive governance, the present controversy-mapping account demonstrates how positions along the chain are not hierarchically fixed, but rather fluid and agile, contested, ambiguous, and unpredictable. As a result, rather than offering an account of the results/outcome in terms of governance and upgrading, after the fact, so to speak, this book seeks to uncover their socio-material micro-foundations and controversies, as a state of *becoming*. Summing up, this book goes further than conventional accounts of upgrading and governance in Economic Geography, as it breaks down structural, hierarchical, path-dependent, and deterministic accounts more than has been seen previously. This has been possible through moving into the wind turbine, disassembling it into some of its constituting components, and tracing relations around seemingly mundane and innocent artefacts. In turn, by tracing the micro-relational, a much broader macro-relational story, not only about Chinese greening but also about Chinese upgrading and governance, and its socio-material grounding, has been revealed, namely as new assemblages sometimes manage to break free and temporarily crystallise, as evidenced in the shift from an assemblage qualified by high growth and quantity to one qualified by consolidation and quality.

Extending the budding conversation between STS and China Studies

Lastly, although the account offered in this work is one that is prone to capture the shifting quality of relations, the book is not a manifest against structural or spatial perspectives. They all have their merit. As Czarniawska (2013) says, there 'is no need to abandon studies of formal organizations, so dominant in contemporary life' (Czarniawska 2013:10). The ambiguous positioning of this book in the space between a relational and structural lens reflects not only the 'theoretical promiscuity' inherent in mapping controversies (Venturini 2010), but also a pragmatic acknowledgement of how different approaches and ways of conceptualising organisation each have their advantages and shortcomings (Czarniawska 2013:13). The point here is that there is potential for fruitful cross-fertilisation between relational and structural perspectives, acknowledging the coexistence of genesis and structure as well as disorder and order (as also argued in the accounts of, e.g., Derrida 1978; Fligstein & McAdam 2011; Stark 2009). This is particularly relevant in a Chinese context of fragmented authoritarianism and of electromagnetic wave fluctuations where things seem fluid and stable at the same time. Indeed, marketisation in Chinese wind power has proved a constant process of solidification and disruptiveness, of institutionalisation and transformation, where everything is 'constantly reformed and built up from scratch: it never ceases to emerge and re-emerge in the course of long and stormy negotiations' (Callon 1998 in Lohmann 2009:503). Accordingly, accounts of Chinese greening should refrain from dichotomous accounts of either structure or agency, control or fragmentation, stabilisation or transformation, or organisation/institution or disruptive processes. The fertile space in the middle between a structural and relational-dynamic perspective derives from the book's embeddedness in the triangular relationship between three main literatures within New Economic Sociology that depicts China's potential greening, as shown in Figure 10.1 – namely the Anthropology of Markets, contemporary China Studies, and Economic Geography, which may be synergistically cross-fertilised.

An ambition arising from this investigation is thus to extend the emerging conversation between China Studies and the Anthropology of Markets to New Economic Sociology (and Institutional Theory) more broadly, in order to benefit from the synergies gained by such cross-fertilisation. The Anthropology of Markets within STS has already made such move, by embedding itself in the broader literature of New Economic Sociology (Caliskan & Callon 2009, 2010). Further there are already traits within China

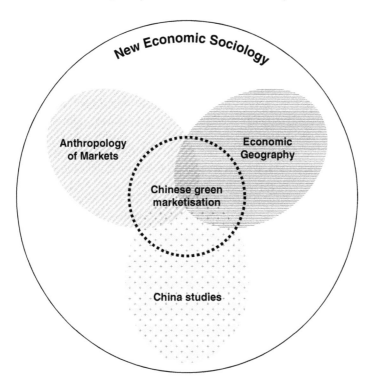

Figure 10.1 Potential cross-fertilisation between perspectives in New Economic Sociology.

Studies (Ang 2016; Gorm Hansen 2017; Heilmann 2010; Kirkegaard 2015, 2016; Korsnes 2015), Economic Geography (Bair 2008; Dicken et al. 2001:93; Grabher 2006), and Industry Studies (Herrigel 2010; Herrigel, Wittke & Voskamp 2013) that indicate what may be coined a potential '(micro-)relational turn', and in some cases even a socio-material turn. At the same time, organisational neo-institutional theory has opened up towards more dynamic and controversial accounts of field emergence and transformation (Fligstein & McAdam 2011), whilst others have opened up towards an STS-lens and its constructivist performativity approach as a potential building block to 'make the microfoundations of institutional theory more explicit' (Powell & Colyvas 2008:276). In New Economic Sociology more broadly, Smith-Doerr & Powell's (2005) network approach calls for '[m]ore process-oriented, case-based approaches [that can] provide rich accounts of why ties are created, how they are maintained, what resources flow across these linkages, and with what consequences' (Smith-Doerr & Powell 2005:394). This request is echoed in recent market studies within New Economic Sociology, which have called for new ways to better capture market genesis, dynamics, and agency to account for the 'first act' of market construction, rather than only accounting for the 'second act' (Powell, Packalen & Whittington 2012: 434). This study offers a response to these calls and openings, namely proposing a lens founded in the Anthropology of Markets within STS.

Keeping epistemological and ontological divides in mind, though, between structural, spatial, and positivist accounts versus relational, lateral, and constructivist accounts, such potential cross-fertilisation and interdisciplinary approach will require innovativeness and the use of analytically pragmatist 'tunnels' (e.g. see Kirkegaard 2015:82–87, and as mentioned in Chapter Three and briefly elaborated here): having hinted at a growing common affinity for 'the relational' (and 'socio-material') in some of the above fields – signifying certain common affinities with the relational and micro-processual lens of American pragmatism (e.g. Dewey 1927; Elias 1978; Whitehead 1978) - one of the main contributions of this study is the indicative and pragmatic proposition of such 'pragmatist tunnel'. That is, while STS has roots in American pragmatism, current streams within China Studies, Economic Geography, and New Economic Sociology also display affinities with the micro-relational and processual lens of American pragmatism. These commonalities may make it possible to dig out an 'underground tunnel' that can serve to bridge and cross-fertilise perspectives. The hope is thus that future studies in the aforementioned fields (and beyond, such as Innovation Studies, International Business, and Sustainable Transition Studies) can use such pragmatist tunnel to bridge and cross-fertilise relational perspectives with certain streams in more structural perspectives. Such cross-fertilisation should help to account better for the simultaneous processes of stabilisation and destabilisation, change and transformation, and of framing and overflowing. Indeed, it is by coupling and extending the perspectives of STS, China Studies, and New Economic Sociology (of which (parts of) Economic Geography form a part) that it has been possible to contribute to and extend not only China Studies and Economic Sociology, but also other fields – potentially even engineering and other practice fields – and STS. That is, whilst the STS lens is based on a modest sociology, this work has had bolder ambitions, including attempts at some degree of generalisation and comparison, by engaging in a broader account of Chinese greening, upgrading, and catch-up through fragmented and experimental marketisation.

Comparisons and future research – on Chinese arts of marketisation mixing bricolage and breakthrough

Taking this bold attempt even further, it is now time to reflect for a final time on the potentially unique mode of Chinese green marketisation. Indeed, it is worthwhile considering carefully if it could be that some of China's other strategic industries have witnessed traits of the same mode of disruptive development and governance, and/or whether other nations have experienced the same type of experimentalism with marketisation.

This is all primarily up to future studies to reveal. However, a few reflections follow below. First, the issue of overcapacity – largely a result of poor and fragmented coordination – has also been witnessed in other Chinese manufacturing industries, with severe issues of environmental degradation and waste resulting (Rock & Toman 2015), as has been described at length in relation to China's investment-driven growth model and stimulus package (Kroeber 2016; Lardy 2016; Naughton 2014). In turn, the politicised and sensitive nature of wind power development marketisation is likely to bear a resemblance to other state-controlled strategic sectors in China, such as renewable energy or high-tech industries. Whether China has engaged in a similar pragmatics of green marketisation, allowing for iterative stages advancing towards the brink of disruption and stalemate, with the same amount of overflowing, in other strategic pillar industries, is however an avenue for future studies. There are indications, though, that in other industries, such as the LED and solar photovoltaic industries, experimentalism has allowed new quite successful growth leaps (e.g. Butollo & ten Brink 2017; Lam, Branstetter & Azavedo 2018). Whilst comparison with the solar photovoltaic industry can only be limited as there are various idiosyncratic differences such as the wind industry's initial concentration on the vast domestic internal market and the solar industry's focus on the global exports market from the outset, it is interesting to reflect on potential implications of different levels of technological complexity, advancement, and computerisation. The rapid industry build-up and export success in solar photovoltaics – although instigating a trade and anti-dumping war with the US – happened without the same amount of quality issues and wasted resources as we have witnessed in wind power. It can thus be argued that the model of experimental marketisation would work better in terms of being less 'wasteful' in less technologically advanced sectors (e.g. solar photovoltaics but particularly in infrastructure projects). Indeed, this reflects how Chinese experimentalism, accelerated by China's invest-ment-model, has been a successful approach in building up and upgrad-ing China's infrastructure, such as the construction of bridges, highways, buildings, grid infrastructures etc., but that this model may reach its limit in more high-tech sectors with thousands of computerised interdependencies, such as in today's modern grid-connected wind turbines and wind farms, which require relatively advanced tools for system integration. We may hereby be witnessing how China's experimental model of marketisation, when expanded to the sectoral level of accelerated industry development and corporate level of risk-prone innovation processes, and when acceler-ated by the Chinese growth model, bears within it a potential Achilles heel that threatens to constitute it as 'too wasteful'. Indeed, wasted resources in China's wind power sector are so dramatic that they raise the question of 'contested failures', that is, the negotiation of whether or not Chinese marketisation of wind power development should be framed as a failure or a success. This negotiation also raises the question of whether the metaphor of a 'turbine wave attack' and the 'Chinese way' is more of an after-ration-alisation promoted by certain actors, or indeed a reflection of actual gov-ernment intent or not. While there is no straight-forward or black-and-white answer, it could be argued that China would benefit from developing a more fine-grained innovation and investment strategy, targeting specific sectors with experimental fragmented development, whilst others are developed in a more gradual, cautious, and small-scale manner, and more in accordance with the original Chinese mode of cautious local experimentation with new market policies before they are rolled out on a national scale. In short, the Chinese model of experimental green marketisation could potentially be less wasteful in some sectors than others.

Along the same lines, whilst marketisation of wind power development in China may seem unique in its degree of pragmatism, fragmentation, and experimentation, there are also specific similarities to other countries. That is, although the Chinese way of experimentation and risk-prone investments is largely regarded as 'impossible in Europe', owing to its constitution largely as a 'very special' 'political project' (interview with Chinese government advi-sor and wind industry association 2013), there are both similarities and differ-ences to the experience of other wind power nations. Indeed, there is no doubt that the Chinese investment-driven growth model has been instrumental to the development of Chinese wind power, but also that such an investment model would never be allowed by commercial risk-averse banks or govern-ments in 'the West', and that the instigation of a 'quality crisis' would most likely have killed not only the entire sector but also delegitimised the demo-cratically elected government behind if set in another context.

This does not preclude experimentalism as part of marketisation in these contexts, however. Take for instance the case of Denmark – a globally renowned wind power pioneer, and a leader both in wind power integration and in the establishment of a wind power electricity market. The early stages of industrial development were marked by a high degree of technological entrepreneurship, local experimentation, and 'resourcefulness and improvisation on the part of involved actors' (Garud & Karnøe 2003:278). The Danish mode of wind turbine industry development has accordingly been argued to be characterised by a path-creating bricolage-like mode of technology entrepreneurship that started out with low-tech design (Garud & Karnøe 2003; Karnøe & Garud 2012), as entrepreneurs muddled forward, creating a new path for wind power into the existing power system. This enabled innovators to dis-embed from existing institutional relevance structures and break free from path dependence, thus engaging in 'path-creation' (Garud & Karnøe 2001). China, in turn, has also engaged in bricolage-like behaviour, such as experimenting with copying and reverse engineering from foreign design licences. Meanwhile, a sense of urgency to catch up has not allowed as much time for gradual learning, cumbersome experience, and basic research, but has instead laid the ground for a strategy of disruptive learning through large-scale trial and error and applied science. At the same time, just as Danish actors had to create a new path for penetration into the grid, creating new relevance for the existing power system and political support system, China's wind power sector has struggled over access to the grid. However, the vested interests of China's state-controlled and heavily coal-based power system, along with the severity of the curtailment issues co-produced by fragmented experimentation, have caused other and sometimes politically more contentious controversies and constraints over wind penetration when compared with the Danish case, even to the extent of threatening a lock-in to fossil fuels.

Therefore, there are both similar and dissimilar traits to the Danish experience. The same is true for the American wind turbine industry, which was founded on an opposite type of strategy, namely a planned high-tech breakthrough, which resulted in the Californian 'wind gold-rush' in the early 1980s (Garud & Karnøe 2003). This was spurred on by market subsidies and tax credits for users and producers, though largely without proper attending to the interplay between wind power deployment and grid expansion or the implications of giving credits only for installed capacity, rather than generated electricity. And so, much as China is now facing curtailment issues, the American wind power sector has also had

> this long discussion, a 'chicken-and-egg discussion': Like – what's coming first? Is it the wind turbines, and then the grid afterwards, or is it instalment of lines to areas of wind and then hoping that someone will install [wind turbines]? (Interview with Chinese think tank 2013)

The American high-tech approach, however, did not lead to long-term success in technology entrepreneurship or gradual sector buildup, as micro-learning processes were stifled (Garud & Karnøe 2003, 2001; interview 2018). It seems, therefore, that China has also borrowed traits of the

Californian wind gold-rush, for instance through its planned approach, incentives for installed capacity, and the (later) Chinese state-led focus on high-tech breakthrough through indigenous innovation and scientific development in core technologies.

What may be unique, then, about Chinese wind power development marketisation is the adoption of a strategy of simultaneous, or oscillating, moves between bricolage and breakthrough, owing to China's fragmented authoritarianism. This is also what has rendered the pace and scale with which China has been able to construct a wind turbine industry and emerging wind power sector unprecedented, whilst also creating unprecedented numbers of controversies and struggles – a contested situation spurred on by enhanced global competitive (algorithmic) pressures. Indeed, China's mode of deploying ambiguous and lofty visions and imaginaries of the country's high-tech future, linked to wind power development, has played a mobilising role in the development of Chinese wind power, leaving ample room for local interpretation in terms of implementation. This has resulted in a Chinese mode of fragmented 'crowdsourcing 2.0' through a 'turbine wave attack', where bottom-up and top-down processes come together to enact the future in distributed bricolage-like path creation at sector level. And so, having 'dived deeper' into the algorithmic universe of the wind turbine, we have got the chance to explore how '[m]arkets have a history; they also have a future that cannot be reduced simply to an extrapolation of the past' (Caliskan & Callon 2010:24).

Rather than representing technological path creation such as in the Danish case, the present study can be argued to present an account of path creation in Chinese wind power development marketisation, or a certain 'arts of marketisation'.[4] Such 'Chinesified' traits of green marketisation in wind power may eventually prove it possible for China to dis-embed from existing relevance structures (Garud & Karnøe 2003), positioning itself as a potential role model for other newly industrialising countries, as it embarks on the long and windy march of its 'sustainability journey' (Garud & Gehman 2012) towards an Energy Revolution (Chung & Xu 2016). Indeed, China may, through experimental breakthrough, be able to engage in innovative manufacturing and greening. For instance, China's international commitment to peak its CO_2 emissions around 2030 already seems a conservative upper limit from a Chinese government that is known to have a preference to underpromise and overdeliver (Green & Stern 2016; Mathews 2016:4).

Meanwhile, marketisation always constitutes a tension; between designing and experimenting, reflecting a certain blend of agnosticism and experimentation (Callon 2009:536) and continuous work. Thus, rather than arguing that experimentation with market design is unusual or unique to China, what we need to understand is how marketisation is done, on the ground, and how it differs from market to sector, from context to context, from technology to technology, and from situation to situation, as well as how it depends on the very socio-material nature of the object of exchange, being co-produced by, and co-producing the specific economic system and mode of energy governance. Future research would benefit from looking further into potential similarities and differences between controversies over the marketisation of wind power development, in developing and developed country settings, and in different political regimes (as argued by Kirkegaard, Caliskan & Karnøe forthcoming). And so, as we descend from the nacelle, past the substantial bearings, our journey takes us out of the wind turbine, where we can, once again, take off the safety hat, stand back, and picture the turbine as a simple and graceful machine. Having traversed the electromagnetic waves of the winds of change in Chinese wind power development marketisation, our algorithmic research journey through the wind turbine has come to an end. Whilst the courage and rationality of this enquiry can only be evaluated by its conclusion, it is also only at the end of the journey through this seemingly precarious strategy of fragmented and pragmatic green marketisation on the brink of collapse that we will be able to determine whether or not China and the Chinese state – having dared greatly – should be credited with the courage and rationality necessary for the journey's completion, having engaged in taming the powers of the wind(s).

Notes

1. Kirkegaard (2017) has dubbed the notion of 'disruptive upgrading', which links up with this line of thought.
2. Opening up the multiple worths of wind power, this book indirectly also relates to the more sociologically and institutionally oriented sociology of worth of French convention theory, which is concerned with how actions are justified and valued through different sociologically and institutionally constructed economies of worth (e.g. Boltanski & Thévenot 2006; Stark 2009; Thévenot 2009). However, convention theory is founded on a social constructivist perspective on the role of economies of worth, which seems to pre-exist and be relatively stable, and as such to some extent bears resemblance to the notion of institutional logics (Friedland & Alford 1991). Thus, although convention theory does acknowledge that potentially contradictory economies of worth may overlap (Stark 2009; Thévenot 2009), this book instead demonstrates the dynamically contested nature of ontologies, worth, and qualities, and how they must be myopically followed as they differ across sites, and how they are being socio-materially constituted.
3. Where there are low transaction costs, relations will be market based, and where transaction costs are high, relations tend instead to be internalised through vertical integration, that is, through corporate hierarchical control (hierarchy) (Gereffi, Humphrey & Sturgeon 2005:83–84). Between these two ideal types of the continuum, that is, between the governance modes of the market and hierarchy, three different network types of governance are identified, namely modular, relational, and captive. In turn, the specific choice of governance mode depends on the level of transaction costs associated with the specific buyer–supplier relations, which in turn relies on the level of supplier competencies, knowledge codification, and transaction complexity (Gereffi et al. 2005:83–84).
4. Paraphrasing the notion of 'the art of interessement' in innovation processes (Akrich, Callon & Latour 2002).

References

Ang, Y. Y., 2016, *How China Escaped the Poverty Trap*, Cornell University Press, New York.

Bair, J., 2008, 'Analysing Economic Organization: Embedded Networks and Global Chains Compared', *Economy and Society* 37(3), 339–364, Special Issue: Governing Global Value Chains.

Blok, A., 2013, 'Pragmatic sociology as political ecology: On the many worths of nature(s)', *European Journal of Social Theory*.

Boltanski, L. & Thévenot, L., 2006, *On Justification: Economies of Worth*, transl. C. Porter, Princeton University Press, Princeton, NJ.

Bourdieu, P., 2005, *The Social Structure of the Economy*, Polity Press, Cambridge.

Butollo, F. & ten Brink, T., 2017, 'A Great Leap? Domestic Market Growth and Local State Support in the Upgrading of China's LED Lighting Industry', *Global Networks* 18(2), 285–306, https://doi.org/10.1111/glob.12160.

Caliskan, K. & Callon, M., 2010, 'Economization, Part 2: A Research Programme for the Study of Markets', *Economy and Society* 39(1), 1–32.

Callon, M., 1991, 'Techno-Economic Networks and Irreversibility', in J. Law (ed.): *A Sociology of Monsters: Essays on Power, Technology and Domination*, pp. 132–161, Routledge, London.

Callon, M., 2009, 'Civilizing Markets: Carbon Trading between *In Vitro* and *In Vivo* Experiments', *Accounting, Organizations and Society* 34(3–4), 535–548.

Chung, S-w. W., & Xu, Q., 2016, *China's Energy Policy from National and International Perspectives – The Energy Revolution and One Belt One Road Initiative*, City University of Hong Kong Press, Hong Kong.

Czarniawska, B., 2013, 'On Meshworks and other Complications of Portraying Contemporary Organizing', *Managing Overflow*, Gothenburg Research Institute, GRI-report, 2013(3), http://hdl.handle.net/2077/34252.

Derrida, J., 1978, '"Genesis and Structure" and "Phenomenology"', in J. Derrida (ed.), *Writing and Difference*, pp. 154–168, Chicago: Chicago University Press.

Dewey, J., 1927, *The Public and its Problems*, Holt, Oxford.

Dicken, P., Kelly, P. F., Olds, K. & Yeung, H. W-C., 2001, 'Chains and Networks, Territories and Scales: Towards a Relational Framework for Analysing the Global Economy', *Global Networks* 1(2), 89–112.

Elias, N., 1978, *What is Sociology?*, Columbia University Press, New York.

Ernst, D., 2006, 'Innovation Offshoring: Asia's Emerging Role in Global Innovation Networks', East-West Center Special Reports: 10.

Fligstein, N., 2001, *The Architecture of Markets: An Economic Sociology of Twenty-First Century Capitalist Societies*, Princeton University Press, Princeton, NJ.

Fligstein, N. & McAdam, D., 2011, 'Toward a General Theory of Strategic Action Fields', *Sociological Theory* 29(1), 1–26.

Friedland, R. & Alford, R. R., 1991, 'Bringing Society Back in: Symbols, Practices, and Institutional Contradictions', in W. W. Powell & P. J. DiMaggio (eds.), *The New Institutionalism in Organizational Analysis*, pp. 232–263, University of Chicago Press, Chicago.

Garud, R. & Gehman, J., 2012, 'Metatheoretical Perspectives on Sustainability Journeys: Evolutionary, Relational and Durational', *Research Policy* 41, 980–995.

Garud, R. B. & Karnøe, P., 2001, 'Path Creation as a Process of Mindful Deviation', in R. Garud & P. Karnøe, *Path Dependence and Creation, Lawrence* Erlbaum Associates, Mahwah, NJ.

Garud, R. B. & Karnøe, P., 2003, 'Bricolage versus Breakthrough: Distributed and Embedded Agency in Technology Entrepreneurship', *Research Policy* 32, 277–300.

Gereffi, G., 1994, 'The Organization of Buyer-Driven Global Commodity Chains: How US Retailers Shape Overseas Production Networks', in G. Gereffi & M. Korzeniewicz (eds.), *Commodity Chains and Global Capitalism*, pp. 95–122, Greenwood Press, Westport, CT.

Gereffi, G., 1999, 'International Trade and Industrial Upgrading in the Apparel Commodity Chain', *Journal of International Economics* 48(1), 37–70.

Gereffi, G., 2005, 'The Global Economy: Organization, Governance, and Development', in N. Smelser & R. Swedberg (eds.), *The Handbook of Economic Sociology*, Princeton University Press, Princeton, NJ.

Gereffi, G., Humphrey, J. & Sturgeon, T., 2005, 'The governance of global value chains', *Review of International Political Economy* 12(1), 78–104.

Gibbon, P., Bair, J. & Ponte, S., 2008, 'Governing Global Value Chains: An Introduction', *Economy and Society* 37(3), 315–338.

Gibbon, P. & Ponte, S., 2008, 'Global Value Chains: From Governance to Governmentality?', *Economy & Society* 37(3), 365–392.

Gilson, R. J., Sabel, C. F. & Scott, R., 2008, 'Contracting for Innovation: Vertical Disintegration and Interfirm Collaboration', ECGI, Law Working Paper 2008(118).

Gorm Hansen, L. L., 2017, *Triggering Earthquakes in Science, Politics and Chinese Hydropower. A Controversy Study*, PhD thesis, Dept. of International Economics and Management, Asia Studies Centre, Copenhagen Business School.

Grabher, G., 2006, 'Trading Routes, Bypasses, and Risky Intersections: Mapping the Travels of "Networks" between Economic Sociology and Economic Geography', *Progress in Human Geography* 30(2), 163–189.

Green, F. & Stern, N., 2016, 'China's Changing Economy: Implications for its Carbon Dioxide Emissions', *Climate Policy* 17(4), 423–442.

Haakonsson, S., Kirkegaard, J. K., & Lema, R. forthcoming, 'China's catch-up in wind power – a case study on decomposition of innovation', Sino-Danish Center for Education and Research, mimeo.

Heilmann, S., 2010, 'Economic Governance: Authoritarian Upgrading and Innovative Potential', in J. Fewsmith (ed.), *China Today, China Tomorrow. Domestic Politics, Economy, and Society*, pp. 109–128, Rowman & Littlefield Publishers, Plymouth.

Helper, S., MacDuffie, J. P. & Sabel, C., 2000, 'Pragmatic Collaborations: Advancing Knowledge while Controlling Opportunism', *Industrial and Corporate Change*, 9(2).

Herrigel, G., 2010, *Manufacturing Possibilities: Creative Action and Industrial Recomposition in the United States, Germany, and Japan*, Oxford University Press, Oxford.

Herrigel, G., Wittke, W. & Voskamp, U., 2013, 'The Process of Chinese Manufacturing Upgrading: Transforming from Unilateral to Recursive Mutual Learning Relations', *Global Strategy Journal* 3, 109–125.

Humphrey, J. & Schmitz, H., 2002, 'How Does Insertion in Global Value Chains Affect Upgrading in Industrial Clusters?', *Regional Studies* 36(9), 1017–1027.

Haakonsson, S. & Kirkegaard, J. K., 2016, 'Configuration of Technology Networks in the Wind Turbine Industry. A Comparative Study of Technology Management Models in European and Chinese Lead Firms', *International Journal of Technology Management*, 70(4), 281–299.

Karnøe, P. & Garud, R. B., 2012, 'Path Creation: Co-creation of Heterogeneous Resources in the Emergence of the Danish Wind Turbine Cluster', *European Planning Studies* 20(5), 733–752.

Kirkegaard, J. K., 2015, *Ambiguous Winds of Change – Or Fighting against Windmills in Chinese Wind Power: Mapping Controversies over a Potential Turn to Quality in Chinese Wind Power*, PhD thesis, Department of Business & Politics, Copenhagen Business School.

Kirkegaard, J. K., 2016, 'China's Experimental Pragmatics of "Scientific Development" in Wind Power: Algorithmic Struggles Over Software in Wind Turbines', *Copenhagen Journal of Asian Studies* 34(1), 5–24.

Kirkegaard, J. K., Caliskan, K. & Karnøe, P., forthcoming, Comparative Marketization: Making Wind Power Investments attractive in Danish democracy, Chinese totalitarianism, and Turkish authoritarianism, presented in earlier versions at Copenhagen Business School, 6–8 July 2017, and at the International Market Studies Workshop, Copenhagen Business School, 6–8 June 2018, to be submitted in *Organization Studies*, mimeo.

Korsnes, M., 2015, *Chinese Renewable struggles: Innovation, the Arts of the State and Offshore Wind Technology*, PhD thesis, Department of Interdisciplinary Studies of Culture, Norwegian University of Science and Technology (NTNU).

Kroeber, A. R., 2016, *China's Economy – What Everyone Needs to Know*, Oxford University Press, New York, NY.

Lam, L. T., Branstetter, L. & Azavedo, I. L., 2018, 'A Sunny Future: Expert Elicitation of China's Solar Photovoltaic Technologies', *Environmental Research Letters* 13, 1–10.

Lardy, N. R., 2016, 'The Changing Role of the Private Sector in China', Conference Volume.

Lohmann, L., 2009, 'Toward a Different Debate in Environmental Accounting: The Cases of Carbon and Cost-Benefit', *Accounting, Organizations and Society* 34, 499–534.

March, J. G., 1991, 'Exploration and Exploitation in Organizational Learning', *Organization Science* 2(1), 71–87.

Mathews, J. A., 2002, 'Competitive Advantages of the Latecomer Firm: A Resource-Based Account of Industrial Catchup Strategies', *Asia Pacific Journal of Management* 19, 467–488.

Mathews, J. A., 2016, 'China's Continuing Renewable Energy Revolution – Latest Trends in Electric Power Generation', *The Asia-Pacific Journal, Japan Focus* 14(17).

Mol, A., 1999, 'Ontological Politics. A Word and Some Questions', in J. Law & J. Hassard (eds.), *Actor Network Theory and After*, pp. 74–88, Blackwell, Oxford.

Morrison, A., Pietrobelli, C. & Rabellotti, R., 2008, 'Global Value Chains and Technological Capabilities: A Framework to Study Learning and Innovation in Developing Countries', *Oxford Development Studies* 36(1), 39–58.

Naughton, B., 2014, 'China's Economy: Complacency, Crisis & the Challenge of Reform', *Dædalus, the Journal of the American Academy of Arts & Sciences* 143(2), 14-25.

O'Connor, G. C., 2006, 'Open, Radical Innovation: Toward an Integrated Model in Large Established Firms', in H. Chesbrough, W. Vanhaverbeke & J. West (eds.), *Open Innovation. Researching a New Paradigm*, Oxford University Press, New York.

Ponte, S. & Cheyns, E., 2013, 'Voluntary Standards, Expert Knowledge and the Governance of Sustainability Networks', *Global Networks* 13(4), 459–477.

Powell, W. W., Packalen K. E. & Whittington, K. B., 2012, 'Organizational and Institutional Genesis: The Emergence of High-Tech Clusters in the Life Sciences', in J. Padgett & W. W. Powell (eds.), *The Emergence of Organizations and Markets*, pp. 434–465, Princeton University Press, Princeton, NJ.

Ponte, S., 2009, 'Governing through Quality: Conventions and Supply Relations in the Value Chain for South African Wine', *European Society for Rural Sociology, Sociologia Ruralis* 49(3).

Powell, W. W. & Colyvas, J. A., 2008, 'Microfoundations of Institutional theory', in R. Greenwood, C. Oliver, K. Sahlin & R. Suddaby (ed.), *The SAGE Handbook of Organizational Institutionalism*, pp. 276–298, SAGE, London.

Rock, M. T. & Toman, M. A. 2015, *China's Technological Catch-Up Strategy: Industrial Development, Energy Efficiency, and CO_2 Emissions*, Oxford University Press, New York.

Schmitz, H. (2004): *Local Upgrading in Global Chains: Recent Findings*. DRUID Summer Conference 2004, Denmark.

Smith-Doerr, L. & Powell, W. W., 2005, 'Networks and Economic Life', in N. Smelser & R. Swedberg (eds.), *The Handbook of Economic Sociology*, pp. 379–402, 2nd edn., Russell Sage Foundation and Princeton University Press, co-publishers, Princeton, NJ.

Silva, P. C. & Klagge, B., 2013, 'The Evolution of the Wind Industry and the Rise of Chinese Firms: From Industrial Policies to Global Innovation Networks', *European Planning Studies* 21(9), 1341–1356.

Stark, D., 2009, *The Sense of Dissonance. Accounts of Worth in Economic Life*, Princeton University Press, Princeton.

Thévenot, L., 2009, 'Governing Life by Standards: A View from Engagements. Postscript to the Special Issue', *Social Studies of Science* 39(5), 793–813.

Venturini, T., 2010, 'Diving in Magma: How to Explore Controversies with Actor-Network Theory', *Public Understanding of Science* 19(3), 258–273.

Whitehead, A. N., 1978, *Process and Reality*, Free Press, New York.

Appendices

Appendix I   Data overview

Table I Overview of collected data

Data source	Type of data	Usage in the analysis

Archival data	Company-related documents:
	  – Company presentations
	  – Product catalogues
	Policy documents and plans:
	  – Renewable energies
	  – Wind power
	  – Innovation
	  – Statistical websites and
	    yearbooks
	Pictures and drawings:
	  – Wind turbines
	  – Control system
	    technologies
	  – Grid system
		General background on
		  companies and their products
		Familiarise with issues and new
		  actors and entities
		Familiarise with political
		  strategies and plans
		Keep record and produce a map
		  of the development of new
		  discourses and instruments in
		  policies and plans
		Familiarise with control systems
		  and their function in the wind
		  turbine
		Support and integrate with
		  interview data

Observations and field diary	Field notes from interviews
	Field notes from visits to wind
	  farm, test and certification sites
	Field notes from conferences
	Field diary
	Participation in and
	  observations at three industry
	  conferences (China 2012,
	  Denmark 2012, Germany 2012)
	Participation in and observations
	  at one academic seminar on
	  materials for wind energy
	  application (China 2011)
	One industrial workshop for State
	  Grid and Asian countries on
	  grid integration (Asian
	  Development Bank, China 2013)
	Informal conversations and
	  notes with interviewees, e.g. at
	  conferences and workshops
	Arranging workshop with
	  researchers on wind power in
	  China, 2012
		Support reconstruction
		Support and integrate with
		  findings from interviews
		Use as basis for further
		  investigation in formal
		  interviews and in archival data
		Support and integrate with
		  analytical findings from
		  interviews

(Continued)

Table I (continued)

Data source	Type of data	Usage in the analysis
Interviews	108 interviews (and conference/workshop proceedings) in total, representing 60 different organisations: — companies (wind turbine manufacturers, component suppliers related to wind power, control system suppliers, design companies, service companies, companies related to renewable energies, component suppliers' meeting) — research institutions and universities; — Ministries; — think tanks; — different interest organisations/industry associations; — certification bodies; — test laboratories; — Banks; — Development programs; — multinational finance institution; — grid companies (and research institutions within it); — Power generating companies	Familiarise oneself with issues and new actors and entities Support reconstruction Keep record of new controversies, issues, actors, and entities Use for further investigation in the following interviews Detect and map relations between actors Map network configurations and their dynamic changes over time Map controversies and issues and their changes over time

Appendix II   Data coding

In order to identify relevant, recurring actors, themes, issues, matters of concern, controversies, and so on, in order to enable a narrative storyline, intensive data coding has been conducted both during data collection as well as during breaks between field trips and during and after writing sessions. With some resemblance to coding processes characteristic of the method of grounded theory, engaging in a constant comparison between data and theory (Glaser & Strauss 1967), rather than being interested in general theory making and dividing data into first and second order codes, the data has been coded along themes and sub-themes. This thematic coding enabled the progressive work on categorisation and grouping together of themes, identifying potential storylines in the process of controversy mapping. The resulting coding documents worked as a basis for preparing interview guides for later field trips, as I tried to gradually fill in some of the holes in the data material, and to verify some of the statements in the data from various sources, as a matter of triangulation (Erzberger & Prein 1997). Later, the thematic coding was repeated several times, to sharpen the story line. Table II renders examples of some of the codes used for developing the story line.

Table II Thematic controversies

Thematic controversies ('2nd order codes')	Thematic issues (subcategories) ('1st order codes')
I: Controversy over 'qualification struggle'	– Issue of poor and fragmented planning – Phases of development – Stages at the brink of impasse – Quality crisis and turn to quality – Contestation over Chinese experimentalism – Legitimacy crisis in Chinese wind power development – Experimental policy-making in China – Contested Chinese pragmatics of experimental, fragmented market construction – Chinese exploration in a 'Big Laboratory' – bad planning or adaptive governance?
II: Controversy over access to power grid	– Struggle for allowing wind power on to the grid – Resistance from wind park owners and utilities – Curtailment delegitimising wind power – Issue of fluctuating wind due to poor quality wind turbines, weak grid, and powerful coal-fired power plants – Issue of poor and fragmented planning and implementation – Issue of political resistance and vested interests against wind power – Power of calculative tools (e.g. support levels, cost and price calculations) – Power struggles with conventional power sources – Controversy over potential socio-material lock-in to fossil fuels
III: Controversy over money and China's system problem	– Issue of politicised market conditions in state-controlled power sector – Consolidation and liquidity constraints – Contested growth model underlying overcapacity issues – Managing the Chinese spider's web of 'common pockets' – Issue of interlinked state-owned companies and corruption – Issue of emerging 'agents' – Quality as personal relations (guanxi) – Destabilised network relations – Issue of dealing with the headquarter for Danish control system suppliers – Issue of (lacking) trust and respect – A skewed market and how to survive as foreign wind turbine manufacturer in China – Controversy over 'system problem' of lacking 'pure market economy'

Table II (continued)

Thematic controversies ('2nd order codes')	Thematic issues (subcategories) ('1st order codes')
IV: Controversy over intellectual property	− Qualifying control system software as 'core' − Collaborations configuring around control system technologies and algorithms − Dilemma between sharing and protecting algorithms − Negotiated access to core algorithms, negotiated boundaries of 'coreness' − Relating core algorithms to issues of quality problems in the industry − Cases of IPR infringement − Issue of (potential socio-material barriers to) upgrading and catchup through leapfrogging − Issue of (in)dependence from foreign technologies and technology transfer
V: Controversy over standardisation and certification	− Difficulties of obtaining international certification of Chinese wind turbines − Indigenous standards − Certification requirements and industry standards − Issue of the right to define quality, construing quality through tools of certificates and standards − Issue of price versus quality − Applied science versus basic research − Emergence of Chinese certification system − Issue of Indigenous Innovation − Potential socio-material limits to upgrading − Contested quality/qualities (negotiating 'quality by algorithm')

References

Erzberger, C. & Prein, G., 1997, 'Triangulation: Validity and Empirically Based Hypothesis Construction', *Quality & Quantity* 31(2), 141–154.

Glaser, B. G. & Strauss, A. L., 1967, *The discovery of grounded theory: strategies for qualitative research*, Aldine, Chicago.

Appendix III Interview overview

Table III List of conducted interviews (anonymised) (chronologised order)

Number	Organisation / type	Date of interview	Place of interview	Interviewee / Position
1	Foreign wind industry association1	Oct. 2010	Denmark	Consultant on China issues
2	Chinese wind turbine manufacturer (WTM) / WTM1	Sep. 2011	China	Chief Strategist, Strategy
3	Chinese research institute1	Sep. 2011	China	Senior Consultant
4	Chinese WTM2	Sep. 2011	China	Vice President; Director
5	Chinese research institute2/ministry	Sep. 2011	China	Professor(s)
6	Foreign WTM1	Sep. 2011	China	Policy Advisor, Government relations; System Engineer, Pitch and Yaw Systems, Technology R&D); IPR
7	Chinese wind industry association1	Sep. 2011	China	Vice Secretary General (main respondent)
8	Chinese WTM3	Mar. 2012	Denmark	Chief engineer
9	Chinese WTM4	Mar. 2012	Denmark	Innovation Manager
10	Foreign wind industry association2	Jun. 2012	Denmark	Vice Director
11	Foreign wind industry association3	Jun. 2012	Denmark	Chief consultant
12	Foreign ministry of science and innovation	Jun. 2012	Denmark	Deputy Director General
13	Foreign WTM1	Jun. 2012	Denmark	Director, Policy Advisor, Group Government Relations
14	Chinese wind turbine (WT) component supplier1	Jun. 2012	China	Senior Manager
15	Chinese WT component supplier2	Jun. 2012	China	Manager
16	Chinese WT component supplier3	Jun. 2012	China	Senior Manager

Table III (*continued*)

Number	Organisation / type	Date of interview	Place of interview	Interviewee / Position
17	Chinese manufacturer3 (other industry)	Jul. 2012	China	Vice-General Manager
18	Chinese WT component supplier4	Jul. 2012	China	Senior Manager
19	Foreign Energy Agency	Jul. 2012	Denmark	Programme manager; programme manager
20	Chinese manufacturer1 (other industry)	Jul. 2012	China	General Manager Assistant
21	Chinese manufacturer2 (other industry)	Jul. 2012	China	General manager
22	Chinese manufacturer4 (other industry)	Jul. 2012	China	CEO
23	Chinese manufacturer5 (other industry)	Aug. 2012	China	CEO; HR Director
24	Chinese manufacturer6 (other industry)	Aug. 2012	China	General Manager; International Sales Section Chief; International Sales Manager
25	Foreign control system supplier1	Sep. 2012	China	General manager
26	Chinese WTM3	Sep. 2012	Germany	Vice president, CEO
27	Development program for Renewable Energy	Sep. 2012	China	Research Associate
28	Chinese research institute2/ministry	Sep. 2012	China	Researchers, business managers
29	Chinese agent/broker	Sep. 2012	China	Agent
30	Chinese WTM4	Sep. 2012	China	R&D Director, Blade and Innovation
31	Foreign control system supplier2	Sep. 2012	China	Director; Department Manager, App. Support and Development Department
32	Foreign and Chinese research institutes and universities	Sep. 2012	China	Scientists, researchers, business people
33	Foreign Innovation Center	Sep. 2012	China	Investment Manager
34	Foreign embassy in China	Sep. 2012	China	Diplomat
35	Foreign embassy in China	Sep. 2012	China	B2B & development program
36	Foreign embassy in China	Oct. 2012	China	Embassy secretary
37	Foreign control system supplier2	Oct. 2012	China	Director; Relations manager

(*Continued*)

Table III (continued)

Number	Organisation / type	Date of interview	Place of interview	Interviewee / Position
38	Chinese WTM4	Oct. 2012	China	International Business Manager
39	Chinese WTM4	Nov. 2012	China	Investment/software engineer
40	Foreign control system supplier3	Nov. 2012	China	Sales manager
41	Chinese WT component supplier1	Nov. 2012	China	Commodity & Project Manager
42	Foreign control system supplier4	Nov. 2012	China	Sales Manager
43	Chinese WTM4	Nov. 2012	China	R&D Director, Blade and Innovation
44	Chinese WT component supplier2	Nov. 2012	China	Board Chairman, Assistant Marketing Director
45	Chinese WTM6	Nov. 2012	China	Chief engineer, R&D
46	Foreign control system supplier1	Nov. 2012	China	Sales Manager, Wind
47	Foreign WTM2	Dec. 2012	China (Skype)	Software engineer
48	Chinese control system supplier5	Dec. 2012	China	Manager
49	Chinese WTM4	Dec. 2012	China	R&D director
50	Chinese WTM4	Dec. 2012	China	R&D, engineer, leader of load calculation team
51	Chinese WTM4	Dec. 2012	China	Software engineer
52	Chinese WTM4	Dec. 2012	China	R&D engineer, blade innovation
53	Chinese WTM4	Dec. 2012	China	Project manager
54	Foreign control system supplier2	Dec. 2012	China	Director
55	Chinese WTM4	Dec. 2012	China	Software engineer
56	Chinese WTM4	Dec. 2012	China	Secretary for R&D manager
57	Foreign control system supplier1	Dec. 2012	China	Regional Sales Account Manager
58	Chinese manufacturer7 (other industry)	Dec. 2012	China	Sales manager China
59	Foreign control system supplier5	Apr. 2013	Denmark	Marketing & Communication Director; Electrical Power Engineer, Tender & System
60	Foreign control system supplier5	Apr. 2013	Denmark	Vice president, China Operations
61	Foreign design house/ certification consultant	Apr. 2013	Denmark	Director

Table III (*continued*)

Number	Organisation / type	Date of interview	Place of interview	Interviewee / Position
62	Foreign research institute	Apr. 2013	Denmark	Engineer/grid integration and wind farm development
63	Foreign research institute	Apr. 2013	Denmark	Engineer/grid integration and control
64	Foreign research institute	Apr. 2013	Denmark	Program manager, aeroelastic design; senior researcher
65	Foreign control system supplier1	Apr. 2013	Denmark	R&D engineer, software engineer
66	Foreign embassy in China	May 2013	China	Diplomat
67	Chinese think tank	May 2013	China	Director
68	Chinese agent/broker	Jul. 2013	China (Skype)	Agent
69	Foreign WT component supplier	Jul. 2013	China	Manager
70	Focus Group Interview – foreign WT component suppliers	Jul. 2013	China	WT component suppliers in China
71	Chinese certification body	Jul. 2013	China	Deputy General Manager Wind Energy Business Dept. Structure Evaluation
72	Chinese ministry	Jul. 2013	China	First secretary
73	Chinese research institute	Jul. 2013	China	Chief engineer PhD; PhD, project manager
74	Chinese certification body	Jul. 2013	China	Director
75	Chinese university	Sep. 2013	China	Former advisor for Chinese Government on MLP S&T, former employee
76	Chinese agent/broker	Sep. 2013	China	'Agent'/'broker'
77	Chinese WTM6	Sep. 2013	China	Vice Director of Wind Power R&D, Director of wind power, Research & Development Centre
78	Chinese agent/broker	Sep. 2013	China	'Agent'/'broker'
79	Joint venture, foreign partner, control system technology	Sep. 2013	China	Chief Technologist/ Doctor; Vice General Manager Chief Finance Officer
80	Chinese wind industry association2	Sep. 2013	China	Director
81	Chinese grid company	Sep. 2013	China	Senior engineer

(*Continued*)

Table III (*continued*)

Number	Organisation / type	Date of interview	Place of interview	Interviewee / Position
82	Development bank, grid companies, generating companies, WTMs	Sep. 2013	China	TSOs, engineers, scientists
83	Chinese grid company	Sep. 2013	China	Chief engineer
84	Chinese power generating company	Sep. 2013	China	Chief engineer
85	Foreign WTM2	Sep. 2013	China	Operations and Dispatch engineer
86	International bank	Sep. 2013	China	Investment banker
87	Chinese Test laboratory	Sep. 2013	China	TSOs, engineers, scientists, test laboratory scientist
88	Grid workshop presentation	Sep. 2013	China	Chief engineer, grid connection
89	Chinese grid company	Sep. 2013	China	Senior engineer
90	Chinese grid company	Sep. 2013	China	Chief engineer
91	Chinese WTM7	Sep. 2013	China	Manufacturer
92	Chinese power generating company	Sep. 2013	China	Director
93	Chinese WTM8	Sep. 2013	China	Engineer
94	Chinese grid company	Sep. 2013	China	Scientist
95	Chinese grid company	Sep. 2013	China	R&D engineer
96	Foreign university1	Sep. 2013	China	Professor
97	Chinese research institute	Sep. 2013	China	Professor
98	Foreign control system supplier6	Nov. 2013	Denmark (Skype)	Sales manager
99	Foreign control system supplier1	Feb. 2015	Denmark (Skype)	Sales Manager, Wind
100	Foreign control system supplier1	Feb. 2015	Denmark	Director
101	Foreign WTM3	Feb. 2015	Denmark	Director
102	Foreign WTM4	Nov. 2015	Denmark	Director
103	Chinese think tank	Dec. 2016	Denmark	Director
104	Chinese agent/broker	Jan. 2017	Denmark	Director
105	Foreign university2	Nov. 2017	USA	Professor
106	Foreign university3	Feb. 2018	USA	CEO
107	Foreign Innovation Center	Mar. 2018	USA	Director
108	Foreign research institute	May 2018	USA (Skype)	Chief engineer, consultant

Index

actor 49–50, 51, 280; actor identity 299; actors in China's standardisation system 243–4; actors in the international standardisation system 241–2; agents and 'go-betweens' 181; Chinese actors 4, 130, 215, 299–300, 301, 303; Chinese actors as inferior partners 216, 252, 253, 258, 262, 299, 305; marketisation 50; micro/macro-actors 46; non-human actors 40, 290, 302, 303; socio-material actors 280; socio-technical assemblage, actors in 41–2, 280, *281*; state–business actors 52, 177, 299; state-endorsed actors 56; *see also* agency; ontology

aeroelastic code 8, 225, 226, 230, 303; certification triangle 247, 248, *249*, 251–2, 253, *254*; competition around aeroelastic codes and algorithmic quality 251–3; lack of basic research in aerodynamics and quality control 255–6; R&D of 257; simulation tool and 4, **58**, 59–60, 132, 233, 247, 248, *249*, 251–2, 253, 254, 277; turbine's performance 252

agency: distributed agency 41–2, 61n4, 136; *see also* actor

agent/*guānxì* (broker) 196, 276; buffer for non-payments 181–2; *guānxì* 181–4; as market intelligence 183; need of 187–8; outsourcing the spider's web and relations as a source of agency 183–4; resistance to 188; using agents to connect to others 182–3; *see also* interpersonal relations; money, access to; Sino-foreign supply chain relations

algorithm 6, 7, 31, 207, 227, 279, 286, 293; algorithmic controversy study 11, 59; 'algorithmic intelligence' 6, 8–9, 284; 'algorithmic power' 10; algorithmic struggles around standardisation 245–53; Chinese wind power and 10–11; contested and controversial in Chinese wind power 30–1; defining the equation/algorithm 227; encryption 7, 30, 132, 213; as framing devices 50, 266; power struggle and 267, 286; renewable energy, sustainability and 9; seeing the universe in an algorithm 47, 58, 279–82; socio-technical assemblage and 46–7; technical lock 7, 30–1, 132, 213, 223, 253; tracing marketisation through algorithms 279–82; 'turn to (algorithmic) science' 285; uncertainty and 11, 31, 50, 57, 267; wind turbine 7, 280; *see also* core algorithm; quality; software algorithms; software IPR; source code

American pragmatism 25, 44, 48, 61n1, 88, 308; micro-relational, processual lens of 48, 308

AMSC (American Superconductor) 214, 218–20, 223

Andersen, Hans Christian 56, 57, 63n16

Andrews-Speed, P. 73, 78, 114, 233

Ang, Y. Y. 27, 75, 77

ANT (Actor-Network Theory) 38, 39, 40, 42, 44, 46, 49, 60, 62n8, 89, 292, 296n6; *see also* Anthropology of Markets

system 200, 210; *see also* supervisory control system
wind turbine industry 68, 104–105, 108; American wind turbine industry 311–12; Denmark 6, 104, 310–11; Germany 6, 104; *see also* Chinese wind turbine industry; WTM
Windey 143n5
Windtec 214, 219
WIPO (World Intellectual Property Organisation) 202
World Bank 242
WTM (wind turbine manufacturer) 4, 29, 50, 113; bankruptcy 178; foreign/ Western WTM 113, 160, 203, 305; private sector 73, 178; *see also* Chinese WTM

WTO (World Trade Organization) 105, 110, 268; China's accession to 68, 71, 78, 201, 202, 235, 263, 287; standards and 235, 239, 263, 268n2; TBT/ Technical Barriers to Trade agreement 243, 268n2; *see also* TRIPS

Xi Jinping 11, 18, 72, 184, 195, 228–9, 262, 287, 290

Yaneva, A. 41, 52, 88

Zhang, J. 290
Zou, Y. 70, 76, 196

For Product Safety Concerns and Information please contact our EU
representative GPSR@taylorandfrancis.com
Taylor & Francis Verlag GmbH, Kaufingerstraße 24, 80331 München, Germany